The Architecture and Planning of Classical Moscow:
A Cultural History

Albert J. Schmidt

American Philosophical Society
Independence Square • Philadelphia
1989

MEMOIRS OF THE

AMERICAN PHILOSOPHICAL SOCIETY
Held at Philadelphia
For Promoting Useful Knowledge
Volume 181

Copyright 1989 by the American Philosophical Society
for its *Memoirs* series, Volume 181

Library of Congress Catalog Card No: 88-71549   ∞
International Standard Book No. 0-87169-181-7
US ISSN: 0065-9738

Illustration for dust jacket: Red Square as restored after 1812. Donskoi v 23759

Illustrations for end papers:

> Front: Ivan Martos's monument to Minin and Pozharskii.
>   Donskoi   v 7018
> Back: Bol'shoi Theater interior, mid nineteenth century.
>   Donskoi   viii 19932

Illustrations at the beginning of chapters from architectural drawings of the period.

For Kathy, Chris, and Betsy

Table of Contents

Preface

This book is addressed to those who find enchantment in discovering the past in the present, specifically, in architectural artifacts that mirror a past epoch. While it is improbable that a single work of architecture would do this, a well-preserved "historic district" could and does. I have tried to persuade the reader that despite enormous destruction of historic Moscow over the last half century there is still a significant remnant from the city of the early nineteenth century. To do so, I have proceeded as a cultural historian, not an architectural one, with a focus on the architectural artifacts and landscape rather than stylistic criticism. The organization of this book is chronological and to an extent approximates an atlas of central Moscow's principal streets, plazas, edifices, ensembles, and even unrealized plans.

This study of classical Moscow has been anything but a solo enterprise. Many scholars, colleagues, and friends have contributed to the final draft. Professor Robert Byrnes of Indiana University facilitated my first visit to the USSR more than two decades ago. In the Soviet Union the late Professors Vladimir I.

Piliavskii, M. A. Il'in, Nicholai Brunov, and in this country, Arthur Voyce were my early mentors. Readers of the several drafts—Professors Thomas Juliusburger, Richard Garner, S. Frederick Starr, and, especially, Professor Charles Cannon and Elizabeth and Kathryn Schmidt—have all given to me invaluable advice. A number of typists have labored on this project over the years: Nina Kendall, Olga Milin, Marlene Baumann, and Irene Palazzo were especially crucial to its completion. I also gratefully acknowledge assistance in translation from Alexander Almasov, Diane Garner, Nina Kendall, Olga Milin and Olga Svetlik.

I am indebted also to the staffs of the Lenin Library in Moscow, the Library of Congress, the Oost-Europa Institut, University of Amsterdam, the Sterling Memorial Library at Yale, the New York Public Library, the libraries at the University of Illinois, the University of Iowa, Indiana University; the Architectural Institute Library on Zhdanov Street in Moscow, the Library of the Town Planning Institute on Dmitrovskoe Highway in Moscow and the Architectural Archive at Donskoi Monastery. I wish especially to thank Victor Baldin,

Director of the Shchusev Museum of Architecture in Moscow for facilitating my obtaining copies of old prints and photographs from the Donskoi Archive, which is under his supervision, and for permission to publish them. Grants from the American Philosophical Society, the American Council of Learned Societies, the University of Bridgeport, and sabbatical leaves from Coe College and the University of Bridgeport also facilitated progress on the project in its various stages.

Although these individuals and institutions have contributed significantly to the work, I take responsibility for all errors and shortcomings.

August 25, 1986
Greenfield Hill,
Fairfield, Connecticut

Introduction

That the eighteenth century was one of change for Russia, especially as it pertains to Peter and Catherine the Great, is hardly a novel theme. Imperial Russia did acquire at least a veneer of Western culture. This study takes account of an aspect of, almost literally, this facade—the architecture and layout of cities in accordance with the principles of classicism. The baroque and rococo of the early and mideighteenth century are discussed only by way of introduction; the focus is on Russia's neoclassic era, from approximately the 1760s until about 1840.

Classicism with its aura of order became an ideal mode for eighteenth-century architects and planners when they tidied up the clutter of medieval cities: city walls became concentric boulevards; radial highways, widened, were given grand perspectives; river banks were straightened with stone embankments. Great squares were embellished with monumental sculptures and masonry architecture, although more often than not the masonry consisted of luxuriant *stucco* plastered over wattle, daub, and log.

The intent of eighteenth-century architects was to improve cities both in function and beauty. Although majestic thoroughfares and plazas did this quite nicely, buildings, in particular, fulfilled this classical mystique. The architecture of classicism has generally been defined in terms of its Doric, Ionic, and Corinthian orders, the arch and the dome. "The

Greek temple," wrote one authority, "is the most perfect example ever achieved of architecture finding its fulfillment in bodily beauty."[1] The Roman architect Vitruvius discerned this beauty "when its [the edifice's] members are in due proportion according to correct principles of symmetry."[2]

Classicism in the Europe of two or three centuries ago had a very special meaning. It served as a vehicle for transforming old cities into new ones: London after the Great Fire of 1666, and later Edinburgh, Munich, Vienna, and Paris. Princes of well-ordered police states, appreciating the classical emphasis on order and monumentality, used it in their new urban creations. The Whigs in England found the Palladian style an apt expression of their aesthetic tastes and symbol of their economic and political dominance. The fact is that grandees, whether building in town or country, appropriated classicism and thus made it the mark of aristocratic taste and power.

What had all this to do with eighteenth-century Russia? Russia, like Europe and England, employed the architecture of classicism for her new cities. Peter's St. Petersburg, built in the northern swampland, and old Tver, demolished by fire in the mideighteenth century, were prototypes for other Russian cities.

[1] Nikolaus Pevsner, *An Outline of European Architecture* (Middlesex, 1963), 19.

[2] Vitruvius, *The Ten Books on Architecture*. Transl. by M. H. Morgan (New York, 1960), 16–17.

Catherine II by the 1770s and 1780s had become obsessed with founding new cities. Doubtless, she hoped that they rather than the monastery would symbolize her new Russia, even though these cities were usually administrative rather than commercial centers. In Catherinian Russia the nobility also found classicism to their taste. Emancipated from servitude in the 1760s, whether they congregated in Moscow or remained in the country, they built in the classical manner. Russian classicism reflected European classicism. Throughout the eighteenth century European architects worked extensively in Russia, and Russians studied in Europe. By 1800 Russian architects had their own brand of Palladian, Romantic, French (Ledoux), and Empire styles.

This book attempts to explain Russia's, specifically Moscow's, appropriation and adaptation of European classicism. Its initial phase in Moscow followed from the genius of the architects Kazakov and Bazhenov late in the eighteenth century; its second phase coincided with the era of reconstruction after the Great Fire in 1812. That this historic center of xenophobia should adopt cosmopolitan classicism as its badge gives plausibility to the thesis that classicism became a vehicle for incipient nationalism. If so, then its location in Moscow is hardly surprising.

The present study is primarily descriptive, a cultural history: how did Moscow move along its way toward classicism after 1750, what prompted this development, who was responsible? This narrative, essentially an atlas, is structured to capture the character of Moscow's streets, plazas, and districts. The great fire of 1812 is presented as a watershed in classical Moscow's history. The many plans before 1812, described in some detail, would simply have remained plans had not the fire made them important antecedents to the plan adopted for restoring Moscow in 1817.

The Soviets have been ambivalent about classicism. Their scholars over the last several decades have dealt generously with Russian classical architecture, lauding both its beauty and scale. They have also found ideological satisfaction in the uniquely Russian, democratic, and heroic dimensions of classical edifices and ensembles. On the other hand, the authorities have been less careful about their preservation. Over the last half century, many classical buildings have disappeared. In Moscow the reconstruction projects of the 1930s and 1960s took a great toll of classical as well as preclassical Moscow: the once majestic and aristocratic Tverskaia has been transformed into a tasteless Gorkii Street; the focal point of the old Arbat is now the un-Russian, though fashionable, Kalinin Prospekt. What remains of its classical face is encompassed in a newly constructed pedestrian mall. Present Soviet emphasis on historical preservation, precipitated, in part, by resurgent Great Russian nationalism and widespread distress over the huge loss of monuments since 1917, has been evidenced by legislation in 1976 and 1982 and an inclusion in the 1977 Constitution. These factors all bode a better future for those amber-, blue-, green-, and cherry-washed buildings that punctuate the city center.

How Moscow's classical face originated some two centuries ago this book purports to tell.

List of Illustrations

CHAPTER I
The Architectural World of the Late Eighteenth Century

Classicism in modern architecture came to fruition in the second half of the eighteenth century. In contrast to the rococo in France and Palladianism in England, it laid claim to a certain authenticity, first Roman and then Greek prevailing in successive revivals. If Renaissance classicism had accentuated beauty, neoclassicism ca. 1800 strove to recapture what was perceived as the essence of the art of antiquity—sublimity, elevation, dignity, honor, simplicity, and grandeur. Aside from its reliance on Roman and Greek models, this new classicism appeared preoccupied with Egyptian motifs, especially those depicting the majesty of death. Recoiling from frivolity, ostentation, and the baroque conception of the building as a living organism, it gave to architecture an intellectual dimension, its romantic aspects notwithstanding. Reduced to basic geometric forms and smooth surfaces, new structures denied all baroque articulation and decoration and accented instead structural expression through its posts and lintels. Architects took pride in the functionality and diversity of their edifices, whether banks, legislative assemblies, churches, fire stations, private homes, or exquisite garden pavilions.

Neoclassicism, like the baroque, often became synonymous with town planning on a grand scale.

Eighteenth-century classicism, influenced by the English garden and temple and the excavations at Herculaneum (1738) and Pompeii (1748), won its way variously. Robert Adam applied Roman forms in his interiors. Thomas Jefferson used Palladian concepts in designing Monticello, but for Virginia's new capitol he recommended the exquisite Maison Carrée in Nîmes as a model. The archeological discoveries which magnified and authenticated the vision of classicism also spurred its publicists. Winckelmann proclaimed the virtues of Greece and Greek art, and Piranesi's etchings of romanticized Roman ruins inspired young architects to travel in Italy in order to recreate its antiquities.

In France the quest for classical sublimity resulted in both a rejection of the aristocratic rococo and the creation of a new classic. The principal proponents of the *style Louis XVI*, as classicism was called in France, were Boullée and Ledoux. Boullée wrote: "Tired of the emptiness and sterility of irregular forms, I have passed to the study of the regular. . . .

1

2

CLASSICAL MOSCOW: ARCHITECTURE AND PLANNING

These captivate by simplicity, regularity, and reiteration."[1] His contemporary, Ledoux, avoiding both the fanciful and the imitative, worked in a world of spheres, cubes, and pyramids—none of which had any clear antecedent in antiquity. His new classic proved admirably utilitarian, serving the current need for such monumental structures as banks, hospitals, barracks, stock exchanges, and opera houses, to say nothing of factories. Neither Boullée nor Ledoux exercised any considerable influence in Western Europe during the era of the French Revolution; however, their ideas were carried to Russia by the émigré Thomas de Thomon, who designed and built the Petersburg bourse.

The clarity of the *style Louis XVI* surrendered to increased surface ornament during the Bonapartist era. Napoleon's most ambitious urban scheme linked the Place de la Concorde, the colonnaded porch of the Chamber of Deputies, the new and magnificent Madeleine Church, and his triumphal arches in an ingenious design, which extolled the martial glory of the First Empire. Imperial, not republican, Rome triumphed in Napoleon's Paris.

But Paris notwithstanding, Greek models dominated classicism for the first thirty years of the nineteenth century. Germany, belatedly taking its cue from Winckelmann, led the way. Karl Langhans and Friedrich Gilly were among the first; but the greatest German masters were Gilly's student Schinkel in Berlin and Klenze in Munich. In England the break between the early Roman classic and that of the post-revolutionary period, the Greek, was best expressed in the highly original works of Soane, Nash, and Smirke. In the United States in 1799, Benjamin Latrobe designed the Bank of Pennsylvania as a Greek temple, applied the Ionic order, and gave it a dome. When Nicholas Biddle determined after his trip to Greece that "a chaste imitation of Grecian architecture" with "a portico on each front"

should be the mode for his new Bank of the United States, he obtained designs from Latrobe and his pupil William Strickland, who had both used the Parthenon as a model. Classicism, having achieved its greatest authenticity during this Greek phase, became increasingly eclectic by the 1830s, when it proved unequal to the competition from a Gothic revival.

In urban design classicism was epitomized most simply by the straight line. Pronounced "the very expression of human reason and will," it received theoretical affirmation by the sixteenth century when acceptance came both in the dominance of the axis and the increased prevalence of gridiron patterns in urban design. The line as an axis both organized the environment and dominated the plaza, which was only an extension of the longitudinal axis. Radial street buildings, uniform in both their facade elements and unbroken horizontal roof-line, accentuated this linear precision.

The public square was an essential element both as organized space and for the conclusion of a monumental perspective. Planners also reserved space for greenery which related the monument to the spatial treatment of the plaza. The classical planner carefully molded this void rather than allow an indiscriminate building mass to arise. Whether located in an oval, circular, rectangular, or square plaza, the monument was flanked symmetrically by important public buildings, uniform in character. Radial streets converging on the monument, pierced the open space in the middle rather than at the corners.

The classical city joined symmetry to perspective: the uniform and harmonious buildings on the radial streets and plazas accomplished this. This program, so to speak, was "the obligation imposed on all the houses of a certain part of the town—street, square, district—to . . . conform to a general design." One regarded as near perfection was that on the west side of the Rue de Rivoli in Napoleon's Paris.

Eighteenth-century planners employed these tested elements of town design in creating new towns as well as in renovating

[1] Quoted from Emil Kaufman, *Three Revolutionary Architects: Boullée, Ledoux, and Lequeu. Transactions of the American Philosophical Society*, N.S., vol. 42, pt. 3 (Philadelphia, 1952): 471.

existing ones. Besides articulating linear thoroughfares and symmetrical plazas, they constructed bridges and stone embankments along straightened rivers, dug and paved canals, and replaced crooked alleys with gridiron blocks. Their landscaping followed the same formulae: major and minor axes, which created beds of parterres, terminated at fountains or other monuments, and precisely clipped hedges or trees were substituted for facade uniformity.

This regulated town design in baroque and classical Europe carried with it a political message. The city of royalty symbolized order, power, secularism and political absolutism. That the great palace should occupy a central plaza allowed for the kind of pageantry which exalted power. Bureaucratic and military edifices, cloaked in columns and pediments, also claimed imposing sites in the new city; ecclesiastical buildings, in turn, lost theirs. This linear development of the city was more than symbolic: besides facilitating traffic flow, wide boulevards and avenues denied protection to street revolutionaries and otherwise impeded social intercourse—except, of course, promenading by the aristocracy. The baroque-classical city ceased being the historic haven of the people.[2]

Classicism and Russia

Classicism, with its orders, unique town design, and accent on masonry construction, was antithetical to old Russian building modes. Thus, when the baroque style was utilized by Peter the Great in his new capital St. Petersburg, it symbolized his intended Western orientation. Determined to promote a more sophisticated absolutism than that he had inherited, Peter chose for his seat of power a location far removed from that relic of Russia's past, Moscow. This northern capital, built in a harsh wasteland at a terrible cost in human life and suffering, emerged as one of Europe's most splendid cities. The emperor's employment of the French architect Leblond and the Italian Trezzini set a precedent for his successors, who sponsored the Rastrellis, Vallin de la Mothe, Giacomo Quarenghi, Charles Cameron, William Hastie, Thomas de Thomon, Avgust Mon[t]ferran[d], and others—all of whom embellished the city over the course of a century and more.[3]

Although initially baroque, by the early nineteenth century Petersburg was renowned for its rococo and classical structures. Perhaps the greatest creations were those of the Empress Elizabeth's favorite architect, Bartolommeo Rastrelli, who about midcentury built the sprawling Winter Palace, the Smolnyi Sobor, and the imposing Stroganov Palace on the Nevskii Prospekt. Catherine commissioned Quarenghi, who came from his native Como to design the Smolnyi Institute; even earlier she had sanctioned Vallin de la Mothe's building the Academy of Fine Arts, the initial stimulus to classicism in St. Petersburg. Alexander I, during whose reign Empire classicism was ascendant, inspired a broad building program which included: Kazan Cathedral, a modest classical rendition of St. Peter's in Rome, by Andrei Voronikhin; the imposing Admiralty of Adrian Zakharov; and Thomon's *style Ledoux* Bourse and Voronikhin's Academy of Mines (Gornyi Institute), both on Vasil'evskii Island. Alexander's preference for the French style was not prejudiced by his recent conflict with Napoleon; he even appointed a former French general and engineer, Augustin Béthencourt, to head the Committee for Construction and Hydraulic Works which passed on the designs of all public and private building in the capital.

As the taste for Greek classicism ebbed,

---

[2] See Pierre Lavedan, *French Architecture* (Baltimore, 1967), 236–39 for a full discussion of classical urban design.

[3] The best works in English on this subject are I. A. Egorov, *The Architectural Planning of St. Petersburg.* Transl. and ed. by Eric Dluhosch (Athens, Ohio, 1969) and George H. Hamilton, *The Art and Architecture of Russia* (Baltimore, 1983). See also R. Lucas, "Innovation in Russian Architecture in Early Modern History," Study Group on Eighteenth Century Russia *Newsletter* 4 (1976):17–24 and L.A.J. Hughes, "The West Comes to Russian Architecture," *History Today* 36 (1986):28–39.

about 1815, the Russian architect Karl Ivanovich Rossi led Petersburg toward Roman classicism. His General Staff building and hemicycle helped enclose Winter Palace Square, and his Senate and Synod partially encased what is now Decembrist Square. These edifices and his ambitious planning schemes in St. Petersburg marked him as the most influential Russian architect-planner of late classicism.

In a monumental style akin to Rossi's, Avgust Avgustovich Montferrand built St. Isaac's Cathedral, finally completed in 1857; moreover, his Alexander Column in Winter Palace Square endowed Petersburg with a colossus on the order of Paris's Colonne de Juillet and the Washington Monument. Classicism was not, however, to be confined to this radiant city on the Neva. Both Catherine II and Alexander I perceived themselves as builders, and they looked farther afield to fulfill their destiny.

Although Catherine's Enlightenment is often dismissed as little more than her superficial communication with an international coterie of thinkers, publicists, and reformers such as Voltaire and Diderot, she appeared to have a genuine interest in the arts. In her correspondence with Falconet she insisted that he personally should cast the bronze statue of Peter the Great in St. Petersburg ("Further, who has convinced you that a professional foundryman would be better than yourself?").[4] In the same way, she spent hours with her architects, reviewing plans. Like her predecessors, she considered the choice of architectural styles a royal prerogative. She dispensed with the rococo of Rastrelli and Prince Ukhtomskii, was for a time enthralled with Bazhenov in Moscow and Cameron in Tsarskoe Selo, but finally settled for the classic of Matvei Kazakov in Moscow and Quarenghi and Ivan Starov in Petersburg. Catherine was

to change her mind about both styles as her brief flirtation with Gothic indicated (see, for example, the work of Vasilii Bazhenov at Tsaritsyna and Kazakov's Petrovskii Palace in Moscow). But these interludes did not diminish her excitement for classicism.

While the Empress displayed indecision in some of her projects, she alone was responsible for much of the construction that did occur during her reign. These included individual buildings, ensembles, and larger city-planning enterprises. James Billington has observed that "more than any other single person prior to the Leninist revolution, Catherine cut official culture loose from its religious roots and changed both its physical setting and its philosophical preoccupations." In doing so, she "substituted the city for the monastery as the main center of Russian culture."[5]

Catherine's involvement in city-building has often been overlooked.[6] As early as the second year of her reign, she had to cope with the burning of Tver (Kalinin). Her decision to reconstruct it along classical lines led her to similar undertakings in Tula, Kolomna, Kostroma, Kaluga, Iaroslavl, Vladimir and elsewhere. Encouraged by Voltaire, she dreamed of civilizing New Russia, that is, the Ukraine, won by her lover Potemkin.[7] The virgin and fertile steppes begged for all kinds of utopian schemes. Voltaire had once even made his visit to Russia contingent upon the empress's making Kiev the capital of her vast empire; another time she herself toyed with the idea of resurrecting a Byzantium under Russian auspices. In new Ekaterinoslav (Dnepropetrovsk) on the Dnieper, she envisioned a mag-

---

[4] Catherine to Falconet, 18 September 1769 in Louis Reau, ed., *Correspondance de Falconet Avec Catherine II, 1767–1778* (Paris, 1921), 100–101, transl. by L. Jay Oliva. *Catherine The Great,* ed. L. Jay Oliva (Englewood Cliffs, N.J. 1971), 51.

[5] James Billington, *The Icon and the Axe* (New York, 1967), 227. Hereafter cited as *Icon.*

[6] One of Catherine's decrees read: "From the very first establishment of settlements, all peoples recognized the advantages of building towns. . . . From the dawn of history, beginning with antiquity, we meet everywhere the memory of the founders of cities equally with the memory of lawmakers." Quoted from Hans Blumenfeld, "Russian City Planning of the Eighteenth and Early Nineteenth Centuries," *Journal of the Society of Architectural Historians* 4 (1944):26.

[7] Cf. Wm. H. McNeill, *Europe's Steppe Frontier 1500–1800* (Chicago, 1964) and Billington, *Icon.*

nificent center of culture and commerce.[8] On the northern shore of the Black Sea, where ancient Greek cities once stood, she planted the new classical ones of Azov, Taganrog, Nikolaev, Odessa, and Sevastopol.

Catherine's aspiration to create new cities was more than a whim or a consequence of expansion into new areas. Truly significant changes, which related to her urban schemes, were occurring in Russia's society. First, Peter III in 1762 lifted a number of long-existing controls on commerce and restricted the rights of serf ownership to the nobility; in the same year, Catherine, having succeeded Peter, began liberalizing manufactures. These separate physiocrat-inspired gestures nearly destroyed whatever existed of a Russian urban bourgeoisie, which faltered before noble and even peasant entrepreneurs in the villages. Thus, when speaking of Catherine as a builder of cities, we are forced to seek an explanation for urban development distinct from the economic.[9]

A partial explanation may be found in Peter III's having freed the nobility from state service. Once emancipated, many left St. Petersburg and the watchful eye of the court to reside in the country or perhaps in Moscow. The famed Legislative Commission of 1767–1768 supported the wishes of the nobility for more autonomy in local administration. The empress, in turn, confronted by the failure of local government during the Pugachev uprising (1773–1774) and moved by liberal *philosophe* political ideas, eventually accepted the Commission's counsel. She issued during the course of a decade three separate decrees: the Law on the Administration of the Provinces of the Russian Empire in 1775 and the Charter of the Nobility and Charter of the Cities in

1785.[10] The first two decentralized government and placed power in the hands of the local nobility to whom the governors belonged. The Charter for the Cities, hardly the enlightened act it is made to seem, really complemented the first two, leaving the nobility firmly in control and establishing Catherine's "cities" as essentially administrative centers.

Thus provincial and urban administrative reform, not commerce, influenced building and town planning throughout the empire. Catherine's regulations directed provincial governors "to establish towns either in existing villages or in new places."[11] The act divided the realm into fifty provinces, an increase of twenty, each consisting of a maximum of twelve and a minimum of eight districts. Besides "provincial" cities, four hundred and ninety-three were designed as "district" cities, and eighty-six were placed under the supervision of the State. Such instant urbanization stimulated Russia's architects as nothing else could.[12]

---

[10] Geo. Vernadsky, et al., eds., *A Source Book for Russian History from Early Times to 1917*, 3 vols. (New Haven, 1972), 2:410–11; 413–18 and Paul Dukes, ed., *Russia under Catherine the Great: Select Documents on Government and Society* 1 (Newtonville, Mass., 1978):136–70. Cf. also Isabel de Madariaga, *Russia in the Age of Catherine the Great* (New Haven, 1981), 277–307. J. Michael Hittle has written on the service city in eighteenth-century Russia and how it can be understood "only as an integral part of a polity dominated by a powerful, centralized state." ("The Service City in the Eighteenth Century" in Michael F. Hamm, ed., *The City in Russian History*, Lexington, Ky., 1976), 53. See also J. M. Hittle, *The Service City* (Cambridge, Mass., 1979). Catherine's urban reform was motivated by increased tax revenues and improved law and order.

[11] Blumenfeld, "Russian City Planning," 27; cf. also Paul Dukes, *Catherine the Great and the Russian Nobility* (Cambridge, 1967); Thomas M. Poulsen, "The Provinces of Russia: Changing Patterns in the Regional Allocation of Authority 1708–1962" (unpublished Ph. D. dissertation, Univ. of Wisconsin, 1962); and Robert E. Jones, *The Emancipation of the Russian Nobility* (Princeton, 1973) and "Urban Planning and the Development of Provincial Towns in Russia, 1762–1796," in *The Eighteenth Century in Russia*, ed. J. G. Garrard (Oxford, 1973), 321–344.

[12] It should be remembered that settlements with hardly more than a hundred dwellings were often labeled cities. The following works are important for a study of Russian urbanization and economic development during the eighteenth century: Blackwell, *Industrialization*; Hamm, ed., *The City in Russian History*; J. Michael Hittle, "The City in Muscovite and Early Imperial Russia" (unpublished Ph. D. dissertation, Harvard Univ., 1969); Jerome Blum, *Lord and Peasant in Russia from the Ninth to the Nineteenth Century* (Princeton, 1961); E. A. Gutkind, *International History of City Development* 8, *Urban Development in Eastern Europe: Bulgaria, Romania, and the USSR* (New York,

---

[8] Cf. Albert J. Schmidt, "William Hastie, Scottish Planner of Russian Cities," in *Proceedings of the American Philosophical Society* vol. 114, no. 3 (Philadelphia, 1970):226–43.

[9] See Richard Pipes, *Russia Under the Old Regime* (New York, 1974), 211–18 and William L. Blackwell, *The Beginnings of Russian Industrialization 1800–1860* (Princeton, 1968), 96–101, herafter cited as *Industrialization*.

Catherine II imposed on these towns her own preference in style and design, resorting to her favorite pastime of appointing commissions. In 1768, for example, she charged the Commission for the Building of the Capital Cities of St. Petersburg and Moscow (*Komissiia dlia stroeniia stolichnykh gorodov Sankt-Peterburga i Moskvy*), established in 1762, to assume responsibility for town building throughout Russia; by the end of the century it had either approved or reviewed more than four hundred city plans. New town design usually conformed to one, or a combination, of four types: radial-concentric, fan-shaped, rectangular, and diagonal. Because planners were ever cognizant of fire and hygienic problems, they conceived cities consisting essentially of a center with suburbs: with regulated streets and alleys, administrative and commercial plazas, blocks, and plots.[13] They designated certain squares for wooden construction, others for masonry. "*Obraztsovye*," or standardized, facade designs were deemed essential not only to accomplish a classical program but also to reduce construction costs.[14]

These many new cities, or administrative centers, in accordance with the reforms, were systematically placed throughout Russia. In some cases populous centers were appropriately designated cities; in other instances villages with perhaps a hundred dwellings acquired the same distinction. Richard Pipes has noted that "the administrative relabeling of the population clearly had not the slightest effect on the quality of life in the cities or on the mentality of its inhabitants, which (except for Moscow and St. Petersburg) remained indistinguishable from the rural. The tripling of urban inhabitants, allegedly accomplished between 1769 and 1796, was a figment of the bureaucratic imagination."[15] Thus, even an insignificant administrative center was often the object of meticulous planning. Where the plan became a reality, the city generally was structured around administrative buildings, a governor's mansion, and whatever else was appropriate to autocratic authority and aristocratic comfort. The mode for such building and planning was invariably classical.

In Russia, as elsewhere in Europe, squares and radial thoroughfares leading into them were at the heart of the new design. Grand monuments like a kremlin, cathedral (*sobor*), or palace naturally terminated a radial at the plaza's center.[16] Both the thoroughfares and squares conveyed a new spatial dimension. Whereas old Muscovy's wooden cities, silhouetted by tent spires and bulbous domes, rose vertically, the new classical towns, conforming to a required 2:1 or even 4:1 ratio between the width of street and height of buildings facing on the street, projected horizontally.[17] Masonry residences of the affluent usually occu-

1972):323–67; Arcadius Kahan, "Continuity in Economic Activity and Policy during the Post-Petrine Period in Russia," *The Journal of Economic History* 25 (1965):61–85. John T. Alexander, *Bubonic Plague in Early Modern Russia* (Baltimore, 1980) and "Catherine II, Bubonic Plague, and the Problem of Industry in Moscow," *American Historical Review* 79 (1974):637–71, hereafter cited as "Catherine II"; in Hamm's volume on the Russian city, see Gilbert Rozman, "Comparative Approaches to Urbanization: Russia, 1750–1800"; Gilbert Rozman, *Urban Networks in Russia 1750–1800* (Princeton, 1976); Roger Portal, "Manufactures et classes sociales en Russie au XVIIIᵉ siècle," *Revue historique* 201 (1949):61–85. T. Efimenko, "K istorii gorodskogo zemleustroistva vremeni Ekateriny II," *Zhurnal ministerstva narodnogo prosveshcheniia*, N.S. 54 (1914). Iu R. Klokman, *Sotsial'no-ekonomicheskaia istoriia russkogo goroda: vtoraia polovina XVIII veka* (Moscow, 1967), and *Ocherki sotsial'no-ekonomicheskoi istorii gorodov severo-zapada Rossii v seredine XVIIIv.* (Moscow, 1960); F. Ia. Polianskii, *Gorodskoe remeslo i manufaktura v Rossii XVIII v.* (Moscow 1960). E. A. Zviagintsev, "Slobody inostrantsev v Moskve XVIII veka," *Istoricheskii zhurnal*, no. 2–3 (1944):81–86; and N. M. Druzhinin, et al., eds., *Goroda feodal'noi Rossii* (Moscow, 1966) contains useful articles for this period. Drushinin is reviewed in Samuel H. Baron, "The Town in 'Feudal' Russia," *Slavic Review* 28 (1969):116–22. P. G. Ryndzivinskii, *Gorodskoe grazhdanstvo doreformennoi Rossii* (Moscow, 1958).

[13] Blumenfeld, "Russian City Planning," 27.

[14] See V. Shilkov, "Raboty A. V. Kvasova i I. E. Starova po planirovke russkikh gorodov," *Arkhitekturnoe nasledstvo* 4 (1953):30–34.

[15] Pipes, *Old Regime*, 216.

[16] This mix of old buildings with the new in architectural ensembles was a notable feature of classical Moscow and distinguished it especially from St. Petersburg. For a fuller discussion of this theme, see N. F. Gulianitskii, "O kompozitsii zdanii v ansamblevoi zastroike Moskvy perioda klassitsizma," *Arkhitekturnoe nasledstvo* 24 (Moscow, 1976):20–40, hereafter cited as Gulianitskii, "O kompozitsii."

[17] See Billington, *Icon*, 228. The minimum widths for Moscow in 1752 were 64 and 40 feet respectively. In Tver the width for main streets was established at 80 feet and the height of buildings at 40. Blumenfeld, "Russian City Planning," 30.

pied those streets leading into administrative plazas. Separated from one another by fences and gates, these edifices achieved the effect of a continuous facade, which gave uniformity and order to the streets and plazas of the city center.

Because the importance of classicism usually diminished in proportion to the distance from the city center, planners designed commercial squares to link the administrative center with the suburb; furthermore, they relegated to outlying areas beyond these great market squares the mélange of wooden cottages of clerks, tradesmen, artisans, and peasants, together with breweries, tallow boilers, hide tanneries, soap-making plants, cemeteries, and other polluters of earth, air, and water. For this segment of Moscow's population classicism appeared to offer very little indeed.

Classicism in Russia was not, however, an exclusive property of the idle rich; its utilitarian adaptability and endless variety were exploited throughout the provinces. True, classical residences—those of gentry (*dvoriane*), princes, and well-to-do merchants—sprang up in both town and country. The style was also applied to the edifices of the bureaucracy and military, to universities, hospitals, almshouses, fire stations, river embankments, bridges, and triumphal arches—all of which exemplified accelerated building in an increasingly sophisticated society.[18] Although provincial classicism generally imitated that of Petersburg and Moscow, resourceful local architects frequently adapted standard designs to local conditions. Often serfs, these provincial builders incorporated elements of folk architecture in their creations. Regional variations gave provincial architecture endless variety and distinguished it from that of Petersburg and Moscow.

In summary, Catherine's building of cities resulted in sometimes majestic, but frequently artificial, creations. Instead of providing an environment for commerce, her "cities" often mirrored aristocratic affluence or served as administrative centers for recently established provincial governments. Under such circumstances, planners of boulevards often concerned themselves more with promenading than traffic and envisioned plazas for military reviews rather than commerce. Nor was it a fiction that the classical facades of a regulated street often obscured the misery of old Russia behind it. To a very considerable degree Catherine's classicism was a facade, a vast "Potemkin village."

Classicism and Moscow

Although eclipsed by St. Petersburg, Moscow became almost as much a part of the European classical scene as the new capital on the Neva.[19] Early classical Moscow resulted largely from the inventiveness of Vasilii

---

[18] The infinite varieties are discussed in George K. Lukomskii, *Arkhitektura russkoi provintsii* (Petrograd, 1916). More on late eighteenth-century Russia's preoccupation with western ideas in architecture is included in several recent articles: N. F. Gulianitskii, "Tvorcheskie metody arkhitektorov russkogo klassitsizma pri razrabotke ordernykh kompozitsii," *Arkhitekturnoe nasledstvo* 22 (1974):30–52, explores interest in the theory of the classical orders and notes in particular the Russian awareness of Vignola, Palladio, Vitruvius, Serlio, Blondel and others late in the eighteenth century. A. A. Kiparisova, "Stat'i ob arkhitekture v russkikh zhurnalakh vtoroi poloviny XVIII veka," *Arkhitekturnoe nasledstvo* 22 (1974):19–26, examines articles on varied architectural subjects published in Russian journals in the late eighteenth century. The maturity of Russian architectural thinking was further evidenced by the growth of critical literature as explored by A. F. Krasheninnikov, "Redkii dokument arkhitekturnoi kritiki v Rossii XVIII v.," *Arkhitekturnoe nasledstvo* 22 (1974):27–29. See L.A.J. Hughes, "Westernization in Russian Architecture, 1680–1725," Study Group on Eighteenth Century *Newsletter* 6 (1978):8–11; Hughes, "Russia's First Architectural Books," *Architectural Design* (1983).

[19] James Billington has stressed that Moscow became the home of anti-Enlightenment and anti-western intellectuals, Moscow "a center for the glorification of Russian antiquity and a cultural Mecca for those opposed to the Gallic cosmopolitanism of the capital." Billington further suggested that "even though [Moscow] accepted the visual veneer of classicism, it resisted the Neo-Classical culture that was being superimposed on Russian cities by Catherine" (*Icon*, 244). An opposing interpretation is that classicism and incipient nationalism were not incompatible. Cf. also Madariaga, *Russia in the Age of Catherine The Great*, 327–42 and Sidney Monas, "St. Petersburg and Moscow as Cultural Symbols," *Art and Culture in Nineteenth-Century Russia*, ed. T. G. Stavrou (Bloomington, Ind., 1983), 26-39. For more on Western influence see P. Clendenning and R. Bartlett, *Eighteenth Century Russia: A Select Bibliography* (Newtonville, Mass., 1981).

Bazhenov and Matvei Kazakov. They and their colleagues, keeping their distance from Petersburg, refurbished the Kremlin and took their commissions from Moscow's grandees, whose good life Tolstoi portrayed in *War and Peace*. The Great Fire of 1812 destroyed much of their work, yet it provided an opportunity for a later generation of architects to mold their city, perhaps more faithfully than ever, to a classical ideal that in its unique way rivaled St. Petersburg. And like the latter, like Berlin, Munich, and Vienna, classical Moscow became an exemplar for the architectural tradition of early nineteenth-century Europe.

Although Moscow had hovered in the shadow of Petersburg for the first six decades of the eighteenth century, it was only deceptively barren of resources and vitality. Fires, defense, and normal building and expansion forced authorities to review constantly the city's form and function. Architects from abroad altered the old city in the baroque and rococo idiom and were emulated by their Russian students. After 1760 Moscow truly reemerged as a kind of microcosm of the divergent and vital currents of Russian life. The influx of aristocrats stamped it a "nest for the nobility," while its extensive serf population reflected how few changes had occurred in the previous century. The city became in fact a hybrid—truly old Russian in one sense, yet new in that a dynamic breed of Russian aristocrats through their building completely altered central Moscow.

Classicism in Moscow after 1750 appears to have been a vehicle for awakening national consciousness. Although the emergence of an incipient nationalism in eighteenth-century Russia, a subject studied by Hans Rogger, has not been linked specifically with classicism, it does conform to the model which he has constructed.[20] Rogger describes this sense of awareness as "a striving for a common identity, character, and culture by the articulate mem-

bers of a given community," which is "characteristic of a stage of development in which thinking individuals have been able to emerge from anonymity, to seek contact and communication with one another." What is original in Rogger's thesis is his insistence that "national consciousness presupposes extensive exposure to alien ways; it presupposes a class or group of men capable of responding to that exposure; it requires, moreover, the existence of a secular cultural community or an attempt at its formation." Such conditions for Russia, he concludes, could only have been met in the eighteenth century.[21]

National consciousness could not emanate from either a burdened peasantry or a service nobility, but in late eighteenth-century Russia the latter had been emancipated and endowed with both corporate rights and consciousness. New privileges and distinction encouraged the nobility to develop its own culture. Having savored the foreign, it took what it liked and began to fashion symbols and an ideology.[22] Classicism became its hallmark.

The linkage of national consciousness with Catherine's classical Moscow appeared even more pronounced in the time of Alexander I. During that heroic epoch classic and romantic imagery were employed to publicize the national valor displayed against the French. Contemporaries naturally depicted resurrected Moscow as the embodiment of Russian greatness and in this instance the columned portico and the colonnaded ballroom, not the onion dome, became symbolic. That official and privileged Russia had in the course of the century following the reign of Peter the Great subsumed classicism in the Russian aesthetic was, indeed, a notable development and appropriately introduces this historical account of classical Moscow.

---

[20] Hans Rogger, *National Consciousness in Eighteenth Century Russia* (Cambridge, Mass., 1969), 3–7, 276–77.

[21] Ibid., 3.

[22] Rogger (276–77) elaborated: "National consciousness . . . was particularly the product of the articulate, the educated, the literate portion of society—that is, its most highly Westernized sector. . . . Its, Russia's, search for a national identity was not a rejection of Europe; it was itself another aspect of the Westernization of Russian society."

Chapter II

Moscow Before Classicism

Moscow is a huge warehouse,
Petersburg a brightly lit shop.
Moscow is indispensable to Russia,
Russia is indispensable to Petersburg.

Gogol, "St. Petersburg,"
Notes of 1836

The city lies in the middle
of the country, in its bosom,
as it were.

Adam Olearius, *Travels*

Old Moscow: Origins and Early Growth

Moscow is one of the intriguing cities in the world. Once the incarnation of "Holy Russia," then relegated to a provincial capital, the city has since emerged as the exemplar of the Communist order. Situated deep within European Russia, it had not seemed destined for distinction. In this respect, the historian Robert Kerner's words are apt:

> The history of Moscow is the story of how an insignificant *ostrog* [stockade] built in the first half of the twelfth century on an insignificant river by an insignificant princeling, became in the course of time the pivot of an empire extending into two, and even three, continents.

The city's origins have been traced to the twelfth century when an overflow of peoples in the Kliazma River valley north and east of Moscow brought them by both river and land into the region. Migrating Russians heading south and west floated down the Voskhodnia (now the Skhodnia) and the Iauza; others forged roads from Novgorod through Volokolamsk in the north or from Kiev and Smolensk in the south to Rostov, Vladimir, and Suzdal north and east of Moscow.[1] The Volokolamsk Road approached Moscow at the site of the future Great Stone Bridge; the Kiev-Vladimir Road traversed the city where the future Novodevichii Monastery rose and followed the Moscow River to the latter's juncture with the Neglinnaia. There on high ground Russians built their *ostrog*, Moscow's first kremlin, which was to become the center of the city and eventually the Russian empire.

---

[1] See P. V. Sytin, *Istoriia planirovki i zastroiki Moskvy 1147–1762*, 1 (Moscow, 1950; hereafter cited as *Istoriia*), for Moscow's early development along these highways and waterways.

Moscow passed through many phases between the twelfth and eighteenth centuries. In large part its history of fire, terror, lawlessness, Tatar attack, Polish occupation, and Old Believer persecution was Russia's history. During these centuries no plan was consciously devised to govern the city's growth, direct its traffic, or zone its various activities, yet in a very real way it had one.

Like other cities, medieval Moscow's design was of concentric walls and intersecting radial thoroughfares (fig. 1). From the close of the fifteenth century, when Ivan III embellished his decaying Kremlin, the city acquired an increasing number of masonry structures such as churches, monasteries, palaces, walls, and towers to define its silhouette. Despite these developments, and despite even the fires and sieges, the city's appearance had not changed greatly by the turn of the eighteenth century. On the eve of the accession of Peter the Great, a full two centuries after Ivan III, the old capital still was very wooden and Asian.

When Peter I became tsar in 1682, Moscow was a large city by European standards, its 150,000 or 200,000 inhabitants preoccupied with defense and commerce. Those of its populace who were tradesmen and artisans lived in what were, for the most part, primitive dwellings. Adam Olearius, a secretary in the Russian embassy of the duke of Holstein, described at mid-century what very likely was the case at the end of the century. Houses were of "pine and spruce logs laid on top of one another and crosswise (at the ends)" and contained shingled roofs plastered with sod or covered by birch bark. Exceptions were the boyar noble homes, located principally in the Belyi Gorod from which industry and the poor were banished. Broad dirt streets, easily transformed into a sea of mud during the thaw, also impressed Olearius. Such impassable streets were "covered with round logs, laid parallel to one another, so that one can walk across as readily as on a bridge."[2]

An English seaman named John Perry, who journeyed to Russia at the turn of the eighteenth century, was especially struck by the mixure of wealth and penury in the city:

> Whenever any traveller comes with a fair view of the city, the numerous churches, monasteries, and noblemen's and gentlemen's houses, the steeples, cupolas, and crosses at the tops of the churches, which are gilded and painted over, make the city look to be one of the most rich and beautiful in the world . . . but upon a nearer view, you find yourself deceived and disappointed in your expectation.

Like Olearius he noted the endless picket fences between the streets and houses and the by-streets, which "instead of being paved with stone are lined with wood." These were

> fir baulks of about 15 or 16 foot long, laid one by the side of another across the street, upon other baulks that lie underneath them lengthways on the street and lie generally above the dirt which is on each side so that the water presently runs off from them and they lie dry.[3]

Moscow at best appeared a portrait in wood, a mixture of the exotic and the shoddy.

Moscow's kernel was the Kremlin[4] (fig. 2),

Olearius). For Olearius's description of wooden Moscow, see 111–17. For a related work, see W. Benesch, "The Use of Wood as a Building Material in Pre-Modern Russia: Its Extent and Potential Cultural Implications," *Journal of World History* 8 (1964):160–67.

[3] John Perry, *The State of Russia Under the Present Czar* (London, 1716; reissued N.Y., 1968; hereafter cited as *State*), 263–64. Moscow in Peter's day, according to Friedrich Christian Weber, Hanoverian foreign minister, possessed about 3,000 masonry buildings, "durable" and "for the greater part sumptuous." He suggested that they would make Moscow "a fine city if they stood regularly together, but they lie dispersed up and down between thousands of wooden houses. Besides that they do not face the streets but are hid in yards and surrounded with walls to secure them against fire and thieves." Like the houses, the streets, too, followed an irregular pattern and were generally not paved. (*The Present State of Russia . . . 1714 to 1720*, 2 vols. [London, 1722–23; reissued N.Y. 1968], 1:217).

[4] As Moscow became by the end of the fourteenth century a major communications link with cities in the general area, new radial streets—the Tverskaia, Dmitrovskaia, New (*Novaia*) Smolenskaia, Stromynskaia, Vladimirskaia, Kolomenskaia, Riazanskaia, and Kaluzhskaia—connected with old streets leading from the city center. L. M. Tverskoi, *Russkoe gradostroitel'stvo do kontsa XVII veka* (Leningrad and Moscow, 1953), 135–48; Hans Blumenfeld, "Theory of City Form Past and Present," *Journal*

---

[2] Samuel H. Baron, ed., *The Travels of Olearius in Seventeenth Century Russia* (Stanford, Calif., 1967, 112; hereafter cited as

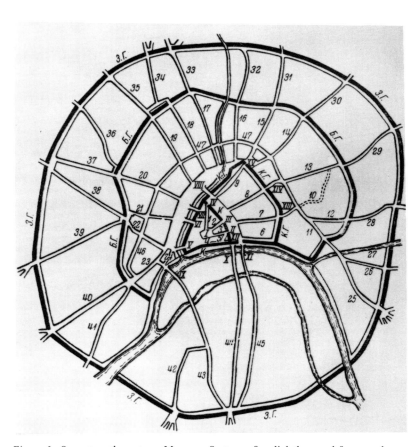

Figure 1. Seventeenth-century Moscow. System of radial thoroughfares and concentric walls (L. M. Tverskoi, *Russkoe gradostroitel'stvo do kontsa XVII veka.* Moscow,
Leningrad, 1953).

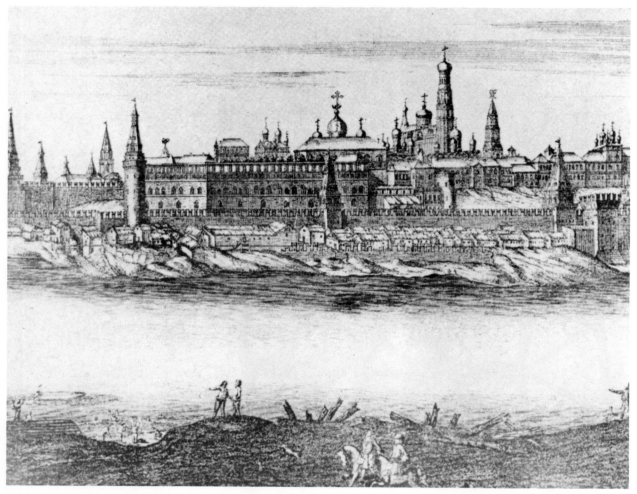

Figure 2. Moscow Kremlin and Embankment. Detail of an Engraving by P. Pikar, ca. 1707 (S. V. Bakhrushin, et al., *Istoriia Moskvy*, 6 vols. 2: Moscow, 1953, frontpiece).

and beyond it lay the Kitai, Belyi, and Zemli-anoi Gorods.[5] The first Kremlin, constructed about the midtwelfth century, was finally expanded and essentially rebuilt during the

reign of Ivan III at the end of the fifteenth century. Its towers, excluding their seventeenth-century superstructure, and some of its most famous churches were creations of Italian architects and engineers, who added a Renaissance aura to this "Third Rome." At the beginning of the eighteenth century the Kremlin held within its walls the tsar's and the Granovitaia Palaces, cathedrals, churches, the Chudovyi and Ascension (*Voznesenskii*) Monasteries, and numerous administrative buildings of brick and stone. Wooden buildings of the nobility, the monasteries, and the clergy contrasted markedly with the five white church cupolas, each overlaid with smooth,

of the *Society of Architectural Historians* 8 (1949); and Robert S. Lopez, "The Crossroads Within the Wall," in Oscar Handlin and John Burchard, eds., *The Historian and the City* (Cambridge, Mass., 1966), 27–43 contains useful comment for the radial-concentric scheme of Moscow.

[5] Kitai Gorod, frequently assumed to mean Chinatown, is a name derived from *Kit* or *Kita*, woven baskets that were filled with dirt to reinforce the wall around it (Arthur Voyce, *Moscow and The Roots of Russian Culture* [Norman, Okla., 1964], 42). Belyi Gorod (White City) took its name from the "white people," or nobility, who lived there and not from the white wall which embraced the city. The Zemlianoi Gorod (Earthen City), once surrounded by a wooden wall, acquired an earthen rampart in 1591 and thus a new name.

thick gold leaf and surmounted by a many faceted cross.

Beyond the Kremlin Gates, Red Square unfolded but was abruptly terminated by *riady*, or market stalls. The square, an oblong expanse, smaller than it is now, dated from Ivan III's time, when it was a *place d'armes*.[6] It was the realm's political, social, and economic nerve center. If memories of Tatar attacks and serf uprisings had faded for those who lived there at the turn of the eighteenth century, executions of the *streltsy* had not. The square had always teemed with idlers, serfs, prostitutes, artisans, clergy, princes, and above all, hawkers—all of whom spilled over into the alleys and shops nearby. Olearius there in the 1630s described "sellers of silk and cloth, goldsmiths, saddlemakers, shoemakers, tailors, furriers, belt or girdlemakers, hat makers, and others each [of whom] have their special streets where they sell their wares." There was an icon market and an open air barber shop widely called the "louse market."[7]

The Kitai Gorod was principally of wooden construction although there were a few masonry churches, monasteries, and buildings in the Ambassadors', Merchants', Cow-branders', and Printers' Yards (*dvory*). Some markets on Red Square were also of brick and stone. The Kitai Gorod radials that continued east and northwest from the Kremlin were the best articulated of any in the city and subsequently proved adaptable to a classical plan.

The Belyi Gorod, like the Kremlin and Kitai Gorod, had a long history. By the fourteenth century radial streets west of the Neglinnaia (*Zaneglimen'e*) housed settlers from Rzhev, Velikii Ustiug, Novgorod, and Tver. A thick forest enveloped that portion of the suburb east of the river, through which passed only one main road. During the fifteenth century the Belyi Gorod became identified with the nobility and church: in Zaneglimen'e, especially, boyar estates and monasteries had replaced smaller houses, and forced a working people's settlement into the forest. Then during the sixteenth and seventeenth centuries, a series of calamities struck the Belyi Gorod. The Crimean Tatar attack and fire of 1571 laid waste much of it. This at least resulted in a new and durable white masonry wall built in 1586–1593 to replace the old earthen rampart. Fire ravaged the area again in 1611, when the Poles occupied Moscow; and still another fire nearly destroyed this noble habitat in 1629.

Some commerce existed in this largely residential Belyi Gorod. Olearius remarked upon the number of artisans, especially bakers, and was impressed by the "bread and flour stalls, the butchers' blocks, the cattle market, and taverns selling beer, mead and vodka."[8] In the seventeenth century, the tsar's stables and a Neglinnaia casting works for guns and bells were built. A half century later one hears of the sale of wheat, meal, flesh, cattle, beer, hydromel, and brandy, prompting the judgment that this suburb "is in a most flourishing state in respect of the variety of trades in which its inhabitants are engaged."[9]

Rivers as well as the concentric walls and radiating streets helped shape Moscow. The

---

[6] Its west side was bordered by the Kremlin Wall and a nearly dried up moat; on its east, by rows of shops; and on the south terminated by St. Basil's Cathedral. At the north end, where the Historical Museum now stands, towered the Main Apothecary Shop, erected in 1699. The Execution Place (*Lobnoe Mesto*), a circular stone slab which still stands alongside St. Basil's, historically served both as a forum for tsar and churchmen to make important declarations and as the site for public executions.

[7] Baron, *Olearius*, 114–15. The Austrian Johann-Georg Korb more than a half century later described the riady in front of the Kremlin as "a series of ambulatories round about with stalls behind." He noted separate markets for silk, for other kinds of cloth, gold jewelry, furs, shoes, linen, pictures, garments, fruit, fish, birds, and for barbering. There were cellars for wine brought by sea into Archangel, and the Gostinyi Dvor where Persians, Armenians, and other foreigners displayed their merchandise. (*Diary of an Austrian Secretary of Legation*, 2 vols. in one. Transl. Count MacKonnell [Latin, 1700; English, London, 1863; reissued New York, 1968], 169.) Weber, nearly three-quarters of a century after *Olearius*, observed that booths in the Kitai Gorod "were ranged into separate quarters and streets according to the goods sold in them." (*Present State of Russia*, 125).

[8] Baron, *Olearius*, 115. Shops, taverns, and hotels clustered not only near the Belyi Gorod Gates and in the place d'armes along its walls, but also in the alleys and radial streets.

[9] Korb, *Diary*, 169.

Neglinnaia River, which approached the city from the north, snaking along the Kitai Gorod and Kremlin walls to the Moscow River, was an important element in the Belyi Gorod.[10] But by 1700 the Neglinnaia, which had begun to run dry along these ramparts, was little more than a series of ponds with water mills situated where the bridges passed over it.[11] Commercial riady on the present site of the Lenin Museum and the snack and game shops, north of the Resurrection (*Voskresenskie*) Gates (site of the Historical Museum), cluttered the left bank. Flour and granary riady occupied the opposite bank (presently the site of the Moskva Hotel). So by the turn of the century the drab brown image of the Belyi Gorod was changing as more and more palaces, shops, mills, and hotels were sharing space with private residences.

The Zemlianoi Gorod by the end of the seventeenth century had for three hundred years quartered streltsy, palace servants, tradesmen and craftsmen, horsemen, gardeners, and Tatars. Their settlements, grouped mainly on radial streets, were separated by gardens and fields. Building plots were smaller than those in the Belyi Gorod and housing, invariably of wood, was consequently denser. The Zemlianoi Gorod was once called *Skorodom*, or "quick house," because the market for building supplies existed there. Olearius observed that one could purchase a prefabricated house in Zemlianoi Gorod and have it constructed elsewhere in the city in several days.[12] That sector of Zemlianoi Gorod touching the Kremlin in the south was called *Zamoskvorech'e* ("beyond the Moscow River"), an area often beset by flooding. From the Great

Stone Bridge to the Zemlianoi Gorod Wall in the southeast, this right bank was inhabited mainly by gardeners, whose plots stretched to the river and whose houses faced the main street, the Sadovnicheskaia.

East of the Neglinnaia, an old and shallow trench carried water from the river past the Nikol'skie Gates of the Kitai Gorod to the Moscow River. In this area, between the Neglinnaia and Rozhdestvenka, stood the Cannon Court (*Pushechnyi dvor*), or armaments works. Another streltsy settlement was located near the Nikol'skie Gates, and on the Horse Market Square blacksmith shops predominated. The ditch emptied into the Moscow River by Vasil'evskii Meadow, site of the future Foundling Home (*Vospitatel'nyi dom*) that rose early in Catherine's reign.

On the west side of the Kremlin, between the Moscow and Neglinnaia Rivers, there were five radial foci, each of which was better articulated than those in either Zamoskvorech'e or along the north and east sides of the Kitai Gorod. They were 1) the Kremlin Borovitskie (or Predtechenskie) Gates, from which Lebiazhii Alley led across the Great Stone Bridge into Zamoskvorech'e; 2) the Borovitskie, as a focus for the Znamenka; 3) the Trinity (*Troitskie*) Gates and Bridge, where the old Volotskaia Road from Novgorod had once converged, as a source for the Vozdvizhenka; 4) the Middle Arsenal Gate, as the origin of the Great Nikitskaia; and 5) the Iverskie, or Resurrection, Gates and Bridge leading into Red Square. This was also the location of future Okhotnyi Riad Square and focus for the Tverskaia, Great Dmitrovka, and Petrovka.

Between the Kremlin and Belyi Gorod Wall lay numerous concentric alleys. Although some had disappeared when settlers were forced from the Belyi Gorod to permit expansion and consolidation of estate holdings during the seventeenth century, the overall appearances had scarcely changed by the mid-eighteenth century. That the disposition of concentric streets frequently resulted in relatively equal blocks suggests conscious planning

---

[10] The Neglinnaia really cut across what is presently the southern half of Sverdlov (formerly Theater) Square to Revolution Square and through Aleksandrovskii Garden.

[11] The Resurrection Bridge (*Voskresenskii Most*) linked Red Square to the Tverskaia; the Trinity Bridge (*Troitskii Most*) drew traffic from the Great (*Bol'shaia*) Nikitskaia and the Vozdvizhenka; the Predtechenskii, from the Znamenka and Prechistenka.

[12] These were really prefabs, for the "logs are already joined together and one needs only to assemble the parts and to chink [the cracks] with moss." (Baron, *Olearius*, 116; repeated almost verbatim in Weber, *Russia*, 125–26).

and regulation of streets even before the age of classical precision. By the sixteenth century Muscovites possessed a definite system of measuring streets and setting them out in straight lines.[13] In the Kitai Gorod between the Nikol'skaia and Mokrinskii Alley, for example, there were several reasonably precise and parallel concentric passages equidistant from one another. This hint at order was possibly the result of planning efforts undertaken after large fires in 1493 and 1501, when Zaneglimen'e was devastated. Conversely, the irregular concentric pattern of the eastern Belyi Gorod resulted from random development and the topography. Regular planning evidently occurred in the western sector, in the Prechistenka and between Streletskii and Trubnyi Boulevards (north of Trubnaia Square); in Zamoskvorech'e, however, only fragments of circular streets appeared.

The Belyi Gorod Wall extended from the Moscow River, below the Neglinnaia, in the west to the confluence of the Moscow River and the Iauza in the east. Originating in the fourteenth century as earthworks and a moat, these ramparts became in the late sixteenth century a white masonry wall, constructed under the direction of the architect Fedor Kon. Beyond this defensive perimeter an area 350 yards wide was cleared to deprive would-be attackers of cover, serve as a barrier against fire, and provide for markets and communications.[14] Open space within the walls was designated a place d'armes. This barrier and its components stood until the second half of the eighteenth century when the area was gradually transformed into that Boulevard Ring which encircles a broad section of central Moscow today.

A Zemlianoi Gorod wall, erected late in the sixteenth century and measuring just over nine miles (fifteen kilometers) in circumference, had earthwork fortifications surmounted by a wooden wall more than sixteen feet (five meters) high with a moat beneath it. This rampart consisted of nearly a hundred closed towers and thirty-four gate towers, all of which burned when the Poles occupied Moscow in 1611, during the Time of Troubles. Afterwards, in 1618, and again in 1638–1641, the earthen rampart was enlarged. Where it appeared vulnerable, especially in the southern sector between the Iauza River and the Krymskii Ford, earthen bastions and an ostrog (1659) were added. By the end of the seventeenth century the name Zemlianoi Gorod, or Earthen City, applied not only to the wall but to the entire area enclosed. The earthen walls, towers, and ostrog survived into the eighteenth century but in a deteriorating state.

Beyond the Zemlianoi Gorod ramparts lay clusters of settlements, and beyond these, estate lands and a half-dozen fortified monasteries—the Andronikov, Simonov, Danilov, Donskoi, Novospasskii, and Novodevichii—which, with their settlements, guarded the arterial approaches to the city and, in a sense, constituted still another concentric defense system. In the second third of the eighteenth century, the government moved the municipal boundary beyond the Zemlianoi Gorod into this sector, but by that time the determinant for locating the walls was the collection of revenue, not defense.

Moscow in Eclipse

Despite Moscow's strategic importance for Russia, Peter I at the beginning of the eighteenth century clearly had no intention of retaining it as his capital city. His reasons were both personal and official. He had always despised Moscow, in particular the Kremlin. Whenever possible, he had escaped the dreary fortress for the freer life among his cronies in Preobrazhenskoe on the Iauza. After the wars with Sweden had won for Russia a toehold on the Baltic, he founded at enormous

---

[13] See Tverskoi, *Russkoe gradostroitel'stvo*, 145.

[14] The Lumber Market, for example, was located at the Neglinnaia River and Belyi Gorod. The Belyi Gorod Wall possessed many towers, ten of which formed entrance gates for radial streets. These were the Vodianye, Chertolskie, Arbatskie, Nikitskie, Tverskie, Petrovskie, Sretenskie, Miasnitskie, Pokrovskie, and Iauzskie.

human and financial cost a new capital there. Although there were strategic risks in shifting Russia's capital from its bosom to an unprotected limb, it suited his purpose personally and politically to have a "window to the West." Moving the capital from Moscow to Petersburg affirmed Peter's goal of breaking decisively with the Muscovite past and establishing a "well-ordered police state," modeled after those of Europe.

Although St. Petersburg overshadowed Moscow throughout the eighteenth century, particularly during the first half, the old capital by no means lost its significance. It remained the largest city in the realm, both in its expanse and populace, although it was to lose perhaps a quarter of its 200,000 population from the plague of 1771. While Petersburg acquired the imperial trappings of a capital city, Moscow retained her historic and preeminent role as an ecclesiastical and administrative center. The sovereign, after all, did journey to Moscow for the ancient coronation rites. Despite the removal of the capital, many governmental agencies remained in Moscow, which, in any case, continued as the capital of its *guberniia*, a substantial territory that included eleven provinces.[15] Nor had Moscow relinquished her essential role in commerce and industry. The College of Manufactures, which oversaw all non-metallic industry, remained there from 1719 until 1779. The city's economy continued to depend upon production of military supplies for the Arsenal and the Military Commissariat. Textiles for uniforms came to dominate Moscow's industry, and the Great Cloth Court became its economic hub.

Toward a Planned City

If Peter had no intention of embellishing his Old Capital, he was forced, nonetheless, to provide for its inhabitants' needs. He did, in fact, show concern for public health and safety, fire prevention, and defense. In the first decade of the new eighteenth century Moscow acquired eight pharmacies and a hospital, while the Dutch physician who directed the latter was also named to head a medical school. That the tsar's concerns about health were justified may be seen in the havoc caused in Russian cities by recurring epidemics. Peter also attempted to deal forcefully with the hordes of beggars, orphans, and illegitimate children who infested Moscow; but decrees against begging and attempts to improve conditions for the children achieved little success. Crime, too, was widespread in Moscow, and the tsar's efforts to reduce it proved equally inadequate. As one of Peter's officials observed: "There is nothing pleasant to report about Moscow. . . . It is a hotbed of brigandage, everything is devastated, the number of lawbreakers is multiplying and executions never stop." In 1723 its citizenry were ordered to organize into night patrols for their own protection.[16]

The greatest threat to Russian urban life, however, came from fire, a frequent visitor to Moscow since early times. Olearius observed in the midseventeenth century that in this city of log houses

> not a month, or even a week, goes by without some homes—or if the wind is strong, whole streets—going up in smoke. Several nights while we were there we saw flames rising in three or four places at once. Shortly before our arrival, a third of the city burned down, and we were told that the same thing happened four years earlier.[17]

Such conflagrations were difficult to contain. Their spread was usually prevented, not by water, but by pulling down houses in their path and carting off the wood before it could ignite.[18]

---

[15] Alexander, "Catherine II," 639–40.

[16] Michael Florinskii, *Russia*, 2 vols. (New York, 1953) 1:400.

[17] Baron, *Olearius*, 112. This observer added: "So that the stone palaces and cellars may be spared from spreading flames, they have very small windows, and these may be sealed by sheetmetal shutters." (ibid.).

[18] John Perry, *State*, 264–65; he also observed that the wood from razed houses often ignited and "gives train to the fire so that I have known it in less than half a day's time, when there has been a gale of wind, to burn above a Russ mile in length and destroy many thousand houses before it has been quenched."

Moscow in flames was also a way of life during the eighteenth century.[19] In late July, 1699, fire gutted virtually all of the Kitai Gorod and Belyi Gorod east of the Neglinnaia. Just two years later, on 19–21 June 1701, the Kremlin itself and the embankment from the Great Stone Bridge to the Moskvoretskie Gates were devastated. The most destructive fire of the Petrine epoch occurred little more than a decade later, on 13 May 1712. Beginning in the Prechistenka at the Belyi Gorod Wall, it swept through both the Zemlianoi and Belyi Gorods to the Sretenka and ravaged, in particular, many estates.

Tsar Peter responded to these fires with a characteristic display of energy. As early as 1698, he ordered the demolition of the mass of timber buildings in Red Square, though he left near the Nikol'skie Gates a wooden theater that stood until 1737, when fire finally consumed it. Then he issued a series of edicts on building and planning.[20] Muscovites in the city center were henceforth required to construct masonry houses, even though shortages in fire-resistant materials usually weakened such decrees. One, dated 17 January 1701, stated that buildings destroyed in 1699 should be replaced, preferably with stone or brick or otherwise with clay. Later in 1701, the Kremlin fire necessitated masonry reconstruction in the Kremlin, Kitai Gorod, and parts of the central city. That same fire destroyed the Tsar's Garden in Zamoskvorech'e and led to the laying out of Bolotnaia Square several years later.[21]

The masonry structures that Peter prescribed were certainly fire-resistant. John Perry, writing at the beginning of the eighteenth century, described their thick walls bound with iron bars and arched over at the top, their iron doors, and their shutters. In time of fire, only the roof burned, and sometimes even that loss was averted by substitution of tile or sheets of iron for the usual fir boards.[22] But, alas, few such sturdy structures were ever erected. Material and labor costs were prohibitive; more importantly, Petersburg's insatiable appetite for building materials during these years left little for Moscow. What often passed for masonry, and so designated below, was stucco over wattle and wood, no less vulnerable to fire than the old log houses. Peter's edicts to make Moscow fireproof were well-intended but largely unfulfilled.

After the great fire in May 1712, the tsar brought the Belyi Gorod under his scrutiny. He prohibited construction of wooden buildings there and decreed that either tile or sod roofing be used on those of masonry and clay. In an edict of June 1712, he required owners of masonry and clay houses in both the Kitai and Belyi Gorod to bring their building facades to the street or risk dispossession of their land.

Like the earlier ones, Peter's edicts of 1712–1714 failed to achieve the desired results. Once again the flow of masonry materials to Petersburg reduced to a mere trickle those available for the Belyi Gorod. Edicts lifting the ban on wood construction (1714 ff.) there cited the necessity to limit masonry building until the New Capital was completed.[23] One decree required clay for building in central Moscow, including the Belyi Gorod; another stressed brick or stone but specified their use

---

[19] The fires of eighteenth-century Moscow are enumerated in Sytin, *Istoriia* 1:187 ff. Perry reasoned that the constant firing of the city was a principal factor in the poverty of the people and was five times more harmful to the city than taxes and war. (*State*, 264–66).

[20] The edicts are recorded in Sytin, *Istoriia* 1:188 ff. and S. V. Bakhrushin, et al., *Istoriia Moskvy*, 6 vols. (Moscow, 1952–1959) 2:84 ff. Hereafter cited as *Istoriia Moskvy*.

[21] On occasion these decrees appeared to contradict their general intent. One in 1705 sought to conserve fire-resistant materials by forbidding their use, except for churches, outside the Kremlin and Kitai Gorod; moreover, edicts were often ignored. That of 28 January 1704, requiring masonry buildings in the Kremlin and Kitai Gorod to front on the street, had to be reaffirmed in both 1709 and 1710. In the midst of these reissues there were especially serious fires in 1709 in the Belyi Gorod, Zemlianoi Gorod, and beyond, and in 1710 in the Kitai Gorod. (Sytin, *Istoriia* 1:198).

[22] Perry, *State*, 267.

[23] The ban on masonry construction was in effect from 1714–1728, but an exodus of architects and skilled workmen to St. Petersburg during these years had a numbing effect on building in Moscow for years after. Weber concluded that Peter's restriction on rebuilding resulted from the diverting of funds to construction in Petersburg; Moscow, he assumed, would simply deteriorate. (*Present State of Russia*, 126–27).

for the Kremlin and Kitai Gorod.[24] Such contradictions simply left a loophole for continuing wooden construction in the Belyi Gorod and elsewhere. Moreover, each new edict virtually repeated the substance of an earlier one; evidently, no one listened.

Although the government retreated to its position of 1704–1705 after its notable failure to improve the Belyi Gorod between 1712–1714, Peter I and his architects continued their efforts to safeguard central Moscow from fire through regular planning. Besides his 1704 edict on masonry houses, Peter had decreed that stone should replace wood pavements. Although this measure was abandoned in 1709 as impractical, house owners were, nonetheless, responsible under pain of fine or the knout, for repairing their wooden pavements. A decree in 1718 specified that an architect supervise all construction in Moscow, but the evidence suggests that property owners continued to circumvent building regulations. In January 1722, the Office of Police assumed responsibility for such supervision. At the end of the same year a special Instruction, which remained a fundamental document for the rest of the century, set forth a code for both police and architects.

The Instruction of 1722 fostered the concept of regular planning by requiring that the fronts of all Moscow houses be placed along a specified line of the street. Property owners in the Kremlin and Kitai Gorod had to construct masonry houses within four years or face the loss of their holdings through dispossession or exchange. The directive also required clay ceilings, tile roofs, and, for houses in the Kremlin and Kitai Gorod, basements.

The Instruction did not rid Moscow of fire. Conflagrations in 1730, 1736, and 1737 did convince officials of the urgency of implementing Peter I's decrees, most of which had been either rescinded or ignored. Prohibitions against chimneyless houses in the Kremlin, Kitai Gorod, and Belyi Gorod, and those against houses without foundations in the first two locations were about the only edicts which had been enforced. In 1730, fire in the Novinskii (now the Chaikovskii Garden Ring) and beyond the Moscow River persuaded officials that future building in these locations must conform to specifications and that a plan for the area should be prepared with that in mind. They further recommended streets with standard widths of 56 to 70 feet, nearly twice as wide as had been considered a few years earlier. The fire that swept the Arbat and spread to the Novinskii in 1736 hurried this planning process. One such plan projected straightened and widened streets and alleys (streets from 56 to 63 feet and alleys at least 21 feet wide) and specific types of buildings such as one-story frame with mezzanine and two-story masonry or masonry and wood. Similar projections were made for other parts of the city. The following year a fire swept from the Kremlin eastward, past the Iauzskie Gates to Lefortov and beyond, destroying 2,527 private houses and many churches and stores.[25]

Besides precautions against fire, the Instruction of 1722 emphasized the regulation of river banks, which were to be lined with "wood and . . . be packed with earth solidly so that there be free passage on these banks."[26] Peter's Instruction and the many decrees preceding it foreshadowed the kind of regulated city that possessed Moscow planners a half century later. Moscow was simply too important to ignore, however disagreeable it was to Russia's rulers.

Defense measures as well as fires were changing the face of central Moscow in Peter's day. What appeared as an imminent attack on Moscow by Charles XII of Sweden in 1707–1708 caused the tsar to order eighteen earthen

---

[24] Perry marveled at the "stupidity and injudiciousness of the Russ lords and counsellors" for not coping better with the fire hazard. Convinced that losses from fires over a twenty-year span exceeded what might have been spent for masonry rebuilding, he was especially critical of the state's tax upon brick which inhibited the very kind of construction so desperately needed. (Perry, 266).

[25] *Istoriia Moskvy* 2:334–35.
[26] Ibid., 86.

pentagonal bastions to be raised before both the Kremlin and Kitai Gorod to reinforce their decaying walls. Earthen fortifications buttressed the Nikol'skie and Savior (*Spasskie*) Gates in Red Square, as well as those walls between the Vodovzvodnaia (Water) Tower and the Tainitskie Gates along the Moscow River.

To facilitate erection of these bastions, the course of the Neglinnaia along the west side of the Kremlin and Kitai Gorod was altered. Peter's engineers channeled this river into a newly excavated moat; and after filling its old bed with refuse and dirt, they laid rows of logs there to support the earthen bastions. When these encroached on the commercial streets and shops on the congested left bank, some, like the snack and game shops, were transferred to the right bank (site of Manezh Square); others were razed. The Apothecary Garden was moved to another location; and the meal stalls, previously on the right bank (site of the Moskva Hotel), were, in part, demolished. East of the Neglinnaia, the bastions eliminated the old ditch and diverted the waters to a new one in front of the defense works. Although war, unlike fire, was not a recurring menace, the prospect of Moscow under siege created great apprehension and led to physical changes in the city's center which obstructed planning endeavors for more than a century. Not until the bastions were demolished after 1812 did substantial building occur in the Kremlin area.

The city's growth and embellishment, no less than fire and defense, accounted for some notable construction in Moscow at the turn of the eighteenth century. One of the most important of these edifices was the new Arsenal (1702–1736), situated along and rising above the interior wall of the Kremlin between the Nikol'skie and Trinity Gates. In an architectural sense it foreshadowed Moscow's classical future.

Aside from the Arsenal, the Kremlin and environs received little embellishment during the early eighteenth century. Hitherto the great repository of Russian architectural treasures and residence of the tsar, the old fortress rather ingloriously became a government office complex. Under such circumstances, its old palaces fell into decay, except when a royal visit or coronation required hurried renovation.

A few new structures did rise beyond the Kremlin Walls. One of these, the Great Stone Bridge (1687–1692) could hardly claim to be a harbinger of classicism, although it became a fixture in the changing city. Near it, a triumphal arch commemorated the conquest of Azov in 1696. The stone Cloth Court (1705), a two-story, rectangular predecessor to Michurin's Court of 1746, exemplified the latest in industrial architecture. Removed from the center of the city, near the Zemlianoi Gorod Wall, stood Mikhail Choglokov's monumental Sukharev Tower (1692–1701), which, like the Great Stone Bridge, was inspired by Russia's National Style. The Main Apothecary was another Petrine creation in Moscow. Erected in the early years of the new century between the Resurrection and Nikol'skie Gates in Red Square, it was three-storied with a small tower and a columnar facade, an interesting blend of the national and proto-classical.

Russia's first theater, a wooden one, was built in 1702 near these Nikol'skie Gates, while across the square by St. Basil's appeared Russia's first book shop, the facade of which, curiously, suggested buildings of a century later. The two most important proto-classical monuments erected in central Moscow during Peter's reign were the Church of the Archangel Gabriel, commonly known as the Menshikov Tower and the Church of St. Ivan The Warrior in Zamoskvorech'e. Built near the Pokrovskie Gates, in the first decade of the eighteenth century, the Menshikov Tower was designed by the Ukrainian Ivan Petrovich Zarudnyi. It and the Sukharev Tower added two soaring elements to the Moscow silhouette during this relatively dormant period.

The Church of Ivan the Warrior (1709–1713, on the Iakimanka), another of Zarudnyi's creations, drew on Russia's past for its octagonal bell tower, pyramid of tiers, and faceted facade but allowed for innovation in its gables, large windows with decorated architraves, classical pilasters, and volutes by the oval windows at the top and the two tiers below. Such baroque-classical elements in both the Menshikov Tower and Church of St. Ivan could only surprise anyone convinced that Moscow was destined for obscurity.[27]

The Iauza River area assumed especial importance in the building that occurred in Peter's reign. Initially, peasant manufactures there necessitated the construction of factories, barns, and warehouses along its banks. One such industrial complex, the Cloth Court, had been the admiralty's sailcloth factory since 1696. The Iauza, however, achieved significance in Russian architecture and planning as a site for palatial rather than industrial architecture.

At the end of the seventeenth century the Iauza, the village of Lefortov especially, had already developed a reputation as an idling place for aristocracy and royalty alike. Lefortov had come into being when one of Peter's favorites, Francis Lefort, established quarters for troops there.[28] Peter himself had been drawn to the camp to seek the protection of his Semenov and Preobrazhenskii regiments from an unreliable streltsy. As Lefortov village acquired status and appropriate embellishment, it emerged as a prototype for classical planning and building in Russia, even before

St. Petersburg. One authority has called it "the birthplace of regulated planning and building of eighteenth-century Russia" and cited the historian Solov'ev's remark that Moscow's Foreign Suburb on the Iauza was "a first step to Petersburg just as Vladimir was one to Moscow."[29]

Building along the Iauza actually accelerated during the first half of the eighteenth century. Just before his death, Peter I had begun, but failed to complete for himself, restoration of the palace of Admiral F. A. Golovin. New palace-park ensembles did appear there in the 1730s. In 1731, the promising young architect Bartolommeo Rastrelli built next to the Golovin complex the summer Annenhof for the Empress Anna Ivanova. Even the Winter Annenhof, built by Rastrelli in the Kremlin the previous year, was dismantled and moved to the Iauza; but, alas, both burned in 1746. Significant in the planning of these two ensembles had been the laying out of the Annenhof groves. Two royal dwellings constructed on the site of the original Golovin palace were, in turn (1753 and 1771), ravaged by fire. Besides palaces, other edifices relating to the royal presence portended classicism on the Iauza. A Senate building in the Foreign Suburb (1702) was the first. A military hospital, begun in 1706–1707, graced the river with its main facade by 1720. Its octagonal cupola bore a greater resemblance to the silhouette of new Petersburg than to any ornament in old Moscow.

---

[27] Cf. also Igor E. Grabar', *Russkaia arkhitektura pervoi poloviny XVIII v.* (Moscow, 1954), 19–38, hereafter cited as *Russkaia arkhitektura*. Although the spire and upper portions of the original Menshikov Tower burned in 1723, the structure was restored in the 1770s. The present tower dates from the late 1830s. Kathleen Berton, *Moscow: An Architectural History* (New York, 1977), hereafter cited as *Moscow*, has noted Bazhenov's admiration for the Church of St. Ivan the Warrior (111). The Gateway Church of the Tikhvin Mother of God (1713–14) in Donskoi Monastery and Zarudnyi's (?) and I. Michurin's Zaikonospasskii Monastery (1711–20, 1742) are other examples of transitional churches, which reflected both the Moscow and European baroque. Examples of transitional secular architecture are the palace of Averki Kirillov and the late seventeenth- and early eighteenth-century dwellings in the Staraia Basmannaia.

[28] Cf. Samuel H. Baron, "The Origins of Seventeenth Century Moscow's Nemeckaja Sloboda," *California Slavic Studies* (1970):1–17.

[29] A. V. Bunin, *Istoriia gradostroitel'nogo iskusstva* (Moscow, 1953), 434. An important forerunner of the classic in Lefortov was the Petrovskii (also called Lefortovskii or Menshikov) Palace, the work of the architects Dmitrii Vasil'evich Aksamitov and probably Giovanni-Maria Fontana. Although initially in the Muscovite style when completed in 1697–1698 or 1699, the Petrovskii was completely rebuilt after passing into the hands of Peter's favorite, Menshikov, in 1707. It received additions from the original rectangular block, forming a great square court, within which the new facades constituted a striking array of columns, pilasters, and arched galleries. This palace, which was joined by a regulated park that descended to the Iauza, became the first in a succession of royal dwellings, baroque and classical, to grace that area. See N. I. Brunov, et al., *Istoriia russkoi arkhitektury* (Moscow, 1956), 258, 274, for drawings of both. R. Podol'skii, "Petrovskii dvorets na Iauze," *Arkhitekturnoe nasledstvo* 1 (1951):15–62 and Igor E. Grabar', *Russkaia arkhitektura*, 17–21. Cf. below, 113

By the end of Peter's reign in 1725, Moscow's growth beyond the Zemlianoi Gorod made that barrier obsolete as a realistic boundary for the city, and, at the same time, caused that area, like the Iauza, to change dramatically in appearance. In 1722, the city officials in an effort to regulate trade, impose duties, and, above all, reduce smuggling, transferred the toll gates to points on the main roads beyond this barrier; but smugglers persisted, using secondary roads.[30] In 1731–1732 Moscow wine sellers, in an attempt to thwart such abuses, erected the Kompaneiskii Wall, extending from these toll gates. Because this wall deteriorated in the course of a decade, the wine sellers persuaded the Kamer College, which supervised the collection of revenues through the spirits monopoly, to construct an earthen wall with eighteen toll gates and a moat before it. This barrier became in 1742 the toll boundary of the city, and in 1754 its overall boundary; but not until the beginning of the nineteenth century, in 1806, did it receive recognition as Moscow's official city limits.[31]

Moscow changed strikingly with the incorporation of lands beyond the Zemlianoi Gorod. Its meadows, groves, grazing land, gardens and fields, and scattered settlements—despite proximity to urban Moscow—made this sector distinctively rural in the first half of the eighteenth century.[32] The area newly enclosed by the Kamer College Wall, primarily along the radial streets, included many of the settlements that had long constituted a part of the city population. Since the sixteenth century, some roads leading into Moscow had been settled by carriage drivers.[33] The foreign enclave on the Iauza, the sizable

Polish and White Russian Meshchanskaia community of craftsmen and tradesmen beyond the Sretenskie Gates, and the military settlements of the Preobrazhenskii, Semenovskii, and Lefortovskii regiments beyond the Iauza appeared during the course of the next century. The roads twisting through these villages also passed the monasteries that guarded the approaches to the city and the estates of large landowners, who earlier had moved beyond the city limits. They had established themselves principally in the south between the Great Kaluzhskaia Road and the Moscow River, and in the west between Great Gruzinskaia Street and the Zemlianoi Gorod Wall.

A land revolution occurred in the Zemlianoi Gorod and beyond during the first half of the eighteenth century. Nobility, in increasing numbers, acquired settlement lands and consolidated these into large estates. In retrospect, building on the Iauza was but an initial step in this process. Streltsy land in Zamoskvorech'e, as early as 1698, had gone to merchants and artisans. When the capital was transferred in 1713, the Tsar's Settlement, where the palace servants resided, lost its purpose; thereupon, the land was sold and the populace dispersed. After their emancipation from state service in 1762, members of the nobility came in large numbers to Moscow—particularly to its suburbs—where they, too, succeeded in wresting settlement lands from previous occupants. Not surprisingly, these new residents turned to the architecture of classicism as they embellished these lands and their beloved city.

The Old Capital at the outset of the eighteenth century was large and important in many ways. Its unique dynamism resulted in changing configurations of settlement, which in turn influenced building and the disposition of alleys and streets. Expansion was a third factor portending the emergence of classical Moscow.

The Michurin Plan of 1739

All of the factors described in the previous section prompted some orderly planning,

---

[30] A wooden wall was erected in 1722 between the turnpikes but was dismantled by peasants in search of fuel.

[31] Internal customs were abolished in Russia in 1754. That established in 1806 was the police boundary; the city was separated from the district in 1864.

[32] The open space here included the Deviche, Miusskoe, and Kalanchevskoe Pole, or fields.

[33] The five settlements of the coachmen were the Kolomenskaia, Dorogomilovskaia, Pereiaslavskaia, and Rogozhskaia, whose populations were very much engaged in the urban life nearby.

which culminated in the Michurin plan of 1739. As early as the spring of 1731, an edict had appeared "concerning the drawing of a plan for the city of Moscow." It stated that "as there is no accurate plan of Moscow, our residence and houses are built without order; therefore, we require that an accurate plan of Moscow, of large streets and small, be drawn."[34] This task eventually fell to two young and talented Petersburg architects, Ivan Aleksandrovich Mordvinov, and, after his premature death in 1734, to Ivan Fedorovich Michurin.[35]

The plan of 1739 offered an entirely new perspective for transforming Moscow and its suburbs as far as the Kompeneiskii Wall.[36] Based on a geodesic survey and thereby exhibiting the actual topography of the city, the plan showed streets, alleys, blocks, fortress walls and towers, churches, large estates, groves, and fields. Although small in scale, the plan served as a basis for regulating streets, issuing permits, and approving plans for new construction until 1775.

Michurin, who depicted Moscow's streets and alleys exceptionally well, made few changes from earlier plans in the Kitai Gorod and the arterial and concentric thoroughfares of the Belyi Gorod. He reduced the number of Belyi Gorod alleys from those appearing in the late seventeenth-century Petrov plan and increased the size of the blocks, principally because of consolidation of land holdings by the nobility. More than his predecessors, Michurin detailed the Zemlianoi Gorod, representing new radial streets and over four hundred others not appearing on seventeenth-century drafts. The innumerable alleys suggested settlement plots with connecting passageways. That many of these streets appeared regular and precise represented pious hope rather than reality. Beyond the Zemlianoi Gorod, Michurin plotted main streets, some alleys, squares, open spaces, and even houses fronting on straightened streets. Although these, too, were designated as regulated and completed, for the most part such was not the case.

The Michurin plan did surpass previous ones in depicting Moscow's landmarks and its changing configuration of settlement, especially in the Belyi and Zemlianoi Gorod, where the number of settlements diminished. A 1737–1745 housing census revealed that the Moscow poor, for the most part, lived in and beyond the Zemlianoi Gorod.[37]

Implicit in Michurin's plan was the need to supervise building. Such monitoring had actually existed from the beginning of the century when Peter I charged the office of architect and the police with this responsibility. Edicts in April and May, 1742, specified codes for building and street and alley width (56 and 28 feet respectively) and authorized an "architectural staff" to assist the police in their execution. Although this staff possessed authority to issue building permits, it often was ignored by the police, who really held the reins of power. The architectural staff, initially consisting of an architect and four assistants, was later supplemented by additional assistants and architecture students. From May, 1742, until his death in 1745, Ivan Iakovlevich Blank held the post of architect; subsequently, Prince Dmitrii Vasil'evich Ukhtomskii served in it for fifteen years. The inclusion of the architectural staff in the police office lasted until 1780, when supervision of building

---

[34] *Istoriia Moskvy* 2:334.

[35] Before his death in 1734 Mordvinov had worked in the Kremlin, Kitai Gorod, and parts of the Belyi Gorod. (Brunov, *Istoriia russkoi arkhitektury*, 296 and Igor E. Grabar' et al., *Istorii russkogo iskusstva*, [Moscow, 1960] 5:153–55; hereafter cited as *Iskusstva*).

[36] The Michurin Plan was not a project design. The best and most detailed account of it is in Sytin, *Istoriia* 1:261–79.

---

[37] *Istoriia Moskvy* 2:337. The number of yards (*dvory*) were as follows:

Parts of the city	1701 No.	%	1737–1745 No.	%
Kreml	43	.25	10	.1
Kitai Gorod	271	1.75	171	1.4
Belyi Gorod	2532	15.5	1249	10.4
Zemlianoi Gorod	7394	45.2	5351	44.6
Beyond Zemlianoi Gorod	6117	37.3	5203	43.5
	16,357	100	11,984	100.0

passed briefly to the Kamennyi Prikaz, or Masonry Bureau. After the dissolution of the Kamennyi Prikaz this responsibility fell to another office, the so-called *Uprava blagochin-ia.*

The rash of fires in mideighteenth century Moscow impelled such planning as Michurin's. Hardly had the city recovered from a conflagration in 1737, when another in 1748 devastated sizable portions of the area beyond the Iauza, including the village of Pokrovskaia and the Foreign Suburb.[38] Tatishchev, the head of police, urged the straightening of streets to reduce the hazards of fire.[39] An edict of 2 July 1748, for example, stated that "buildings in burned-out areas be constructed according to the means and desires of the builder, whether of stone or wood, large or small, with a notice given to the police with a presentation of the plans for the approval of such."[40] Principal streets and alleys projected for straightening were marked in red, thus making "red lines" (*krasnye linii*) a part of the official vocabulary of planning in Moscow after midcentury. An edict passed on 30 June 1752 required that plans approved by the Empress Elizabeth use red lines for streets and alleys and set the width of primary streets at seventy feet and alleys at forty-two. These

dimensions remained standard through the nineteenth century.

Despite talk for half a century of the benefits of masonry construction, stucco and wood, especially, fulfilled most building needs at midcentury. Constant shortages in brick and stone caused either delays or neglect. When Tatishchev reported to the Empress Elizabeth in 1750 that the decaying walls of the Belyi Gorod created a hazard, she ordered their partial dismantlement. This salvageable brick from razed sections was immediately used to repair both government and private structures. The demand for building materials also resulted from the accelerated construction in both the city and its suburbs.[41] In the Kitai and Belyi Gorods, intensive building (often of splendid town houses) proceeded more rapidly than in the Zemlianoi Gorod, where wealthy landowners were consolidating their properties. The latter built masonry mansions; however, the Zemlianoi Gorod occupants whom they displaced invariably embraced traditional wooden modes of construction farther from the city.

At midcentury Moscow confronted essentially the same problems that it had a half century earlier. Despite the city's first coherent plan, that of Michurin, fires, changing population configuration, and materials shortages left Elizabeth's officialdom as bewildered and as unsuccessful in coping with Moscow's problems as Peter's had been. The need existed for a coordinated effort by trained personnel and for an efficient organization. When both appeared in the second half of the century, the results were remarkable.

---

[38] The Ostozhenka, Volkhonka, and Miasnitskaia areas also burned.

[39] A. Tatishchev (the Moscow general policemaster; not V. N. Tatishchev, the historian) designated that old streets be traced in black on the plans; new construction was to be marked in red. In this way began the practice of representing straightened streets also in red and referring to them as the "*krasnye linii,*" or the "red lines," on which the facades of new housing were placed.

[40] Cf. *Istoriia Moskvy* 2:340.

[41] Cf. ibid., 341.

Chapter III

Planning Classical Moscow 1762–1812: The Task and the Resources

The half-century before 1812 proved trying for Moscow's architects. In endeavoring to change the city's appearance from a traditional to classical idiom, they were confronted by the quantitative dimensions of the task, uncertain commitment, and funding. At times it seemed that planners were forced to vent their frustrations simply by drafting more plans while chaotic old Moscow persisted.

Catherine's Moscow

The magnitude of ordering Moscow was confirmed by visitors, foreign and domestic, who wrote of what they perceived. The Englishman, William Coxe, spoke in 1778–1779 of a "vast city . . . stretched in the form of a crescent to a prodigious extent" with "innumerable churches, towers, gilded spires and domes, white, red and green buildings, glittering in the sun forming a splendid appearance yet strangely contrasted by an intermixture of wooden hovels."[1] Edward Daniel Clarke, another English traveler, concluded that the city was a mass of contradictions, "everything extraordinary as well as disappointing in expectation." Like Coxe, Clarke

gazed upon glittering spires, burnished domes, and painted palaces; within the gates he found "nothing but wide and scattered suburbs—huts, gardens, pigsties, brick walls, churches, dunghills, palaces, timber yards, warehouses, and a refuse as it were of sufficient materials to stock an empire with miserable towns and villages."[2] Russians themselves confirmed these paradoxes. The poet Konstantin Nikolaievich Batiushkov described Moscow as "that strange mixture of old and newest of architecture, misery, and riches."[3] Truly, the city at midcentury was a conglomeration: stately palaces beside the meanest hovels; commerce and industry at once in their midst and yet spilling into the suburbs; expansive estates of the nobility; and sprawling monasteries encompassed by white masonry walls and crowned with glistening bulbous cupolas. Small wonder that travelers exclaimed of Moscow as if it were of the exotic East.

During the reign of Catherine II, despite both that sovereign's personal dislike for the city and the aura of St. Petersburg, Moscow's

---

[1] *Travels in Poland, Russia, Sweden, and Denmark,* 5 vols. (London, 1802) 1:277.

[2] *Travels in Russia, Tatary, and Turkey* (Edinburgh, 1839), 17. Hereafter cited as *Travels.*

[3] Quoted from *Istoriia Moskvy* 3, *Period razlozheniia krepostnogo stoia* (Moscow, 1954):142.

importance was reestablished. Large, industrial, disordered, and with a populace often unruly and impoverished, Moscow had become an essential commercial, administrative, and cultural center as well as a habitat for the nobility recently emancipated from state service. Its new Foundling Home and university represented the best of humanitarian and enlightened intentions. The university, located appropriately near the Nobles' Meeting House and Maddox Theater, gave Moscow an intellectual focus. The versatile scholar Mikhail Lomonosov had been a founder, and the poet Mikhail Kheraskov was its curator after 1778. Nikolai Novikov, who became manager of the university press in 1779, probably had the greatest intellectual impact of any. Besides editing a weekly satirical journal and the official *University Gazette*, he headed the controversial Free Mason movement and won notoriety for criticizing Catherine for her failure to enact social and political reform. With Kheraskov, the architects Bazhenov and Kazakov, the historian Shcherbatov, and others, he helped establish in Moscow a promising, if not pulsating, intellectual and artistic environment.

The manufacture of textiles, as noted above, dominated Moscow's industry at this time, and its center was Michurin's Great Cloth Court in Bolotnaia Square. At its peak production, about 1771, this factory employed some 1,400 workers, mainly bondaged, and operated 140 looms. It produced principally woolen "soldier cloth" for uniforms and kersey for linings—all for the Military Commissariat nearby. Other woolen mills were located on the Iauza, east of the Kremlin, and outside of the city. The Sailcloth Court in Preobrazhensk and Ivan Tames's factory, located in the Khamovniki sector of the Zemlianoi Gorod, both produced linen cloth. Other textile factories were located in the old mint in Kadashevskii Court, near the Great Cloth Court, and in the Ambassador's Court in the Kitai Gorod east of the Kremlin.[4] This industry, especially the

large factories with a hundred or more workers, was a mixed blessing socially and economically. Its contribution to the city's disarray and social problems made it a major consideration in any planning endeavor.

While manufacturing and commerce required factories, wharves, warehouses, and well-planned marketing areas, it remained for Moscow's privileged class to exercise the greatest influence on the allocation of space within the city. The nobility required spacious accommodations, which meant mansions, granaries, and cookhouses for themselves and their servants. In effect, they transferred the comforts and expectations of rural estate living to the city's very center. Moscow's aristocracy, like that in Western European capitals,

> expected the city to provide them with elegant squares to set off their homes, with picturesque monuments, and with parks and boulevards that would supply a backdrop for the May Corso, for the Spring Parade, for the *ausflug* or Sunday excursion, for the gentleman on horseback and the lady in her carriage.[5]

As town walls gave way to wide concentric boulevards, spacious plazas unfolded across the sites of the old city gates. These changes, which cost Moscow some of her inscrutable alleys and meandering streams, also allowed new classical facades to encroach upon those of "wooden" Moscow.[6]

Grandees and gentry, collecting in the Belyi Gorod, required such amenities as a Gentlemen's University Boarding House, Nobles' Meeting House, university, and Maddox's Theater on the Petrovka. Splendid estates soon bedecked both the city center and its

---

[4] John Alexander, "Catherine II," 645–53 passim.

[5] Oscar Handlin, "The Modern City as a Field of Historical Study," in Handlin and Burchard, eds., *The Historian and the City*, 21.

[6] In theory, at least, provincial architects had little opportunity to create their own brand of classicism; instead they were obligated to conform to standard facade designs of prominent Petersburg and Moscow architects. The "model facades" were published and distributed through the realm. The best account is E. Beletskaia, N. Krasheninnikova, L. Chernozubova, I. Ern, "*Obraztsovye*" *proekty v zhiloi zatroike russkikh gorodov XVIII–XIX vv* (Moscow, 1961; hereafter cited as Beletskaia, "*Obraztsovye*" *proekty*).

outskirts. Situated within deep courts these edifices consisted of great central blocks, colonnaded porches, and expansive lateral wings—all washed in pastels and secured behind ornamental fences and gates. This architecture of affluent Moscow, less massive and better integrated with the environment than that of St. Petersburg, consequently radiated greater warmth and intimacy.

The outer reaches of the city, by contrast, were hardly affected by these initial planning efforts. Although the nobility absorbed lands of tradesmen and craftsmen in the suburbs and occasionally built Palladian mansions in the midst of wooden cottages, the area remained cluttered in places and traditionally rural.[7]

While planning was required both to order industrial Moscow and beautify the aristocratic city, the decisions required to move it along a classical path came only gradually from a reluctant empress. Catherine II, like Peter I, detested the Old Capital. She remembered, perhaps, her unhappy experiences there as a grand duchess; moreover, her conception of well-ordered European cities, real or imagined, was assaulted by both the disordered environment and seditious and rude Muscovites. She admitted her disdain for its alien architecture, polluting industry, and congested wooden hovels and her disgust for its many filthy beggars and bondage laborers. She was convinced that the perpetual threat of pestilence, fire, and civil insurrection in Moscow was undermining her entire realm. Dread of this city led Catherine to stay away from it during most of her reign; failing, however, to wish it away, she reluctantly set herself to the task of improving it. Her efforts

on behalf of the Old Capital, then, were definitely a labor of necessity, not of love.

Catherine II's arrival in 1762 for her coronation, celebrated by the customary placing of triumphal arches at various entrances to this "originally enthroned capital," impressed upon her the need to do something. She and her entourage remained in Moscow until the middle of the following year. Her decree of 23 October 1762, called for the repair of bridges and a greater cleanliness in the city. She reiterated the ban on new factories in both Moscow and Petersburg. Decrees prohibiting workshops that used fire in their production actually had been in effect for the Belyi Gorod and Zemlianoi Gorod since early in the century; moreover, in 1754 the Empress Elizabeth had sought a reduction of industry in Moscow in order both to conserve wood fuel and avoid deforestation of the environs of the city.[8] But if in her initial decree Catherine seemed only to be following the policies of her predecessors, she clearly broke new ground in that of 11 December 1762, which enlarged the 1737 Commission for Building to include Moscow.

This Commission, a Senate auxiliary, supervised planning for all cities and included many prominent figures. The architect-draftsman Aleksei Kvasov headed its operational department from the time that he transferred to the Commission in April, 1763, until his death in 1772. His successors were the architect I. E. Starov and in 1774 Ivan Lemm, or Lehm. The Commission also had within its ranks architects' helpers recruited from the Office of the Academy of Sciences and "architectural draftsmen" from the Academy of Arts. Experienced geodesists came to the Commission from the Engineering Corps and the Surveying Office of the Senate. City and provincial geodesists and architects, appointed by provincial governors, frequently collaborated with the Commission in the planning of cities in late eighteenth-century Russia. The Commission was responsible for most of the

---

[7] See V. Snegirev, *Moskovskie slobody* (Moscow, 1947) and P. V. Sytin, *Iz istorii moskovskikh ulits* (Moscow, 1959), 338. Hereafter cited as *Ulits*. The nobility, particularly, moved into the Foreign Suburb and Basmannaia settlements east of the Zemlianoi Gorod on the Iauza, appropriating empty lots between the city and the settlements as well. Extensive surveying during Catherine II's reign ordered the former suburbs by imposing limits on the land holdings and facilitating the abolition of "taxable lands" and their transfer to private ownership.

[8] Alexander, "Catherine II," 654–55.

plans and "model" projects for home building at this time. These plans, which originated in the provinces in accord with guidelines set forth by the Commission, were sent to the Commission which approved or corrected them, or even sent architects into the provinces to make the necessary adjustments.[9]

In effect, the decree of 1762 promised equal treatment for Moscow and Petersburg. Catherine ordered that "the same thing should be done for Moscow, which, because of the age of its construction, has not yet come into any order and has not been freed from the hazard of fire." Fire, she added "brings great destruction to the city because of its cramped and disordered wooden buildings." She further directed that the Commission function as the seventeenth-century Kamennyi Prikaz had for her predecessors, "so that those who wanted to build masonry houses could do so without difficulty" and that "all the materials under its supervision . . . be sold to those demanding it and not at a punishing price."[10]

Lest this stilted language obscure her real feelings, the empress stated elsewhere her opposition to the concentration in Moscow of big industries, especially textile. These she concluded contributed to the city's overpopulation, disorder, and pollution; Moscow's water, incidentally, was too dirty even for dyeing.[11] Plague, no less than fire, she perceived as a prospect for her city.[12] Despite such premonitions Catherine did little in the next decade to remove industry of any sort from central Moscow. Even the ban on new building seems to have been relaxed at an early date: in February 1763 permission was granted to establish a silver and gold tapestry factory. Other such approvals followed.

Reordering Moscow: A Cadre of Pioneering Architects

Catherine's Russia did not lack entirely the resources to plan Moscow's refurbishment. Steps had been taken several decades earlier to develop a cadre of architects experienced in the field and acquainted with the problems of materials procurement and architectural education. As it turned out, these early developments proved valuable for Catherine's Moscow enterprise.

Among the architects working in Moscow during the 1730s and 1740s, Ivan Kuz'mich Korobov, Michurin, Mordvinov, and Ivan Grigor'evich Ustinov had been the most important. These men, having studied in the Netherlands as "pensionaries" of Peter I, returned to work in Russia, perhaps unexpectedly to Moscow.[13] Korobov was probably best remembered for his masonry gostinyi dvor, or arcade of shops, in Red Square. It remained until 1813, at which time its charred shell was in part utilized by Bove for his splendid new bazaar. Mordvinov, perhaps the most promising of this quartet, died in 1734 at the age of thirty-four. Undoubtedly, the best known was Michurin. He is credited with the Trinity Church in the Arbat, the church over the gate of Zlatoustovskii Monastery, the Sinodal'naia Tipografia Palace, the Church of Paraskeva-Piatnitsa (1739–1744) in Okhotnyi Riad, and in Bolotnaia Square (after 1746) a new Cloth Court, replacing the one built there some forty years earlier.[14] During these decades the Petersburg architect Rastrelli also came to Moscow. Besides working at Annenhof, he completed in 1753 a new Kremlin grand palace on the foundations of the old one of Ivan III.

Contemporaneous with Rastrelli's sojourn in Moscow was the rise of Prince Dmitrii Vasil'evich Ukhtomskii.[15] Before 1745, the year that he was named architect, he had served apprenticeships with Michurin and Ko-

[9] Beletskaia, *"Obraztsovye" proekty*, 60. The beginnings of Catherine II's planning activities are described in Sytin, *Istoriia* 2:8; *Istoriia Moskvy* 2:342; and briefly in M. Budylina, "Planirovka i zastroika Moskvy posle pozhara 1812 goda (1813–1818 gg.)," *Arkhitekturnoe nasledstvo* 1 (1950), hereafter cited as *"Planirovka i zastroika."* See also V. Shkvarikov, *Ocherk istorii planirovki i zastroiki russkikh gorodov* (Moscow, 1954), 92–93.

[10] Sytin, *Istoriia* 2:8–9.

[11] Alexander, "Catherine II," 659.

[12] Ibid., 655.

[13] Grabar', *Iskusstva* 5:152 ff.

[14] Ibid., 165 ff. and Grabar', *Russkaia arkhitektura*, 256–59.

[15] Cf. especially A. Mikhailov, *Arkhitektor D. V. Ukhtomskii i ego shkola* (Moscow, 1954).

robov. By the early 1750s, after the students of Michurin, Korobov, and Ivan Iakovlevich Blank had come under his direction, Ukhtomskii became the city's most influential architect and teacher. His first notable venture was the bell tower, begun in 1741, in Trinity-Sergei Monastery at Zagorsk. In Moscow, he projected a four-story tower, some 262 feet high, at the Resurrection Gates of Red Square. Had this been built, it would have closed the plaza and added a significant architectural monument to the entire Kremlin ensemble. Both of these towers by Ukhtomskii were notable in that they retained a traditional plan beneath a rococo facade.

Ukhtomskii's Moscow monuments frequently had broad city planning implications. This was especially true of his splendidly rococo Red Gates (*Krasnye vorota*), at the intersection of the Miasnitskaia and the Zemlianoi Gorod Wall (1753–1757), and his Kuznetskii Bridge (*most*), built across the Neglinnaia in 1753–1757.[16] Of all his Moscow creations, Ukhtomskii's Church of St. Nikita the Martyr (1751) in the Old Basmannaia, beyond the Zemlianoi Gorod, established him as Moscow's premier rococo architect. His most ambitious undertaking, on the other hand, was a massive invalid hospital ensemble to be built overlooking the Moscow River at the Simonov Monastery. But this did not pass beyond the design stage.

Aleksei Evlashev and Ivan Zherebtsov were Ukhtomskii's contemporaries. During the 1750s Evlashev designed and built the three-story bell tower of brick and stone over the main gate of Donskoi Monastery. Zherebtsov worked at Annenhof on the construction of the Catherine (or sometimes called Golovin) Palace. His four-story bell tower in the Novospasskii Monastery, begun in 1759 and completed in 1784, was hailed at the time as one of Moscow's important monuments. Doric, Ionic, and Corinthian tiers marked it as clas-

sical despite its traditional cupola and Greek-cross plan. In addition to Zherebtsov's works, the Church of St. Clement, Roman Pope, in the Piatnitskaia (1750s–1770s), Apraksin House (1766) at the Pokrovskie Gates, and Karl Blank's Church of St. Nicholas "in Zvonari" (1762–1781) and bell tower of the Trinity Church "in Serebrenniki" (1781) were among the most notable accomplishments (and present survivals) of this late rococo era.[17]

Creating Instruments for Planning, Building, and Schooling

As Moscow's architects from Michurin to Ukhtomskii perfected their craft and artistry and breathed new life into the old city, they also performed a pioneering work in nurturing a bureaucracy for planning, building, and training. Their efforts came to fruition in Catherine's reign when in 1768 the jurisdiction of the Building Commission for St. Petersburg and Moscow was extended to all Russian cities.[18] As the supreme agency for planning and building in Russia, the Commission, as noted above, developed and inspected city plans, supervised building projects of masonry construction, and encouraged uniform design of both towns and private dwellings. The records, perhaps incomplete, showed that of 416 plans considered, the Commission approved 306, mostly after the new administrative division of

---

[16] The Red Gates (*Krasnye vorota*) were only another casualty of the Stalin era. Cf. Palmer, "Restoration of Ancient Monuments in the USSR," *Survey* 74/75 (1970):168.

[17] Cf. Brunov, *Istoriia*, 321–29 and Grabar', *Russkaia arkhitektura*. Recent photographs of these rococo edifices may be found in Mikhail Il'in, et al., *Moscow Monuments of Architecture 18th-the first third of the 19th century*, 2 vols. English and Russian text (Moscow, 1975) 2:31, 32, 43, 44, 47. Hereafter cited as *Monuments*. Volume 2 of this work has outstanding photographs of most of the important eighteenth and early nineteenth century classical edifices in Moscow. The reader is urged to refer to this work.

[18] Catherine II was responsible for the expansion of the Commission to include *Komissiia dlia stroeniia Peterburga i Moskvy* on 11 December 1762, and later the Commission was charged with supervision of all planning operations in all Russian cities. Cf. Beletskaia, *"Obraztsovye" proekty*, 60 ff. The Commission endured until 1796, when it was disbanded by the Emperor Paul I.

1775.[19] Town plans, conceived by provincial architects, went to the Commission for modification, approval, or rejection. When unusual problems arose, the Commission created separate departments to resolve them. The rebuilding of Tver in 1763 and the preparation of a plan for Moscow in 1775 required such special attention.

Responsibility for these various functions rested with a Commission which consisted of a director and a staff of architects, their helpers, and some geodesists. The draftsman-architect, Aleksei Vasil'evich Kvasov, became its first director in April, 1763.[20] Kvasov died in 1772, and his successor, the prominent architect Ivan Egorovich Starov, remained in charge for only two years. From 1774 until the demise of the Commission, the architect Ivan Lehm headed it. The helpers, recruited from the Academy of Sciences, were students who had finished courses in architectural drafting. The geodesists came from the Engineering Corps and Surveying Office of the Senate. Captain Mikhail Fonvizin, their commander, had collaborated with Kvasov in 1763 in the drafting of plans for both Petersburg and Moscow. City and provincial geodesists and architects joined the regular staff, as needed, to produce plans for Russian cities.

By the mid-1770s, when Moscow's urban planning problems loomed large, a Separate Department (*Otdelennyi*) for Moscow was established to coordinate planning and building under the supervision of Moscow's governor-general. Petr Nikitich Kozhin was named to head the department. Having participated in the construction of St. Isaac's Cathedral (predecessor to Montferrand's) in St. Petersburg, Kozhin had served as a member of the Commission since 1772 and had helped focus attention on the needs of Moscow.

This department, which began to function in mid-June, in turn spawned the *Kamennyi Prikaz* to implement planning policy for Moscow, oversee production and distribution of building materials, and train architects to cope with the considerable building contemplated. Although notable progress had been achieved in greater diversity, standardization, and production of masonry materials, the need was ever-present for ingenuity. That Kozhin was also appointed director of the Kamennyi Prikaz came as no surprise because his expertise in materials procurement was crucial for the Moscow project. Some years earlier he had discovered for St. Petersburg a rich source of stone building materials in the Lake Ladoga and Onega region. In Moscow he soon achieved success manufacturing refractory brick in the state-owned plant which he helped found in Ust-Setunsk.[21] This factory, intended as a model of efficiency for privately owned ones, greatly facilitated private construction. Kozhin also introduced a machine for kneading clay and standardized the size of bricks produced in all state plants. In the Moscow region, too, Kozhin participated in discovery of new materials, lodes of white and other kinds of stone.

The scarcity of masonry materials was a constant concern for Moscow's architects. While the Ust-Setunsk plant produced only for private construction, state and private factories declined from thirty in Moscow in 1774 to sixteen in 1810; consequently, building needs were not being filled. An edict of 2 June 1808, permitting peasant manufacturers to sell brick in both Moscow and Petersburg, belatedly sanctioned what had probably been a long-standing practice. Muscovites also found new ways to reuse old materials. Brick and stone from the dismantled Belyi Gorod Wall were often used for government buildings like the Foundling Home and the Arsenal; less frequently private home builders also drew upon this source.

Besides procuring materials, the building

---

[19] Between 1776 and 1788 some 287 plans were approved (Beletskaia, "*Obraztsovye*" *proekty*, 61).

[20] The first members included I. I. Betskii, Z. G. Chernyshev, N. Chicherin, and later A. I. Shuvalov, and P. Zavadovskii.

[21] Besides brick and tile factories a state bank was established to provide credit for private parties engaged in masonry construction.

bureaucracy tried to develop a skilled man-power reserve. The complexity and scope of building required an expertise which early eighteenth-century Russia did not possess. Architects and builders from abroad had offered their services, which were often accepted; but the hope persisted that Russia could and would train her own cadres of skilled architects and technicians. That classicism was eventually mastered by Russians who gave it a peculiarly Russian quality is indicative of the success of these early efforts.

Although Peter I developed no coherent program of formal architectural education, some progress resulted. A distinction evolved between a trained architect and a master builder. This recognition of the architect as a professional, fostered by the presence of foreign artists and a wider reading of such Western architectural classics as Vignola and Palladio, spurred ambitious young Russians to excel in the building arts. Aspirants naturally learned something of both the art and craft by working as helpers, assistants, or apprentices to foreign architects. The more promising of these were, as noted above, packed off to Western Europe to sit before the masters, particularly the Dutch. Upon returning to Russia pensionaries like Ustinov, Mordvinov, Korobov, and Michurin contributed significantly to the training of a new generation of architects.[22] In 1731–1741, Korobov, with Petr Mikhailovich Eropkin and Mikhail Grigor'evich Zemtzov, wrote a treatise on architectural education that led to the establishment of an architectural school in the Chancellery of Building in Petersburg.[23]

Of these "pensionaries," Michurin achieved the greatest fame in architectural education. During the 1730s, in his capacity of inspecting and repairing decayed monastic buildings, he assembled a group of student assistants. Because this venture proved a successful practicum Michurin enlarged and even formalized it. The fire of 1737, in particular, caused such demands on him that he organized the so-called Moscow Architectural Office which rivaled the Chancellery in Petersburg. His students included such architects as Aleksei Petrovich Evlashev, Vasilii Obukhov, Ivan Zherebtsov, and, in particular, Prince Ukhtomskii. For this reason, historian Igor Grabar' regarded Michurin and his "school," which continued through Ukhtomskii to Vasilii Ivanovich Bazhenov and Matvei Fedorovich Kazakov, to be the source of architectural education in Moscow.[24]

Ukhtomskii, Moscow's leading practitioner in the rococo style, was largely responsible for training Moscow's first generation of classicists, who included both Vasilii Bazhenov (fig.3a) and Matvei Kazakov (fig. 3b). Ukhtomskii's school, created to impart both theoretical and practical knowledge to prospective young architects, achieved its outstanding success in rebuilding Tver after 1763.[25] Reduced to ashes in a single day (12 May 1763), that city became at once a laboratory and model for planning throughout Russia. Four days after the city had burned, Petr Romanovich Nikitin, assistant director of Ukhtomskii's staff and school, was charged to draft a plan for the city and its buildings. Working under Nikitin in this enterprise was Kazakov, whose endeavors in Tver won high praise from Catherine II and led directly to his lifetime assignment to Moscow.

[22] Cf. Grabar', *Iskusstva* 5:153–55.

[23] Architectural education in Petersburg during the first half of the eighteenth century was a function of the Chancellery of Building, the major architectural office. Initially foreign architects performed most of the teaching, but later one Mikhail Grigor'evich Zemtzov played a major role in the Chancellery instructional program. In 1723 Peter I had sent him to Stockholm to study Swedish building techniques. By the late 1720s, when foreign architects were no longer invited in great numbers to Russia, Zemtzov not only assumed a prominent role in completing old buildings and planning new ones but attracted students of many foreign architects to him. The architects I. Blank, P. Eropkin, and V. V. Rastrelli all drew upon the talent of the Zemtzov cadre in the Chancellery. For more on architectural education in Petersburg, see E. A. Borisova, "Arkhitekturnoe obrazovanie v Kantseliarii ot stroenii vo vtoroi chetverti XVIII veka," in *Ezhegodnik Instituta istorii iskusstv 1960* (Moscow, 1961), 97–131.

[24] Grabar', *Iskusstva* 5:155–56; see Grabar', *Russkaia arkhitektura*, 369–411, for the works of Evlashev, Obukhov, Zherebtsov, and Ukhtomskii.

[25] Mikhailov, *Ukhtomskii*, 243–329.

Figure 3a. Vasilli Ivanovich Bazhenov (1737–1799) by an unknown artist (A. V. Bunin, *Istoriia gradostroitel'nogo iskusstva.* Moscow, 1953).

Figure 3b. Matvei F. Kazakov (1738–1812) by an unknown artist (E. Beletskaia, *Arkhitekturnye al'bomy M. F. Kazakova* Moscow, 1956).

Others of Ukhtomskii's school acquired fame in planning and building Russian cities in the second half of the eighteenth century. Kazan was rebuilt under the supervision of Vasilii Kaftyrev, while Aleksandr Filippovich Korkorinov planned cities in Smolensk province. Korkorinov, who himself became a force in architectural education as the first professor of architecture and first rector of the Russian Academy of Arts in St. Petersburg, was the son of an architect or draftsman in a Demidov plant in Siberia. Having initially studied architecture under Ivan Blank, Korkorinov moved with Blank's entire staff into the fold of Ukhtomskii after his teacher's death. His stay with Ukhtomskii in this instance was brief, just a month and a half; he then apprenticed under Korobov and joined the staff of Vasilii Obukhov before returning once again to the school of Ukhtomskii. Another whose career was indirectly influenced by Ukhtomskii was Vasilii Ivanovich Bazhenov, who first affiliated with Ukhtomskii, not as a student, but as a painter for Korkorinov. In such diverse ways did architects learn from one another when architectural education in Russia was on anything but a firm basis.

The founding in 1757 of the Academy of Fine Arts in St. Petersburg proved a milestone in the training of artists in Russia. The moving force behind its establishment was Elizabeth's favorite, Count Ivan Ivanovich Shuvalov, although it had remained an unfinished project of Peter I. The Academy was finally organized in 1764 when Catherine II replaced Shuvalov with Count Ivan Ivanovich Betskoi. Even before this, however, Shuvalov had seen to the design and construction of the imposing edifice on the Neva by Vallin de la Mothe and Kokorinov.

From the time of its founding, the Academy asserted its leadership in all of the arts. Unlike the French Academy, where the separate arts were taught in various institutions, in Russia all instruction occurred in the single Academy building. Even when students studied abroad, they did so under the auspices of the Academy. The young Bazhenov was one of the first who did, and he went to the French Academy. The Russian Academy was similar in most ways to its French counterpart. There existed the same three grades of membership—associate, academician, and professor. The absence of public schools in Russia fostered the development of an Academy school, which admitted students as early as their sixth year.

The Academy of Fine Arts in Russia was more than a mere school for artists and to a greater degree than other national academies it was an arbiter of art. S. Frederick Starr has recently observed that

> from the time of its foundation down to the middle of the nineteenth century, the Academy of Arts exercised direct control over the process of design and execution of every major state-sponsored architectural project in Russia. Special commissions constituted from among its professors monitored the planning of new ensembles in the capital and approved standard building designs for provincial centers. The Academy, in short, was the only union and the Russian state a closed shop. . . . To be sure, its control did not extend to private construction, but until mid-century there was so little free capital for major private construction projects that this limitation meant very little in practice. Also, by virtue of the high visibility of governmental projects, the style in which they were executed was naturally adopted by architects engaged in private practice.[26]

While the Academy clearly did not exercise the direct influence on Moscow and its architects that it did in Petersburg, its indirect influence was considerable. Above all, it placed art in Russia on a sound academic foundation, which led inevitably to a refinement in architecture throughout the realm.

During the 1770s, when the demand for building expertise exceeded the supply in Moscow, both the Kamennyi Prikaz and Krem-

lin Departments assumed responsibility for architectural education as well as for building.[27] The Kamennyi Prikaz developed a sophisticated program of instruction, operating according to well-defined rules and recruiting both faculty and students. The students ranged in age from nine to sixteen, and, in contrast to those in the aristocratic Ukhtomskii school, came from the low rung of society. For that reason, its graduates served most often as architects' apprentices or helpers, rather than as architects.

The Kamennyi Prikaz school provided a stark existence for its pupils. Classes began at six in the morning, sometimes lasting until seven in the evening. The pupils, who by 1780 numbered 33, wore uniforms, answered roll call, and experienced severe discipline for deviating from the rules. Initially, housing consisted of an old residence hall, but in 1778 students acquired their own house in Sverchkov Alley near the Pokrovskie Gates. The students' daily routine was punctuated by occasional variety. Instruction was erratic, judging from the casual attitude of the architect-instructors. Occasionally they shirked their duties and/or misbehaved: fighting and especially drinking were charged against faculty and students alike. The authorities whipped or expelled students for drunkenness and drafted them into the army for forgery and theft.

The instructional staff of the Kamennyi Prikaz consisted principally of the administration. In addition to the energetic and resourceful Kozhin, Nikolai Nikolaevich Le-Grand, the principal architect in the Separate Section in 1775, was appointed senior Kamennyi Prikaz architect in January, 1777, and thereafter taught design. Captain Christian Ivanovich Roseberg, who held the post of minor architect in the Kamennyi Prikaz, taught architectural theory. A veteran of army

---

[26] "Russian Art and Society 1800–1850" in Theofanis G. Stavrou, ed., *Art and Culture in Nineteenth-Century Russia* (Bloomington, Ind., 1983), 102–103. Article hereafter cited as "Russian Art."

[27] See M. V. Budylina, "Arkhitekturnoe obrazovanie v kamennom prikaze (1775–1782)," *Arkhitekturnoe nasledstvo* 15 (Moscow, 1963):111–20, hereafter cited as "Arkhitekturnoe obrazovanie."

building projects in Moscow, he had received special commendation in 1769 for rebuilding the Troitskii Bridge over the Neglinnaia to the Kremlin. When Roseberg left the staff in 1778 and LeGrand shortly afterwards, the pupils were forced to rely on apprentices and helpers for instruction. An architect's helper named Krylov taught drawing to both classes of students for eighteen hours each week.

The Kamennyi Prikaz school offered its students some extremely limited opportunities in the theory and practice of architecture. Of the texts on architecture in the library, most were in either French or Latin; other holdings included scientific and educational works. The pupils also engaged in a practicum, that is, learning while working in the field. Both LeGrand and Roseberg, who supervised construction of facades and streets, had several students assigned to them. The practicum, which formally began only in 1780, also involved drafting plans for private homes and working in brick plants at Ust-Setunsk. The names of the Kamennyi Prikaz students have, for the most part, been lost, or there is simply no record of achievement. Some continued their work in the Kremlin Department (*Expeditsiia*). The brothers Ivan and Nikolai Uriupin and Nikolai Petrovich Kuzmin worked under Bazhenov in the Kremlin and on Tsaritsyna Palace outside Moscow. After Bazhenov retired, they continued under Kazakov in the Kremlin Department.[28]

The Kremlin Department, created in 1768 for the purpose of transforming the Kremlin into a classical ensemble, was quite separate from the Commission and its Separate Department. Like the Kamennyi Prikaz, it offered training opportunities, practical and theoretical, for young architects. Elizvoi Semenovich Nazarov wrote in 1773, while still a student, that Bazhenov, the first head of the department, had him prepare "plans and facades, profiles, etc." Making models doubtless consumed these students' time; one may imagine budding young architects working long hours on Bazhenov's wooden model of a Kremlin Palace.[29] Formal instruction usually occurred in a classical model home erected within the Kremlin walls. Although Bazhenov's time for teaching was limited, his friend, F. V. Karzhavin, taught physics, mathematics, history, and architectural theory and translated architectural treatises. Matvei Kazakov, Bazhenov's first assistant, dubbed "vice-architect," was also an instructor.

Ivan Vasil'evich Egotov was an especially prominent alumnus of the Kremlin school.[30] After working under Bazhenov and Blank, he aided Kazakov in 1777 in preparing a plan for Kolomna. The following year, having been promoted from apprentice to "architectural assistant, 14th class," he worked in the Kremlin until he joined Kazakov in the new city of Ekaterinoslav.[31] Both Egotov and Kazakov returned to the Kremlin Department in 1788, Kazakov to take charge, and Egotov as his second. Egotov left it again during the 1790s when there was little activity, but returned in 1801 to direct the Kremlin architectural school. By 1813 and 1814, probably the year he died, Egotov was "director of the draft shop, councillor of state (*statskii sovetnik*), and cavalier."[32] His career, one largely associated with the Kremlin Department, exemplifies the progress of a student who climbed to the highest level in his profession and who contributed significantly to classical building and architectural education.

Although Egotov and many others began their schooling under Bazhenov, they discovered in Matvei Kazakov their outstanding mentor.[33] As successor to Bazhenov in the Kremlin enterprise and master practitioner of

---

[28] Ibid., passim.

[29] This model is presently in the Museum of the Academy of Construction and Architecture of the USSR in Donskoi Monastery, Moscow. Cf. M. I. Domslak, *Nazarov* (Moscow, 1956), 5. cf. below p. 38.

[30] Cf. A. P. Sedov, *Egotov* (Moscow, 1956), 9.

[31] Wrote Kazakov: "For the task that I have been charged, I am taking as my assistant Ivan Egotov."

[32] *Sedov*, 18.

[33] See A. I. Vlasiuk, A. I. Kaplun, and A. A. Kiparisova, *Kazakov* (Moscow, 1957), 311–12, hereafter cited Vlasiuk, *Kazakov*; M. A. Il'in, *Kazakov* (Moscow, 1955), 23–24.

Moscow classicism at the end of the century, Kazakov was inevitably involved in architectural education. In reality, he promoted it with marked success. His biographer has recorded that he "regenerated in a new manner the architectural school of Ukhtomskii."[34] P. S. Valuev, who headed the Kremlin Department when Kazakov retired, observed that

> the most famous and able architect Kazakov, who gained glory all over Russia by his outstanding knowledge of his art and his creative and practical accomplishment, directed his talent to the architectural school instituted by him, thereby filling not only Moscow but all Russia with good architects.[35]

Kazakov's school, which dated from his return to the Kremlin Department in the 1780s, was eventually housed with the draft shop in his house in Zlatoustovskii (now Komsomolskii) Alley. His students, who were recruited from literate public school boys, learned arithmetic, geometry, drafting, and drawing in the architectural school.

Kazakov's commitment to architectural education extended also to those in the building trades. In 1792 he even proposed the establishment of another school—one for masons, carpenters, joiners, and locksmiths, who during the winter months would receive instruction in drafting, drawing, and architectural theory. Kazakov observed:

> Before this day imported foreigners were assigned to masonry building in our cities at a very great cost. But there are those who, even though calling themselves craftsmen, are completely deficient in these arts. They appear not even to have been trained abroad but to have finished their training here. If they appear well-based in the art, they still know nothing of the quality of our materials or of what our climate can do to most construction, especially brick. Therefore, for very great pay there is very little profit.[36]

In 1805 Kazakov's Kremlin School acquired

the official title of Architectural School. Although retired by that time, Kazakov continued teaching and developing curriculum, which eventually consisted of classes in "drawing, mathematics, mechanics, perspective and art (landscape and ornamental), art from plaster figures, civil architecture, and the theory of the Russian language." Connected with the school was Kazakov's draft shop, where the veteran architect had amassed drafts and drawings of

> the best buildings and views of all four parts of the globe, the drafts and drawings of all the buildings belonging to the Department, views of the ancient buildings of Moscow, including even those which were not saved and demolished, and also those built by the efforts of the Kremlin Department, as well as models of the better buildings.[37]

The graduates of Kazakov's school were worthy of their master. They included besides Egotov, Osip Ivanovich Bove and Aleksei Nikitich Bakarev, both of whom participated in the restoration of Moscow after 1812. Kazakov's son wrote:

> Loving his art and passionately working on important operations, M. F. Kazakov zealously instructed young architects. He left the Fatherland not a small number of architects sufficiently supplied with instruction and usefully performing their task. Thus, he aided the perfection of architecture in Russia.[38]

Training programs for architects and artisans such as that initiated by Kazakov in eighteenth-century Russia indicated a realistic approach to broad-based urban planning and building. Although foreign architects dominated the scene, Russians increasingly assumed key roles. The stature of the architects of the Moscow School—Bazhenov, Matvei and Rodion Rodionovich Kazakov, Egotov, Bove, Bakarev, LeGrand, Nazarov, Karl Ivanovich Blank, and Semen Karin—reflected the modest success of both formal and informal in-

[34] Il'in, *Kazakov*, 23.
[35] Vlasiuk, *Kazakov*, 311.
[36] As quoted ibid.

[37] As quoted ibid., 312.
[38] As quoted ibid., 311.

struction during these formative years of classicism in Moscow.

Clearly, Catherine's Moscow of the 1760s, exhibiting a new vitality after long neglect, required renovation. It fell to this group of young architects, trained for the most part in Russia, to replan Moscow and build in its regulated streets and plazas edifices which, paradoxically, both reflected an incipient national feeling and cast Moscow in the mold of similarly refurbished European cities. That classicism became the vehicle for these young Moscow architects to plan a new Moscow is the subject of the next chapter.

CHAPTER IV

Planning Classical Moscow 1762–1812: Plans and More Plans

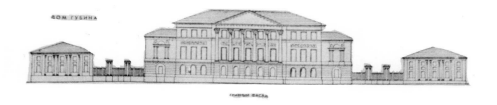

Creation of a classical city required setting it out geometrically, with precision. If Moscow appeared to defy this orderly process, it was hardly the fault of its planners. They drafted plan after plan in the half-century before 1812. These were of various kinds: some detailed existing conditions; others offered an entirely new design, a goal to be achieved. Some were of little consequence; others made a difference. In all, they left Moscow on the eve of the Great Fire with diverse designs, none of which was entirely fulfilled.

Despite this failure to implement any one design, parts of several did alter the Moscow landscape. What emerged from these plans constituted an incipient classical city, circa 1810. Perhaps more important than any material fulfillment were the thought and inspiration which they stimulated. Thus, when confronted with Moscow's restoration after 1812, her architects drew upon ideas that had been germinating for half a century. The planning of classical Moscow, 1762–1812, for all its apparent shortcomings, marked the beginning of an endeavor which continued into the third and fourth decades of the nineteenth century and allowed Moscow to become a classical city of European dimensions.

The Plan of 1775

Although the responsibility for planning lay with the Building Commission for St. Peters-

burg and Moscow as established in 1762, the initial undertaking occurred on 25 July 1763. On that date the Senate directed the architect, Aleksandr Frantsevich Wüst to draft a plan for Moscow and provide a cost estimate of those buildings designated for masonry construction. Both the plan and the estimate were to have been forwarded to the Kamer College, but apparently the plan was never implemented. In response to a Commission directive, one Lt. Petr Ivashev, called quartermaster-general, composed in 1763 an informational plan of Moscow "and the area lying around it for thirty versts." The scale was too small to articulate the streets and especially the buildings within the Zemlianoi Gorod; however, beyond it the numerous settlements, monasteries, and other details were clearly indicated.[1]

In 1767 the Commission for Building required the architect Aleksei V. Kvasov "to place on a general plan . . . all the settlements beyond the Zemlianoi Gorod." This work, projected from local survey plans, was never finished.[2] More meaningful was another plan

---

[1] Sytin, *Istoriia* 2: 10–14. A *verst* equals .66 miles or 1.067 km. A *sazhen'*, or *sàgène*, equals about 7 feet. The scale of Ivashev's plan was 3,500 feet (500 *sàgènes* to the inch). This plan of 1763 evidenced few changes between the Zemlianoi Gorod and Kamer College Wall from Michurin's of 1739; however, it was, as noted, much more detailed for the area beyond the customs barrier. In 1765 what was essentially a copy of Ivashev's plan, but on a still smaller scale, was engraved by the artist-engraver M. I. Makhaev. There is no indication that anything came of it either.

[2] Ibid., 41.

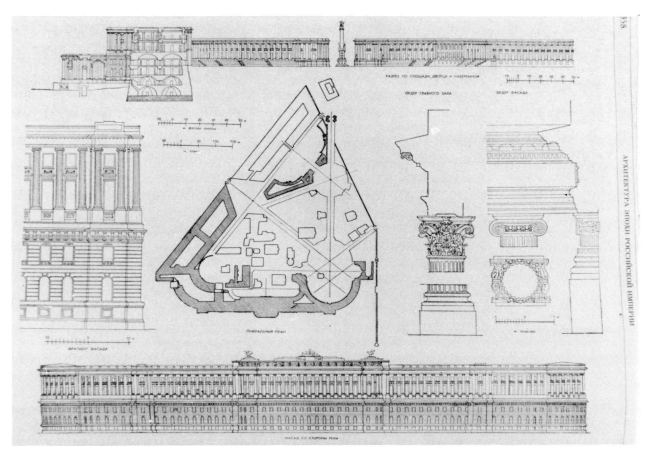

Figure 4. The Great palace in the Moscow Kremlin (planned 1767–1775), architect V. I. Bazhenov (N. I. Brunov, et al., *Istoriia russkoi arkhitektury.* Moscow, 1956).
Upper: Profile of palace along embankment and view from square.

Left: Fragment of the facade.
Right: Order of the Great Hall and order of the facade.
Center: General plan.
Lower: Facade from the Moscow River side.

drafted the same year under the supervision of "Engineer-major S. G. Gorikhvostov." This plan was prepared in two variants,[3] the first of which designated city walls, streets and alleys, streams, plantings, gardens, and important existing masonry structures but excluded their out-buildings. The second variant, which added existing wooden structures to the plan, denoted land plots within the Zemlianoi Gorod and the outlines of city blocks, streets, alleys, and fields beyond it. Within the Zemlianoi and Belyi Gorods even

specific masonry buildings were designated. Small settlement plots were still represented in the Zemlianoi Gorod, where wooden buildings lined the streets and alleys. Gorikhvostov's preparatory plan, a logical antecedent to any future project plan, was, in effect, the fulfillment of the directive to the architect Wüst four years earlier.

As it turned out, the greatest impetus for a classical Moscow in these years came, not from any of the above plans or planners, but rather from a Kremlin palace project devised by the architect Vasilii Ivanovich Bazhenov (fig. 4). When Catherine became empress in 1762, she indicated her distaste for Rastrelli's and Ukhtomskii's rococo style by turning to the architecture of classicism. For building in St.

---

[3] The complete title of the plan was the "General Plan of the Imperial Capital City of Moscow." For a description of the legend of this plan and a comparison of it with that of 1739 see ibid., 21–37; cf. also *Istoriia Moskvy* 2: 344.

Petersburg and environs she most frequently gave commissions to the German Iurii Matveevich Fel'ten, the Italian Antonio Rinaldi, and, eventually, the Scotsman Charles Cameron. But in Moscow it was the Russian Bazhenov who prevailed during the early years of her reign, and he was certainly the most talented of the lot.

For a Russian of that day Vasilii Bazhenov possessed unusual and impeccable credentials. As noted above, he moved from his studies at the Academy of Fine Arts in St. Petersburg to the Academies in Paris and Rome before returning, not yet thirty, to Russia in 1765. After spending several years in Petersburg, he left for Moscow in 1769, where he spent most of his remaining years giving a Russian

reality to the French Classical and Italian Palladian modes to which he had been exposed. In Moscow transformation of the city's center became his overriding concern; to this end he devised a plan to alter the Kremlin in an unprecedented way (fig. 5).

As early as 1767 Bazhenov, heedless of ancient architectural monuments, proposed converting the medieval Kremlin into a vast classical ensemble, which in its sheer mass would have dominated the city architecturally even more completely than did the old citadel. In boldness and scale Bazhenov's Kremlin was the most inventive planning effort of Catherine's reign. Central to the plan was the enormous palace with auxiliary buildings conforming to the generally triangular shape of

Figure 5. Moscow at the End of the Eighteenth and Beginning of the Nineteenth Centuries
Kremlin walls and towers, 1485–1495; Kitai Gorod walls and towers, 1535–1538; Belyi Gorod walls and towers, 1585–1593; Zemlianoi Gorod walls, late sixteenth century. 1. Arsenal (Ivanov), 1702–1736. 2. Senate, now Supreme Soviet Building (Kazakov), 1776–1787. 3. Great Kremlin Palaces: (Rastrelli), finished 1753; projected by Bazhenov, 1767–1775; projected by Kazakov, 1797; projected by L'vov, 1797; undertaken by Stasov in 1816 and Tiurin in 1822. 4. Nikol'skie Gates (Rossi restoration), 1817–1818. 5. Commercial Rows (restored by Bove), 1814–1815. 6. Gostinyi Dvor (Quarenghi and Kazakov [?]), 1790–1805. 7. Foundling Home (K. Blank), 1764–1770. 8. Adoption Council, or Opekunskii Soviet (D. I. Giliardi), 1823–1826. 9. Pashkov House, now part of Lenin Library (Bazhenov), 1784–1786. 10. Old Moscow University (Kazakov), 1786–1793; restored (D. I. Giliardi), 1817–1819. 11. The Manezh, or Manège (Béthencourt), 1817; decoration 1824–1825 (Bove). 12. Aleksandrovskii Garden, built over the encased Neglinnaia River and on the site of Peter's Bastions (Bove), 1821–1822 or 1823. 13. Site of Petrovskii or Maddox's Theater and after 1812 Theater Square. The Bolshoi Theater (A. A. Mikhailov and Bove), 1821–1825; rebuilt (Kavos), 1851–1856. The Malyi Theater, 1821–1840. 14. Dolgorukov House, later Nobles Meeting House, 1780s; Hall of Columns within (Kazakov), 1784–1786. 15. Kuznetskii *Most*, or Bridge (Ukhtomskii), 1753–1757. 16. Temple of Christ the Savior or Redeemer (Ton), 1838–1880. 17. Ensemble of houses on Tverskoi Boulevard, 1790s and early 19th century; Lunin House (D. I. Giliardi), 1818–1823 at Nikitskie Gates. 18. Talyzin House, presently Museum of Russian Architecture, 1787 (Kazakov School) and restored 1816; and Sheremetev, or Razumovskii, House (Bazhenov?), 1780 on Vozdvizhenka (Kalinin Prospekt). 19. Tverskoi or Chernyshevskii House (Kazakov), 1782–1784. Rebuilt in 1940s; now *Mossovet*, or City Hall. 20. Gubin House (Kazakov), presently Institute of Physical Therapy, 1790s. 21. Iushkov House on the Miasnitskaia (Bazhenov), 1780s–1790s. 22. Baryshnikov (Kazakov), 1797–1802, and Lobanov-Rostovskii House, 1790, on the Miasnitskaia. 23. Church of the Archangel Gabriel, or Menshikov Tower (Zarudnyi), 1705–1707. Zemlianoi walls and towers, 1591–1592. 24. Gagarin House on Novinskii (Bove), 1817. 25. Seleznev (Khrushchev) House, now Pushkin Museum (Grigor'ev), 1814 or 1820, on

the Prechistenka. 26. Dolgorukov House (Kazakov), 1780s, on the Prechistenka. 27. Lopukhin (Stanitskaia) House (Grigor'ev), now Tolstoi Museum, 1817–1822, on the Prechistenka. 28. Provision Warehouses (Stasov), 1832–1835. 29. Gagarin House on the Povarskaia, now Gorkii Museum of World Literature (D. I. Giliardi), 1820s. 30. Church of All Sorrows (*Vsekh Skorbiashchikh*), 1790? (Bazhenov); altered, 1828–1833 (Bove). Dolgov House, late 18th century; restored, 1817 (Bove). 31. Church of St. Ivan or John the Warrior, 1709–1713. 32. Church of St. Clement (Evlashev), 1740s–1770s. 33. Military Commissariat (Le Grand), 1778–1779. 34. Batashov House (R. R. Kazakov and M. Kisel'nikov), 1798–1802, and nearby Tutolmin House (Starov?). 35. Gagarin House or Catherine Hospital at the Petrovskie Gates (Kazakov), 1786–1790; restored (Bove), 1820s. 36. Razumovskii House or English Club, 1780; reconstructed after 1812 (Menelas). 37. Widows' Home, 1812–1823. 38. Volkonskii or Protkov House (Bove), 1809. 39. Usachev House, now "Vysokie gory" Sanitarium (D. I. Giliardi and Grigor'ev), 1829–1831. 40. The Sheremetev Hospital or Indigents' Home, now Sklifosovskii Institute (Nazarov and Quarenghi), 1794–1807. 41. Church of Philip the Metropolitan (Kazakov), 1777–1788. 42. Triumphal Gates (Bove), 1827–1834, dismantled and subsequently (1968) moved to southwest Moscow. 43. Catherine Institute, now Soviet Army Building (altered by I. and D. Giliardi), 1802–1818. 44. Aleksandrovskii, now Tuberculosis Institute (A. A. Mikhailov or I. Giliardi), 1807 or 1809–1811. 45. Mariinskaia (now Dostoevskii) Hospital (Mikhailov or I. Giliardi), 1803–1805. 46. First City (*Gradskaia*) Hospital (Bove), 1828–1833. 47. Golitsyn Hospital (Kazakov), 1796–1801. 48. Neskuchnoe Estate, c. 1756; restored (Tiurin), 1830s. 49. Razumovskii House in Gorokhovoe Field, later Institute of Physical Culture (Menelas), 1801–1803; restored (A. G. Grigor'ev), 1842. 50. Demidov House with "Golden Rooms" (Kazakov), 1789–1791, in Gorokhovskii Lane. 51. Ascension (*Voznesenie*) Church (Kazakov), 1790–93. 52. Lefortov ensemble: Annengofskii Palace (Rastrelli), 1730–31; the Military Hospital (Egotov), 1798–1802; the Catherine, or Golovin Palace (Quarenghi), 1773–1796; Lefortov, or Petrovskii, Palace (Aksamitov), 1697–98; (Kazakov), 1775–1782; and *Slobodskii* Palace (Kazakov), 1788–1789, in Leforov. 53. Vitberg's projected monument to the fallen of 1812, 1817. 54. Znamenka Church (Nazarov), 1791–1795, Novospasskii Monastery.

MOSCOW

Late Eighteenth and Early Nineteenth Centuries

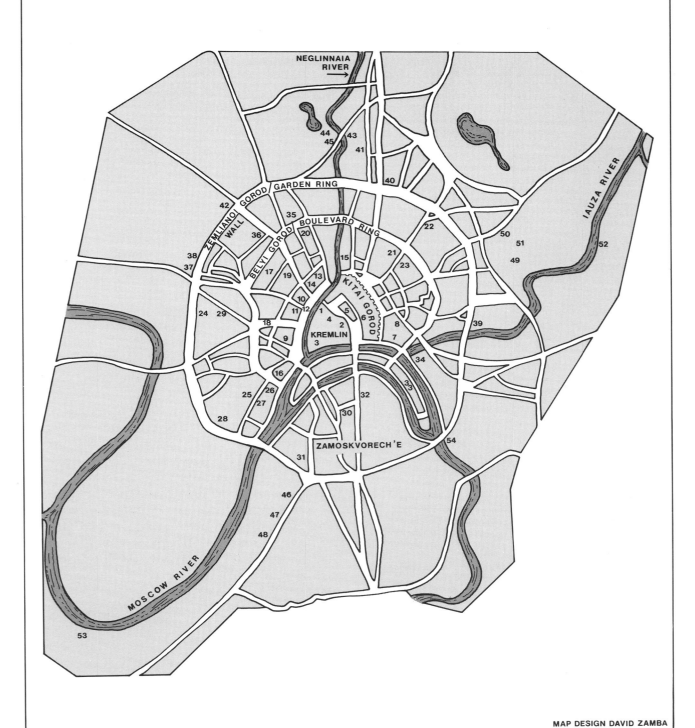

the fortress. Its long (more than 2,100 feet) four-story Moscow River facade was to have been linked to the water by majestic staircases and terraces.[4] Instead of soaring, this new monolithic palace would have created a horizontal Kremlin, one which could consort stylistically with the Foundling Home in Vasil'evskii Meadow down the river.

The Kremlin palace from Zamoskvorech'e was intended to provide a dramatic river prospect: its four-story front facade, the two lower rusticated and the two upper encased by huge Corinthian columns, designed to contrast with Doric and Ionic facades on the other two sides. The edifice itself was conceived to provide the most lavish accommodations for royalty: salons, picture galleries, a theater, and living quarters. From its inner approach, the palace was projected as a mass of columns, the fullest realization of Bazhenov's aspiration to make it "a hymn to the column."[5] An elegant oval plaza was to be before the palace entrance with three streets—the arteries from Petersburg (Tverskaia), Iaroslavl (Vozdvizhenka), and Vladimir (Il'inka)—converging upon it. These three radiating streets were projected as the architectural axis for the city and, symbolically, the basis for subordinating both city and country to the Kremlin.[6]

Bazhenov envisioned the oval court before the palace for public celebrations and therefore designed it in monumental proportions. For its center he planned a triumphal column and an equestrian statue of trumpeting glory. Elsewhere in this great square he proposed other buildings of equal height. Their protruding ground floors were to have been utilized as a stepped podium when great crowds gathered in the plaza on national holidays. The architect intended to place beyond this platform the most impressive structure of the entire ensemble, a colossal colonnade enclosing the entire court. Beside the main oval court Bazhenov planned several lesser ones, each as an ensemble linked by splendid colonnaded entrance ways. Edward Clarke believed that "had the work been completed, no edifice could ever have been compared to it. It would have surpassed the Temple of Solomon, the Propylaeum of Amasis, the Villa of Adrian, or the Forum of Trajan."[7]

Bazhenov's Kremlin project went beyond planning a palace. The congested and disordered construction in both the Zamoskvorech'e and Belyi Gorod marsh land near the Kremlin walls prompted him in early 1770 to draft plans for regulating that stretch. He proposed canals on the Moscow River to reduce flooding and a bridge on the main axis of his palace. Eventually, he hoped to transform the old bed of the river into a canal as well as straighten and reinforce the river banks with stone.

Despite extensive and, at times, feverish preparations, a classical Kremlin palace was never built. Clearing the expanse had begun as early as 1769, but actual construction never progressed beyond the solemn ceremony of laying the palace cornerstone in 1773. By 1775 the entire project was abandoned by the empress, who evidently had lost interest. Even the razed portions of the citadel walls were rebuilt. The reasons for discontinuing the operation are obscure. The estimated cost was admittedly exorbitant, but initially the proposed expenditure had been used to dramatize the resources of the Russian Empire as it pursued its war against the Turks. Perhaps the successful conclusion to that conflict in 1774 convinced Catherine that she had nothing more to prove. Officially, it was reasoned that the Kremlin hill simply could not support such a huge ensemble.

---

[4] The main section of the palace was to have covered 11.12 acres, or an area of 1.5 million cubic meters. This was twice the area covered by Zakharov's Admiralty Building in St. Petersburg and four times its cubic capacity. A wooden model of Bazhenov's classical Kremlin edifice may be seen in the Architectural Museum in Donskoi Monastery.

[5] Arthur Voyce, *The Moscow Kremlin: Its History, Architecture, and Art Treasures* (Berkeley, Calif., 1954), 60–61.

[6] Despite this extensive transformation of the Kremlin, the cathedrals in it were slated to be preserved. The arterial streets mentioned are now Gorkii, Kalinin, and Kuibyshev Streets respectively.

[7] *Travels*, 32.

Real progress in altering Moscow was minimal during the 1760s, despite the prospects early in that decade. By 1770 the Commission had only two variants of the plan of 1767, nothing more. At that time natural forces accomplished what human beings could or would not: the plague infested Moscow in the autumn of 1771, and fires destroyed large sections of the city in 1773. Both catastrophes served to counteract bureaucratic inertia.

The plague was a calamity of the first magnitude, for Moscow lost perhaps a quarter, nearly sixty thousand, of her inhabitants. Catherine, ever scornful of the city and easily convinced that overcrowded and filthy conditions caused the epidemic, determined to rectify the matter. The authorities systematically destroyed some three thousand wooden houses, but in Catherine's mind the big textile factories with their unsanitary working conditions and masses of bondaged laborers were the culprits.[8] At least, a secret memorandum by Catherine dated 4 September 1771, suggested as much. In this document, she demanded of the Senate "that all big factories be removed from the city of Moscow and not a single one left except for handiwork in homes."[9] In an earlier statement, entitled *Réflexions sur Pétersbourg et sur Moscow*, the empress stated similar arguments against industry in Moscow. Her portrayal of Moscow as "a seat of sloth," her criticism of its excessive size, and her diatribes against its various social classes reveal the consternation the city caused her, especially during the plague riots of 15–17 September.[10] Although Catherine failed to remove the big textile factories from the city, they were so debilitated by the plague that they could not continue on the same scale as they had before 1771.[11] So the plague of 1771

spurred her, as little else could, to do something about her unruly and ungainly city.

The plague was followed by fires. The first of these occurred on 22 June 1773, south and southeast of the Zemlianoi Gorod Walls in the Kozhevniki and Taganka areas beyond the Moscow and Iauza Rivers. The second, in mid-July, engulfed the Tverskaia. The resourceful governor-general of Moscow, Prince M. N. Volkonskii (1771–1780), reacted swiftly by submitting proposals for preventing recurrence of such disasters.[12] He made the now familiar recommendation that future Belyi Gorod construction be masonry, including tile roofs, and that those Zemlianoi Gorod wooden buildings standing on stone foundations also be roofed with tile. Noting the limited number of tile and brick factories, he urged that the government build more and enlarge those already existing. Prices, as set by the government, could permit purchase of bricks and tile directly from such factories. He preferred tile roofs to metal, because overheated metal often ignited wooden roof beams. Volkonskii also promised Catherine that he would submit plans for restoring the burned areas.

The first of these was entitled, "Plan Composed at the Moscow Police Station of the Holy Churches, Shops, etc. and the Second Part of the Belyi Gorod, Burned Down on the 14th of July of this Year, 1773." This plan, drawn on 31 July 1773, by an architect named P. Bortnikov, encompassed portions of the Tverskaia and Great Dmitrovka within the Belyi Gorod. Although the draft revealed no rerouted alleys, the arterial and lesser streets, except dead-end ones, were widened and straightened, even severing masonry buildings in their new paths.

A second proposal, "The Plan at the Moscow Police Station of all the Churches, Public Buildings, etc., Burned Down on the 14th of July of this Year, 1773, in the Sixth Part of the Zemlianoi Gorod," focused on the entire

---

[8] In 1775 there were, reputedly, in Moscow 8,878 houses compared to 12,538 in 1770. The sharpest drop, about 40 percent, was outside the Zemlianoi Gorod where many of the poorest homes were located. (*Istoriia Moskvy* 2: 344. See Alexander, "Catherine II").

[9] Quoted from Alexander, "Catherine II," 637.

[10] Ibid., 659.

[11] Ibid., 661 ff.

[12] Sytin, *Istoriia* 2: 495.

Zemlianoi Gorod region west of the Petrovka-Karetnyi Riad. In this plan, all projected alleys and streets were represented, and the Tverskaia and Little Dmitrovka emerged widened and straightened. A number of ponds and vacant lots were included within the blocks.

Still another draft, the "Plan Composed at the Moscow Police Station of all the Churches, Public Buildings, etc., in the Fifth Part, beyond the Zemlianoi Gorod Burned Down the 14th of July of this Year, 1773," centered on the Zemlianoi Gorod at the Tverskie Gates. The many streets and alleys, which had in former days served the Tverskaia-Iamskaia (Coachmen's) Settlement, were, with the exception of Great Tverskaia-Iamskaia Street (now Gorkii), altered or replaced with new thoroughfares. There was, of course, no square at the Zemlianoi Gorod Wall (present-day Maiakovskaia Square), only large lots; and beyond these lay the Iamskoe Field. The reasons for the complete replanning of the Tverskaia-Iamskaia Settlement were contained in the report to Catherine II by the Commission for the Building of St. Petersburg and Moscow. Dated 8 October 1773, this document revealed how the fires in 1773 had devastated the Tverskaia Coachmen's Settlement, causing severe property losses. Because the fires had spread rapidly through the crowded wooden hovels, the Commission replanned the settlement with more space between buildings. The proposal called for the building of 116 masonry houses instead of wooden ones.

A fourth proposal, the "Plan of the Buildings Burned on the 22nd, 23rd, and 24th of June of this Year of 1773 in the Twelfth Part, Beyond the Moscow River in the Kozhevniki Composed on June 23rd, 1773," projected straightened and widened streets and alleys and even two new alleys. No complete plan has survived for the burned-out Taganka, but three partial ones do exist. One, in referring to houses that burned, designated "two-story masonry shops with arches and columns before them," to replace those "to the east and south of the burned church of St. Nicholas on the Bolvanovka in the Zemlianoi Gorod."

Another plan projected meat, fish, bread and flour shops on the site of the future Taganskaia Square, where government-employed masons then resided. These plans were drawn and signed by Bortnikov, who also drafted facade plans for wooden and masonry houses of one, one and a half, and two stories with half floors, all of which were intended for vacant lots in the Taganka in 1773.[13]

Upon receiving these plans for restoring the Taganka and Tverskaia, Catherine reaffirmed her intention (4 September 1773) to create an entire masonry "city" as well as to establish state-owned brick and tile factories and a bank to extend credit for private construction. On 2 December, she approved Volkonskii's report of the fires and his plans, thus forcing the Commission for the first time to give priority to Moscow's needs over those of St. Petersburg.[14]

Because of this new orientation, some of the Commission's membership had to be transferred to Moscow. A Commission report, approved by Catherine II on 14 March 1774, recommended, as noted above, creation of a Separate Department (the *Otdelennyi*) to attend to that city. Headed by Petr Kozhin, it began functioning on 16 June 1774; by April of the next year the Department had prepared (1) a project plan for Moscow (fig. 6); (2) a scheme for increasing production of building materials; and (3) a proposal for a Kamennyi Prikaz to implement the plan and oversee production and distribution of building materials.[15] These proposals were submitted to the empress who by 7 July approved all of them.

The general plan of 1775, the most important one produced for Moscow in the late eighteenth century, became a model for those

---

[13] See Sytin, *Istoriia* 2: 58–63.

[14] The planning developments at this stage are described in several places: Grabar', *Iskusstva* 6: 250; Budylina, "Planirovka i zastroika," 135; *Istoriia Moskvy* 2: 346; Sytin, *Istoriia* 2: 66 ff., 481–83, 497–504; S. A. Zombe, "Proekt plana Moskvy 1775 goda i ego gradostoitel'noe znachenie," *Ezhegodnik Instituta Istoriia Iskusstv 1960* (Moscow, 1961), 55.

[15] The Separate Department (*Otdelennyi*) continued to function so long as did the Commission; both were dissolved by the Emperor Paul on 21 December 1796. (Ibid., p. 88).

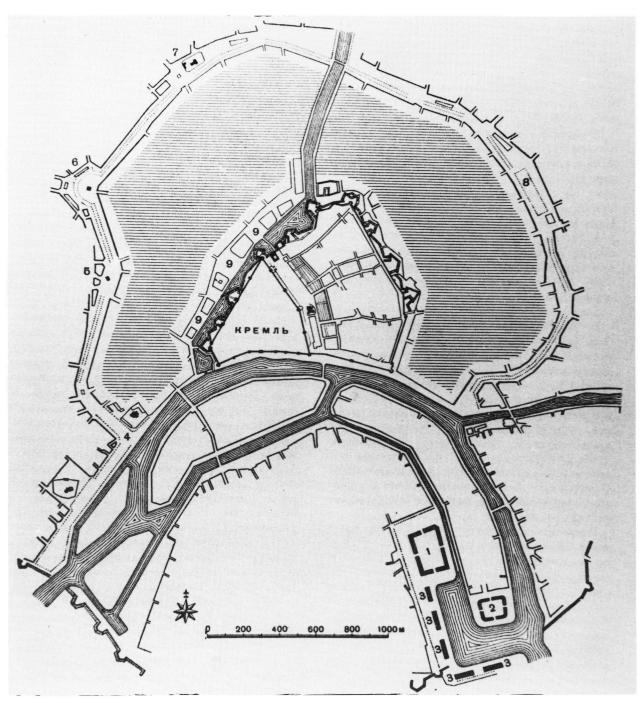

Figure 6. Projected changes in the central district of Moscow, according to the plan of 1775. Details (Bunin, *Istoriia gradostroitel'nogo iskusstva*). . . . 1 and 2-Gostinye dvory of the grain market; 3-Warehouses; 4-Southwestern end of Boulevard Ring (on the site of the demolished walls of Belyi Gorod); 5-Arbatskaia Plaza; 6-Plaza at the Nikitskie Gates; 7-Plaza at the Strastnoi Monastery; 8-Plaza at the Pokrovskie Gates; 9-North to south: the projected Okhotnyi Riad, Moiseevskaia, and Mokhovaia Plazas on the banks of the Neglinnaia.

working to create a classical city. Kozhin and his architect LeGrand played the key role in adapting the plan to Moscow realities, but this grand design probably was a collective effort of that enterprising Moscow coterie of Blank, Kazakov, and Bazhenov rather than of the anonymous members of the Separate Department.[16] Based on that of Gorikhvostov (1767), this plan divided Moscow into the "city" of the Belyi Gorod, the "suburbs" of the Zemlianoi Gorod, and "outlying lands" within the Kamer College Wall.[17] In this way, the design left intact the historic radial-ring pattern and the limits of Moscow but permitted revamping the "city," notably with elegant plazas and public buildings.

Significantly, the men responsible for the plan of 1775 were determined to disassociate it from any new Kremlin venture:

> Moscow has as a center the town *Kreml'*, and construction within it . . . has been placed upon the Department of the Kremlin Palace and did not enter into the inspection of the Commission.

These planners sought, specifically, an enlargement and architectural enrichment of the city center exclusive of the Kremlin and increase in the scale of building in its central district, the main throughways, and squares.[18]

In the Kitai Gorod, where the plan called for three squares, Red Square was to be left unchanged and the Il'inskaia simply widened. Alongside St. Basil's, however, a new square was planned. For the Belyi Gorod, the planners proposed a chain of plazas embracing in semicircular fashion the Kremlin and Kitai Gorod. This ring, with the Moscow River as

both its origin and termination, was etched in space cleared of ancient defenses and congested wooden structures. The squares were designed to reduce the hazard of fire and accent their classical edifices, which would become part of the greater Kremlin ensemble.

The planners also sought to improve the Neglinnaia, a shallow and filthy mudhole which served mainly as a refuse dump, in order to enhance the appearance of these central squares and make it an integral part of the urban composition. They proposed not only to pump more water into the river but to widen and deepen its bed, straighten its banks, and line its quays with trees in order to bring it into harmony with the central plazas.[19]

In addition to well-ordered squares ringing the Kremlin and Kitai Gorod and a straightened and scoured Neglinnaia, the 1775 plan called for another ring in the Belyi Gorod, at the site of old ramparts. The Commission proposed linking new plazas at the gates with a tree-lined, concentric Boulevard Ring, on which splendid classical edifices would be erected. These distinctly administrative plazas would be supplemented by two new commercial ones in Zamoskvorech'e, on the Moscow River for the city's grain market. The plan seemingly overlooked nothing, specifying for these commercial plazas good port facilities, granaries, merchants' stalls, even trees and shrubbery.

The planners of 1775 also addressed the problem of Moscow River flooding. To improve drainage of the river's right bank, opposite the Kremlin, Kitai Gorod, and Foundling Home, they proposed a drainage canal system from the Great Stone Bridge to the Krymskii Ford, to be separated from the main channel of the Moscow River by two islands. As with the Neglinnaia the planners would level the banks, reinforcing them with stone,

---

[16] Bazhenov's conception of the Kremlin palace coincided with the formative period of the general plan of 1775. That it and subsequent plans for the city incorporated such Bazhenov ideas as a system of canals for the Moscow River, a Neglinnyi Canal, and other elements giving order to the city center comes therefore as no surprise.

[17] This concept of a masonry "city," a mixed wood-masonry "suburb," and wooden "outskirts" represented Catherine II's more than Kozhin's ideas for town planning. (Cf. Sytin, *Istoriia* 2: 481).

[18] Zombe, "Proekt plana Moskvy," 56.

---

[19] This "new" Neglinnaia was projected for a deepened moat alongside the bastions of Peter I; however, the northern course of the river was abandoned in 1777. (Cf. Zombe, "Proekt plana Moskvy," 61–62, 82).

and eventually laying out tree-lined thorough-fares on these embankments. The right bank, once drained, was to have been divided into regular city blocks, accommodating attractive buildings (fig. 7).

That the plan of 1775 portended a classical city did not preclude its blending the new with the old. Indeed, there was no escaping the historic "city" and its topography. Concentric boulevards and passages were clearly drawn for both aesthetic and utilitarian reasons; so, too, were the waterways. The planners intended that Kitai Gorod and Kremlin plazas would bring to the "city" a spaciousness to enhance its beauty as well as to deter fire. They based their spatial organization on the ensemble, distinguished by the singular character of its architecture. Individual ensemble facades, extending forward to measured limits, were related in scale and proportion to those of the square or street as a whole. The planners differentiated important administrative or public buildings from lesser edifices by monumental scale and magnificence. Such great structures, their expressive facades punctuated by gigantic porticoes and capped with flat cupolas and belvederes, demanded that grand perspective which classical planning promised.

Whatever its aesthetic and practical merit, the plan of 1775 possessed obvious shortcomings. It emphasized excessively the administrative center and the highways leading to it, and too little the suburbs and outskirts. Such a formula seemed destined to exacerbate the differences between these divisions of the city. Locating important governmental and economic operations on these "city" plazas would, in effect, have removed them from most of the population. Proponents of the plan, who claimed that it would make Moscow fire-proof, also had to face the reality that the masonry "city" would contain only 13 percent of Moscow's houses.[20] The crush of frame structures beyond the city center would continue the fire hazard there. Moscow, unlike St. Petersburg, had constantly to contend with her past.

There were other obstacles to the fulfillment of this plan: the wealthy opposed encroachment upon their property rights; the dispossessed bemoaned their difficulties in locating new housing. As various segments of the populace, the church, and local authorities joined to contravene the plan, mansions of the rich continued to rise in the midst of wooden hovels, while prescribed street and alley widths were ignored.

Meanwhile, the Kamennyi Prikaz, responsible for implementing the plan, had been empowered to supervise building, procure materials, and recruit skilled workmen, qualified engineers, and architects. Under Kozhin, this agency seemed destined to play a decisive role in Moscow's future. In reality, it lasted only eight trying years. From the outset, a shortage of funds restricted its distribution of building materials: after the first year most of its funds were exhausted. Half of the brick and tile produced in the Ust-Setunsk factory, moreover, went for state rather than private use. City officials, for reasons noted above, impeded the agency, seeking to divest it of its supervisory functions and eventually stripping it of its jurisdiction over Kremlin, palace, church, and state construction.

Any one of these obstacles might have been overcome had Kozhin received proper backing, but from the beginning he had to contend with the College headed by the Governor-general Volkonskii, the reputed defender of vested interests in the city.[21] With its resources diminished and authority challenged, the Kamennyi Prikaz had few supporters. It only remained for the empress to lose interest. When she did, the agency's opponents had no difficulty in convincing her to abolish it. Dissolution of the Kamennyi Prikaz in 1782

---

[20] The "city" contained 1,116 of the 8,878 homes of Moscow; therefore, the Kamennyi Prikaz was severely limited in its ability to alter the appearance of Moscow.

[21] Because the governor and the police permitted evasion of planning rules set forth in 1775 and administered by the Kamennyi Prikaz, the latter in reality had lost its authority long before it was officially abolished. (Cf. Sytin, *Istoriia* 2: 95–97, 483; Zombe, "Proekt plana Moskvy," 92).

Figure 7. Kremlin Embankment at the end of the eighteenth century (Donskoi, V-13527). Prints labeled "Donskoi" are from the . . . A. V. Shchusev Museum of Architecture, Photo Archive, Donskoi Monastery.

46

struck a severe blow to coherent planning in Moscow and consequently delayed the emergence of a classical city.

The Kamennyi Prikaz had issued two reports, which revealed the extent of its activities. The first, dated 22 August 1776, accounted for its work in ordering the rivers and setting limits on estates in order to regulate city blocks. This latter kind of activity naturally brought the bureau into conflict with vested interests. Kozhin's second report—which outlined such projects as regulating the Neglinnaia, leveling Peter's bastions, laying out new streets and plazas in their places, erecting a new Gostinyi Dvor in the Kitai Gorod, planning a canal to the south of Moscow between the Andreevskii Ravine and the Danilov Monastery to reduce flooding, and building brick and tile factories—was ignored completely, although many of these goals were realized at a later time.

The planning of Moscow was sporadic after 1775. The plan of 1775, which served as a model for just over a decade, was subjected to important modifications by 1786. These changes occurred after the abolition of the Kamennyi Prikaz, when successive governors of the city with Catherine's acquiescence began nibbling away at the original plan.

Z. G. Chernyshev (1782–1784) did so when he permitted the erection of a commercial building along the Neglinnaia River, a flat contradiction of a clause in the plan. The governor's ruling that land between the Serpukhovskie Gates (now Dobryninskaia Square) and the Arsen'evskii Alley beyond the Kamer College Wall be partitioned into blocks also violated a stipulation which required approval of the Senate for use of land in such a manner. Chernyshev's successor, Ia. A. Brius (1784–1786), carried revision a bit further. On 3 February 1786, he passed on to Catherine recommendations to reduce the number of squares to fourteen, most of which had already existed or could easily be created from vacant areas or in thinly populated sectors of the city. He urged utilization of the open stretches of the dismantled Belyi Gorod Wall and existing space in the Zemlianoi and Kitai Gorod, thereby avoiding the demolition of residential buildings. Brius retained in the revised plan the three public squares in Kitai Gorod, but projected Red Square around the Execution Place rather than around St. Basil's. Before the Gostinyi Dvor (near the present site of Old and New Squares), along the Kitai Gorod Wall from the Nikol'skie Gates to the Moscow River, Brius proposed small markets. He designated another plaza by the Trinity Monastery within the Kremlin, opposite Trinity Gates. In the Belyi Gorod he proposed three squares—at the Tverskie Gates, in the Mokhovaia, and one from the Okhotnyi Riad to Moiseevskaia Almshouse; in Zamoskvorech'e, he designated the Bolotnaia and Polianskaia Squares. At the Zemlianoi Gorod Wall, he proposed plazas (1) at the Serpukhovskie and Kaluzhskie Gates, (2) at the Red Gates, and (3) at the triumphal arch in the Tverskaia. Brius also pleaded for deletion of the proposed concentric boulevard in the Belyi Gorod, urging instead that the space be paved and used for market places. Catherine gave her "supreme approval" to Brius's proposals on 27 March 1786.

The area which received especial scrutiny both in 1786 and 1790 was that of the Kremlin and Kitai Gorod. The 1775 plan had recognized the need for rejuvenating the Neglinnaia along the Kremlin's west wall and eliminating the clutter of wooden houses along its banks. The solution had been the ordering of the river and the building of a chain of three central squares. The 1786 variant proceeded in this direction but with minimal progress.

It projected these plazas (Okhotnyi Riad, Moiseevskaia, and Mokhovaia) from the far reaches of the Okhotnyi Riad (approximately the center of Sverdlov Square) in the north to Trinity Bridge in the south. Realizing them was another matter. Not only did the melange of deteriorating shops and stalls remain, but additional commercial building in the vicinity of the Resurrection Bridge had been permitted by the then governor Count Chernyshev. This spilled over into what is presently Revolution Square and the northern edge of the Okhotnyi Riad. Subsequently, the new blocks and streets, laid out to continue the radial ones, were oriented toward this illegal construction.

Because both the old and this illegitimate new building stalled implementation of the 1775 plan, architect Fedor Kirillovich Sokolov, at the urging of Governor Brius, concentrated in 1786 on the central squares and river. He proposed increasing the length of the proposed Okhotnyi Riad Square to 1,456 feet, thereby extending it from the center of today's Sverdlov Square to the site of the former Moiseevskaia Almshouse, presently that part of Manezh Square opposite the Hotel National. The width of 175 feet (25 ságènes) he retained. The Mokhovaia he projected in dimensions of 1,120 × 210 feet (160 × 30 ságènes), subsequently reduced by Kazakov. Sokolov proposed using the plots of land on the new blocks (*kvartaly*) oriented toward the illegal structures for private construction and intended a single classical facade for both old and new commercial riady facing the Neglinnaia. This facade would at once have obscured the disorderly array behind it and decorated and dignified the quay; its classical motif, moreover, would also have complemented the Kremlin ensemble. For his second task, that of ordering the Neglinnaia, Sokolov proposed a system of precision-contoured basins (four oval and one rectangular) of various sizes, joined by open canals. Although Sokolov's recommendations, for reasons left unexplained, were not implemented, they, at least, were not discarded. In fact, Kazakov drew on them just a few years later when he sought to resolve the same Neglinnaia dilemma.[22]

The northeastern limits of the Kitai Gorod also figured in these revisions. Whereas the plan of 1775 had designated squares and city blocks there and a Neglinnaia canal alongside the bastions down to the Moscow River, the canal had been deleted in 1777. Only a square "from the Nikol'skie Gates to the Moscow

River" was reaffirmed in the variant of 1786.

In the last decade of Catherine's reign several additional plans for the Neglinnaia appeared. The first successor to the one of 1775, discounting the variants, was drawn in 1789 by the "architectural assistant first class Lieutenant Ivan Marchenkov." Appearing just fifty years after the first geodesic plan of 1739, his draft in an illuminating manner represented both the projections from the plan of 1775 and the streets, alleys, and rivers as they existed in 1789. Marchenkov attempted, moreover, to account for all construction during the intervening fourteen years. He focused on Moscow within the Kamer College Rampart, although he also included certain areas beyond it. Between the Kamer College and Zemlianoi Gorod Walls, Marchenkov identified only significant buildings located on important streets and left the remaining area in vegetable gardens, fields, and vacant space. He recorded both the Neglinnyi Canal and Mytishchinskii Aqueduct as being under construction. Although he depicted Moscow River locations, the Vodootvodnyi Canal appeared as projected in 1775 rather than as completed. Concentric boulevards, projected in 1775 but nearly eliminated by Brius in 1786, appeared as planned. Parts of the Zemlianoi Gorod (Zaiauz'e and Zamoskvorech'e up to the Krymskii Bridge) retained their earthen bastions. The Boulevard Ring, articulated by two rows of trees, embraced the center of the city from the Moscow River to the Iauzskie Gates. Not surprisingly, Marchenkov also revealed in his plan significantly more masonry buildings in the Belyi Gorod than in the Zemlianoi Gorod; those in the latter were virtually all churches. Peter's earthen bastions and moats along the walls of the Kremlin and Kitai Gorod were still there. Rectangular forms projected as public buildings in 1775, but never built and subsequently deleted in 1786, reappeared both along Mokhovaia Street's northern edge and in the Okhotnyi Riad.

Two additional plans followed Marchenkov's. The first, quite inferior to his, was completed in the Survey Office and signed by

---

[22] Grabar', *Iskusstva* 6: 258; Budylina, "Planirovka i zastroika," 136–37; Zombe, "Proekt plana Moskvy," 67–87.

one Kazmin in 1790. Apparently derived from a survey begun in 1786, this "Plan of Moscow of the XVII and XVIII Centuries" depicted the outskirts of Moscow within 4 versts (about 2.7 miles) of the Zemlianoi Gorod wall. That it recorded land ownership was probably the purpose of its release.[23]

Another plan of 1790 stemmed from the activities of Prince A. A. Prozorovskii, who in July, 1790, became governor of the city. Impressed that vested property interests had virtually immobilized renovation of the city, he responded quickly to the devastation caused by a fire which had swept the Neglinnaia in 1790.

In a report to Catherine, Prozorovskii requested an updated plan to determine property holdings; that is, all existing houses, names of owners, and dates of construction. While the fire on the Neglinnaia had eliminated much of the congested construction there, a clear designation of property limits was critical for planning and new building.[24] In addition to his report, Prozorovskii submitted to Catherine II three plans of the Neglinnyi region from the Kuznetskii Bridge to its estuary. The first two were copies of the plan of 1775 and its 1786 variant; the third identified structures existing in 1790 with their construction dates and proper locations on the landplots. Although this last plan fell short of the governor's need for a complete and exact plan for the entire city, St. Petersburg did respond.[25]

A special planning group established under the Commission for the Building of St. Petersburg and Moscow was directed to prepare an addendum to the plans of 1775 and 1786, or the kind of draft requested by Prozorovskii.[26] Despite the comprehensive view taken

by this planning body and Kazakov's plan for the Neglinnaia and what was to become Theater Square, this group's work was disappointing.[27] Any account of the burned out Neglinnaia after 1790 inevitably built upon Sokolov's efforts of 1786. A 1790 draft, probably that of Kazakov, plotted buildings, blocks, plazas, canals, and basins in a similar but more artistic and detailed manner than Sokolov had four years earlier. The basins were redrawn and the canals joining them given a new direction on the Kremlin-Kitai Gorod axis. The ordered Neglinnaia, indeed, received clearer articulation in both 1786 and 1790 than it had in 1775. Implicit in regulating the river were the "red line" limits, established for buildings on the blocks adjacent to the river. Kazakov, attentive to this precision, used the line of the squares. Farther down the Neglinnaia his proposed Mokhovaia perspective impressively closed on the Pashkov House, high on Vagan'skii Hill. He represented Moiseevskaia Square as a small rectangle, close to where the monastery had once stood.

The plan of 1790 identified what was to become, after Red Square, Moscow's most famous plaza: the Theater (Sverdlov) Square. Located between the Dmitrovka and the Petrovka, it had its origins in the planning of the 1780s and events of the decade before that. When a private home there had burned in 1773, the Petrovskii Public Theater (later Maddox's) was erected in its place. Although Kazakov in 1790 proposed widening and regulating the open space in front of this building's plaza, the 1790 draft depicted only a small plaza, merely the limits of a residential block. The 1790 planners also proposed shifting commerce to the Varvarskie Gates, where the market, built with Governor Chernyshev's permission, contained vacant shops. Because commercial rows were prohibited along the Neglinnaia, the planners designated this newly

[23] *Istoriia Moskvy* 2: 352–54.

[24] See Zombe, "Proekt plana Moskvy," 67–70; Sytin, *Istoriia* 2: 271 and A. Kiparisova, "Chertzhi i proekti M. F. Kazakova v Tsentral'nom voenno-istoricheskom arkhive," *Arkhitekturnoe nasledstvo* 1 (1951): 117.

[25] Cf. Sytin, *Istoriia*, 2: 560.

[26] This special body for composing a "Plan of the Capital City of Moscow" (*Plan stolichnogo goroda Moskvy*) was established 11 July 1790.

[27] Cf. Budylina, "Planirovka i zastroika," 172–73 n. and E. A. Beletskaia, *Arkhitekturnye Al'bomy M. F. Kazakova* (Moscow, 1956), 27 n, hereafter cited as *Al'bomy M. F. Kazakova*. A. Kiparisova, "Chertezhi i proekty M. F. Kazakova," 116–17.

regulated river site for private housing to accommodate those uprooted in the laying out of the central plazas.

From the outset, shortages of equipment and skilled labor, inexperienced personnel, and Prozorovskii's indecision prevented the planners from meeting scheduled deadlines. Then in 1794 the governor died; two years later death claimed Catherine before she could react to the Commission's proposal. Paul, not unexpectedly, reversed his mother's general policy on city building as well as in other matters. He dismissed the special 1790 planning body and even the Building Commission for St. Petersburg and Moscow, which had first drawn attention to Moscow more than three decades earlier.

Catherine's passing marked the end of an era in city planning and building. Though the empress disliked Moscow, she had not neglected it. Prodded by occasional natural disasters, she had at least nudged the old city along its classical way. Her chief accomplishment, the general plan of 1775, served for over a decade as a model for refurbishing if not rebuilding the old city. Any departures from it seemed merely to stimulate new plans. What would have resulted from the new plans and from the new Commission is difficult to say, but Catherine's death clearly brought a temporary respite in town planning as a royal concern.

Matvei Fedorovich Kazakov: Architect of Classical Moscow

Despite the Emperor Paul's disposition to dismantle his mother's planning apparatus, building in Moscow did occur.[28] It was fostered principally by that city's most accom-

plished architect, Matvei Fedorovich Kazakov (fig. 3b). Kazakov had actually been on the Moscow architectural scene for many years and was nearing sixty when Catherine died. If less talented than Bazhenov, he was immeasurably more successful in obtaining approval for his projects and bringing them to fruition. One historian has even labeled the classical era the "Kazakov Period" (1770–1860) in recognition of his and his students' impact on the city's physical transformation.[29]

Unlike Bazhenov, Kazakov had not studied in Rome, Paris, or even St. Petersburg; rather he graduated from Ukhtomskii's Moscow school where he had served for years as an apprentice. Except for a brief stint in rebuilding Tver, Kazakov spent his entire professional life in Moscow. In 1768 he joined the Kremlin Department as an aid to Bazhenov, thus beginning his long love affair with Moscow.[30] Under Bazhenov, Kazakov demolished, repaired, and rebuilt the Kremlin, and in so doing, acquired an unsurpassed knowledge of that ancient ensemble. During these years he also acquainted himself with the problems of materials procurement, even to the extent of planning brick factories and probing existing stone quarries. After 1770 Kazakov's role equaled that of Bazhenov in the Kremlin undertaking. He supervised the razing of the *prikazy* buildings and the Cathedral of the Chernigov Saints (located where the main facade of Bazhenov's palace was projected), oversaw the digging and laying of the palace foundation, and even prepared financial estimates for the palace construction itself. From 1786 Kazakov headed the Kremlin Department, which under his direction became a focal point for all important governmental building in Moscow and, as noted above, he utilized his organizational talents to resurrect the architectural school of Ukhtomskii.[31]

---

[28] Two *fin de siècle* planning efforts of little consequence were those by the Provincial Surveyor Khomiakov and the merchant Polezhaev. The former, charged on 17 February 1797, to complete a city plan, accomplished very little. Polezhaev's plan in 1796 was a slightly modified version of Gorikhvostov's of 1767 and Marchenkov's of 1789. Although it failed to discriminate between what actually existed and what had been projected in 1775, Polezhaev's contained information about buildings and streets and statistics. (Sytin, *Istoriia* 2: 310, 493).

[29] Berton, *Moscow*, 135. Bunin also referred to these years as "Kazakov's Epoch."

[30] *Istoriia gradostroitel'nogo iskusstva*, 276; see also Kiparisova, "Chertezhi i proekty M. F. Kazakova," 116–18. The best existing biography of Kazakov is Vlasiuk, *Kazakov*. The information appearing here is drawn largely from it and Il'in, *Kazakov*.

[31] This institution continues today in the Moscow Institute of Architecture. (Il'in, *Kazakov*, 23–24).

At the invitation of the Moscow governor, Prince Prozorovskii, Kazakov in 1790 had entered into the planning of central Moscow. After completing the Moscow River embankment, he redesigned his Tverskoi House, the governor's mansion, and laid out in 1792 a plaza on the Dolgorukov properties before it. Although this project on the Tverskaia evoked little interest from Catherine, it proved to be one of the most important ensembles planned in Moscow before 1812.[32]

Kazakov returned to the unfinished task of fashioning a classical Kremlin in 1797. The demise of Bazhenov's monumental scheme had left unresolved the matter of a palatial residence for the royal family: Kazakov's palace on the Prechistenka, regarded as temporary, appeared to be destined for demolition, while Rastrelli's old Elizavetinskii Palace in the Kremlin was no longer adequate for the royal family's needs.

The design by Kazakov for remodeling the Kremlin merits attention because, like Bazhenov's, it had broad planning implications. This latest Kremlin venture grew out of a project for a new palace, riding school, and hanging garden—all commissioned by the Emperor Paul.[33] Kazakov retained Bazhenov's focus on the southern approach to the Kremlin, but opted not to obscure the central group of Kremlin churches by a huge palatial facade (fig. 8). The southeast corner he reserved for the riding school, the main facade of which would have been on line with the facade of the central palace. These two edifices were to have framed the cathedral group and the bell tower of Ivan the Great, thereby forming a balanced three-part composition. Kazakov designed additional palace buildings for the rear of the Kremlin opposite the Trinity Gates. One of these, a three-story grand ducal residence, faced both the plazas by the Senate and the cathedrals, while his proposed three-story residence for the princesses just south

of the Trinity Gates was intended to shape that space as a trapezoid.

Kazakov, like Bazhenov, envisioned a palace embellished with columns. The main section, as viewed from the south, was to have rested on an arcaded lower story (retained from Rastrelli's old palace) that contrasted sharply with the soaring eight-column central portico, pediment, and cupola. Kazakov emphasized more than Bazhenov had done the external appearance of the Kremlin structures, the panoramic view from the south. For him the plazas were neither primary nor unique, but they did provide a uniformity for the whole composition. Despite Kazakov's care for this project and his stature as Moscow's chief architect, the plan was not approved.

In April 1797, the Emperor Paul turned instead to the architect L'vov (fig. 9) and instructed him to compose plans, not for a new, but for a reconstructed Rastrelli palace. L'vov went further, however, suggesting a vast ensemble, which incorporated the old structure (fig. 10) and integrated his palace with the existing Kremlin buildings. He, too, proposed that his palace occupy the prominent southern approach to the Kremlin. It resembled Kazakov's plan in that it represented a three-part palace composition with finished side wings. In his plan, L'vov treated Rastrelli's palace as the left wing of the new palace and accentuated a new central structure, which consisted of a six-columned portico and colonnaded rotunda, capped with a cupola. In one unapproved variant, L'vov even designed an essentially Gothic Kremlin, while employing a classical mode only for the new central edifice and the Rastrelli palace. To effect a Gothic look he proposed elevating a hanging garden to the substructure of the assemblage and then allowing it to trail off as a natural garden, through which the sweeping staircases of the central palace structure would have led.

A comparison of the Kazakov and L'vov plans shows the former as much larger in scale, really a major planning scheme. Kazakov had intended that his building would front on a street within the Kremlin, whereas L'vov projected his building in a garden surrounded

---

[32] Cf. below, 000.

[33] For more on Kazakov's Kremlin project, see Vlasiuk, *Kazakov*, 287–96; the best account of L'vov's Kremlin palace is M. V. Budylina, O. I. Braitseva, and A. M. Kharlamova, *Arkhitektor N. A. L'vov* (Moscow, 1961), 152–56.

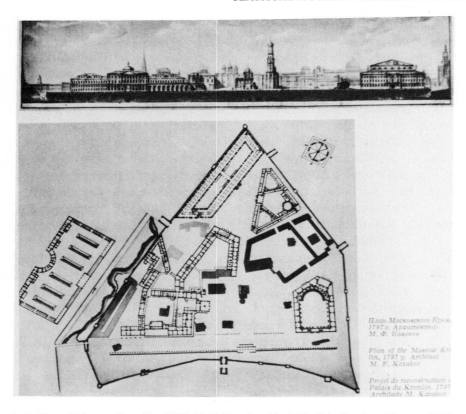

Figure 8. Plan of Moscow Kremlin, 1797, M. F. Kazakov (A. I. Vlasiuk, *Kazakov.* Moscow, 1957).

by high walls. Kazakov's horizontal assemblage would have presented a striking silhouette; L'vov's design, on the other hand, was for a single building rather than a complex. Instead of contemplating reconstruction of the entire Kremlin as did Kazakov, L'vov sought to harmonize his new buildings with the old.

The distinctions between L'vov's and Kazakov's plans resulted from different programs. Kazakov's plans assumed that the second-floor rooms of the west wing would be used for administrative purposes and the central building, a huge central hall, for gatherings. He would have replaced the ancient Sretenskaia Church with a new, well-lighted one. L'vov proposed small second-floor apartments, no central hall, and retention of the church. He designated the left side of the central corpus as quarters for the royal family. L'vov's intimate royal villa in a park-like setting failed, like Kazakov's monumental structure dominating the river front, to receive royal sanction—for reasons left unstated.

Although these two plans for a classical Kremlin constituted the last efforts of their kind for more than two decades, the streets and buildings in its vicinity continued to be a central concern as a new century dawned. Once again, Kazakov was the principal in the matter. Despite infirmity from illness and old age, in October 1800 he began still another project, the creation of a "facade plan" for Moscow.[34] Admirably suited for such a task as a result of his intimate knowledge of Moscow, he accepted the charge that he draft an axonometric plan, showing the city blocks in perspective, with plans, facades, profiles, and descriptions. In truth, this facade plan probably was intended to facilitate work on a general plan.

A precedent for this perspective plan had been completed some forty years earlier for

---

[34] See M. A. Il'in, "'Facadicheskii' plan Moskvy M. F. Kazakova," *Arkhitekturnoe nasledstvo* 9 (1959): 5–14, and Vlasiuk, *Kazakov,* 303–10.

Figure 9. Nikolai Aleksandrovich L'vov (1751–1803), D. G. Levitskii, 1789 (M. V. Budylina, et al., *Arkhitektor N. A. L'vov*. Moscow, 1961).

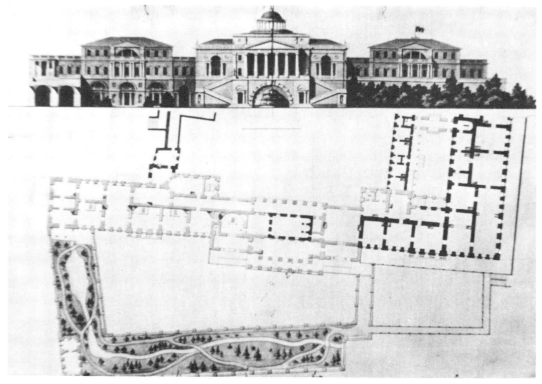

Figure 10. Design for Moscow Kremlin Palace, N. A. L'vov, 1797 (Budylina, *L'vov*).

St. Petersburg.[35] Furthermore, Bazhenov, before his death in 1799, had begun collecting drafts of "all large buildings existing in both capitals," with the idea of publishing them in a series entitled *Russian Architecture*. Although unfinished, this work was reflected in Kazakov's facade plan. Evident interest in Moscow's architectural appearance had also been indicated by the drawings of Giacomo Quarenghi and Francesco Camporesi, the engravings and lithographs from Dela Barthe's and Cadolle's paintings, the watercolors of Fedor Alekseev, and the drawings by Kazakov himself. It was not surprising, therefore, that the Moscow governor, I. P. Saltykov, should have given to the ailing Kazakov this facade project. Although no trace remains of the facade plan, a related project by Kazakov has survived. In the summer of 1802 Kazakov informed Saltykov that he was at work on drawings of "plans, facades, and profiles of private Moscow buildings."[36]

In complying with Saltykov's command, Kazakov chose as assistants his former students, Semen Kesarino (Cassarino), Fedor Sokolov, Ivan T. Tamanskii, I. S. Selekhov, and his two sons, Pavel and Matvei. Surveyors and a detachment of soldiers were also placed under his supervision. The facade plan was to have consisted of 187 (later reduced to 185) tablets or parallelograms, with axonometric drawings of objects within the Kamer College boundaries (subsequently limited by the Zemlianoi Gorod). At the outset, the scale was 1 inch 70 feet, but eventually it was made to conform to the St. Petersburg plan, 1 to 15. The tablets were to have measured 39 inches × 28 inches, and 500 copies of each were projected. Through a precise measurement of the general plan and the buildings on the plots, exonometry was to have been achieved. The general plans of the lots were drafted in one scale from south to north to facilitate moving them onto the plans. The latter con-

formed to the sectors and streets of the city and were themselves to have been superimposed on a general plan of the city. Drawings were made of the measured buildings. After the final drafting of each tablet, the drawings were painted in watercolor and given an explanatory text. The atlas as a whole was designed to include additional description of the buildings and a map-key.

By 1804, after forty plates had been completed, the project lost the support of the Emperor Alexander, who had succeeded Paul, his father, in 1801. Kazakov, perhaps anticipating this prospect, had sought to hasten work on it by personally engraving and coloring two plates of the Moscow Kremlin; however in 1805, he was informed by the Moscow governor, Bekleshov, that the emperor "in order to escape large expenses necessary for the engraving of the facade plan of Moscow has stated that the expenditure of such a sum for a purpose in which there is no special worth is unacceptable."[37] Other factors—the Russo-Persian war, a renewal of the conflict with Napoleon, and Kazakov's illness—probably also influenced the decision. Initially, Alexander intended to deposit the unfinished portion of the plan in the Hermitage, but Kazakov urged that the drafts remain in Moscow in order to facilitate on-going street planning. Such was the fate of the most ambitious planning endeavor since that of 1775.

Kazakov's facade plan won praise from contemporaries despite its rejection. The architect Selekhov wrote that:

> The Commission, having composed the facade plan of Moscow, will prepare a large geometric plan of this capital, and . . . this plan together with the facade plan will remain the only one and a model for all plans known in Europe.[38]

Perhaps the true measure of this plan was that

---

[35] Cf. D. Arkin, "Perspektivnyi plan Peterburga 1764–1773 gg," *Arkhitekturnoe nasledstvo* 9 (1959): 13–20.

[36] Il'in, "'Facadicheskii' plan," 7. These drawings have been published in Beletskaia, *Al'bomy M. F. Kazakova*.

[37] Sytin, *Istoriia* 2: 364–65 and Il'in, "'Facadicheskii' plan," 12; cf. also Vlasiuk, *Kazakov*, 310. The amount involved was 61,050 rubles, according to Sytin.

[38] As quoted in Vlasiuk, *Kazakov*, 310; cf. also Il'in, "'Facadicheskii' plan," 7. Alexander I evidently had high regard for the project after all, for he bestowed upon Kazakov the medal

Kesarino, Nikolai Gorchakov, Petr Evreinov, and others of Kazakov's school who helped develop it, eventually played key roles in rebuilding Moscow after 1812. Nevertheless, the abandonment of the plan proved an unworthy finale for Kazakov, who lingered until the end of October, 1812, when he died perhaps from the shock of the burning of his beloved Moscow.[39]

In addition to Kazakov's facade plan at least four additional plans of Moscow appeared in the decade before the Great Fire of 1812. The first, a slightly corrected version of the draft plan of 1775, was issued from the Surveying Office even before Kazakov began his facade plan. It mistakenly represented tree-lined boulevards along the Neglinnyi Canal from the Samoteka to its estuary when, in reality, this planting was only contemplated. A second, Courtener's (Kurtener's) plan in 1805, used Marchenkov's of 1789 and that of 1800 for its model. Although larger in scale than any of these, Courtener's draft, nonetheless, repeated anachronisms present in the 1789 plan. Sytin, commenting on the origins of this plan, rejected the view that it was the so-called "Ancient plan of Moscow of the XVIII Century," merely published by Courtener. Nor did he date it 1800–1801; rather its anachronisms suggest that it was essentially the plan of 1789. The third plan, dating from 1806–1808, carried with it the inscription: "Plan of the ancient capital city of Moscow composed during the leveling of its heights and ravines." This plan evidently resulting from the planning efforts between 1792–1797 and Kazakov's between 1800–1804, consisted of six diameters which passed through the plan from one end to the other. Each diameter, shown separately in watercolor drawings, served as a profile of Moscow, depicting Moscow's main

buildings in relationship to others and to fields and gardens. *An Atlas of the City of Moscow*, a hand-drawn work prepared in 1806 and containing plans of nearby areas and Moscow homes, is known to have existed; however, it apparently was destroyed in the fire. So far as is known, nothing came of this draft.

The fourth plan, composed in 1810 in the Committee for the Equalizing of City Obligations (*Komitet po uravneniiu gorodskikh povinnostei*), proved to be by far the most influential. This Committee, in some respects the successor to the Commission for the Drafting of a Facade Plan for the Capital City of Moscow, served principally to equalize or balance the land tax of 1802 for the building of barracks. Having become involved in planning that year, it subsequently undertook the composition of a city atlas. When the Committee issued a plan for Moscow, it did so in two variants. Because the first bore the signature of Kesarino, director of drafting for the Committee, it generally is identified with him. Both variants limited Moscow to the Kamer College Rampart but they differed in scale, the first 1,400 feet to the inch and the second 840 feet. The former also contained an extensive legend, enumerating the twenty police districts of the city, a few words on the founding of the city 663 years earlier by Prince Iurii Vladimirovich, and some not very relevant measurements.

The second existing variant had the usually cumbersome title, "General Plan of the Capital City of Moscow, Composed in the Committee for Leveling City Obligations in Moscow with the Indication in Some Places of New Limits of the Kamer College Wall and Parts of the City, 1810." It differed from the first only in the new boundaries of the police districts and Kamer College Wall. The importance of this draft, to be discussed below, was the use made of it by the Scottish architect-planner William Hastie and the Commission for Building when they undertook the restoration of Moscow after 1812.[40]

---

of Anna, second degree; gave to Selekhov and Sokolov diamond rings; and to Kazakov's two sons and to other architects gold snuff boxes.

[39] "The news was the death blow. Having devoted his entire life to architecture, having graced the throne city with superb buildings, he could not imagine without shuddering that his many years of labor turned into ash and vanished with the smoke of the fire." These were the words of Kazakov's son as quoted in Il'in, *Kazakov*, 45.

---

[40] Sytin, *Istoriia* 2:382–83, 396, 493–94.

Building during the Planning Years

Although elaborate plans for Moscow were carefully drawn but left largely unimplemented, the architectural contours of Moscow did change during the late eighteenth and early nineteenth centuries. Just how much is the question.

The two principal Soviet writers on the subject differ sharply. P. A. Sytin regarded the period 1762–1812 as significant for Moscow because of the "origin, creation, and completion of the draft plan of Moscow." But he insisted that the plan in itself constituted no guarantee of a planned city. Instead "the plan, the abundance of orders and the editing completing and altering it, led to a planless, mainly spontaneous building of the city." Sytin criticized Catherine and her planners for exaggerating the diversity of Moscow's parts and consequently proposing distinctive architecture for each part. After all, rich nobles as well as impoverished artisans lived beyond the Zemlianoi Gorod and in the western sector of the Zemlianoi Gorod. In fact, nobles there often lived more splendidly than some inhabitants in the eastern portion of Catherine's masonry "gorod." In resorting to a tri-partite division, Catherine, he believed, took no account of the scarcity of building materials. While she forbade the construction of wood building in both the Kitai and Belyi Gorod, she did not preclude masonry in either the Zemlianoi Gorod or beyond. She consequently spread her materials too thinly and encouraged a lax policy of enforcing building codes within the "gorod." In the face of shortages in funds, building materials, and opposition from vested interests, Moscow's building continued "uncontrolled" despite the proclaimed aura of planning that characterized the period.

S. A. Zombe, in disagreeing with Sytin, construed the plan of 1775 as "one of the most interesting examples of such planning composition." Even into the nineteenth century this project remained "a planning document on the basis of which were conducted city planning operations. It introduced a dis-

ciplinary principle into the planning and building of the city." Zombe took Sytin to task for "diminishing the practical significance of the draft of 1775" and "explaining the principles placed in the plan by the whim of the Empress, Catherine II." More than Sytin, Zombe emphasized that this period in the history of town planning was significant because of the "movement to regularize the planning and construction of the city . . . and to bring its network of streets to a determined, rationally built system." The draft of 1775 was hailed as outstanding "for its great comprehension of realistic ideas over 'ideal' ones. . . . Its brilliant continuation of its historically-composed system of the city determined its role in the ensuing formulation of the planning and architectural-artistic appearance of Moscow."[41]

These arguments notwithstanding there were some solid accomplishments. In the Kitai Gorod the alterations of Red Square were completed by 1795. In the 1790s a new Moskvoretskaia Street, linking the Moscow River quay to Red Square, was begun. Efforts to regulate other parts of the Kitai Gorod and eliminate its commercial clutter met with opposition from the tradesmen there. Attempts to widen the Varvarka and the Il'inka, for example, provoked a storm from those whose property was threatened. This opposition resulted in the building of new commercial stalls, not where the 1775 planners had prescribed, but at various locations in Red Square. The two-story building for shops on the west side of Red Square, for example, obscured view of the walls and towers of the Kremlin and isolated them from St. Basil's. Some setbacks to planning may, however, have worked out for the best. In 1804 attempts to dispose of the Kitai Gorod's decaying walls and buildings from the Nikol'skie to the Varvarskie Gates and to replace them with an Aleksandrovskii Prospekt were vetoed by Alexander I, who decided that the ancient monuments in the area ought to be renovated and preserved.

---

[41] See Sytin, *Istoriia* 2:481 ff. and Zombe, "Proekt plana Moskvy," 53–54, 96.

Related to this Aleksandrovskii Prospekt was a plan by I. V. Egotov, architect of the Kremlin Department, and F. K. Sokolov. Entitled "Commercial square near the wall of the Kitai Gorod" and on the other side "Along the wall of the Kitai Gorod in Moscow in 1804 under no. 25," it embodied some of the principles of 1775. The authors urged demolition of the deteriorating parts of the Kitai Gorod and Peter's bastions, filling the moats, and razing buildings which crossed the limit lines. On the empty space the architects projected four market places, each alike in size and architectural style—with massive porticoes and colonnades. They intended to retain the wall of the Kitai Gorod from the Varvarskie Gates to the corner tower and along the Moskvoretskaia Quay. In the central part was a semicircular building with columns around its perimeter and its facade oriented toward the corner tower of the Kitai Gorod. The widening of the Kitaigorodskii Passage (*proezd*) as planned would have improved the view of the new ensemble from the river and, as it does today, joined the quays of the city with its central plazas.[42]

In the Belyi Gorod, the Okhotnyi Riad, Moiseevskaia, and Mokhovaia Squares as projected in the plan of 1775 had more or less materialized before the close of the century. That ambitious enterprise of ordering the banks of the Neglinnaia to its confluence with the Moscow River made some progress during these years, although completion had to wait until after the Great Fire. The beginnings of the great Theater Square may be traced to the 1770s and the city blocks north and east of the Kremlin and Kitai Gorod Walls to the 1780s. The New Square and the Old Square, both east of the Kitai Gorod, date from the years between 1782 and 1796. That space which became Varvarskaia Square was occupied by private estates as late as 1806, but a new street, intended in 1775 to link it with the Moscow River quay, was laid out in the 1790s. The plan of 1806–1808 indicated that

trees had already been planted on it. A portion of the area north of the Cannon Court had been cleared as early as 1780; between 1803 and 1804 the factory itself was razed, a leveling which created an expanse from Peter's Bastions at the Kitai Gorod to the northern line of Cannon (Pushechnaia) Square. Private homes on the latter site were removed after 1806.

The upper reaches of the Belyi Gorod and the Zemlianoi Gorod underwent modest changes before 1812. The Belyi Gorod Walls and Towers were dismantled between 1750–1792, but the boulevard projected for their site was hardly begun by the century's close. Brius, as Governor General of Moscow, proposed paving the space vacated by the Belyi Gorod Wall and using it for a market. His successor, Eropkin, urged plotting avenues only along those streets where the walls had stood. Neither proposal was approved by Catherine II, but in 1796 Governor M. M. Izmailov authorized completion of the Tverskoi Boulevard as a promenade between the Tverskaia and Nikitskaia.

The image of Zemlianoi Gorod, especially the Moscow River area of Zamoskvorech'e, changed notably by the end of the century. Alongside the already existing Bolotnaia and Polianskaia Squares appeared Sepukhovskaia and Kaluzhskaia after 1798. The Vodootvodnyi Canal, paralleling the arc of the old Moscow River bed, was built in the years 1784–1786 to reduce flooding in the area.[43] In many respects, this river sector was the most altered part of central Moscow. Late in the 1780s construction on the quays from the Great Stone Bridge to the mouth of the Iauza began. The Kremlin Embankment, completed by 1791 or earlier, became a favorite for the strolling aristocracy before the Tverskoi Boulevard opened. Between 1795 and 1800 the primary stone siding of this Kremlin Embankment was replaced by a capital support wall, and between 1801 and 1806 Moskvoretskaia

---

[42] Zombe, "Proekt plana Moskvy," 92–94 and Sedov, *Egotov*, 18.

[43] Instead of the four canals called for by the plan of 1775, A. I. Gerard built this one. (Zombe, "Proekt plana Moskvy," 82. Also see below, 107, 171.

Embankment, by the Kitai Gorod, was faced with stone. Four years later, a stone quay before the Foundling Home was completed. Southwest of the Kremlin, the Bersenevskaia Embankment's wooden support walls dated from 1737–1745; these walls, however, and those on the Sofiiskaia and Raushskaia, were not replaced with stone siding until long after 1812. Trees may have been planted along these quays as early as the 1790s.

Progress on the Neglinnye canals and basins was slow, despite the very considerable attention given to them. The 1786 plan had called for a canal and pools with boulevards alongside, but this canal was not completed until 1791, some forty feet east of the river's original bed. At that time the city's trials with the Mytishchinskii Aqueduct had only begun. In effect, the Neglinnaia solution was deferred until after the Great Fire.

Perhaps more than any single element in Moscow, the Kremlin acquired greater clarity in perspective. As viewed from its southern approach, it benefited when old buildings obscuring its magnificent churches were dismantled. To this extent Kazakov's impact on the Kremlin was greater than Bazhenov's, for as chief Kremlin architect he not only cleared the Kremlin of deteriorating structures (Preservation was not a consuming passion with the classicists!) but designed the Senate, which was built in 1776–1787. His Moscow University and Bazhenov's Pashkov House facades strikingly framed the Kremlin on its west side. This Neglinnaia border was completed on the south side by the Foundling Home, the Military Commissariat (the long facade of which extended along the flat bank of Zamoskvorech'e), and the Shapkin (later Tutolmin) House even farther down stream.

In addition to these Neglinnaia and Moscow River ensembles, one on the Iauza River east of the Kremlin and another farther along the Moscow River accentuated the Kremlin.[44] The first consisted of the huge Catherine (Golovin) Palace (Antonio Rinaldi and Giacomo Qua-

renghi), the new Military Hospital (Ivan Egotov), and the refurbished Petrovskii-Slobodskii, or Suburban, Palace complex (Kazakov). Below Lefortov on the Iauza, Menelas's Razumovskii Palace, Ascension (*Voznesenie*) Church, and Demidov House linked the Lefortov ensembles with the Kremlin. The second of the major ensembles, which included the Dolgorukii, Trubetskoi, and Demidov mansions and Kazakov's Golitsynskaia Hospital unfolded along the Khamovnicheskaia Loop of the Moscow River.

New residential housing, although limited, resulted from late eighteenth-century planning efforts. Despite a prevalence of dilapidated wood cottages in most parts of Moscow, occasionally masonry dwellings did replace frame ones lost to fire or razed to bar the plague in the early 1770s. In these the classic style prevailed, for they were placed on the "red lines" of streets and conformed to model designs issued by the Kamennyi Prikaz. Some of the best of Moscow's old buildings and monuments were incorporated into Moscow's new urban design.

A notable occurrence in the late eighteenth century was the appearance of rental property, especially in the Kitai Gorod, for artisans and tradesmen. Much of this building, undertaken by lesser architects or merely master carpenters, distorted classical models. They successfully moved away from the rococo styles of midcentury by creating more symmetrical structures, embellished with purely classical motifs. Pilasters decorated the facades and masonry houses were often trimmed with stone socles and cornices. On two-story buildings the windows were often united by vertical panels (*filenka*) and wooden houses often possessed various kinds of imitation masonry trim. Most houses of Moscow, especially those in the outskirts, possessed no design or ornamentation at all.[45]

The reign of Catherine II, then, was a period of extensive town planning in Russia. The empress's disdain for old Moscow and

---

[44] For a fuller discussion, see below 113–121, 182 ff.

[45] Cf. Brunov, *Istoriia russkoi arkhitektury* 351 ff., 391 ff.

her enchantment with classicism persuaded her to foster various planning and building schemes to alter its appearance. The general plan of 1775, a watershed in the city's history despite its immediately meager yield, continued as a model for planning before 1812 and, particularly, afterwards. Although Moscow's architects dreamed more easily than they achieved, Catherine's "classical" Moscow was more than a blueprint. It was a city with an ever-increasing number of edifices in the new style. Their striking ochre and amber pastels would cause Napoleon on the Sparrow Hills in fateful 1812 to marvel at the sight of a *European* city beneath him.

CHAPTER V

Construction in Moscow's City Center Before 1812

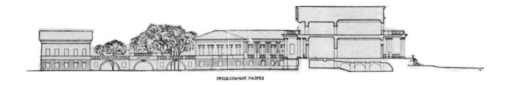

Although Moscow had undergone notable change late in the eighteenth century, its architects fell short of creating a classical city in the fullest sense.[1] Attempts to transform both the Kremlin and Kitai Gorod had met with little success. While preliminary efforts to convert the old fortress into a classical Kremlin, in fact, had shorn it of many ancient buildings, the elegantly conceived palaces by Bazhenov, Kazakov, and L'vov failed to materialize. Only a graceful Senate building gleamed in the midst of still very old Kremlin surroundings. The Kitai Gorod benefited from a new *gostinyi dvor*, an arcade of shops; but the continuing presence of earthen bastions and ancient moats in and around Red Square somehow belied any rush to the classical orders.

This mixed architectural image prompted a varied reaction from contemporaries. Foreigners, awed and disgusted by the old city, often deprecated what they saw, especially after an initial visit. On the other hand, those who returned were impressed by the changes. The scientist and traveler Peter Simon Pallas

was struck by the "magnificence" of Moscow's buildings and the vastness of some of the architectural ensembles: "Every object we behold in Moscow is, like the city itself, in a certain degree gigantic." He was referring specifically to the Foundling Home, but he also marveled at the beauty of Kazakov's Hall of Columns in the Nobles' Meeting House.[2] The Englishman, Linney Gilbert, like so many visitors, perceived the contrast in riches and poverty, the old and new: "Wretched hovels," he observed, "blended with large palaces; cottages of one story stand . . . next to most superb and stately mansions." Remarking that some parts of Moscow were like a desert and other parts densely populated, that some sections resembled a village and others part of a great capital, he concluded that "this Asian city was gradually becoming European."[3]

Central Ensembles: The Kremlin

Transforming the Kremlin, doubtless the most "Asiatic" element in the city, proved an on-going process with responsibility vested in the Kremlin Department. Although estab-

---

[1] Good general descriptions of Moscow's architecture during the second half of the eighteenth century may be found in N. Kovalenskaia, *Istoriia russkogo iskusstva XVIII veka* (Moscow, 1962), 135–160; Brunov, *Istoriia russkoi arkhitektury*, 351–93; *Al'bomy M. F. Kazakova*; Grabar', *Iskusstva* 6, which contains a section on Moscow city-building (250–265) and separate chapters on Bazhenov and Kazakov; *Istoriia Moskvy* 2: 623–41. The reader is here referred to M. Il'in, *Moskva, Pamiatniki arkhitektury XVIII-pervoi treti XIX veka/Moscow Monuments of Architecture*. 2 vols. (Moscow, 1975), cited as *Monuments*.

[2] *Travels through the Southern Provinces of the Russian Empire in the years 1793–1794*. 2 vols. Transl. from the German by P. S. Pallas (London, 1812) 1: 7. Pallas was in the pay of the Russian state during the course of his travels. In particular, he described Russia's fauna and flora.

[3] Linney Gilbert, *Russia Illustrated* (London, 1844), 158.

lished to facilitate Bazhenov's plan, it remained a force in renovating the Kremlin long after Bazhenov's classical scheme had been set aside. Many old buildings were replaced during these years. Decaying buildings from the sixteenth century—most of which were located in the Kremlin's western section between Trinity Gates and the grand palace in the south—were among the first pulled down. The Sretenskii Cathedral by the palace, Trinity Podvor'e, facing the Trinity Gates, along with the Epiphany and Sergievskaia Churches and buildings in between were all demolished. The Godunov Palace was sold at an auction in 1806.[4] In 1802 repair of the decaying walls commenced. The tottering Water (*Vodovzvodnaia*) Tower was dismantled and rebuilt in 1806. In that year, too, and for reasons left unexplained, the Nikol'skaia Tower in Red Square received a tent-shaped superstructure, adapted to the pre-classical seventeenth-century mode. Its author, surprisingly, was the St. Petersburg classicist Karl Ivanovich Rossi.

Architectural additions to the Kremlin at the *fin de siècle* were really quite few, far short, indeed, of Bazhenov's vision of the 1760s. For the new Senate Square, the former site of Trinity Podvor'e and Godunov Palace, Ivan Egotov designed and built (1806–1809) a two-story classical armory to house the palace treasures. In addition to having a rusticated ground floor and an upper one finished in two colors, this edifice was faced with a Corinthian portico and an elevated attic with a cupola. Its elegance was enhanced by bas-relief figures over the second-story windows and Gavriil Tikhonovich Zamaraev's sculptures of Russians, triumphant in enlightenment, clustered around the attic.

An unexpected alteration occurred in the grand palace: a version of Rastrelli's original edifice, approximating the design of L'vov, appeared on Kremlin hill after 1800. A second floor was added to the palace over the middle portion on the river side, and the center section of the first floor received a colonnade with a balcony. The mezzanine balcony was, in turn, crowned with a pediment. Such remodeling of the Rastrelli palace represented the extent to which the ideas of Bazhenov, Kazakov, and L'vov were fulfilled before 1812. In still another Kremlin change Rossi, employing the seventeenth-century National Style, designed the Ekaterinskaia Church in the Ascension monastic complex. That church, unfinished in 1812, was finally completed in 1817 by the architect Aleksei Nikitich Bakarev.[5]

More than any of the above, Matvei Fedorovich Kazakov's Senate Building was the most important classical monument erected in either the Kremlin or Kitai Gorod at this time (fig. 11, 12a,b). Built between 1776 and 1787, while Kazakov was a member of the Kremlin Department, it linked a proliferating government to the architecture of classicism. The building's shape was that of a triangle, its exterior corners severed and with an inner court. It was further conditioned by its proximity to the Kremlin Wall, the former Chudov Monastery, and the Arsenal. Central to its composition was a cupola-capped rotunda, wedged into the apex of the triangle and on the main entrance axis. This rotunda (fig. 13), encompassed by a monumental Doric colonnade, touched upon the entire Kremlin ensemble. Located midway between the Savior and Nikol'skie Gates, it imposed a diametrical axis on Red Square and became a landmark for future building there.

The overall external appearance of the Senate was one of simple grandeur. Its amber facade had a rusticated lower portion and pilasters without capitals. This favorite Russian device accentuated the severe and flat vertical projection of the wall in order to compensate for the extended facade. A powerful cornice balanced a generally plain exte-

---

[4] Also sold in this manner were the Kolymazhnye (or Gerbovye) Gates at the entrance of the *Perednii* Imperial Court and the "Lion" Gate of the Poteshnyi Palace.

[5] It was demolished in 1929. Cf. illustr. N. Ia. Tikhomirov and V. N. Ivanov, *Moskovskii Kreml'* (Moscow, 1967), 209.

Figure 11. The Senate Building, Arsenal, and Nikol'skie Gates after a painting by F. Ia. Alekseev, about 1800 (Donskoi, V-5639).

Figure 12a. The Senate (1776–1787), M. F. Kazakov (Schmidt).

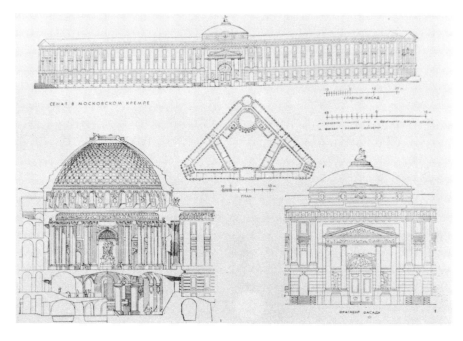

Figure 12b. Drawing, Kazakov's Senate (Brunov, *Istoriia*).

63

Figure 13. Senate rotunda from the inner court (M. A. Il'in, *Moskva pamiatniki arkhitektury XVIII- pervoi treti XIX veka.* 2 vols. Moscow, 1975, hereafter cited *Monuments*).

rior. Kazakov employed the Doric order for the facade, but chose Ionic for the portico. A four-columned portico with a pediment, placed in the center of the main facade, emphasized the smaller cupola over the entrance arch and also opened a view to the formal pentagonal court and compositional center of the building, the cupola rotunda hall.

The Senate's interior offered a dazzling elegance quite apart from its quiet exterior.

Within the rotunda was, first of all, the meeting place of the Senate, a hall measuring 89 feet in height and 81 in width.[6] The most impressive element here was a Corinthian colonnade, above which stretched a gallery and the cupola embossed with rosettes and squares. Light filtering through three tiers of

[6] See *Monuments* 2: 56–60, for recent photographs of the Senate.

windows bathed the hall and highlighted Kazakov's bas-relief decorations, which extolled the virtues of his empress and the ideals of the Enlightenment. This Senate rotunda hall, the most splendid in Russia, became a model for classicism throughout the realm.

Beneath the Senate and beyond the Kremlin Wall lay Red Square, which, too, had changed during the course of the century. Though smaller in 1800 (fig. 14) than it is today, it was, nonetheless, Moscow's busiest plaza. Pedestrian and equestrian jostled each other and overflowed to every corner of it. Mideighteenth century prints depict the Resurrection Gates choked with people on foot, in coaches, wagons, carts, and carriages making their way across an unpaved plaza (fig. 15). Portable pancake (*bliny*) stands and hawkers of most anything in their loaded carts dominated commerce in the square. Stalls along the Kremlin Wall from the Nikol'skie to the Savior Gates and on the east side, where GUM now stands, controlled trade on the periphery. Between St. Basil's and the Savior Gates tradesmen with their stands, men on horseback, well-dressed ladies and gentlemen, army officers, and beggars intermingled; this configuration was repeated across the square where merchants' stalls cluttered the entrance to the Kitai Gorod. The glut of dwellings and shops around St. Basil's and along the Moskvoretskaia down to the river denied the viewer that sense of spatiality that may be experienced there today (fig. 16).

Although this disordered scene had by no means disappeared by the end of the century, perceptible changes were occurring. While remaining virtually enclosed and oblong in form, the square benefited from new commercial rows constructed in 1786. These bracketed both the east and west sides of the square, accentuated its naturally longitudinal axis, and obscured from the plaza the malaise of Kitai Gorod shops. On the Kremlin side of the plaza a stone bridge at the Nikol'skie Gates spanned the dried moat, overgrown with weeds and trees, and offered a perspective of tortured St. Basil's. From the stunted tent

spire of Nikol'skie Gates to the soaring Savior Gates along the Kremlin moat, a colonnaded arcade replaced rickety, wooden stalls. The longitudinal axis extended from St. Basil's to the Resurrection Gates; the diametrical one, from the cupola of the Senate to the shops on the opposite side of the square.

Beyond Red Square, the rest of the Kitai Gorod burgeoned haphazardly. Here, too, a superabundance of people and vehicles invaded the Il'inka, Varvarka, Nikol'skaia, and their interconnecting alleys, pushing and shoving past the wooden shops and stalls. The potential for fire in this sector, despite all the planning, had not diminished with the years. The notable exception to this disorder was a new and massive Gostinyi Dvor (fig. 17), erected in 1790–1805 between the Il'inka and the Varvarka, an area occupied by some 4,000 shops of the Higher and Middle Commercial Riady.[7]

Designed along classical lines by Giacomo Quarenghi and possibly Matvei Kazakov, the Gostinyi Dvor was built by Semen A. Karin and I. S. Selekhov in the form of a rectangle with an interior court. Various architectural devices such as side projections, a finely orchestrated pattern of openings, and alternating rusticated and smooth walls obscured the drop from the Il'inka to the Varvarka. Encompassed by a two-story open arcade, since closed, the building on its street sides was embellished by what was essentially a Corinthian colonnade. The pillars composing it were really free standing and gave great power and spaciousness to the building; the single cornice gave it the unity of a single block. In its interior court, where deliveries were made, pilasters without capitals substituted for the columns with little loss of elegance. Nowhere in Moscow was the classical idiom more consciously bestowed on a commercial building. Considering the Kitai Gorod's central role in Moscow's economy, the Gostinyi Dvor was appropriately located in its busiest streets.

---

[7] See *Monuments* 2: 73–76, for recent photographs of the Old and New Gostinyi Dvory (Merchants' Yards).

Figure 14. Red, or possibly Old (*Staraia*), Square at the end of the eighteenth century. Engraving from a drawing by J. Dela Barthe (Donskoi, V-24655).

Figure 15. The entrance into Red Square through the Resurrection Gates (Donskoi, V-8225).

Figure 16. Moskvoretskaia Street with St. Basil's in the background, c. 1800. Painting by F. Ia. Alekseev or his school (Donskoi, V-1599).

68

Figure 17. The Gostiny Dvor in the Il'inka (1790–1805), Giacomo Quarenghi and M. Kazakov(?). (Schmidt).

Some years later, 1839–1842, a new gostinyi dvor was erected just opposite this earlier one. Although both survive, the earlier one remains architecturally superior.

Other classical edifices were constructed in this area. Sometime after 1785 two grandiose houses with some sixty shops beneath—the Kalinin and Pavlov House and that of the Khriashchevs'—were constructed on the Il'inka (fig. 18). Designed by Kazakov to house haberdasheries on the ground floor, they greatly improved the appearance of their neighborhood. The Kalinin and Pavlov House was built on the site of the old Ambassador Court. Essentially rectangular, its gallery of twenty-two arched portals punctuated the main facade with its massive six-column Co-

rinthian portico on a podium.[8] The Khriash-chev House, undistinguished with its rusticated facade, eventually received a Corinthian portico, perhaps after 1812.[9]

Just a short distance from these houses, where the Il'inka crossed the Bogoiavlenskii (now Kuibyshevskii Passage), Karuninskaia Square was created between 1776–1782. Seventeenth-century buildings belonging to the Volokolamsk and Trinity-Sergei (in Zagorsk) Monasteries were razed for this plaza, planned by the architect Ivan Egorovich Starov.[10] Com-

[8] The Kalinin and Pavlov mansion was changed significantly in the 1830s. (Cf. *Al'bomy M. F. Kazakova*, 33–35, 245).
[9] In 1838 a gallery was added to the first floor. (Ibid., 36–37, 245).
[10] Sytin, *Ulits*, 97.

Figure 18. The Il'inka, the houses of Kalinin, Pavlov, and Khriashchev by M. Kazakov. From a watercolor by F. Ia. Alekseev or his school at the end of the eighteenth century (Donskoi, V-7020).

70

merce was further assisted by the building in 1804 of a number of two-story, stove-heated shops in Bogoiavlenskii Alley. These brought to Karuninskaia Square the trade that previously had flourished along the Kremlin Wall between the Nikol'skie and Savior Gates.

Like the Il'inka the Varvarka bristled with activity and had an even more wooden appearance. Nor did widening in 1792 save it from the conflagration twenty years later. Its most notable classical edifices were Lushnin House and the Church of St. Barbara the Great Martyr. The Lushnin assemblage of two two-story sections reached to the street. Both had rusticated lower floors and rounded corners, from which wings extended at 90° angles. Within the court created by these street wings a central three-story structure stood apart. The most notable aspect of this asymmetrical ensemble was the contrast it presented to the non-classical surroundings.[11] The same was true of St. Barbara's church within the shadow of the old Gostinyi Dvor. In the form of a Greek cross, it contained bell tower and cupola and a striking four-column Corinthian portico, all of which made it an exception to the older churches surrounding it.

Because Russian sovereigns in the eighteenth century used the nearby radial Nikol'skaia for a grand entrance into the Kremlin, triumphal arches had frequently to be erected where the street entered Red Square. In it resided the wealthy and powerful Cherkasskies and Sheremetevs, for whom Ivan Starov built a classical mansion in 1790–1791. Yet increasingly the Nikol'skaia became identified with bookshops, twenty-six of which were located there by the first quarter of the nineteenth century. Since the architecture in this street was not classical, it had little consequence for the scheme of a new city.

At the far end of Red Square from the Nikol'skaia, Moskvoretskaia Street led from St. Basil's to the bridge of the same name. The street, which originated in the late fifteenth century when the Kremlin walls were

erected, linked with the bridge at the end of the eighteenth century to form a Tverskaia-Piatnitskaia axis.[12] Although the plan of 1739 showed only St. Basil's and two smaller churches on the west side of the Moskvoretskaia and the Cattle-branding Yard and commercial stalls on the east, in reality, the shops lined both sides of the street. In the early 1790s, Governor Prozorovskii ordered the demolition of a corner of the old Cattle-branding Yard that extended into the Moskvoretskaia Street itself and the widening and straightening of the street. After the fire of 1812 destroyed all the Moskvoretskaia's wooden buildings, some were replaced by masonry.

Between the Varvarka and the Moskvoretskaia Embankment of the Moscow River lay *Zariad'e* (beyond the riady). In 1770 this sector was an overcrowded slum of workmen, craftsmen, and lesser tradesmen. Because Peter's bastions, which encompassed the Kitai Gorod, severed the sewage connection with the river, much waste and filth flowing from the Varvarka collected in Zariad'e. Not surprisingly many epidemics, notably the great plague of 1771, originated there. To improve the lot of the Zariad'e and, in particular, to correct the shortcomings of the water system, the Moscow River Embankment was built beneath the Kitai Gorod walls in 1796–1800.

The flow of traffic no less than that of water caused the Kitai Gorod problems requiring the planners' attention. Throughout the eighteenth century Peter's bastions governed Kitai Gorod traffic, blocking old gates and causing the opening of new ones. North of the embankment along the eastern fringe of the Kitai Gorod the bastions necessitated the building in 1739 of the Novo-Nikol'skie Gates (opposite Miasnitskaia, now Dzerzhinskii Square), the first to replace old tower gates. New entrances also pierced the Kitai Gorod Wall south of the Il'inskie Gates and north of the Varvarka.

---

[11] *Al'bomy M. F. Kazakova*, 93, 253.

[12] In 1938 many houses on the Moskvoretskaia were demolished, thereby opening this area behind St. Basil's to a new Moskvoretskii Bridge.

Another entered into New Square, south of the Novo-Nikol'skie Gates. The Il'inskie Tower Gates remained open, but the Nikol'-skie and Varvarskie were sealed. Heavy Kitai Gorod traffic also resulted from new commerce. The removal in 1783 of a sizable market from the Okhotnyi Riad to the east side of the Kitai Gorod and construction three years later of masonry shops to supplement or replace wooden ones already there helped organize New Square, specifically designated for commerce.[13]

Because the Kitai Gorod Wall fell into disrepair in the vicinity of New Square, the authorities considered razing it, even before the Great Fire. The governor, A. A. Bekleshov, proposed in 1804 to demolish that portion of the wall between the Varvarskie and Nikol'skie Gates and to construct in its place a wide Aleksandrovskii Prospekt. Because the tsar did not approve this scheme, it was dropped; however, when fire destroyed the wooden shops near the wall in 1812, a thorough reordering of the area became a necessity.

The Kitaiskii Passage, a circular boulevard skirting the east side of the Kitai Gorod, was opened in 1790, when the moat was filled. In 1806–1808, houses there were demolished and rows of trees planted, but the plan of 1775 was never quite realized. The bastions remained for some years; and when they were dismantled, a succession, rather than a chain of plazas was laid out. Along Kitaiskii Passage, where the Varvarka linked with the Solianka, construction of Peter's bastions had necessitated razing many dvory, but this 1806 plan shows, surprisingly, that some there had, in fact, escaped destruction.[14] Future Lubianskaia Square, for example, late in the eighteenth century was occupied by dvory, shops, the almshouses of the Church of Fedoseevsk, as well as the bastions.

In the southeastern corner of the Kitai Gorod, between the Solianka and Moscow River, lay Vasil'evskii Meadow, which after the middle of the eighteenth century was totally transformed by the famous or infamous Foundling Home. Erected between 1764 and 1770, this structure (fig. 19) became important for both social and architectural reasons. The perceptive Edward Clarke noted that in the twenty years prior to 1786:

> it had received no less than thirty-seven thousand, six hundred, and seven infants. Of this, one thousand and twenty had left the asylum and there remained six thousand and eighty at that time. In 1792 the number of children in the house amounted to two thousand; and about three thousand belonging to the establishment were at nurse in the country. Every peasant that has an infant receives a ruble and a half month's allowance. Every month, such of the children as have been vaccinated are sent into the country where they remain until the age of five years. Before vaccination mortality was much greater.[15]

Edward P. Thompson, in the next century, referred to this institution when he observed that "a premium is offered to the heartless in Russia by opening the doors of an asylum, disguised under a philanthropic name" to fill the ranks of the army and navy.[16]

The work of the architect Karl Ivanovich Blank, the Foundling Home was also a milestone architecturally. It was the first structure in Moscow representing a departure from the rococo to the classical. Designed to accommodate some eight thousand orphans, this ensemble consisted of two important structures, each of which enclosed a rectangular court. These were in turn joined by a central unit projecting toward the Moscow River. The ensemble was framed on three sides by lower (two-story) structures, used mainly for warehouses and living quarters. The color-washed

---

[13] In the midnineteenth century the original New (*Novaia*) was called Old (*Staraia*) and vice versa; this situation somehow righted itself by the end of the nineteenth century. (Cf. Sytin, *Ulits*, 112–13).

[14] After the bastions were leveled in the early 1820s, the Varvarskaia Square (presently Nogin) emerged.

[15] *Travels in Russia, Tatary, and Turkey* (Edinburgh, 1839).

[16] *Life in Russia: Or, the Discipline of Despotism* (London, 1848), 281. For more on foundlings in Russia, see David L. Ransel, *Mothers of Mercy: Child Abandonment in Russia* (Princeton, N.J., 1988).

Figure 19. Center section of the Foundling Home (*Vospitatel'nyi Dom*), 1764–1770, in the Vasil'evskii Meadow from the Moscow River, Karl I. Blank (Schmidt).

facades of the Foundling Home were rusticated at the ground level and embellished above by a cornice which accentuated the building's prevailing horizontal character. The center section, uniting the two principal complexes, consisted of three separate elements, each of which, crowned by a cupola, extended toward the river. Two were small, but the central cupola became one of the identifiable features of the entire assemblage and a Moscow landmark. Although its long facade, measuring 1,243 feet, appeared to face the river, the Foundling Home really turned inward toward its parade ground on the Solianka. In so doing it formed an important link with other ensembles around the Kremlin.

The Belyi Gorod

Although residences appeared in the Kitai Gorod late in the eighteenth century, it remained essentially commercial. The true residential sector was that aristocratic refuge, the

Belyi Gorod, although even there some buildings, particularly those in the central squares, served a public purpose.

In the 1770s planners began conjecturing about central squares positioned along the west side of the Kremlin and Kitai Gorod.[17] In the next decade changes actually began on the Neglinnaia beneath the Kremlin. Okhotnyi Riad Square, projected in the plan of 1775 and modified in 1786, emerged in 1791. Originating at the Nobles' Meeting House (presently *Dom Soiuz*), the plaza eventually stretched across the future Theater Square to the Moiseevskii Monastery almshouses. In the 1780s private dwellings—among them the estates of the Dolgorukovs and Gruzinskies—and several churches, and a cemetery lined the northwest.[18] On the opposite side from

---

[17] Cf. especially Sytin, *Istoriia* 2, Zombe, "Proekt plana Moskvy," and Sytin, *Ulits*, passim.

[18] Before seizure of this land by the Dolgorukovs and Gruzinskies, the meal and flour shops had occupied this area. Fire destroyed them in 1737. The Dolgorukov-Krymskii mansion on the corner of the Great Dmitrovka became in the 1780s the Nobles' Meeting House. See n. 23 below.

the Dolgorukov holdings the press of Okhotnyi Riad shops begged for some kind of order.

When renovation of the Okhotnyi Riad began in the 1780s, estate houses and fences were removed to allow for masonry shops on the "red line" of the south side. In 1786, old shops on the square's north edge were demolished and replaced with two-story ones of brick and stone. Otherwise, progress lagged; execution of the 1786 variant encountered delays when princely and ecclesiastical landowners sued to obtain compensation for their land. Generally, old structures remained interspersed with the new throughout the 1790s. Although Prozorovskii had demanded demolition of remaining buildings in order to realize Kazakov's 1790 plan, the empress permitted the razing of only one church, the removal of its cemetery, and the destruction of the separate belfry and clergy's houses of another.[19] In 1791 an Okhotnyi Riad Square, less than that envisioned in 1775, officially opened, although shops were not built from the square's center to its south side until 1798.

The other central squares were only partially organized in accordance with the plans. It is even questionable whether the Moiseevskaia, projected for the site of the former Moiseevskii Monastery, ever developed into the small rectangle conceived by Kazakov.[20] In any case, it was later absorbed by Manezhnaia Square after 1812. From Moiseevskaia Square to the Great Nikitskaia in the early 1780s, shops of every description—eating places, taverns, a flea market, and scrap shops—jammed the narrow alleys. In 1783 the authorities transferred some of these to Old and New Squares; in 1790, fire destroyed others.[21] After 1790 larger craft shops appeared in this burned out area.

The future Mokhovaia Square (unfolding at what is today the lower end of the Manezh) in the early 1780s was a maze of wooden shops or stalls, which Governor Brius tried to eliminate. His edict, dated 11 February 1786, stipulated that 13,500 rubles be taken from the Kremlin Department treasury funds for their demolition and the construction of new masonry shops, in accordance with Sokolov's plan of 1786. By June, Brius could report that Mokhovaia Square was nearly complete; however, the governor was premature, for work on the square actually dragged into the reign of the Emperor Paul.[22]

Late in the eighteenth century, a number of prominent classical buildings were erected in these central squares. One, Prince V. M. Dolgorukov-Krymskii's splendid property in the Okhotnyi Riad, was altered in 1782, possibly by Matvei Kazakov, to become the Nobles' Meeting House. That edifice used for meetings and glittering social affairs perhaps more than any other symbolized the "golden age of the Russian nobility."[23] Its exterior was undistinguished except for its several Corinthian porticoes and bas-reliefs, but within it gleamed Kazakov's marbled Hall of Columns (*Kolonnyi Zal*) (fig. 20a,b), one of the most spectacular creations of Russian classicism. Pallas, impressed generally by the magnificence of Russian palaces, singled out this "grand assembly

---

[19] The church razed and cemetery removed was that of St. Anastasia; the partially dismantled St. Parasceve was itself rebuilt.

[20] All the Moiseevskie monastic buildings were razed in 1789; the monastery itself had been dissolved in 1765.

[21] When owners of larger shops prevailed upon the governor to remove entirely the taverns and scrap riady, Prozorovskii complied by transferring them to Old (Staraia) Square in the Kitai Gorod and the flea market to the New Square. (Sytin, *Ulits*, 174).

[22] Kazakov's plan reduced the size of the Mokhovaia as conceived by Sokolov in 1786 and thereby enlarged the city block which lay between the square and Okhotnyi Riad Square. Cf. Grabar', *Iskusstva* 6: 256–57, 260–61, for reproductions of Sokolov's and Kazakov's plans of the Neglinnaia area. See also Zombe, "Proekt plana Moskvy," 88–89.

[23] The Nobles' Meeting Hall (now House of Trade Unions) on Okhotnyi Riad antedated Kazakov's building in Moscow; nevertheless, he completely altered both its exterior and interior. Even while drafting plans for the university nearby, Kazakov was called upon by Dolgorukov-Krymskii, governor of Moscow, to transform a rather ordinary mansion into a magnificent one with a hall for official receptions and balls. This governor had purchased the building from one Volinskii in the 1760s and finally sold it on 19 December 1784, to the Assembly of the Nobility. Cf. A. Kiparisova, "Neopublikovannye proekty moskovskikh zodchikh konsa XVIII i nachala XIX vekov: chertezhi i proekty M. F. Kazakova v Tsentral'nom voenno-istoricheskom arkhive," *Arkhitekturnoe nasledstvo* 1 (1951): 114–16, hereafter cited as "Neopublikovannye proekty." The exterior of the Nobles' Meeting Hall was refurbished again in 1793–1801 and was rebuilt in 1896 and 1903–1908. See *Monuments* 2: 87–89 for recent photographs.

Figure 20a. Nobles' Meeting House; Kazakov's Hall of Columns within (Schmidt).

Figure 20b. Kazakov's Hall of Columns, 1784–1786 (Brunov, *Istoriia*)

hall" for balls and masquerades and called it "one of the most spacious rooms in Europe."[24]

Kazakov fashioned interior space—witness his Senate and Golitsynskaia Hospital interiors and the Golden Rooms of Demidov House—by relying upon cupolas, columns, pilasters, cornices, bas-relief sculptures, and paintings. His Hall of Columns, however, with its glistening Corinthian colonnade, surpassed in beauty all the other three. Its enveloping columns supported a small attic with a balustrade that also encircled the room. Above a protruding frieze semicircular windows allowed light to filter through the columns; meanwhile, semicircular mirrors, resembling these windows, created illusions of spaciousness and further magnified the brilliance of transparent crystal chandeliers, which hung between each pair of columns. The frescoed ceiling was one of Kazakov's great interior

---

[24] *Travels,* 9.

masterpieces but it was destroyed by the fire in 1812. An arched doorway pierced the midsection of each of the walls. Although simpler than the Senate Hall, the Hall of Columns emerged as a prototype for palatial ballrooms in Russia. Similar rooms appeared in Kostroma, Tula, and Kaluga. Severely damaged in 1812, the Hall of Columns was restored by Aleksei Bakarev, who probably added the gallery.

After 1784 Kazakov undertook to harmonize the exterior of the Nobles' Meeting House with its splendid hall. Drawings show that he originally contemplated embellishing the central portico and the Dmitrovka facade with bas-relief sculptures and facing the columns and pilasters with stucco. He also pondered enriching the Okhotnyi Riad side with a portico of a semicircular arch with double pillars on each side. Later drawings show that Kazakov ultimately rejected this ornate decor, especially on the Dmitrovka. Except for a small pediment over its columns the initial plans for the Okhotnyi Riad side were not significantly altered either.

Shortly after undertaking his work on the Nobles' Meeting House, Kazakov in 1786 laid the foundation of the main university (fig. 21) building on the Mokhovaia near the Great Nikitskaia and north of the Kremlin. The university had originally been housed some thirty years earlier, in a building by the Resurrection Gates. It acquired rights to the new location just two years after its founding, when the properties of the Repnins, in 1757, and those of the Ivashkins, in 1773, were procured. By 1775, the old structure at the Resurrection Gates had been relegated to dormitory use, even though a new building was far from completion.

Preparations for a new university began as early as 1777.[25] Kazakov, charged with its

design, began work on his first draft in the late 1770s. This plan, complex in its composition, offered a decorative exterior. Compositional stress fell on the building's center, on its great dome, portico, and the usual classical accoutrements—columns, decorative balconies, and allegorical sculptures. For balance Kazakov proposed unadorned wings, which, along with the sumptuous central facade, would have embraced a quadrangular courtyard. Although the plan received approval, a shortage of funds caused work on it to proceed slowly.

Completion of the wing facing the Nikitskaia was the only significant accomplishment by the fall of 1782. At that time Kazakov ordered some changes, notably curving the corners of the wings and altering details in the facade. By 1784, the second wing was completed. For the next two years, the university building would boast of two wings but, alas, no central corpus. On 2 March 1785, an appropriation of 125,000 rubles facilitated construction of this main section; the first stone was laid on 23 August 1786.

Kazakov's university, completed in 1793, inspires interest, not only for what it was, but because it illustrated the evolution of his thinking during its various stages of planning and construction. Although the original draft had typified the style of the 1760s and 1770s, in its modified version it showed the influence of Bazhenov's Great Kremlin Palace, becoming simpler in plan and more severe in decor. The facade's midsection, with its large cupola and small domes, did, however, retain its splendor. In a third plan, Kazakov accentuated the length of the facade by straightening it. He moved the round reception hall to the rear and flattened the dome. By a more even distribution of the decorative elements, he lessened the contrast between the wings and the central facade.

The university complex finally assumed the form of the Greek "Π." It possessed an impressive entrance court formed by enveloping wings of the building, and separated from the Mokhovaia by a fence with two gates. Kazakov

---

[25] Cf. Kiparisova, "Neopublikovannye proekty," 111–14. Kazakov's building is sometimes referred to as the "old" university to differentiate it from the "new" university ensemble (1833–1836) of E. D. Tiurin facing the Mokhovaia on the lower side of the Great Nikitskaia. A still newer university rose in the Lenin (formerly Sparrow) Hills during the Stalin era.

Figure 21. Moscow University (1786–1793) from the banks of the Neglinnaia. Watercolor by architect M. F. Kazakov. (*Monuments* 1: 55).

placed this building on the same line as that of the Nobles' Meeting House thereby articulating the northern fringe of these squares which girded the Kremlin. The building's compositional center was its great assembly hall, a half-rotunda capped with a cupola. Smaller circular halls occupied the ends of the wings while the remaining rooms were rectangular. An eight-column Ionic portico dominated the center of the facade over the rusticated ground floor; four-pilaster Ionic porticoes embellished the extremes of the lateral wings. Kazakov's artistry may be observed today only in the main facade; the cupola and trim in the hall are a part of Domenico Giliardi's and possibly Grigor'ev's masterful restoration in 1817–1819.

Farther along the Mokhovaia from the university, Vasilii Bazhenov created in the mid-1780s one of Moscow's most graceful and handsome residential ensembles, Pashkov House (fig. 22a,b). Placing it on a promontory opposite the Borovitskie Gates of the Kremlin and separating it from the Mokhovaia with an exquisite fence, the architect endowed this urban estate house with a radiant and distinctive central corpus, wings, formal entrance, gardens, and diverse auxiliary buildings. In so doing, he made it an exemplar for princely living and taste in late eighteenth-century Russia. Svin'in, in his description of Moscow, cited the Pashkov House, in particular, for its magnificence and surprises. "It comprehended within itself all the conveniences and delights of life. This little garden situated on a pretty high eminence presented a type of the Garden of Eden." The varieties of statuary to which each footpath in it led, the riding academy, the theater for serf actors, and the lamps—all caught his fancy.[26] By placing this house high above the street, with a panoramic view of the Moscow River at its juncture with the Neglinnaia, Bazhenov insured its exposure

26 Pavel Svin'in, *Sketches of Russia* (London 1814, 2nd ed. 1843), 30–31. The full meaning of Pashkov House as an ensemble is discussed by Gulianitskii, "O kompozitsii," 21–23. The author particularly emphasizes Bazhenov's inclusion of older buildings.

Figure 22a. Pashkov House (1784–1786), V. I. Bazhenov (Schmidt).

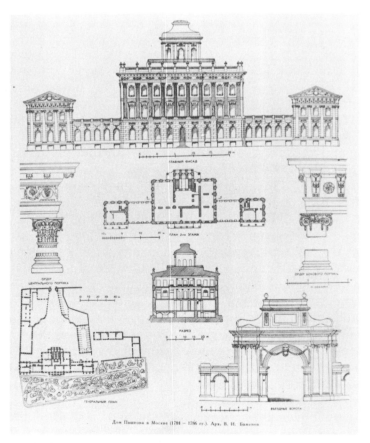

Figure 22b. Drawings of Pashkov House (Brunov, *Istoriia*).

78

from all sides and its inclusion in the larger architectural complex of the Kremlin.

The gleaming white Pashkov edifice rose three stories and was crowned with a belvedere. Single-story galleries extending from both sides of it were linked with two-story wings. The main entrance, facing the formal court within and on the side opposite the Mokhovaia, was placed on the axis of the central building. To the right of the vestibule, a sweeping staircase led to the first floor and main hall of the palace. Lateral pavilions completed the ensemble.

The combination of rococo and Palladian splendor of Bazhenov's Pashkov House was expressed strikingly in its Kremlin facade, dominated by a majestic four-column Corinthian portico. The architect placed a statue beside the first and fourth columns of this portico. The entire building derived a soaring quality from its components—the portico and pilasters on the facade of the lateral porticoes, the diminished height of windows on each successive story of the building, the triangular pediments of the lateral porticoes, and the cubical central structure and cylindrical belvedere. The sloping hill also accentuated the palace's verticality, probably more than anything else. Pashkov House's elegance was enhanced by the twin Ionian columns encompassing the belvedere and the frieze and pediments of its lateral wings liberally endowed with garlands, rosettes, and striking bas-relief figures. All of these and a central corpus were surmounted with a balustrade and urns. A picturesque garden, enclosed by an openwork iron fence and supported by massive pillars, unfolded along the slope of the hill before the main facade and extended nearly to the Neglinnaia. The entrance to Pashkov House from Vagan'kovskii Alley was a splendid Ionic gate and enclosed court. Twin Ionic columns flanked both sides of the main entrance; small ones rose beneath the arch of Tuscan order.[27] Bazhenov's Pashkov House,

like Kazakov's university was a monument of early Moscow classicism, yet it carried with it the ornateness of the rococo. Built originally for P. E. Pashkov, a member of Catherine II's household, then ravaged by fire in 1812, it was restored thereafter with some modification by Osip Bove. Today it retains its importance as part of the Lenin Library.

In the Soviet capital today two additional ensembles complete the line of eighteenth-century facades that begin with Pashkov at one end of the Kremlin and conclude with the Nobles' Meeting House opposite the Kitai Gorod wall. Although these ensembles did not exist late in the eighteenth century, the refined architecture and spatial composition of Theater and Manezh Squares did, indeed, have their origins in the last quarter of the eighteenth century. The new university, Maddox's (the Petrovskii) Theater, the Nobles' Assembly, Pashkov House, and rows of new commercial buildings marked an area which eventually ranked in importance second only to the Kremlin and Red Square.[28] Beyond Maddox's Theater and the Neglinnaia, where the old Cannon Court (demolished 1803–1804) and a mass of private dwellings had stood, space was opened almost to Maroseika Street.

Ordering the Neglinnaia

The Neglinnaia River, long at odds with the concept of a classical Moscow, entered the Belyi Gorod Wall due north of the Kremlin through a wide arch and beneath a closed tower. It followed a course similar to that of the radial streets, converging on the Kitai Gorod, and thereafter trickled along the west side of the Kremlin bastions to the Moscow River.[29] By midcentury the Neglinnaia, in

---

[27] The fire in 1812 destroyed all of Bazhenov's interior and the belvedere. The restoration except for the belvedere, which

took on an early nineteenth-century look, was faithful to the original design. In 1938 a staircase was built before the main facade. The building, as part of the Lenin Library, houses the Rumiantsev Collection.

[28] This theater was named for the Englishman Maddox; it opened in 1780 and burned in 1805. It was located approximately on the site of the Bol'shoi Theater of today.

[29] The opening created by this arch, guarded by an iron grille, was about sixteen feet. (Sytin, *Ulits,* 314). Because Neg-

deference to the bastions, had been rerouted to a new bed; the old one, meanwhile, collected refuse. At the Kremlin, three bridges—the Resurrection leading into Red Square, and the Trinity and Borovitskii nearer the Moscow River—reminded Muscovites of the river's earlier importance.

Resurrection Bridge, opposite the Okhotnyi Riad and the university, was the busiest intersection along the Neglinnaia's entire course[30] (fig. 23). On this stone bridge leading into Red Square, mingled the rich and poor: noble, soldier, priest, tradesman, serf, and beggar. Some rode, some walked, most loitered; beneath the bridge, maids washed their assorted laundry. In the background towered twin tent spires that identified the Resurrection Gates, and farther to the right a single spire designated the Nikol'skie. The Senate dome barely exposed itself, but nearer at hand stood the Main Pharmacy, or Zemskii Prikaz, and below the Kremlin walls bulged Peter's bastions.

In the north, too, the Neglinnaia was shallow, although it occasionally flooded the Petrovka in the spring. Flowing past the gardens of Rozhdestvenskii Monastery, it gave a bucolic cast to that quarter. Around Kuznetskii Bridge this rural character lessened as the Bridge became a place for smart shops. Adjacent land holdings, especially to the north, were consolidated as the Cannon Court blacksmiths and stable keepers were displaced by gentry and such princely newcomers as the Vorontsovs.[31]

Moscow planners, contemplating a clear and sparkling Neglinnaia, proposed in 1775

regulating and cleansing it. They talked of widening and deepening the river's bed, straightening it, and planting trees along its banks. Flanked by stone quays and symmetrical boulevards, this new Neglinnaia would enhance both the ancient Kremlin and the new ensembles opposite it; moreover, it could serve Muscovites as both a major transportation artery, foreshadowing later Neglinnaia Street, and as a source of fresh water.

The proposed linking of the Neglinnaia to an aqueduct from the village of Mytishch (about sixteen miles north of Moscow) joined the issues of the river's beauty and utility. Moscow's water supply had reached crisis proportions by the late eighteenth century. The Moscow River and its tributaries were polluted, and well water, long tapped for drinking and cooking, had also become contaminated. In 1779, Catherine II named a Commission for the Construction of a Water Works in Moscow and appointed the engineer F. V. Bauer as its head. Sent to Moscow with orders "to inspect all suitable sites to supply this city with pure water and to make a project and monetary estimate suited for this purpose," Bauer conceived of constructing an aqueduct to bring water from Mytishch into the city, along the west side of the Neglinnaia to the Kuznetskii Bridge, and even beyond to the Moscow River. In his appraisal of the situation he wrote:

> Having inspected carefully all these surroundings, I present not only my project for leading sufficient, pure water into this city but also for transporting from the city some of its impurities, for which the River Neglinnaia itself gives us an opportunity. Besides that I propose to fill in part of the abovementioned ravine, which divides the city [for the length of the Neglinnaia]. This could provide free and uninterrupted communication among all the streets of the city and would create such good and suitable places for strolling in parts of the city from which most people [now] move as far as possible because of evil odors arising from the Neglinnaia. The streets as well as the gardens which lie on both banks of the river will

---

linnaia Street did not exist before the late eighteenth century, no gate, of course, had been cut through the Belyi Gorod Wall. *Truba*, or pipe, applied to the opening through which the river flowed. After the wall and tower had been dismantled and the river converted into a canal, Truba designated the entire area, and after 1794 even the plaza which opened there. The best accounts of this attempt to order the Neglinnaia are Zombe, "Proekt plana Moskvy," 59–60, 64–65, 71–81; Sytin, *Ulits*, 242–44; and Grabar', *Iskusstva* 6: 252–61.

[30] The bridge was demolished when the Neglinnaia was piped underground after the Great Fire.

[31] The Vorontsov House, built by Kazakov, still stands on the Rozhdestvenka (now Zhdanov) as the Moscow Institute of Architecture.

Figure 23. Resurrection Bridge over the Neglinnaia and entrance into Red Square through the Resurrection Gates, late eighteenth-century print (Donskoi, IV-1248).

receive from this [filling of the ravine] a larger area to develop and will have much easier access to water during fires.[32]

Besides proposing to replace the dead Neglinnaia with a canal and aqueduct, Bauer planned classical trappings: ordered landscaping, stone embankments, bridges, ponds with fountains and cascades, statuary, obelisks, water pavilions, and fountains along the canal.[33]

Work on the Neglinnaia-Mytishch project proceeded fitfully. By 1787, eighteen fountains and twenty-eight basins had been built in Mytishch, and from them water flowed by gravity in a stone aqueduct. For a time the authorities suspended work because of the Turkish war. By the beginning of the nineteenth century, however, the Mytishch waters were carried into Trubnaia Square to a round pavilion, which contained a water-purifying pool, and then on to Kuznetskii Bridge. This pavilion pool served as source for the open Neglinnyi Canal, which began at this point.[34] That canal, built in 1789–1791, was situated about forty-two feet east of the river's original bed, which had been filled with debris. From Trubnaia Square, the quays were sided with stone, and below Kuznetskii Bridge, surmounted by a decorative iron grille. Staircases were placed along both sides of the canal, north and south of Kuznetskii Bridge, and Neglinnaia Street was built along its quays.

Shortly after 1800 the task of completing the Neglinnaia project from the Kuznetskii Bridge and increasing the supply of fresh water fell to A. I. Gerard.[35] In 1804 the Gerards, father and son, proposed a system of three oblong basins, alternating in varied lengths with open and enclosed canals, in the hope of improving the Neglinnaia from the Kuznetskii Bridge to the Moscow River. They plotted the Mytishchinskii Aqueduct along the left bank of the Neglinnyi Canal to the Kuznetskii Bridge at which point it passed to the canal's right side, assuming a position parallel to the Moscow River. Locations for water-purifying fountains to fill the basins were designated. Although several variants of this proposal circulated, these essentials were approved by Alexander I in an imperial edict issued 18 February 1806. This "Moscow Aqueducts" project, assigned to the Department of Water Communications with A. I. Gerard in charge, was expected to take four years to build at an annual cost of 110,000 rubles.[36]

Work on the basins and canals below the Kuznetskii Bridge began in accord with Gerard's plans but for unknown reasons was never completed. The first basin, nearly a half mile long and thirty-five feet wide, lay along the old course of the Neglinnaia, just north of the Kitai Gorod; the second lay opposite the bastions of the Kitai Gorod; the third beneath the Kremlin walls, between the Resurrection and Trinity Gates. Like the canal banks, these basins were planted with two rows of lindens and guarded with a decorative iron railing.

The last section of the canal, that between the Trinity Gates and the Moscow River, was crucial to the success of the Bauer-Gerard project, for the canal-basin system simply could not function properly without it. Not only did it remain unfinished, but even the completed section of canals and basins was defective: both in quality and in quantity the supply of water fell far short of expectations. Late in 1811 General P. L. Carbonier, an engineer from St. Petersburg investigating the water-supply canal, suggested remedies for the flawed system. His proposals came to nothing when in the following year all available funds were earmarked for the restoration

[32] Zombe, "Proekt plana Moskvy," 64.
[33] Although Bauer died in 1783 before completing his work, he had always intended after completing his plan for the aqueduct to turn his project over to architect-planners for development as an architectural project.
[34] Inside the Trubnaia pavilion a vertical cast-iron pipe in the center of a stone-sided pool captured the surplus water and sent it through other pipes and into fountains between Trubnaia Square and the Kuznetskii Bridge. (Sytin, *Ulits*, 315).
[35] In addition to the Sokolov and Kazakov drafts of the Neglinnaia area, that of the Gerards is also illustrated in Grabar', *Iskusstva* 6: 252–53. Noting that the canal had been completed as far south as the Kuznetskii Bridge, A. I. Gerard observed that the area between the Kuznetskii Bridge and the Moscow River, about 5,600 feet in length, "remains most marshy and disgusting as the small current of the Neglinnaia River flows over the marsh and in summer produces a very disagreeable air." (Zombe, "Proekt plana Moskvy," 65).

[36] Ibid., 74.

of burned Moscow. For several years the Neglinnaia River project was set aside.

Then, in 1816, the Committee for Building
and Hydraulic Operations discarded the
scheme of a water-supply canal altogether. It
recommended instead that

> the open canal, filled because of lack of
> hydraulic pressure with impurities and pro-
> ducing an unpleasant odor, be covered with
> arches and paved, and, thus joining the
> squares, would create a thoroughfare around
> the walls of the Kremlin.[37]

Between 1819 and 1823, total elimination of
the Neglinnaia was accomplished under the
auspices of the Commission. In such a manner

Moscow lost the prospect of a tree-lined water
thoroughfare but succeeded, finally, in rid-
ding itself of an eye-sore and sanitation problem.

That the 1775 plan for the central plazas
and the Neglinnaia was even partially implemented emphasized the priority assigned to
the reconstruction of central Moscow. The
grandees of Catherinian Russia—those who
most frequented Kazakov's Hall of Columns,
Senate, and university and Bazhenov's Pashkov house—established their residences in
close proximity. It is to their habitat of porticoed mansions washed in yellow, blue, and
pink that we next turn. Located on the radial
thoroughfares, these urban estates in the Belyi
Gorod gave to the city its sharpest image of
classicism.

---

[37] Ibid., 81.

CHAPTER VI

Moscow's Thoroughfares Before 1812

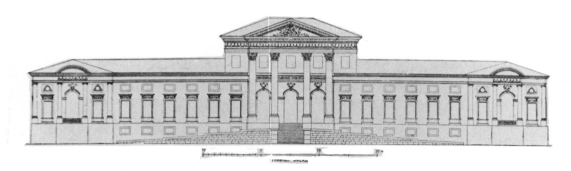

From the beginning of Catherine's reign Moscow was becoming something quite different from what it had been. It continued to be big and dirty and those who lived there as boorish as ever, but the city became vital in a new way. This surge of energy was largely traceable to the emancipation of the nobility from state service in 1762. Finding life far removed from the court in St. Petersburg much to their liking, they discovered Moscow. Thoroughly Russian, it served their purpose both for community and for distance from the Neva. Taking up residence in Moscow, the nobility encouraged the building of public edifices like the Nobles' Meeting House, Maddox's Theater, and the university. They also built great houses along and behind the arterial streets of the Belyi Gorod and the Zemlianoi Gorod. Because Moscow until the great fire was essentially an underdeveloped city, villas also occupied the rural expanses within the city limits. Urban estate houses no less than those townhouses fronting on the streets became a distinctive feature of affluent classical Moscow.[1]

The great houses invariably carried a mon-umental facade, symbolic to those enjoying new status in society. Typically, this facade was divided into three horizontal parts by stringcourses or mouldings, each separating a floor, and usually three bays wide; it was sectioned into nine rectangles. The center, where the middle vertical and horizontal bands intersected, determined the location of the main hall within. The dominance of this central entrance was achieved, frequently, by a majestic Ionic or Corinthian portico of six, eight, ten, or twelve columns; the remainder of the facade extending from the portico had variously five, seven, or nine windows. A large and ornate window, usually on the axis of the portico, was flanked by the remaining three, five, or seven windows in each of the lateral wings. A three-story residence normally had a vestibule and servants' quarters on the ground floor, a center hall, and suites of rooms for entertaining on the next floor, and bedrooms on the floor above.

These estate houses generally followed three distinctive plans.[2] In one, the main block lay beyond the line of the street, with its perpendicular wings forming a court. The L-

---

[1] Some built in unpopulated areas beyond the Zemlianoi Gorod, as noted in the next chapter.

[2] Cf. P. E. Gol'denberg, *Staraia Moskva* (Moscow, 1947), 49–52.

shaped wings reached to the street and were each in turn linked by an ornamental iron fence and gate.[3] A variant of this first type was represented by lateral wings, extending the main corpus to create an exceptionally long facade.[4] In another modification, such extended lateral wings were brought forward to the street, thereby separating the court from the street.[5] A second and fundamentally different type of estate house lay along the line of the street and reserved its main facade for an interior court; thus, unlike the first plan, it backed on the street.[6] A third kind, common to the radial thoroughfares of Moscow, occupied a corner lot. From the main hall on the corner, lateral wings skirted the two perpendicular streets. Usually cylindrical in shape, the exterior of the hall was shielded by a colonnade and appeared externally as a rotunda with a dome.[7]

*   *   *

For centuries Moscow's radial streets had borne the traffic to and from Moscow's historic center: in the west, one led to Volokolamsk and Smolensk; in the north, to St. Petersburg; and in the northeast, to Iaroslavl' and Vladimir. Communities of tradesmen, long having occupied these roads in the Zemlianoi Gorod, were pushed farther out by the noble influx of the second half of the eighteenth century.

Of all the radial thoroughfares the Prechistenka, more than any other, was appropriated by the nobility at this time. Designated Volkhonka-Prechistenka in the Belyi Gorod and Prechistenka-Ostozhenka in the Zemlianoi Gorod, it originated in the southwestern cor-

ner of the Kremlin and also attracted traffic from the Great Stone Bridge, which entered the radial through the Vodianye Gates of the Belyi Gorod. During the seventeenth century such prominent families as the Prozorovskies, Sheremetevs, Iushkovs, and Buturlins lived along the Volkhonka-Prechistenka. Later, Peter's favorite, Prince Aleksandr Danilovich Menshikov, built a palace there; and so did the princely Shakhovskies, Dolgorukovs, Golitsyns, Volkonskies, and Naryshkins.

Building on the Prechistenka continued during the late eighteenth and early nineteenth centuries. Kazakov at the beginning of the 1780s was charged by the empress herself to transform the older Golitsyn and Dolgorukov mansions into a single palace. Catherine originally had entertained such an idea for celebrating the Peace of Kuchuk-Kainarji in 1774. Although she had not built then, the decayed state of her several Moscow palaces required a decision.[8] Eventually, she determined to utilize these Prechistenka residences as the core of a new structure.

By late 1774 Kazakov with his pupils Rodion Kazakov, Nikolai Matveev, and Aleksei Khodov prepared a draft of the middle section which linked these two mansions into a single edifice. As constructed, it contained a columned throne room and an adjacent reception room in the Dolgorukov section. These chambers were decorated with garlands, medallions, and wreaths. A terraced gallery joined this formal part of the palace with the Golitsyn wing. Kazakov even included an iconostasis in the church of the palace.

Catherine, reacting unenthusiastically, referred to the palace in a letter to her confidant, Melchior Grimm, as "a triumph of confusion."[9] The palace did not remain for long on the Prechistenka. After Catherine's departure for St. Petersburg, it was dismantled and

[3] The house of Count Osterman near the Karetnyi Riad was of this type.
[4] Beketov House on the Miasnitskaia and Razumovskii in Gorokhovskii Alley.
[5] Razumovskii House on the Vozdvizhenka and Shcherbatov on the Petrovka.
[6] Examples: Talyzin House on the Vozdvizhenka, Dolgorukov on the Povarskaia, and Pashkov on the Volkhonka-Mokhovaia. Cf. Gol'denberg, *Staraia Moskva*, 50.
[7] Cf. Iushkov House on the Miasnitskaia and Sheremetev on the Vozdvizhenka.

[8] The Rastrelli buildings in the Kremlin and the Annenhof were in lamentable condition and the Ekaterininskii Palace, under construction on the site of the Annenhof summer palace, was proceeding at a slow pace. Cf. Kiparisova, "Neopublikovannye proekty," 109–111.
[9] Ibid., 109.

removed to the Sparrow (*Vorob'evy*) Hills, where it was rebuilt in 1778 on the foundation of old Vorob'evskii Palace.

Kazakov, meanwhile, obtained commissions from both the Princes Golitsyn and Dolgorukov to build in the Prechistenka. In 1778 the Golitsyns had Kazakov design an auxiliary building; two years later the Dolgorukovs charged him to design and build a mansion. The latter, magnificent and expansive, established an assertive position on the thoroughfare with its powerful six-column Ionic portico and a splendid dome on a drum (figs. 24 and 25). Massive entrance gates, surmounted by a balustraded balcony which linked the central block with the lateral wings, led into a park of fountains and ponds. This spectacular town house, although frequently modified since 1812, is still a dominant edifice on the Prechistenka.[10]

Despite destruction caused by the fire of 1812 to the Prechistenka, that street retained its aristocratic appearance through its altered or new edifices. One of the former was the late eighteenth-century mansion belonging to the 1812 war hero, Denis Davidov. Resembling Menelas's Razumovskii mansion in Gorokhovskii Alley, it had a towering pedimented facade and two balustraded half-porches. The variation of arched and square apertures and smooth and rusticated walls further distinguished its Ionic facade.[11]

Another refurbished eighteenth-century structure was the police office. Its Corinthian columnar and pilastered facade, backed by a plain upper and rusticated lower wall, reached to the street and gave the building the aura of authority appropriate to its use. Notably, it had a parapet rather than a pediment and a blank frieze balanced by a moulding of dentils.[12]

On the Znamenka, which crossed the Mokhovaia beside Pashkov House, Moscow's grandees also resided in great splendor. Behind Pashkov House, on the corner of the Krestovozdvizhenskii Alley, Count R. I. Vorontsov had a majestic residence, which, with its colonnaded portico and "court of honor," was another tribute to Kazakov. A theater was housed in a wooden addition to this palace from 1766 until fire destroyed it in 1780. Another Znamenka house, one which also accommodated its owners' love for theater, was that of General S. S. Apraksin, built by Camporesi in 1792 with a stage and quarters for both serf and Italian troupes.[13] An expansive facade with an eight-column Corinthian portico and a dome on a drum over the entrance hall were its most prominent external features. Still standing in the Znamenka is the house of Arsent'ev-Buturlin, built about 1800.[14] Its facade, tastefully divided into smooth-textured and rusticated sections, was dominated by an octastyle Ionic portico and four arched doorways beneath this porch.

The prevailing classicism of the Vozdvizhenka, the high road to Smolensk, was traceable less to individual buildings than to an extensive ensemble at its lower end, a composite of the houses belonging to the Talyzins, Sheremetevs, and Razumovskies. The Corinthian Talyzin mansion on the west side of the street and the Doric Razumovskii and Corinthian Sheremetev (fig. 406) on the opposite side formed a magnificent assemblage with several older churches and the Mokhovaia House of A. I. Pashkov, itself adjacent to the

---

[10] As illustrated in *Al'bomy M. F. Kazakova*, 99–102, 254; and *Monuments* 2: 142–44. This house burned in 1812 and was altered again in 1837.

[11] See *Monuments* 2: 346, for a description and recent photograph.

[12] See *Monuments* 2: 178, for a recent photograph. Near these two Prechistenka edifices stood several notable ones in the Ostozhenka. That of General P. D. Eropkin, built in 1771,

was rectangular and severe. (Illustrated in *Al'bomy M. F. Kazakova*, 95, 253 and in *Monuments* 2: 347). The monotony of an extended facade was broken by pilastered sections, a gabled pediment, and a portal of four pairs of Doric columns supporting a balustraded roof. Just thirty-five years after its construction, in 1806, it was completely rebuilt. The frame Loshakovskii-Vsevolozhskii House, an Ostozhenka classical residence, was erected at the beginning of the nineteenth century. See *Monuments* 2: 347, for a description and recent photograph.

[13] Cf. Sytin, *Ulits*, 188 and *Al'bomy M. F. Kazakova*, 157–59, 262. After the 1812 fire performances were also moved here from the burned-out Arbatskaia Square theater. In the autumn of 1818 the theater moved to the A. I. Pashkov House at the Mokhovaia and Great Nikitskaia.

[14] *Monuments* 2: 160–61, 342.

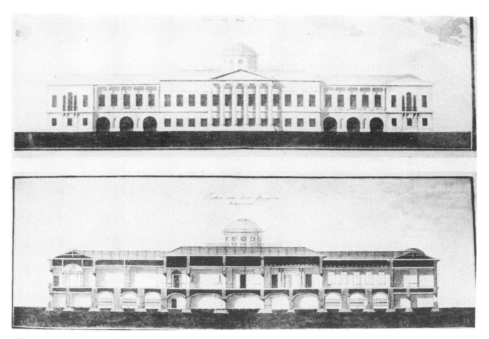

Figure 24. Dolgorukov House (1780s) on the Prechistenka, architect M. F. Kazakov. (E. A. Beletskaia, *Arkhitekturnye Al'bomy M. F. Kazakova*, Moscow, 1956; hereafter, *Al'bomy M. F. Kazakova*).

Figure 25. Dolgorukov House as restored in the 1830s and 1840s and appearing today (Schmidt).

new university.[15] The central corpus of the estate belonging to General Count P. F. Talyzin (1787) lined the Vozdvizhenka. Its facade of three horizontal sections supported a shallow Corinthian portico. Between the main building and the smaller end ones portals opened into an expansive semicircular rear court. This mansion, attributed to the "school of Kazakov," burned in 1812 and was later restored.[16]

Across from this Talyzin block stood Count N. P. Sheremetev's small corner house, designed probably by N. A. L'vov. Originally built for the Hetman K. G. Razumovskii about 1780, it passed to the Sheremetevs in 1800. From the corner rotunda, its wings extended at right angles along the Vozdvizhenka and an intersecting alley. A Doric colonnade laced this building's rounded corner, and a flat cupola on a drum, pierced by round windows, capped it. A pediment and series of medallions over each first-story window enlivened its Vozdvizhenka facade. Although this house burned in 1812, it, too, was restored, in 1814–1816.[17]

Adjacent to this corner house, the Hetman Razumovskii had also owned a more spacious Vozdvizhenka mansion, possibly a creation of Bazhenov (fig. 40b, p.118). Located where a seventeenth-century Naryshkin estate house had stood, it, too, was conveyed to Prince Sheremetev in 1800. Its long and ornate facade with projecting wings was articulated by a portico of Corinthian pilasters and the three arched main entrances. Its interior—the hall in particular—had exquisite wall and ceiling ornament and parquet floors. Auxiliary buildings, extending from the main corpus, formed a magnificent formal court that extended to the Mokhovaia. This estate also burned in 1812.[18]

Beyond the Mokhovaia, the Vozdvizhenka passed through the Arbat Gates before branching into various radial thoroughfares in the Zemlianoi Gorod. After the gates and old buildings had been pulled down, a large square was set out before 1800. Although some wooden structures remained, the Arbat became the hub of aristocratic Moscow.[19] The Counts P. B. Sheremetev and F. A. Osterman and a Golitsyn prince lived there, and in 1807 Karl I. Rossi built the frame Arbat Theater. This high, colonnaded structure with its superb decor and sets was destroyed with the rest of the plaza in 1812.

The nobility also dominated such lesser Arbat radials as the Povarskaia between the Arbat and Garden Ring. There glistened the columns and washed classical mansions belonging to the Dolgorukovs, Volchovs, and Solugubs.[20] In the Great Nikitskaia the houses were similar to those in the Arbat and Povarskaia. In Catherine's day many old Moscow families like the Bezsonovs, Orlovs, and Razumovskies, and grandees like the Princess E. R. Dashkova, Prince S. A. Menshikov, and I. A. Brius possessed properties there;[21] others—the Romodanovskies, Apraksins, and Kolychevs—had resided in it since early in the

---

[15] Cf. Gulianitskii, "O kompozitsii," 24–25.
[16] Cf. Sytin, Ulits, 190. Drawing in Al'bomy M. F. Kazakova, 162–63, 263 and photograph in Monuments 2: 159, 341.
[17] See Al'bomy M. F. Kazakova, 166–67, 263 and Monuments 2: 341.
[18] See Al'bomy M. F. Kazakova, 169–75, 263 and Monuments 2: 90–91, 341.

[19] The author remembers nostalgically this entire area west of the Arbat to the Garden Ring and north to the Great Nikitskaia (Herzen) in the early 1960s. Although decaying, it nonetheless retained its classical purity. Then the bulldozer destroyed much of it to make way for the modern Kalinin Prospekt.
[20] That of Prince A. N. Dolgorukov with its magnificent portico and wings framed a garden and yard, which were separated from the street by a grille. This mansion is now the Union of Writers of the USSR. Reputedly, it was used as a model by Tolstoi for the Rostov House in War and Peace. The nearby Volchov House, situated behind decorative iron fences and gates, achieved compositional symmetry through a careful arrangement of its facade elements—eleven windows across, twin Ionic columns at each end, and a four-column Ionic portico (as illustrated in Al'bomy M. F. Kazakova, 221, 269). The Solugub mansion with a six-column portico and lateral wings was another late eighteenth-century creation in this street (Monuments 2: 136).
[21] The dwelling of Princess Dashkova is presently, in a much altered state, the Moscow Music Conservatory. The Great Nikitskaia (Herzen) is arrayed with classical architecture to this day, from the Square of the Uprising (Vosstaniia) to the university on the Mokhovaia. The narrow streets and alleys between Herzen and Kalinin below the Boulevard Ring are similarly laced with classical architecture.

century. The splendid Brius mansion dating from the 1770s was in the following decade enlarged with a lateral wing and by the end of the century partially rebuilt. Kolychev House, today the Juridical Institute, survives from Catherine's day with its six-pilaster Corinthian portico and side entrance arches between the main and auxiliary buildings.[22]

There were two Orlov houses in the Great Nikitskaia. That of G. N. Orlov, built after 1775 as an expansive rectangular block with seventeen windows across, received vertical articulation from double pilasters at each end and a six-pilastered portico.[23]

The L. K. Razumovskii House, distinctively symmetrical, had an elegant four-pilastered portico and bas-relief medallions between the ground and first-floor windows, each of which was capped with a pediment.[24] The Menshikov mansion, possibly a Kazakov creation, appeared in the 1778 plan of blocks but without the auxiliary buildings that formed its spacious front court. This rectangular edifice was articulated by a six-pilastered Ionic portico and small balcony over the main entrance. The house was altered during the first quarter of the nineteenth century. Near the Menshikov estate, but facing an alley rather than the Nikitskaia, were the A. M. Golitsyn properties. Dating before 1777 and altered after 1782, this estate house appeared modest compared to most in the neighborhood.[25]

On the right side of the Great Nikitskaia in the Zemlianoi Gorod were the estates of the Prince G. A. Potemkin-Tavricheskii, General V. I. Suvorov, Princess A. A. Prozorovskaia, Prince I. P. Gagarin, and Prince N. M. Golitsyn. The Golitsyn House, severe in appearance, was built by the Nikitskie Gates at mid-

century and renovated before the turn of the next.[26] Beyond the Nikitskie Gates on the Little Nikitskaia, gentry and princely comfort was evidenced by the Potemkin, Naryshkin, Orlov, and Bobrinskii holdings. The Dolgorukov (sometimes Bobrinskii or Naryshkin) palace, pedimented but devoid of a portico, compensated with diverse window styles, bas-reliefs, and a grand entrance of three arched portals. Its charming balconies at the sides of the wings were accentuated by Corinthian columns, grille, bas-relief medallions, and apertures of varied shapes.[27] Houses like this one made the Nikitskaia, Great and Little, nearly equal in classical artifacts to the Prechistenka and the Tverskaia.

The incomparable Tverskaia during the eighteenth century was Moscow's busiest and best known thoroughfare (fig. 26). Although dominated by the houses of gentry and grandees, the street was heterogeneous in character. The poet, P. A. Viazemskii, writing of the Tverskaia at the beginning of the nineteenth century, observed that:

... here are miraculous mansions,
With coats of arms where a famous family is crowned,
And near them shacks on chicken legs,
And a garden with cucumbers.[28]

As an arterial highway to Petersburg, the Tverskaia bore heavy traffic and was a site for ceremony and festivity. Coronation and triumphal parades passed through the Tverskie Gates, where wooden arches were customarily raised to welcome honored guests to the city. Such parade gates had been erected for Peter I in 1721 after his success against the Swedes, and for Elizabeth, Catherine II, and Paul I to celebrate their coronations. Another arch was constructed in 1775 to observe the victory of Count P. A. Rumiantsov-Zadunaiskii over the Turks. These ceremonial gates did not last very long; usually they burned, deteriorated, or

---

[22] *Al'bomy M. F. Kazakova*, 180, 264. Corinthian like the Kolychev House, that of the Bezsonovs, possibly by I. V. Egotov, was more pretentious though smaller. (Ibid., 86–87, 252).

[23] Ibid., 176, 264. The other Orlov House, designed possibly by Kazakov before 1778 (presently in a much altered form used by the Moscow University history faculty), had a four-pilastered central Ionic portico. After burning in 1812, it was substantially changed in 1814. Cf. ibid., 187–88, 265 and *Monuments* 2: 137 for a recent photograph.

[24] *Al'bomy M. F. Kazakova*, 155, 261.

[25] Ibid., 164–65, 263 and 151, 260.

[26] Ibid., 220, 269.

[27] Ibid, 216–17, 269; *Monuments* 2: 108–110. This house was altered significantly after 1812.

[28] As quoted in Sytin, *Ulits*, 212.

Figure 26. The Tverskaia in the early nineteenth century. Lithograph from the original by A. Cadolle, 1830s (Donskoi, V-32724).

90

were simply dismantled. The Tverskie Gates had been pulled down in 1720, although the walls remained intact until the destructive fire of 1773. Following their removal, a rather disorganized plaza emerged, cluttered with shops and dwellings.[29]

From the Tverskie Gates to Okhotnyi Riad, the Tverskaia was lined on both sides with majestic classical mansions and ensembles built or restored after the 1773 fire.[30] About midway between lay Tverskaia Square. In 1790 the state purchased lands from the Dolgorukovs in order to enlarge the grounds of the governor's mansion and lay out a square before it. Kazakov, charged with planning this square, suggested a fence around it and a "gallery with columns" before the court of the guard, but these embellishments were not sanctioned by Catherine II. The only immediate accomplishment was the clearing and planning of the plaza in 1792. Because mansions here faced the Tverskaia rather than the square, only low fences with grille gates were in evidence. The sophistication of this setting was tempered by herds of Petersburg-bound livestock driven through the square at night. Just before 1812, this plaza changed significantly as a result of new construction. Miraculously, the square itself—indeed, most of the Tverskaia, for that matter—did not suffer greatly from the fire in 1812. One structure that survived was Tverskoi House, the residence of the governor, which Kazakov had built for Count Z. G. Chernyshev in 1782. In a much altered form, it is the present City Hall (*Mossovet*).

Kazakov designed or restored other Tverskaia mansions in the classical mode. One of these, the Ermolov House belonging to the

Orlovs in 1770, survived the fire of 1773 only as a shell. Preserving in part its original rococo character, Kazakov restored it with a semirusticated facade and four-pilastered Corinthian portico.[31] Sometime after 1778, Kazakov designed for Prince A. A. Prozorovskii a house on the Tverskaia which also showed traces of rococo. An Ionic portico over its center entrance severed the line of windows reaching across the facade. Pedimented and unpedimented windows, windows with balconies, and elevated sections of the facade above the first story windows—all these gave this symmetrical facade a warm and lyrical quality.[32]

The Koznitskii House, built probably by Kazakov in the early 1790s, conformed more to the style of later classicism than to rococo. Its dominant feature, a majestic six-columned Corinthian entrance, rested on a rusticated podium and before a medallion-decorated wall. This same facade had balcony windows with pediments between pairs of twin columns at both ends.[33]

The S. M. Golitsyn mansion lay situated between Georgievskii Alley and the Kuznetskii Bridge. Built after 1765 and escaping the fire of 1773, it consisted of a main block and two lateral wings embracing a front court. Kazakov gave to this rococo-like dwelling a sublime dimension through its interior components—columns in the vestibule, for example. The subsquent addition of a corner section, a rotunda and cupola, and a full complement of circular windows, bas-reliefs, and small pediments over the doors and windows also enriched its classical appearance.[34]

Kazakov also designed the Musin-Pushkin House, built sometime after 1797. Twenty-seven windows punctuated the expansive Tverskaia facade; ten additional windows spanned the central gable. A frontage of such

[29] The fire of 1812 barely touched this square; therefore, many old houses remained until recent times. (Ibid., 302–08).

[30] For a pictorial reconstruction of the Tverskaia as it appeared from the Boulevard Ring to Okhotnyi Riad in 1805, see *Al'bomy M. F. Kazakova*, insert after 278; cf. also Gulianitskii, "O kompozitsii," 25–26. The Tverskaia (Gorkii) today bears little resemblance to its classical past although there are some worthwhile remnants in the alleys behind the facades that line the street from the Garden Ring to Marx Prospekt (the old Okhotnyi Riad).

[31] *Al'bomy M. F. Kazakova*, 38–39, 245.

[32] Ibid., 49–52, 247.

[33] Ibid., 71–75, 249–50.

[34] Ibid., 76–77, 250. The corner building with the rotunda survived the main building which burned in 1812. The significance of the Golitsyn ensemble and others near it is discussed in Gulianitskii, "O kompozitsii," 25–26.

proportions was naturally given both vertical and horizontal articulation. To the left and right of the central portion, dominated by the gable, portals opened beneath two sets of twin Ionic pilasters. These doorways were themselves embellished with rusticated projections, overhanging balconies, and assorted bas-reliefs.[35]

Many dazzling estate houses in addition to those designed by Kazakov lined the Tverskaia. Often they followed a cycle of destruction and restoration as a result of recurring fires. With each restoration these mansions naturally assumed a contemporary mode and emerged as essentially a new structure. Such was the V. P. Saltykov mansion in Gazetnyi Alley, which was originally constructed in the first half of the century, burned in 1773, restored, burned again in 1812, and finally rebuilt in 1829. Its main block, divided by a four-columned Corinthian portico, fronted on the Tverskaia while its side entrance led into a spacious quadrangular court.[36] A palatial Ionic dwelling in Georgievskii Alley, built after 1781, came into possession of the Beketovs by 1793. It burned in 1812, and was subsequently restored between 1815 and 1831.[37] North of the Tverskie Gates the succession of classical mansions continued. Among these, that of the Razumovskies was most striking. Built in 1780, it was reconstructed by the English architect

Adam Adamovich Menelas (Menelaws) as the English Club after 1812.[38]

East of the Tverskaia diverse rococo, Palladian, and classical mansions vied with one another for distinction in the Great and Little Dmitrovkas and Petrovka.[39] On the Great Dmitrovka resided the Counts Saltykov, who had variously served as governors of the city. The estate of N. E. Miasoedov, an assemblage of late eighteenth-century buildings, was highlighted by one which embraced with its lateral wings a splendid court.[40] M. M. Golitsyn's mansion, built near Georgievskii Alley sometime before 1777, was distinctive for a facade of four pilasters terminating beneath an ornate frieze and a balustrade, which edged the entire roof.[41]

Beyond the Dmitrovka, in the Petrovka, the ever-prominent Romodanovskies, Gagarins, Shcherbatovs, Meshcherskies, Gerasimovs, and Menshikovs had resided since Peter's reign. The Princes Lobanov-Rostovskii also lived there, on the present site of the Bol'shoi Theater and near the Sibirskii and Shcherbatov properties. Probably it was Kazakov who, after 1781, built a fairly typical classical mansion for the merchant Kir'iakov on the Petrovka at Bogoslovskii Alley.[42]

In the 1790s Kazakov also designed Gubin House on the Petrovka, just below the Petrovskie Gates. It immediately ranked among the most important buildings of Kazakov and of classical Moscow (fig. 27a,b). Erected on a large, elevated lot, the mansion for the mer-

---

[35] *Al'bomy M. F. Kazakova*, 84–85, 251–52.

[36] Ibid., 152–53, 261.

[37] Ibid., 178–79, 264. Another was the B. A. Golitsyn House at Kamergerskii Alley, erected between 1775 and 1778 for Prince M. I. Dolgorukov. Designed as an "H" with lateral wings projecting to both the front and rear, this palace had a central portal shielded by a balustraded four-columned portico. This house burned in 1812 and was later rebuilt. (Cf. ibid., 181–82, 264). The Zubov mansion standing opposite Briusovskii Alley was also altered after a fire, but one earlier than 1812. Built in the first decade of the eighteenth century as a mansion for the governor of Siberia, Prince M. P. Gagarin, it burned in 1773. Afterwards, its basically rectangular block was restored and modified. Although the facades of its slightly protruding lateral wings carried Corinthian pilasters at each extremity, the central portal and the galleries across the facade retained a distinctly non-classical, even seventeenth-century, look. (Cf. ibid., 184–86, 265, for more on the Zubov House which came into that family's possession in the 1790s).

[38] Cf. below, 165, for more on Menelas's English Club and 117 for Menelas's work on the Razumovskii House in Gorokhovoe Field.

[39] Other than in Chekhov Street (Little Dmitrovka) few classical houses have survived in this sector of Moscow. The intersection of the Boulevard Ring and Pushkin contains several of post-1812 vintage (the present University Typographia by A. G. Grigor'ev in 1817–1821 and another with a columned portico and located on the Ring dating from 1816–1817, the work of N. Sobolevskii. See *Monuments* 2: 353 for a recent photograph). Aside from the Gubin and Gagarin Houses at the Petrovskie Gates the only monument of historic interest below the Boulevard Ring is Petrovka Monastery.

[40] *Al'bomy M. F. Kazakova*, 149, 260.

[41] Ibid., 150, 260.

[42] *Al'bomy M. F. Kazakova*, 90, 252.

MOSCOW'S THOROUGHFARES BEFORE 1812

Figure 27a. Gubin House (1790s) on the Petrovka, architect M. F. Kazakov (Schmidt).

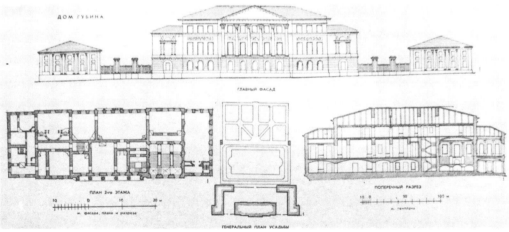

Figure 27b. Drawing, Gubin House.

chant Gubin was situated along the "red line" of the street. Its distinctive external features were a powerful portico, high pediment, loge, and otherwise severe facade. As was typical of townhouses of late eighteenth-century Moscow, the portico rested on a high basement, articulated by rusticated walls. Within, however, it opened into a court and a formal park with a pond. It became, in effect, a rural estate house in Moscow's center. Kazakov arranged the rooms in the usual manner for such houses, the most elaborate ones on the first floor above the ground level and the living quarters on the second. A gate and fence linked the two lateral wings of the main body, which was itself articulated by a massive Corinthian portico of six columns.[43]

At the Petrovskie Gates the rich had always mixed with the not-so-rich. This area was especially identified with Moscow's carriage makers (thus, *Karetnyi Riad*), who had resided there from the late seventeenth century. The burning of the settlement in 1812, apparently by its artisans to prevent the French confiscation of their carriages, forever changed this Moscow neighborhood. Among the nobility who resided there before 1812 was Prince V. N. Gagarin, whose palatial mansion with a mighty twelve-column Ionic portico dominated the space at the Petrovskie Gates. Designed probably by Kazakov and built between 1786–1790, it burned in 1812 and was restored by Osip Bove in the 1820s[44] (fig. 28a,b). Opposite Prince Gagarin's house Bove, apparently, built about 1800 an equally large mansion for Prince Shcherbatov, but no description of it remains. These great houses gave to the Petrovka a classical dimension despite the presence of the seventeenth-century Petrovskii Monastery.

Like the Petrovka, the Kuznetskii Bridge was originally an artisan habitat, but it lost that image early, by the mideighteenth century. As noted, the Cannon Court blacksmith and stable-keeper settlements and even old nobility were after the fire of 1737 forced to make way for fashionable French shops, which transformed the bridge area into a "sanctuary of luxury" for decades to come (fig. 29). Ukhtomskii's Kuznetskii Bridge, built over the Neglinnaia in 1753–1757, provided an ideal setting for these new entrepreneurs. North of the bridge the area changed, too; most of it becoming part of the Vorontsov estate through which the river flowed. Kuznetskii Bridge did not suffer greatly from the fire in 1812, but the enclosure of the Neglinnaia in an underground pipe in 1817–1819 led to the demolition of the span.

The Vorontsov estate typified the rural estate in urban Moscow. It skirted the Kuznetskii Bridge in the north, occupying much of the land between the Petrovka and the Rozhdestvenka. In the mideighteenth century only wooden out-buildings and a fence with a gate faced the Rozhdestvenka. A masonry house of some sort lay within the grounds, and behind it stretched a meticulously attended regulated garden, replete with statuary and gazebos. In 1778 Vorontsov commissioned Kazakov to design a new estate house, eventually realized as a three story one with a colonnaded front portico and two lateral wings. Its grounds stretched to the Neglinnaia River in back and reached forward to the Rozhdestvenka from which it was separated by an iron grille.

At the century's end, this Rozhdestvenka was bounded in the west by the old Cannon Court buildings and in the east by a vast open space reaching almost to the Kitai Gorod Walls. When the Cannon Court was demolished in 1803, this unoccupied expanse extended to the Neglinnaia. In 1782 the old Rozhdestvenskii Monastery walls, near the Zemlianoi Gorod, were razed to permit widening of the street from twenty-eight to sixty-two feet. Although the appearance of the Rozhdestvenka changed by the end of the eighteenth century, this thoroughfare had less a classic look than did the other radials.

New construction reshaped the Great Lubianka-Sretenka east of the Rozhdestvenka. Commerce, which had flourished there since the sixteenth century, retreated—as new houses for the nobility were erected in the eighteenth. On the Great Lubianka, within the Belyi Gorod, lived the Princes Golitsyn, Volkonskii, Khovanskii, and Khilkov, whose fences, stables, and out-buildings were visible from this street. In 1774–1776 Matvei Kazakov designed a light, warm residence for A. N. Golitsyn. A rectangular block with a Corinthian portico, it had atop the block a bal-

---

[43] Ibid., 60–61, 248; *Monuments* 2: 96–97 for recent photographs.
[44] This central section was built between 1786–1790, designed probably by M. F. Kazakov; the building burned in 1812 and was much altered in the 1820s by Bove. (Cf. *Al'bomy M. F. Kazakova*, 222–23, 269).

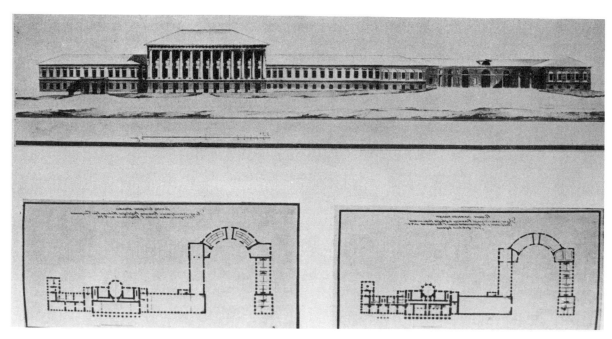

Figure 28a. V. N. Gagarin House (1786–90; restored 1820) at Petrovskie Gates, architects M. F. Kazakov and O. I. Bove (*Al'bomy Kazakova*).

Figure 28b. Gagarin House at the Petrovskie Gates (Schmidt).

Figure 29. View of the Kuznetskii Bridge at the beginning of the nineteenth century. Lithograph from the original by A. Cadolle, 1830s (Donskoi, V-26136).

ustrade that paralleled an ornamental iron fence stretching across its entire front.[45] When it was built, shops and taverns occupied small parcels of land adjacent to it along the Lubianka. Beyond the Belyi Gorod, on the Srentenka, this lord-merchant configuration persisted, permitted probably because of the proximity of the market.

Classical edifices on the Miasnitskaia, which took its name from the sixteenth-century butchers who lived there, surpassed in grandeur any in the Great Lubianka-Srentenka. Most of the great houses lay far to the rear of estates that displayed only fences or stables on the Miasnitskaia; however, there were notable exceptions such as the frame Menshikov and masonry Stroganov Houses, and, especially Bazhenov's Iushkov House (fig. 30), Kazakov's Baryshnikov House, and the Lobanov-Rostovskii mansion.

The Iushkov residence, erected after that of Pashkov in the late 1780s and early 1790s represented the author's turn to a severer French classicism from the Italianate. It occupied a corner lot where its two identical rectangular wings were joined at 90° angles by a half rotunda with a semicircular Ionic colonnade. The deep loggia created by the latter gave the building a striking spaciousness. Rustication of its lower level offered a pleasing contrast to the flat surface of the upper, and a lack of architectural details conveyed the intended severity and power, characteristic of the Empire mode of the next two or three decades.[46]

The elegance of the Baryshnikov Mansion in large part stemmed from its street facade. Unlike Gubin House, which Kazakov built with the entrance court in the rear, that for Major Baryshnikov (late 1790s) included a

---

[45] Ibid., 45–48, 246.

[46] See *Monuments* 2: 93, for another recent photograph.

Figure 30. Iushkov House (late 1780s–early 1790s) on the Miasnitskaia, architect V. Bazhenov (Schmidt).

grand front entrance on the Miasnitskaia. By extending two lateral wings from this structure to the street, Kazakov created a court before the dominant, and only slightly projected, central facade. A soaring Corinthian portico rising from the projected ground floor towered over and dominated all other elements in this building. Lower level rustication countered both the portico height and the soft-textured upper story. The lateral wing facades were each pierced by three windows which in turn were framed by two pairs of pilasters. Various auxiliary buildings beside and behind this main corpus complemented it.

The Baryshnikov interior epitomized Kazakov's tasteful elegance. He gave to the square main hall a Corinthian colonnade border and frescoed ceiling, while another Corinthian peristyle ringed an exquisite oval bedroom. Its richness in detail and its miniature scale made this bedroom one of Russia's most radiant classical interiors.[47]

Lobanov-Rostovskii House, which dated from 1790, was a palatial home of a different sort, distinguished most of all by its central portico and pedimented wings. Two pairs of full-length Corinthian columns on each side both supported and accentuated this ponderous and arching portico. The facades of the wings were identically finished with four Corinthian pilasters and three bas-relief medallions between the capitals. Except for the central and wing facades, the entire front was rusticated. This mansion, as shown on the plan of streets of 1780, was altered at the end

---

[47] *Al'bomy M. F. Kazakova,* 68–70, 248; *Monuments* 2: 130–33 for recent photographs.

of the century.[48] Two other Miasnitskie houses deserve mention. The frame Tatishchev House, built after 1760 at the corner of Miasnitskii Passage in the late rococo mode, had, like other corner edifices, its fulcrum in the cylindrical section from which wings extended at right angles. Sheremetev House near Sretenskii Boulevard dated from the 1770s. It was a work obviously in the new classic mode, as indicated by its Corinthian portico of four pilasters supporting an elaborate pediment.[49]

More than the Miasnitskaia, the eighteenth-century Maroseika was a street of middle-class and artisan dwellings; however, interspersed among them were great mansions as well. During the seventeenth century settlements of kettlemakers and hatters had located there, in the midst of commerce and gentility; by the eighteenth, the street had become a habitat for physicians, apothecaries, and artisans, many of whom were foreigners. Beyond the Belyi Gorod courtiers, physicians, architects, and pharmacists—again mainly of foreign extraction—resided on this street, now called the Pokrovka.

The architecture of the Maroseika was as diverse as its inhabitants. Among its classical artifacts, a house designed probably by Bazhenov and built by M. Kazakov stands out. Located at the Armianskii Alley it was completed in 1782 and came into the possession of N. P. Rumiantsev in the 1790s.[50] It was a rather large structure, the main section of which was a corner rotunda. Its highly articulated wing facades and rotunda conveyed an elegance despite absence of the usual portico. A similar edifice in this street was that belonging to V. P. Razumovskii. Also situated on a corner lot, it had a rotunda and dome.[51]

One of the notable non-residential buildings to rise on the Maroseika before 1812 was the Church of Saints Cosmas and Damian,[52]

designed by Matvei Kazakov and constructed between 1791–1803. Its rotundas, lanterns, bell tower, porticoes, and smooth-textured walls marked it severely classical although its plan was that of a Greek cross. The central rotunda, capped with a lantern, acquired spaciousness from the protruding chapels. In all, this church testified to its architect's virtuosity: Kazakov had only a few years earlier completed the cylindrical Church of Philip the Metropolitan rather more in the decorative Bazhenov mode of classicism.

Classical edifices at the Pokrovskie Gates were generally less ornate than some from midcentury on the Maroseika. Both the Iamanskii and the A. G. Golovkin mansions, erected late in the eighteenth century, typified this relative severity. The former, without portico, possessed a facade pierced by nine windows across its first floor and six windows and three entrances on its ground level.[53] The Golovkin edifice, rectangular in plan and with two lateral wings projecting only slightly in back, was also without notable facade adornment save its windows and tiny gables.[54]

Among those great houses on the Maroseika-Pokrovka reflecting late rococo and early classical styles was that of the Apraksins, built about midcentury. Constructed in 1766 by Ukhtomskii, it had a rococo facade of columns, windows encrusted with bas-reliefs, and precise horizontal stringcourses. Apraksin House really represented a rococo lag into the classical era.[55] That belonging to Field Marshal Prince N. V. Repnin stood three stories, was rectangular in form, had nineteen pedimented windows across it, and a central portal leading into the inner court. The absence of a portico and the pilastered divisions of its facade confirmed its essentially rococo motif, too.[56]

Shakhovskii House nearby, resembled that of the Repnin in style and vintage, but the horizontal and vertical divisions of its facade,

[48] Al'bomy M. F. Kazakova, 224–25, 269; see Monuments 2: 128 for a recent photograph.
[49] Al'bomy M. F. Kazakova, 127–29, 141, 257, 259.
[50] Ibid., 40–43, 246.
[51] Ibid., 138, 258.
[52] See Monuments 2: 148, for a recent photograph.

[53] Al'bomy M. F. Kazakova, 211, 268.
[54] Ibid., 201, 267.
[55] Monuments 2:51–54 for recent photographs.
[56] Al'bomy M. F. Kazakova, 135–36, 257.

window decorations, gables, and a balustrade distinguished it from the Prince's house. The A. A. Dolgorukov Mansion, situated farther along the Pokrovka and dating from 1750, also mirrored the earlier rococo. From a rectangular body, wings stretched to the rear to form an inner court. Like Repnin House, it contained a great central portal which led into a court, but its facade, while distinctly rococo, was markedly less ornate than that of the Shakhovskii. The F. N. Golitsyn House, finished in 1784, despite its late date also seemed essentially rococo in idiom. Its main facade contained fifteen variously adorned windows across both stories. A distinctive cornice, a horizontal division in the center and a central cupola on a drum were its most notable features.[57]

These great mansions on the Maroseika-Pokrovka suggest that it was essentially a rococo street. Such a characterization is inaccurate, for there were later classical houses, and some of the rococo mansions were converted to a less pretentious classicism later in the century.

The remaining radial street was the ancient Solianka through which the heroic Dmitrii Donskoi passed on his way to do battle with the Tatars at Kulikovo in 1380.[58] From early in the eighteenth century until it was replaced by the Foundling Home in 1764, the Cannonball Court, or Munition Works, occupied the west side of the Solianka in Vasil'evskii

Meadow. By this century, too, the Volkonskies, Buturlins, Naryshkins, Istlent'evs, and other noble families resided on the thoroughfare. The Solianka terminated at the stone Iauzskie Bridge and Gates until destruction of the latter at the end of the eighteenth century; then it continued beyond the Iauza River through the old Silverworkers' Settlement.[59]

The A. Istlent'ev Mansion, a rectangular block with two wings extending to the street, was one of the most important Solianka residences before 1812. Its front court, which the wings embraced, was sheltered behind an ornamental iron fence with gates at each end; a six-columned portico, faintly suggesting a rococo motif, dominated the main facade.[60] The numerous porticoed facades along the Solianka made it one of the pleasantest streets in Moscow during this age of Kazakov; after 1812 its classical buildings acquired even greater renown.

On these radial thoroughfares of the Belyi and the Zemlianoi Gorod, Russia's nobility spared nothing to emulate their English counterparts in habit and dwelling. While they perhaps fell short in the former, they often surpassed the English lords in the luxury of their domiciles. Moscow during the half century before 1812, despite its unsavory neighborhoods and suburbs, acquired an aura of classicism from the Prechistenka to the Solianka. In looks, if not spirit, it was, indeed, becoming a part of Europe.

---

[57] Ibid., 112–15, 132–34, 256–58.
[58] The street acquired its name only in the seventeenth century when the salt monopoly was established there.

[59] In 1805 a stone bridge over the Iauza replaced the wooden one. (Cf. below, p. 167).
[60] Al'bomy M. F. Kazakova, 107, 255.

CHAPTER VII

Classical Moscow's Emergence Along The Boulevard Ring and Beyond Before 1812

Classicism was expressed in the architecture of Moscow apart from the radial thoroughfares. Specifically, there were four such sectors of the city: 1) The Boulevard Ring which evolved before 1812 to become the most important concentric element in the new cityscape; 2) the banks of the Moscow River embankment on which classical symmetry was imposed in an effort to exercise flood control; 3) the ancient Zamoskvorech'e, that part of the Zemlianoi Gorod which reached to the Kremlin from the south, where some new construction was undertaken; and 4) beyond Zemlianoi Gorod where a number of significant classical edifices, particularly hospitals, were erected. The building in and organizing of these four areas before 1812 is basic to comprehending the classical Moscow consumed by fire.

The Boulevard Ring

If at the end of the eighteenth century the lines for a classical city were less precisely drawn beyond Belyi Gorod than in the proximity of the Kremlin, the same could also be said of the future Ring. This boulevard was projected to replace the old ramparts separating the Belyi and Zemlianoi Gorods. In

reality the wall, by midcentury long decaying and partially dismantled, had disappeared completely by the 1780s except for stacks of bricks destined for future construction on the same site. But a spacious and splendid thoroughfare had not immediately replaced it. For the most part, the space vacated by the old Belyi Gorod Wall had spawned only hovels and various nondescript buildings and had collected brush and debris. Such disorder was not what Moscow's eminent architects had envisioned.

Indeed, they had intended the Boulevard Ring, poised fan-shaped at the Moscow River, as bedecked with comely facades of mansions and churches and divided by a park-like esplanade. The planners further recommended that the Ring should be well planted with chestnut, linden, and birch to provide an umbrella of shade for promenaders in this the chic sector of the city. Each segment of the Ring was named for the district through which it passed, the Prechistenskii, Nikitskii, Tverskoi, etc.

Progress in construction of the western half of the Ring on the eve of the Great Fire was uneven at best. Destruction on the Moscow River's left bank caused by the great flood of 1783 and a cyclone three years later necessitated reconstruction, some on the unfinished

Prechistenskii Boulevard. Work on this section of the Boulevard from the river to the Arbat commenced fitfully at the beginning of the century and dragged on after 1812. Amidst the houses of minor officials, a tavern and the police headquarters, the classical Tsurikov, A. S. Sheremetev, and Naryshkin mansions dominated the Prechistenskii Ring. Of these the most notable was that of Tsurikov, the work of Kazakov or his school, with its striking facade of fifteen windows across and a towering six-column Corinthian portico.[1]

The Nikitskii Boulevard, contiguous to the Arbat in the east and in process before 1812, opened for use shortly thereafter, but with no remarkable architecture. With respect to the Tverskoi adjoining it, the story was quite different. The fire of 1773, which devastated the Tverskoi area, forced the authorities to assign a high priority to its completion. Completed in 1796, the Tverskoi became the setting for some of Moscow's most attractive town houses. A block of these houses, spared the fire in 1812, is the most important early classical survival of its kind (figs. 31–32). Its continuous facade of harmonious classical elements—columns, balustrades, and grille-work balconies, pediments, voluted and plain pilasters, variously rusticated and smooth walls, bas-reliefs, and diverse window shapes—marvelously exemplifies the stylistic maturity achieved by Moscow's classical architects before 1812.[2]

The Tverskoi, so endowed, became a popular strolling place for Moscow's aristocracy at the turn of the century. The traveler Reinbeck referred to this walk as one "for foot-passengers in the middle of the broadest street and planted with trees"; he complained, however, that dust inhibited growth of vegetation along this Boulevard Ring. Each week two promenading days were designated; on these days "the fashionable and unfashionable on

foot, horseback, and in carriages flock from all quarters of the city to public walks in the Summer Garden and on the Boulevards."[3] Initially, birches were planted on the Tverskoi, and when they died, lindens replaced them. These lindens met a different fate, for during the French occupation they were cut down for firewood or else used for hanging Muscovites suspected of arson. With the departure of the French, lindens, flower beds, fountains, and benches were once again set out, and the strolling resumed on the Tverskoi.

The Strastnoi, Petrovskii, and Rozhdestvenskii Boulevards—those sections of the Boulevard Ring east of the Tverskoi—were delayed, in their opening, more or less, until after the fire. Although the Strastnoi, between the Tverskaia and the Petrovka, was not finished until 1830, mansions of the nobility were erected there. Such was the Benkendorf House, two stories in height, nine windows across, with a great Corinthian portico. Another was Kazakov's previously mentioned palatial residence for Prince V. N. Gagarin at the Petrovskie Gates.

In 1800 little progress had been made on the Boulevard from the Petrovskie Gates to the Neglinnaia River. Only stacks of bricks from the demolished wall suggested the good intentions. By 1812, however, work on the Petrovskii Boulevard, which took its name from the nearby monastery, was well underway if not actually completed. The Great Fire destroyed the various cottages, stables, baths, and mansions which had collected in the open spaces, thus allowing for a fresh start, architecturally. Birches had originally been planted there as on the Tverskoi, but in 1818 a renovated Petrovskii likewise received lindens. As for the projected Rozhdestvenskii Boulevard, it and the adjacent area were at the end of the century still dominated by the four-hundred-year old Rozhdestvenskii Monastery. The dismantling of the Belyi Gorod Wall and filling of the moat had permitted its monks to divert the stream into their kitchen gardens,

[1] *Al'bomy M. F. Kazakova*, 156, 262; see *Monuments* 2: 166, 167, for recent photographs. The house burned in 1812 but was subsequently restored and remains today a house of unusual beauty both within and without.
[2] *Monuments* 2: 168–73, 344.

[3] *Travels*, 60–61, 64.

Figure 31. Houses (late eighteenth century) on Tverskoi Boulevard Ring near Tverskie Gates (Schmidt).

Figure 32. Houses (late eighteenth century) on Tverskoi Boulevard Ring near Tverskie Gates (Schmidt).

but little else had changed. On the site of the wall itself, from the river to the Sretenskie Gates, wooden shops and merchants' houses remained until consumed by fire in 1812, after which work on the Rozhdestvenskii Boulevard was undertaken.

The completion of the Boulevard Ring from the Sretenskie to the Pokrovskie Gates was delayed at the very least for two decades after 1812 and in some places longer. The Sretenskii, for many years the residence of mailmen (even after the removal of the post office in 1783), lay unfinished until the 1830s. Late in the eighteenth century, diverse shacks, shops, and the estate houses of the Zubkovs, Sokolovs, and Deviatovs had edged up to the Miasnitskie Gates. Around the year 1800, enterprising members of these wealthy families even built hotels at both the Sretenskie and Miasnitskie Gates.

East of the Miasnitskie Gates, the Boulevard (present Chistoprudnyi) also remained unfinished until well into the first half of the nineteenth century. For decades the area had embraced the old cattle market and slaughter houses, and so it remained until early in the nineteenth century, when the meat shops were removed from Miasnitskie Gates to a location beyond the Zemlianoi Gorod. Restaurants, inns, and shops replaced them on the site of the future boulevard. Throughout most of these years heaps of bricks and deep holes from the dismantled wall were left undisturbed while the rococo Menshikov Tower rose incongruously nearby.

The open space at old Pokrovskie Gates was left alone until the 1830s. During the previous century attractive frame houses for gentry, surrounded by large gardens, had sprung up there, while picket fences, wooden cottages, stables, and nondescript larger buildings appeared where the walls had been. In the 1790s masonry and wooden shops clustered at the gates. Nearby orchards prompted a contemporary to write that they "made that region pleasant to the eye and the air pure, pleasant, and healthful, so no one dreamed of leaving his home in the summer and going to his dacha."[4] An imposing house with powerful six-column porticoes, designed by Kazakov for the Durasovs, was constructed near the Pokrovskie Gates at the turn of the century, about the same time as a new barracks for a musket regiment. After 1812, appearances in this sector improved when masonry or stucco structures largely replaced the rows of burned wooden shops near the Pokrovskie Gates.

The most easterly boulevard, the Iauzskii, was constructed in or around 1823. In the eighteenth century this area had attracted various noble families, who built their residences on both sides of the dismantled wall. After 1812, however, these properties passed into the hands of new owners, principally merchants. Architecturally, the Iauzskii Boulevard was dominated by Karl I. Blank's expansive Foundling Home complex.

The Boulevard Ring, like the radial thoroughfares, was conceived with Moscow's aristocracy in mind. It was assumed from the beginning that they would reside there in splendid estate and dress in order to see and be seen. Only the Tverskoi was completed in good time for this sort of thing. In addition to the lovely Tverskoi town houses, Kazakov's Corinthian Tsurikov House on the Prechistenskii, his Gagarin mansion with its gardens that embraced the Petrovskie Gates, and the Corinthian Benkendorf House dominating the Strastnoi proved the outstanding *fin de siècle* architectural accomplishments in the Ring.[5] In the interim diverse construction, most often unregulated, filled the breach. The fire of 1812, having destroyed all but the Tverskoi, made the nobility of the Boulevard something of an anachronism afterward. By the 1830s, even their hallmark of identity, classicism, had run its course there, despite some notable construction after the fire.

---

[4] Quoted from Sytin, *Ulits*, 327.
[5] *Al'bomy M. F. Kazakova*, 177, 264.

The Moscow River

From the beginning Moscow's architects assigned even a higher priority to the rivers than to the boulevards. Of the two waterways, the Neglinnaia and the Moscow, the latter was crucial to both the city's economy and appearance. The immediate task was to transform the river at its southern approach to the Kremlin because of the area's commercial importance and the urgent need to reduce spring and autumn flooding there.[6] To this end a branch system of canals within the old bed of the river was planned to control the water level by regulating the current of the river and, consequently, enhance the development between the Moscow River and its old bed. The planners proposed draining the marshy right bank of the river and then dividing it into city blocks, for which they projected a classical program. They also recommended transferring the important bread market from beneath the Kremlin walls to the right bank of the river and developing a port with a good harbor and two new plazas to accommodate commerce. This scheme also called for the construction of tree-lined stone quays, dams, and bridges, in addition to the canals, plazas, and assorted classical edifices.

The Moscow River beneath the Kremlin was at once bucolic and commercial during most of the eighteenth century, though by 1800 commerce and industry were clearly ascendant. On the right bank the streets were unpaved, and the dirt embankment of Zamoskvorech'e offered little protection to flooding. Old prints depict Muscovites strolling along the river or filling barrel carts with water. In winter they skated and sleighed on the river; in milder weather they took to rafts and sail boats. Although the Kremlin and Kitai Gorod side also remained unpaved until the end of the century, it, too, saw much activity. At Moskvoretskii Bridge, a conglomeration of covered wagons and carriages, diverse humanity, and discarded barrels was a common

sight. Provision sheds, constructed of brick, rested against the walls and near the decaying towers of the Kitai Gorod (fig. 33). At the base of the Kremlin walls the embankment was marred by the dump. All these varied elements notwithstanding, it remained for the Kremlin and the Great Stone Bridge with its eight broad arches to dominate this entire area.

The Moscow River's left bank, from the Great Stone Bridge to the mouth of the Iauza River, consisted of the Kremlin Embankment beneath the citadel walls and the Moskvoretskaia Embankment from the Moskvoretskii Bridge to the Iauza. The bridge was, in effect, an extension of the ancient Ordynka, Piatnitskaia, and Balchug Streets in the south, to Red Square in the north. Consisting merely of beams tied together and resting on the water, this bridge, or one like it, had spanned the river at that point since the sixteenth century. After acquiring a cover and handrail in the 1760s, it was raised and placed on wooden piers some twenty years later. Although there was agitation for a stone bridge in the 1780s, one was not built until 1833.

The history of the Kremlin Embankment is inseparable from that of the fortress itself. Throughout the centuries the quay beneath its walls supported commerce. Its complexion changed significantly with construction of the Great Stone Bridge (1687–1693), a glass-making factory at the Tainitskie Gates (1691), and the erection, nearly two decades later, of Peter's earthen bastions. With the transfer of the capital to St. Petersburg in 1713, use of the Kremlin diminished, and its quay lapsed into a garbage dump. Bazhenov in 1770–1771 called for an embankment sided with logs in order to eliminate the dump and regulate the shore, but nothing came of this proposal.

Although the plan of 1775 called for laying out streets along an embankment, the area changed slowly. The police delayed matters by leasing land to private individuals; however, an imperial edict as late as 7 August 1795, reiterated a determination to fulfill the plan. These included, within five years, the

---

[6] See Zombe, "Proekt plana Moskvy," 81–87 and Sytin, *Ulits*, passim.

Figure 33. The Moscow River Embankment late eighteenth century. Commercial warehouses along the Kitai Gorod Wall. Engraving from a drawing by J. Dela Barthe. (Donskoi, VIII-13674).

replacement of "wooden sidings of the quay" with stone, the eventual leveling of the quay, and the construction on it of a street lined with trees. The Kremlin Embankment and street, as designed principally by Kazakov, were actually set out early in the 1790s, essentially for the aristocracy's enjoyment. Organized promenades, accompanied by music from the river boats, proved popular there, although this boulevard was never so popular as the warmer and drier Tverskoi, which opened in 1796.

The first step to recast the shoreline between the Moskvoretskii Bridge and the Iauza was taken in the summer and early fall of 1790. At that time Governor Prozorovskii directed the architect Karin to submit a plan for this embankment, whereupon all buildings along it from the Kremlin and Kitai Gorod walls to the fence of the Foundling Home were razed. Although Karin was subsequently replaced by the French engineer, A. I. Gerard, responsibility for the Moskvoretskii Quay seems to have fallen eventually to Kazakov, who also completed the adjacent Kremlin Embankment.[7]

The Moskvoretskii shore acquired a modern look between 1795–1798, when its bank was reinforced by piles and the street was laid out. Although Peter's aging bastions had long proved an obstacle to regulating this area, an even greater one was the Foundling Home, the back of which towered majestically over the river.[8] Its patrons successfully opposed a street along the embankment from the Moskvoretskii Bridge to the Iauza estuary until

1795, when an imperial edict from Catherine II terminated the Home's special privileges in order to allow for the construction. Between 1801–1806 the quay was sided with stone and sometime later was separated from the river by an iron fence and plantings. When the planting of the Moskvoretskaia and Kremlin Embankments occurred is unclear. The 1806–1808 plan of Moscow depicted trees on both; however, it did not clearly distinguish between what was intended and what was accomplished. Possibly trees had been planted on the quays as early as the last years of the eighteenth century.[9]

Throughout the eighteenth century, the eastern segment of the right, or south, bank, opposite Kazakov's embankments, was without a river road. This side of the river consisted merely of backyards and vegetable gardens for houses along Sadovnicheskaia, which extended southeast from the Balchug. The Koz'modem'ianskaia, Komissariatskaia, and Krasnokholmskaia Embankments occupied this extreme southeast segment. In the western portion of the right bank, the Sofiiskaia Embankment stretched from the Moskvoretskaia to the Great Stone Bridge; the Bersenevskaia Embankment completed the right bank from the bridge to the Vodootvodnyi Canal. Vsekhsviatskaia and Bolotnaia Squares allowed access from the Great Stone Bridge to the Polianka and Great Iakimanka in the Zamoskvorech'e.[10]

---

[7] Zombe, citing the historian of Moscow, M. Gastev, believes that Kazakov planned the Moskvoretskaia Embankment. Gastev wrote that "all the buildings which had been standing along the bank were demolished, first from the wall of the Kreml and then from the wall of the Kitai Gorod to the fence of the Foundling Home," and the quay along the Moscow River was built under the supervision of Kazakov ("Proekt plana Moskvy," 84).

[8] A fence stretching from the eastern wall of the Kitai Gorod to the river marked the Home's domain. During these years this institution also controlled the Vasil'evskie Baths, eleven small buildings which created a sea of mud in the area. An open pipe laid in 1782 to the Kitai Gorod Wall drained away impurities. Eventually baths and fences were removed and the street built. (Sytin, *Ulits*, 284).

[9] The records link Kazakov to the planning of two other projects on the Moskvoretskii Embankment. In a letter of June, 1791, Prozorovskii observed that in addition to work on the quays, it was indispensable "to build a free dock, . . . for the reception and shipment of merchandise" and that "the plan of best adaptability to commerce had been composed by the architect Kazakov." The plan had been dispatched to the mayor "to show to the merchants of Moscow and to inquire of them about their wishes to have a place for grain barns at the wall of the Kitai Gorod." Kazakov also proposed a barn near the dock and suggested attaching it to the Kitai Gorod wall with its roof slanting away from the wall. Although nothing came of the dock, such a barn was built; however, it did not prevent the grain market's subsequent removal to Bolotnaia Square across the river. (Quotes are from Zombe, 84).

[10] This stretch of land between the river and the canal even today possesses some interesting classical survivals, although most were constructed after 1812. The modest facades of the row houses contrast with the massive Military Commissariat.

Since this marshy right bank of the Moscow River was especially prone to flooding, Moscow's planners were forced to attend to it for practical as well as aesthetic reasons. From the Bersenevskaia Embankment at one end to the Koz'modem'ianskaia, Komissariatskaia, and Krasnokholmskaia at the opposite, the land between the old and new river beds suffered recurring inundation.[11]

Construction in 1786 of the Vodootvodnyi Canal, which paralleled the Moscow River along its old bed, finally brought relief. The plan for the canal, an outgrowth of proposals for flood control canals in 1775, was prompted by the destructive flood of 1783. A. I. Gerard, who later worked on the Neglinnyi Canal, supervised the project, reducing the canals in number from four to one, the Vodootvodnyi.

Construction of the Vodootvodnyi Canal proved a difficult task. Gerard initially opted to dam the Moscow River from the Bersenevka to the left bank near the Great Stone Bridge and channel the water into the canal. Even though Gerard had concluded by the spring of 1785 that the canal was too shallow, operations to deepen it proceeded slowly. In August, 1786, high water breached the earthen dam and inundated the right bank once again. After a Petersburg Commission blamed faulty dam construction and shallowness of the canal for this flooding, Gerard did, indeed, deepen the canal and build a new dam with movable locks (wooden shields) that more effectively regulated the flow of water. Simultaneously, he reinforced the canal banks with wooden beams and the right bank of the river with stone posts.[12] In this way the Vodootvodnyi Canal both reduced flooding and assisted in ordering the Moscow River area.

Change came only gradually to this right bank of the Moscow River. During the course of the sixteenth and seventeenth centuries most of it had simply formed the Tsar's Gar-den and his gardeners' settlements. The garden lay along the Sofiiskaia Embankment until its destruction by fire in 1701. The occupants of the Upper Garden Settlement held a part of the Bersenevskaia Embankment; east of the garden lay the Middle and Lower Garden Settlements.

In the eighteenth century much of the area was devoid of housing until the Vodootvodnyi Canal offered reprieve from perennial flooding. After the destructive flood of 1786 and correction of the canal, new residents opened shops along the Sofiiskaia Quay. Michurin's Cloth Court, of declining importance after the plague of the early 1770s, remained but with a depleted work force. In the second half of the eighteenth century the Sukonnye Public Baths were erected beside the Cloth Court. Nearby was the Old Stone Bridge Liquor Yard, an assemblage of vodka storage barns. Originally of wood construction, these barns were eventually replaced by brick ones. Behind the Cloth Court, in Tsaritsyn Meadow, a grain market functioned in the numerous brick and wooden shops. On market days peasants sold their wheat and oats directly to the townspeople from their grain carts. In such a way Tsaritsyn Meadow and the Boloto (marsh) on the Bersenevskaia Embankment became a grain market square; after 1812 this area, named Bolotnaia Square, was the recognized center for grain storage and enterprise in Moscow.

Despite improvements brought by the Vodootvodnyi Canal, the ordering of the Moscow River's right bank progressed more slowly than that of the left. Work on the quays, especially, did not keep pace. The Sofiiskaia and Raushskaia Embankments acquired stone siding only in the 1830s. Evolution of the ancient Balchug, which funneled traffic into Red Square from both the Great Ordynka and the Piatnitskaia, reflected the precarious existence of the entire right bank during the eighteenth century: fires there in 1701 and 1730 and the flood of 1783 destroyed many of its frame houses; the fire of 1812 left nothing.

---

[11] Afterwards flooding proved extremely rare, two exceptions being in 1879 and 1908.

[12] Between 1788 and 1806 this flood-control canal was lengthened.

Although distinctive domestic architecture, generally, was not the hallmark of the right bank, there was an important ensemble of buildings at the eastern extremity of the river's loop. It consisted of two public buildings, the Foundling Home and the Military Commissariat, and several private residences, among them the Tutolmin and Batashov Houses on Shvivaia Hill.

After the Foundling Home, the most impressive element in this ensemble was Nikolai Nikolaevich LeGrand's Military Commissariat (1778–1779 or 1780, fig. 34a,b). The Military Commissariat, one of the largest complexes in the city, consisted of a three-story main corpus pointing toward the river at the Sadovnicheskaia Embankment. Two-story wings, embracing a nearby square court, extended from its center. The cupola-crowned, cylindrical towers at each corner were ammunition warehouses. LeGrand's Commissariat achieved monumentality through its Sadovnicheskaia

Figure 34a. Military Commissariat (1778–1779) as viewed from the Moscow River, architect N. N. Le Grand (Schmidt).

Figure 34b. Military Commissiariat. Corner Ammunition Storehouse (Schmidt).

facade. The powerful Doric portico of six voluted columns, resting on a rusticated ground-floor entrance and supporting an ornate frieze, dominated the rest of the building. Bas-relief sculptures beneath the windows and vertical bas-relief two stories in height at each corner of the building contrasted sharply with the severity of the two-story wings and corners.

On a smaller scale Tutolmin House also gave the river area a classical cast (fig. 35, 36). This three-story mansion with its great Corinthian portico and semicircular wings towered over everything on the Kremlin's east

side in the same way that Pashkov House did on its west. This house on Shvivaia Hill, another component in this river ensemble, was built in the late 1780s and early 1790s. Its architect is uncertain. Grabar' speculated that it was Bazhenov, but later opinion has favored I. E. Starov because of its symmetry, general design, distinctive interior, and various motifs. Tutolmin's main block, capped with a belvedere, was rectangular with a majestic and far-projecting six-columned Corinthian portico. This porch had a balcony on its first floor and a small porticoed entrance on the ground level. The powerful columns used the ground

ДОМ ТУТОЛМИНА НА ШБИВОЙ ГОРКЕ. ЦЕНТРАЛЬНАЯ ЧАСТЬ ФАСАДА
(фрагмент чертежа в размере подлинника)

Figure 35. Detail of the Tutolmin House, architect Starov(?) (*Al'bomy Kazakova*).

Figure 36. Iauzskii Bridge and Tutolmin House at the end of the eighteenth century. J. Dela Barthe (Donskoi, V-28988).

floor as a base, which itself was niched for statuary. From the central corpus, semicircular wings symmetrically embraced the main entrance gate, located on an axis with the great portico.[13]

Batashov House, also on Shvivaia Hill but nearer the Iauza (on Iauzskaia Street), was designed by Rodion Rodionovich Kazakov and probably built by the serf M. Kisel'nikov. Succeeding Matvei Kazakov as head of the Kremlin Department in 1801, Rodion worked on the Batashov project between 1798–1802. Withdrawn from the perimetrical line of the street, the solemn and grand Batashov corpus was embellished with elegant lateral wings. Its grounds were bordered by a fence of openwork cast iron and a gateway famous for its lions ensconced on a Corinthian portico.[14]

Another Moscow River estate, which complemented the Tutolmin and Batashov was that of Klapovskaia in the Goncharnaia, not far from the future Taganskaia Square. Built at the turn of the nineteenth century, it was imposing for its full-length, six-column Ionic portico, bas-reliefs within the semicircles over the doorways, stone block gateways with arched openings, and iron gate leading into the estate. Like Batashov House, it acquired a monumentality from its spacious front court and imposing main gate.[15]

In summary, the efforts exerted by classical Moscow's planners and builders at the turn of the century greatly improved the Moscow River. The area did not become a habitat for Moscow's aristocracy, but it did trade chronic flooding, disreputable if bucolic embankments, and twisting alleys, for dams, canals, stone quays, bridges, ordered streets, spacious plazas, and a pleasant assortment of classical buildings. Such changes greatly enhanced the river prospect of the Kremlin, even though a magnificent classical palace had failed to rise within its walls.

Zamoskvorech'e

South of the Kremlin and the Moscow River lay the Zamoskvorech'e, which until the eighteenth century had been the dwelling place of palace servants, the tsar's streltsy musketeers, merchants, and Tatars. The liquidation of the streltsy and removal of the palace servants and Tatars prompted merchants and tradesmen from the Kitai Gorod quite as much as gentry and grandees to establish themselves there in the eighteenth century. Because of its numerous churches, Zamoskvorech'e also housed many clerics. This sector after 1750 continued as a mix of social classes, albeit of a different configuration from that which had characterized it earlier.

Four ancient radials—the Piatnitskaia, Ordynka, Polianka, and Iakimanka—converged upon the Kremlin from Zamoskvorech'e. The Piatnitskaia, named for the Church Paraskeva-Piatnitsa, dated from the late fifteenth or early sixteenth century. The Great Ordynka had been centuries earlier the principal thoroughfare from the Kremlin and Red Square to the Khanate of the Golden Horde. The Great Polianka, called Koz'modem'ianskaia during the seventeenth century, housed the streltsy until their dissolution. Lastly, the Great Iakimanka led to the Kaluzhskie Gates.[16]

The architecture of Zamoskvorech'e was quite as varied as its population. Two classical edifices in the Piatnitskaia were the residences of the Korobovs and Glebovs.[17] The classic of the Ordynka was strikingly represented by the Church of Our Lady of All Sorrows (*Vsekh Skorbiashchikh*) and the merchant Dolgov's home. All Sorrows, which uniquely combined

---

[13] *Al'bomy M. F. Kazakova*, 108–11, 255.

[14] See *Monuments* 2: 114–17, for recent photographs of Batashov House.

[15] Ibid., 112, for a recent photograph.

[16] Zamoskvorech'e continues to this day to reward one seeking images of old Moscow. The Piatnitskaia is perhaps best in this respect; however, there are fascinating classical survivals on the Great Ordynka and Polianka, especially in the alleys and side streets from the canal to the Garden Ring. (See *Monuments* 2: 185, for a recent photograph of early nineteenth-century houses on the Piatnitskaia).

[17] The former, a rectangular block with projecting rear wings, had a street facade; Glebov House, on the other hand, conveyed warmth through a graceful four-columned Ionic portico with balcony and symmetrical doorways at each end. (*Al'bomy M. F. Kazakova*, 143, 145–56, 259–60).

early and later classicism, was begun by Bazhenov about 1790 and eventually completed in
the elegant style of the Empire by Osip Ivanovich Bove in 1828–1833. The estate belonging to the merchant A. I. Dolgov, brother
of Bazhenov's father-in-law, lay opposite this
church.[18]

When the nobility acquired streltsy plots in
the Great Polianka, they consolidated these
into great estates with gardens and parks. One
of the most charming estate houses in this
street, or in Moscow for that matter, was that
of Prince I. I. Prozorovskii, probably designed
by Bazhenov and built in the 1780s.[19]

The Iakimanka differed from the Polianka
and from the other Zamoskvorech'e thoroughfares, in that it did not attract a great
influx of nobility. In this street merchants and
minor officials who acquired streltsy lands
gave their new dwellings a minimally classical
look. The Iakimanka, through its dwellings
and plank sidewalks, projected a traditionally
wooden image, which even the Great Fire
failed to change. These edifices and streets of
Zamoskvorech'e in mirroring the social diversity left rather an uncertain classical legacy.[20]

Beyond Zemlianoi Gorod

Moscow's architects had not in their draft
plan of 1775 shown the same concern for the

area beyond the Zemlianoi Gorod that they
had for the streets, boulevards, and rivers of
the Belyi and Zemlianoi Gorod. This was true
despite the city's unofficial annexation in the
1740s and 1750s of lands extending to the
Kamer College Rampart. Village life, a rich
mixture of serf agriculture, industry, and commerce, flourished beyond Zemlianoi Gorod
late into the eighteenth century. The village
design, in contrast to the precision of regulated city blocks, was one of gardens, groves,
and fields surrounding existing streets and
alleys. As open land was consumed by continuous building at the edges of the city, these
village streets and alleys frequently linked up
with those emanating from the city center.[21]

Masonry and stucco dwellings, erected beyond the Zemlianoi Gorod in the late eighteenth century, coexisted with but were far
fewer than wooden ones. In the First Meshchanskaia, a continuation of the Sretenka, a
number of substantial homes appeared during
the reign of Catherine.[22] The Nikolo-Iam-
skaia, paralleling the Iauza River, developed
a strong classical cast. Its buildings included
some estate houses, modest masonry and

---

[18] Because its components were constructed at separate times—the main block in the 1770s and the rest in 1780s and 1790s—the ensemble design was dramatically asymmetric. Aux-iliary buildings and an ornamental iron fence partially shielded the center section and undistinguished facade from the street. Cf. below, 173–174, for more on All Sorrows Church and Dolgov House, which burned in 1812. (See *Al'bomy M. F. Kazakova*, 144, 259–60).

[19] Its main buildings, one ornate and the other strikingly severe, were linked by a wall and gates. Refinement of its main facade—a carefully decorated cornice and frieze, tall and exact pairs of Ionic pilasters, balconies with sculptured iron grille, exquisite windows, and a distinctive side entrance—gave it some of the same lyricism as its author's Pashkov House. (Ibid., 62–67, 248).

[20] Where the Zemlianoi Gorod Wall had not disappeared, houses of quality, as well as hovels, rose alongside it, on the site of the future Garden Ring. This was especially true along that northern edge which today is the Sadovoe-Kudrinskii. There the Nebol'sins and Meshcherskies and Protkovs built great houses late in the eighteenth and at the beginning of the nineteenth century, not far removed from Ivan Giliardi's Widows' Home. The Protkov (Volkonskii) mansion, dating from

1809, was designed by Bove. (See *Monuments* 2: 184, for a recent photograph). For a fuller discussion, see below p. 179–80.

[21] The Kamer College Wall, measuring just over 23 miles (37.3 km) around Moscow, bore regional names for the areas through which it passed, i.e. Butyrskii Kamer College Wall, Preobrazhenskii, etc. Such regional names were also applied to the turnpikes at the wall, i.e. Tverskaia, Kaluzhskaia, Serpu-khovskaia, etc. (Cf. Sytin, *Ulits*). That Moscow at the end of the eighteenth century had the "look of a large village, surrounded by a flock of small villages" was the opinion of Gol'denberg, *Staraia Moskva*, 38.

[22] Bazhenov designed a story and a half house in the manner of French Classicism—without columns, pilasters, or pedi-ments—for his father-in-law the merchant L. Dolgov about 1770. This surprising departure from his Italianate inclinations resulted in a rather severe house distinguished by wide and exquisitely decorated window frames. These wide windows barely compensated for the subsequent loss of what was prob-ably an equally beautiful upper story. (See *Monuments* 2: 92, for a recent photograph).
The architect E. Nazarov also built in this street an imposing masonry mansion—eleven windows across its first and second stories, a six-columned Corinthian portico resting on a ground story of five arches, and with facade texture that anticipated Empire classicism after 1812. Farther east toward the Iauza River, on the Elokhovskaia (Spartakovskaia), the Musin-Pushkin city estate house, built at the end of the eighteenth century, followed the usual corner portico design but with extra elegance. (*Monuments* 2: 111, for a recent photograph).

stucco dwellings, the Church of Semen Stolnik (probably by Rodion Kazakov in 1798), and the Church of Sergei in Rogozhka (1796–1838).[23] The New (*Novaia*) Basmannaia, which paralleled the Ring east of the Red Gate (*Krasnye vorota*, now Lermontov Square) and the Old Basmannaia were also rich in classical dwellings.[24]

Of Moscow's suburban dwellings, one of the most intriguing was the Orlov dacha called the "Pigeonry," located near Donskoi Monastery.[25] Its classical elements—bas-reliefs, columns, and a pedimented entrance—were secondary to its idiosyncratic shape—a cylindrical, colonnaded first story resting on a cubed ground floor podium. A gabled roof, moreover, held a still smaller colonnaded second-story room. No structure of comparable design was built in classical Moscow.

Monasteries, palaces, and new hospitals occupied parts of this outlying area. Monasteries generally were exemplars of the Muscovite architectural style, but a partial exception was Novospasskii on the Moscow River below the Iauza. Founded in the time of Ivan Kalita (1328–1340) and moved to its present site in the reign of Ivan III, the Novospasskii Monastery had as its principal structure the seventeenth-century Church of the Transfiguration (*Spasa Preobrazheniia*). But the ensemble also contained two notable eighteenth-century edifices. One was its rococo bell tower, designed by Ivan Zherebtsov and constructed between 1759 and 1762. Soaring some 235 feet over the entrance, it was reminiscent of Ukhtomskii's in Trinity-Sergei Monastery in Zagorsk. Within the Novospasskii's gleaming walls an exquisite edifice in a later classic mode

and of small dimension especially disproved the notion of any incompatibility between the monastery and the classic. This, the Znamenskaia Church, lay situated adjacent to the Transfiguration (fig. 37). Built between 1791 and 1795, probably by Elizvoi Semenovich Nazarov, it was not finished within until 1803. The building is remarkable for its four-column Tuscan portico, a cupola, nearly obscured from the ground, side apses, and very precise cornice which articulates the bulging apses. This splendid building epitomized classical elegance in church design. Because it was the burial vault of the wealthy and powerful Sheremetev family, one may speculate that Nazarov's success in this enterprise was a factor in persuading the Sheremetev family to allow him to undertake the more ambitious Indigents' Hospital.[26]

Palatial ensembles and hospitals—these were the most likely classical aggregations beyond the Zemlianoi Gorod. The palaces on the Iauza, in the Lefortov suburb, offered a setting that especially stimulated both the construction of new buildings and the renovation of the old. Here, the old Petrovskii, the refurbished Suburban (*Slobodskii*, formerly the Bestuzhev) Palace adjacent to it, the new and massive Catherine (formerly Golovin) Palace (1771–1776), and the Military Hospital (1798) on the opposite bank of the Iauza comprised one of Moscow's most important classical assemblages.

The late seventeenth-century Petrovskii (Menshikov or Lefortovskii) Palace in Lefortov, through various eighteenth-century renovations, acquired by the end of the century a classical cast. Fires were, in large measure, responsible for these alterations as well as for those of other Iauza edifices. Just as a fire had destroyed the wooden Annenhof Palace on the opposite bank in 1752, so did another devastate the Petrovskii a year later. Some effort was made at hasty restoration in order to accommodate the Empress Elizabeth for

[23] *Monuments* 2: 339, for a listing of classical edifices on this street.

[24] There stood the late eighteenth-century Kurakin House, with striking bas-reliefs on the facade pediment. (*Monuments* 2: 118–20, for recent photographs).

Other Basmannaia residences were the Plescheev in the New Basmannaia with a facade of four pilasters beneath a pediment and a rusticated ground floor, Matvei Kazakov's Demidov House, a massive block with lateral wings, the wooden Murav'ev-Apostol House in the Old Basmannaia, marked by a six-columned Corinthian portico. (*Monuments* 2: 134, for a recent photograph).

[25] *Monuments* 2: 147, for a recent photograph.

[26] In Novospasskii Monastery E. S. Nazarov also restored the early seventeenth-century Church of the Apparition in a classical mode (1793–1795).

Figure 37. Znamenskaia Church, c. 1791–1795, architect E. S. Nazarov (Schmidt).

her visitation to Moscow, but nothing actually came of it. The palace was abandoned for another decade during which it deteriorated even more.

Attention later focused on the Petrovskii when, early in her reign, Catherine II made known her intention to visit Moscow. It was assumed that she would stay in one of the palaces. A Prince Makulov, charged with reconstructing the Petrovskii, in the summer of 1766 produced a plan for it. After describing the building and the extent of its decay, Makulov recommended improvements as well as repairs. His proposals, drawings, and cost estimates did not win Catherine's approval. Deciding that the estimates were excessive, she opted for housing only lower rank court officials in the Petrovskii, thereby reducing the need for extensive restoration. Windows were cut into the ground floor on the street side, giving it the appearance that it retains to this day. The facade of the main building was plastered, but the wings were left virtually untouched.

The plague of 1771–1772, which caused the palace to be used as a hospital, again brought the Petrovskii to Catherine's attention. By the end of 1772, she once more contemplated renovation; but when Makulov suggested that her ideas were impractical, she wrote:

> I see now that it is impossible to remodel the Lefortovskii house according to my plan as it would make it necessary to break it up almost completely and build anew. Even then it would still be no good as it is placed too close to the land slope and would require the expenditure of up to 900,000 rubles, the sum of which I do not intend to spend on a temporary dwelling.[27]

Once again modest repair was substituted for extensive rebuilding. Years later, Paul I commissioned Matvei Kazakov to renovate Iauza palaces on the right bank—both the old Petrovskii and Suburban—for court use. Kazakov's drawings of 1797 indicate that for a time he contemplated more than the mere improvement of the Petrovskii. One plan was to construct "a high wooden fence in its courtyard for passage to the main building, at the

---

[27] R. Podol'skii, "Petrovskii dvorets na Iauzes," *Arkhitekturnoe nasledstvo* 1(1951):14–55.

same time concealing the sight of the kitchen utilities." A variant indicates that he finally placed the kitchens in two courtyard buildings, obscuring their entrances from the main building. The facades of Petrovskii he kept severe, with only pilasters on a flat surface. When the palace was damaged by fire in 1812, it again had to be extensively renovated. The outside did not change in appearance, but interior construction necessitated installation of new metal staircases and concrete reinforcement of the wings.[28]

Annenhof Park, surrounded by the Catherine and Suburban Palaces and the Military Hospital buildings, proved the unifying element in this ensemble: a diametrical alley through the park linked the middle facades of the Catherine and Suburban Palaces, and a longitudinal alley provided an axis from what had been the old Annenhof Palace entrance to the hospital portico. The stone Palace Bridge, designed by Iakovlev in 1779–1781, became the transportation link between the Catherine Palace and the opposite bank.

The Suburban Palace next to the Petrovskii, won wide acclaim from contemporaries for its elegance, especially with an addition by Kazakov late in the century. The original palace, which belonged to Bestuzhev-Rumin, was built according to a design by Ukhtomskii. The palace's center section and wings were oldest, dating to 1749. A 1759 draft of the Ukhtomskii edifice showed the disposition of statues and ponds in a park extending to the Iauza. Between 1788 and 1801 this ensemble belonged to Prince A. Bezborodko, who twice had charged Quarenghi to prepare plans for rebuilding it, but eventually commissioned Kazakov for the task. Once finished, the palace was given to the Emperor Paul. Kazakov's half-rotunda facing the Iauza was the Suburban's most notable facade element. Joining the wings of the building and possessed of a colonnaded portico, it rested on the elevated basement. This rusticated facade section was pierced by three portals and capped by a modest balustrade. Kazakov linked part of its structure, the church and colonnade, with old Petrovskii Palace. A splendid staircase in the center of the building led to this portico.

When at Paul I's coronation, King Stanislaus Poniatowski of Poland exclaimed at its unsurpassed "fullness and decoration,"[29] he was probably moved by the magnificent Suburban interior—its patterned parquet floor of rare woods, ceiling paintings, walls of mirrors, crystal chandeliers, gilded bronze light fixtures, and furniture upholstered in silken damask. Russian palaces like the Suburban displayed a splendor which matched the best in eighteenth-century Europe.

The two remaining elements in the Iauza ensemble were the Catherine Palace (1773–1796) and the Military Hospital. Although the former had frequently burned and been remodeled during the eighteenth century, not until the end of the century did refurbishing succeed, at least so far as Catherine was concerned. Plans for the Catherine Palace were initially drafted by Vasilii Semenovich Iakovlev; however, those by the Petersburg architect, Antonio Rinaldi, finally prevailed.[30] Giacomo Quarenghi designed the interiors and embellished the facade with a seemingly endless Corinthian colonnade (fig. 38). Comparesi contributed the sculpture, and for a time, at least, Karl Blank was the principal builder. Measuring approximately 756 feet in length, nearly 459 in width, and encompassing 1,272,640 cubic feet, the Catherine Palace was Moscow's largest classical residence. Despite this size, it possessed little trim and ornament. The most unique feature of its street facade was the great loggia with its sixteen-post colonnade topped with a balustrade. An octastyle Corinthian portico, in turn, dominated the court facade. The Emperor Paul, predictably, abused that which had pleased his mother:

---

[28] Ibid., passim.

[29] M. A. Il'in, *Moskva* (Moscow, 1963), 223. Damaged severely in 1812, the Suburban was rebuilt by Domenico Giliardi. (See *Monuments* 2: 264–65, for recent photographs).

[30] Catherine II at first contemplated using Petrovskii by linking it to the Bestuzhevskii Palace and another old structure, the Marlinskii Palace; then she characteristically changed her mind and ordered that the Catherine Palace be reconstructed.

Figure 39. Military Hospital (1798–1802) in Lefortov, architect I. V. Egotov (Schmidt).

Figure 38. Catherine Palace (1773–1796) in Lefortov, architects A. Rinaldi and G. Quarenghi (Schmidt).

after her death he converted this palace into a barracks for soldiers of the Moscow garrison regiment. When this contingent left in 1824, the Moscow Cadet Corps moved in and remained until approximately midcentury.

The Military Hospital (fig. 39), built by Bazhenov's or really Kazakov's student, Ivan Vasil'evich Egotov, between 1798 and 1802, underwent additional changes by F. Shestakov during the 1830s. Its central corpus, the facade of which reached the street, rose three stories with two-story wings extending from it. Although older buildings formed part of this hospital complex, Egotov did succeed in creating a highly integrated whole: the axis for the main building served for the entire ensemble. Projecting slightly from its wing facades, this center section contained a loggia screened by four pairs of Corinthian columns resting on the raised ground floor and in turn supporting a massive pediment encrusted with bas-relief sculpture. On each side of the portico a pair of matching Corinthian pilasters appeared to complement the columnar support of the pediment. Egotov placed semicircular Italianate windows behind the columns and an assortment of semicircular, arched, and conventional windows on the rusticated ground floor. The wing facades also had a variety of window shapes and even a portico without a pediment. The overpowering effect of the central portico was lessened by the smaller Ionic portico on the lateral wing; the miniature columns of the window platbands, bas-relief sculpture, and other facade elements offered an acceptable contrast to the smooth wall. The courtyard facade was plainer, with pilasters substituted for porticoes; however, a variety of round, curved, and pedimented windows characterized this side, too.[31]

Although Lefortov from the very beginning of the eighteenth century was central to the architecture of classicism in Russia, it was challenged later in the century by another classical ensemble, that of Gorokhovoe Pole, or Field, farther down the Iauza. Consisting of the elegant Razumovskii Palace (1801–1803) and Kazakov's Ascension Church (1790–1793) in Gorokhovoe Field and Demidov House (1789–1791) in Gorokhovskii Alley—this group along with the radiant mansions of the Novaia Basmannaia effectively linked Lefortov with the Kremlin.[32]

This Razumovskii Palace, like the one on the Tverskaia, was designed and constructed originally by Adam Menelas and rebuilt in the Empire style several decades later by Afanasii Grigor'evich Grigor'ev. It had a main entrance and court in front and an English park with ponds descending to the Iauza in the rear. The central corpus was rectangular with wings extending the facade. Grigor'ev curved these galleries to form a court. The palace's most impressive feature, which made it one of classical Moscow's most splendid edifices, was its center section. This consisted of a double niche and an Ionic portico. A colonnade placed in front of pavilions, connected to the wings by Grigor'ev's arched, elevated walk, reached to the street and was placed on line with the fence (fig. 40a). The Razumovskii interior, exquisitely arranged and decorated, consisted of centrally located halls, drawing rooms, and a picture gallery. The living quarters were in the wings and on the mezzanine; servants were housed on the ground floor.[33]

In Gorokhovoe Field, Matvei Kazakov's Church of the Ascension, marked especially by its rotunda and bell tower and traditional Greek cross plan, became a focal point. Its classical motifs were similar to those Kazakov later gave to his Church of Philip the Metropolitan (but notably absent in his Sts. Cosmas and Damian). The lantern-topped rotunda as pierced by pedimented gables was a classical

[31] See in particular Sedov, *Egotov*, 24–38. See *Monuments* 2: 82–86 for recent photographs.

[32] The Shepelev House ensemble (Kisel'-nikov, according to the design of Deval, 1798) in the Taganskaia, similarly connected the two.

[33] Gol'denberg (*Staraia Moskva*, 52) has suggested Kazakov as the original author and dated the building 1790–1792. See *Monuments* 2: 121 for a recent photograph.

Figure 40a. Razumovskii House (1801–1803) in Gorokhovoe Field, architect A. A. Menelas (Schmidt).

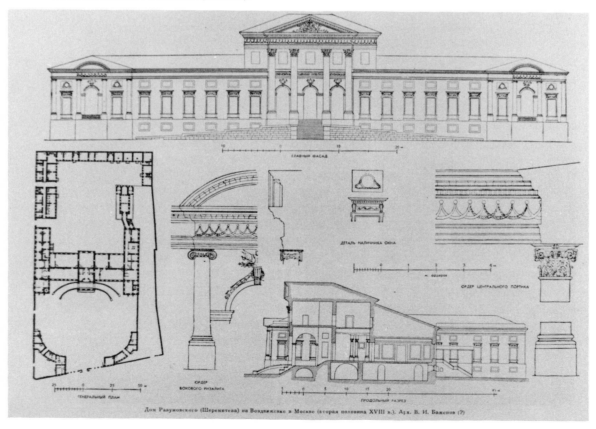

Дом Разумовского (Шереметева) на Воздвиженке в Москве (вторая половина XVIII в.). Арх. В. И. Баженов (?)

Figure 40b. Drawing of Razumovskii House (late eighteenth century) on the Vozdvizhenka, V. Bazhenov(?) (Brunov, *Istoriia*).

118

fixture; however, the bell tower with its accented porticoes, columns, pilasters, and the Ionic colonnade which girded it, gave this complex its distinctive look.[34]

In nearby Gorokhovskii Alley Kazakov had built in 1789–1791 a palatial dwelling for I. I. Demidov, the Ural iron entrepreneur (fig. 41). Its rather severe main body and two lateral buildings led into a magnificently ordered park. The house was marked by a raised and slightly projecting portico of six Corinthian columns. Its pediment, faced with bas-relief sculpture and a rusticated ground facade, had two smooth-textured upper stories. Besides opening the base of the protruding portico with an arched entrance, the architect sought to relieve the monotony of the facade by capping the third of the five middle-story windows on each side of the portico with a small pediment, imposing rosette bas-reliefs across the same tier, and edging the third-story windows with a distinctive moulding. Initially, the roof supported a balustrade above the attic, which added to the building's elegance.[35]

That Demidov House was untouched by the fire in 1812 explains its minimal exterior alteration and completely preserved eighteenth century interior. Its Golden Rooms (*Zolotye komnaty*) set it apart from all other residences of late eighteenth-century Moscow. Richly adorned throughout—as shown by its lower vestibule, circular dining room on the upper floor, and its living and bedrooms—the mansion possessed a decor original in ornament and trim. The living and bedrooms, in particular, glistened with wreaths, flowered cornices, gold-leaf carvings over the windows and doors, dainty vases, and enchanting colors. Demidov's interior confirmed the creator of the Hall of Columns as Moscow's outstanding interior as well as exterior designer.

Figure 41. I. I. Demidov House (1789–1791) in Gorokhovskii Alley, architect M. F. Kazakov (Schmidt).

In addition to those on the Iauza, the most important pre-1812 architectural ensembles beyond the Zemlianoi Gorod lay in the south and north ends of the city. The first of these, essentially a hospital complex, backed onto the Moscow River and faced the Great Kaluzhskaia Road. In the eighteenth century a wooden palace had stood on the high banks of the river at this so-called Khamovnicheskaia Loop; by 1800 these lands belonged to Princes Dolgorukii and Trubetskoi, the Aleksandrinskii Palace, and the Golitsynskaia Hospital. The array of buildings in this commanding position faced the river, utilizing the waters effectively as both a mirror for their beauty and as an axis for the ensemble.

Golitsynskaia Hospital formed the most important single component in this Moscow River—Great Kaluzhskaia complex (fig. 42a,b).[36] Built in 1796–1801 on the estate of Prince A. M. Golitsyn and by his philanthropy, this ensemble was in reality Matvei Kazakov's last important creation. Drawing upon the estate house prototype, he turned the majestic entrance court toward the Kaluzhskaia, permitting the facade of the central building and its wings to envelop this courtly entrance. The park in back descended in terraces to the

[34] See *Monuments* 2: 152–53, for recent photographs.
[35] *Al'bomy M. F. Kazakova*, 80–83, 155 and A. M. Kharlamova, *Zolotye komnaty doma Demidovykh v Moskve*, Moscow, 1955. See *Monuments* 2: 122–25, for recent photographs.

[36] See especially Vlasiuk, *Kazakov*, 256–280 and N. L. Krasheninnikova, *Ansambl' Golitsynskoi bol'nitsy* (Moscow, 1955). See *Monuments* 2: 78–81 for recent photographs.

Figure 42a. Golitsynskaia Hospital (1796–1801) on the Kaluzhskaia, architect M. F. Kazakov. Detail: upper portion of the central portal and dome (Schmidt).

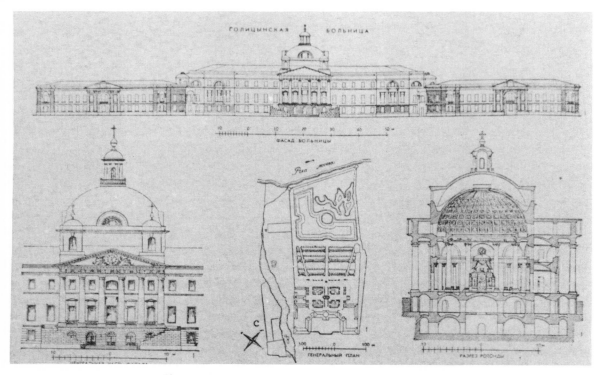

Figure 42b. Drawing of Golitsynskaia Hospital. (Brunov, *Istoriia*).

Moscow River. Kazakov placed the building's powerful central block, marked by an imposing six-column Doric portico, on a podium, while its lateral wings were located in the interior corners of the court. The center section served as a chapel; the ground floor of the hospital contained the pharmaceutical and medical facilities and administrative offices; the patients' quarters, served by a central corridor, were on the upper two floors. The severe and symmetrical facade of the central block and the powerful sweep of those on its wings endowed the structure with a majesty, which was reiterated in the dome over the rotunda. A delicate lantern, capping the cupola and the small tower-like lanterns over the portico, imposed restraint on the building's powerful elements. Ionic porticoes on the wing, like the lantern, offered a respite from the prevailing Doric severity. Inside the center block church an Ionic colonnade encircled the rotunda. Above the choir gallery on the second floor rested the cupola, pierced by rays of light at its apogee. Through its severity, both inside and out, this building anticipated the classicism of the Empire. Kazakov succeeded, above all, in adapting this ensemble to its superb physical setting: the high shores of the Moscow River in back and the street in front, both of which connected the ensemble to the spatial elements around it.

In the vicinity of the Golitsynskaia Hospital and near Donskoi Monastery still another hospital rose late in the eighteenth century. This was the Pavlovskaia, initially a wooden structure built in 1763 and named for the Grand Duke Paul.[37] Although new sections were added, a fire in 1784 destroyed the entire complex. Paul was determined to build a larger masonry hospital and chose Bazhenov to design the edifice. The architect's plan once again proved too extravagant; however, a frame structure was erected and sufficed until replaced by a masonry one by Kazakov between 1802–1807.[38]

Kazakov's Pavlovskaia fell short of his Golitsynskaia as a work of art. Punctuated by a graceful Ionic portico and spacious front steps, its facade is otherwise undistinguished save for the balconies of its lateral wings adorned with bas-relief sculptures, balustrade, and columns. The columns supported a plain frieze and cornice, topped by a semicircular window on the second-story level. The hospital's monumental entrance was derived from its lion statuary. If less dramatic than the Golitsyn Hospital, the Pavlovskaia nonetheless exemplified the considerable artistry and en-

ergy of Kazakov then in the twilight of a long career.

In Moscow's north end at the Zemlianoi Gorod Wall, hospital ensembles and churches left a classical mark on the area. The most striking suburban hospital after Kazakov's Golitsynskaia, was the public Hostel for Indigents, or Sheremetev Hospital (*Strannopriimnyi Dom*, fig. 43a,b), located at the Zemlianoi Gorod Wall and Second Meshchanskaia (a continuation of the Sretenka). The hostel was erected between 1794 and 1807 as a memorial to the deceased wife of Prince N. N. Sheremetev, and in accord with a design by Elizvoi Semenovich Nazarov, one of Sheremetev's serf-architects who earlier had served under Kazakov in the Kremlin Department.[39] In this semicircular, two-story building Nazarov placed at its center a church with a cupola, in its left wing an almshouse, and in its right a hospital. The service staff resided in the basement and the administration occupied the two court wings. Quarenghi (fig. 43c) executed a significant departure from the original design when, in 1803, he placed in front of Nazarov's church portico an imposing peristyle with doubled columns and added portals to the centers of each of the encompassing wings. In focusing on the semicircular courtyard before the house, Nazarov had failed to articulate this central portico. Quarenghi's stress on the church—by pulling it forward and embellishing its entrance with the colonnade—gave it a prominence which it had originally lacked. Both the balustrade surmounting the wings and the Doric pilasters framing each section of windows greatly distinguished the building. The wings themselves were terminated at the street by cubes, which retained the balustrade

[37] See A. Kiparisova, "Proekt Pavlovskoi bol'nitsy v Moskve," in *Arkhitekturnoe nasledstvo* 1 (1951): 119–27. See *Monuments* 2: 186–88, for recent photographs.

[38] Five versions of Bazhenov's plans of May, 1784 provide some indication of the projected structure. All five designs contain a portico on the central corpus. In four of these, columns adorn what was either a semicircular concave facade or one stretched out across a wide front. The building, resting on a low base, was in each variant crowned with a cupola.

[39] Elizvoi Semenovich Nazarov, one of the important architects of the late eighteenth century, was born a serf and accepted into the Kremlin Department in 1768, the year it was established. Since he entered at the personal request of Bazhenov, he probably studied under him and later under Kazakov. Nazarov resigned from the Kremlin Department in 1773. See especially M. I. Domshlak, *Nazarov* (Moscow, 1956), 48–69, for specific comment on the Sheremetev Indigents' Hospital (*Strannopriimnyi dom*, now Sklifosovskii Institute). (See *Monuments* 2: 69–72, for recent photographs).

Figure 43a. Sheremetev, or Indigents' Hospital (1794–1807), architect E. S. Nazarov. Central colonnade by G. Quarenghi (Schmidt).

and pilasters but added a six-post Doric portico without a pediment. Constructed of brick with a stucco veneer, the Hostel was erected under the supervision of Count Sheremetev's serf-architects—Pavel Ivanovich Argunov, Aleksei Fedorovich Mironov, and Grigorii E. Dikushin. Sculptures pervaded the interior while the most notable painting was one by Dementii Karlovich Scotti, which dominated the ceiling of the church. The Hostel was an important urban ensemble, embellished with a vast court in front and a formal park in the rear. Its site was enhanced still more with the completion of the Garden Ring which it eventually faced.

In the same northern sector as the Indigents' Hostel, Kazakov earlier had built, between 1777 and 1788, the double-tiered and cylindrical Church of Philip the Metropolitan (1777–1788).[40] A central rotunda with two four-columned Ionic porticoes without pediments (fig. 44) supported a lantern-capped belvedere on a drum. Its portals led into an elegant interior where four huge Ionic columns and the wall of the altar enveloped the rotunda beneath the cupola. These Ionic columns complemented the smaller Corinthian columns, arranged in a semicircle around a smaller altar rotunda. Between the Ionic columns and the outer wall were the choirs. The interior, which in recent years has greatly deteriorated, was garnished with sculptures and bathed by rays of sunlight pouring

---

[40] See *Monuments*, 2: 149–51, for recent photographs.

Figure 43b. Drawing of the Indigents' Hospital. (Brunov, *Istoriia*).

Figure 43c. Giacomo Quarenghi (1744–1817)

through the cupola windows. Philip the Metropolitan exemplified the best of classical church building in Moscow by the master architect Kazakov.

Another important architectural ensemble beyond the Zemlianoi Gorod was that of the Aleksandrovskii Institute, the Mariinskaia Hospital, and the Catherine Institute—located in Ekaterininskaia (Kommuny) Square, west of both the Indigents' Hostel and Kazakov's Church of Philip.[41] The first of these was a school for merchants' children; the latter for the daughters of the higher nobility. Both

[41] Ibid., 244–47, for recent photographs of the Mariinskaia (now Dostoevskii) Hospital, Aleksandrovskii (now Tuberkulez-nyi) Institute, and Catherine Institute (now Central House of the Red Army).

Figure 44. The Church of Philip the Metropolitan (1777–1788) on the Second Meschanskaia Street, architect, M. F. Kazakov (Schmidt).

the Aleksandrovskii and Mariinskaia supported powerful and extended porticoes. The former's eight Corinthian columns with an unadorned pediment, rose from the ground floor and provided seven portals into the building. The architect of the Aleksandrovskii remains in doubt: some ascribe it to Andrei Alekseevich Mikhailov in 1807; others to Ivan Giliardi sometime later. The equally imposing Mariinskaia, also by Mikhailov or Ivan Giliardi in 1803–1805, received a similarly strong accent from an eight-column Ionic portico and the ensemble entrance. The columns extended to a sweep of steps while the entrance, a decorative iron gate between two arched doorways in stone blocks, was embellished with lions.

Of greater architectural importance than either the Aleksandrovskii or Mariinskaia was the Catherine Institute.[42] Although it dated from the eighteenth century, its many alterations more appropriately place it in the period

after the fire. Once known as the Invalid House, it was acquired for the Catherine Institute in 1802, and Ivan Giliardi was charged to renovate it. In the process of enlarging the building, Giliardi altered the facade several times before 1818. After that date, Domenico Giliardi modified the appearance of both the building and the plaza. The completed edifice (1818), consisting of an extended central corpus with symmetrical wings, reached forward to form a deep central court. The facade was dominated by a full-length Doric portico of ten columns, pierced by nine arched portals; the gate to the grand court was one of exquisite ironwork. Actual rebuilding and widening of the square occurred in 1826–1827.

A classical Moscow had by no means been preordained. The so-called golden age of the Russian nobility, gentry and grandee alike, had produced a remarkably vital society in Moscow, and the classical edifice was its monument. The comfortable life of the nobility, depicted by Tolstoi in *War and Peace*, found expression in the Nobles' Meeting House, in

---

[42] See N. Krasheninnikova, "Byvshee Ekaterininskoe uchilishche," *Arkhitekturnoe nasledstvo* 1 (1951): 199–210.

the university, the Golitsyn and Sheremetev Hospitals, and in the estate and town houses in the Prechistenka, Tverskaia, and Tverskoi as well as the Gubin mansion on the Petrovka, the nearby Gagarin at Petrovskie Gates, the Sheremetev and Talyzin on the Vozdvizhenka, Iushkov on the Miasnitskaia, and Pashkov on the Mokhovaia. Their enumeration and locales suggest that Moscow had undergone a visual transformation, indeed had become classical, before 1812. That was not entirely the case.

Despite the new and elegant masonry and stucco construction in Moscow during the first decade of the nineteenth century, including Andrei Mikhailov's and Ivan Giliardi's Mariinskaia Hospital and Catherine and Aleksandrovskii Institutes, there was a notable lull in great projects. Bazhenov had died in 1799, and Kazakov, who died in 1812, was virtually inactive the last decade of his life. More to the point, Emperor Alexander was deeply engaged in revamping central St. Petersburg, an enterprise which left him little time or means for any ambitious undertakings in Moscow. The Old Capital, having emerged as both an architectural and intellectual force in Russian culture during Catherine's reign, during the first years of Alexander's seemed destined once again to recede within St. Petersburg's shadows.

Although Moscow's rich lived well in their porticoed mansions, they coexisted with the other Moscow, that of the onion domes and wooden hovels. Batiushkov's vignette of Moscow in 1811 captured the essentials of this contrast.

> Right and left we shall see magnificent buildings [of the Kremlin] with shining cupolas, with high towers, and all this surrounded with a great wall. Here everything reminds us of ages past—tsars, patriarchs, great events. Here every place bears the impression of the seal of past centuries. Here everything is opposed to what we see on the Kuznetskii Bridge, on the Tverskaia, on the Boulevard Ring, etc. There are French bookshops, fash-

ionable stores . . . in one word all the elements of fashion and luxury. In the Kremlin all is quiet, everything has a sort of grandiose . . . appearance; on the Kuznetskii Bridge everything is in motion. . . . Notice everything, and you will suddenly see Moscow with all its contradictions. Near great mansions here is a hut, the miserable home of poverty and illness. Here lives a whole family, exhausted by need, hunger, and cold. This is Moscow, a large city, the home of luxury and poverty. But here before us is a palace with high marble columns and extensive front court.[43]

The crooked lanes and alleys abounded, defying reason and order; the half-finished boulevards, starkly denuded of trees, discharged clouds of dust near a new Neglinnaia River which really never ran as it was intended. Central Moscow's street conditions improved, but almost imperceptibly. By the end of the century, lanterns were hung every sixty-six feet on the posts of main streets in the Belyi Gorod. Despite cobblestone paving, even the most exclusive streets were dusty. George Reinbeck, visiting in Moscow in 1805, described the "paving miserable and dust rising from the carriageways intolerable." The cobblestones did not fit properly; moreover, the "practice of filling up the interstices with sand, but particularly with rubbish from old buildings, increases the dust."[44] Linney Gilbert in 1812 observed that some streets were paved "and others, especially in the suburbs, were formed with trunks of trees or boarded with planks like the floor of a room."[45]

Alleys, though reduced in number, were still abundant and identified by their mainly wooden houses, cobblestones, dirt, or plank paving, and lanterns spaced farther apart than on the thoroughfares. A traditional look in both the streets and alleys was fostered by

---

[43] K. N. Batiushkov, *Sochineniia* (Moscow, 1955), 308, 312.
[44] *Travels from St. Petersburg through Moscow, Grodno, Warsaw, Breslaw, etc., to Germany in the year 1805: in a series of letters,* (London, 1807), 60.
[45] *Russia Illustrated*, 158.

numerous flower and kitchen gardens, long a feature in old Moscow.

Moscow in 1812 was still predominantly brown, yet its center and those streets emanating from it radiated with the amber pastels of its classical edifices. This city, burdened with a history of fires, was to experience the worst yet. In so doing, it perpetuated classicism to a degree and for a longer period than had been anticipated.

CHAPTER VIII

Planning a New Classical Moscow After the Great Fire

What a change! Lowly and prostrate it now lies; its crumbling towers falling into decay; its proud banners torn from their burning walls and scattering their shriveled fragments to the hollow winds; its gates demolished; its houses ransacked; its streets laid waste. . . .

Robert Johnston[1]

Whether the French or the Russians themselves set fire to Moscow is a question which has never been resolved. It is certain, however, that the fires of 15 September 1812 were the worst which ever befell the city. Waiting until 19 October in his belief that this destruction would force Tsar Alexander to treat with him, Napoleon finally gave up when no word came. His departure from Moscow left the citizens of Moscow to contend with their shattered city.

The destruction of Moscow in 1812 was nearly total.[2] The Kremlin at the city's core

escaped, although its walls suffered serious damage from explosions at the time of the French withdrawal. Beyond the Kremlin walls lay a smoldering, ruined Kitai Gorod, the once-cramped commercial center. The Belyi Gorod west of the Kremlin from the Neglinnaia River to the Boulevard Ring was thoroughly demolished. Only parts of the far northern and northeastern sections remained intact. In the Zemlianoi Gorod the Zamoskvorech'e lay ravaged. Even substantial parts of the city beyond the Zemlianoi Gorod were consumed.

Contemporaries verified the extent of Moscow's ruin. Robert Johnston, an English observer, recorded not long after Napoleon's departure that

the entrance to the city exhibits a general scene of ruin and appears from those parts of houses now standing to have consisted of brick and wooden houses huddled together without order or neatness. At present nothing more excites the appearance of wretchedness and filth. As we proceeded the streets began

---

[1] *Travels through part of the Russian Empire and the country of Poland; along the southern shores of the Baltic* (London, 1815), 243, hereafter cited as *Travels*.

[2] The best accounts of rebuilding Moscow after the fire are the following: Budylina, "Planirovka i zastroika," 135–74; A. A. Fedorov-Davydov, *Arkhitektura Moskvy posle otechestvennoi voiny 1812 goda* (Moscow, 1953); I. E. Grabar', S. A. Zombe, T. P. Kazhda, "Arkhitektura Moskvy," *Iskusstva* 8, i (Moscow, 1954), esp. 142–60; L. Chernozubova, "Iz istorii zastroiki Moskvy v pervoi polovine XIX veka," in *Arkhitekturnoe nasledstvo* 9 (1959): 15–26, hereafter cited as "Iz istorii zastroiki"; and Gol'denberg, *Staraia Moskva*; A. J. Schmidt, "The Restoration of Moscow

After 1812," *Slavic Review* 40 (1981): 37–48. The fire took its greatest toll in the Piatnitskaia, Prechistenskaia, Gorodskaia, Taganskaia, and Sretenskaia Districts. The Iauzskaia, Iakimanskaia, Basmannaia, Rogozhskaia, and Arbatskaia also suffered severe damage. The least destruction occurred in Pokrovskaia, Sushchevskaia, Miasnitskaia, and Presnenskaia. (Cf. Budylina, "Planirovka i zastroika," 158–59).

to assume a more regular form with the remains of large and splendid edifices divided from each other by mean hovels and gardens; churches of the most singular and gothic forms with numerous gilded spires and domes crowd on each other, it is almost impossible by any description to convey a correct idea of this singular appearance.[3]

John Thomas James, visiting Moscow after the fire, wrote of the pervasiveness

> of horror that far exceeds the utmost limits of fancy. . . . All was not in the same forlorn condition. Street after street greeted the eye with perpetual ruin. Disjointed columns, mutilated porticoes, broken cupolas, walls of rugged stucco, black—discolored with the stains of fire and open on every side to the sky—formed a hideous contrast with the glowing pictures which travelers had drawn of the grand and sumptuous palaces of Moscow.[4]

P. F. Vigel, a perceptive commentator on the city and its citizens, described his entry into the city in the summer of 1814:

> I could see the horrible vestiges of destruction. That part of the city through which I passed, the Taganskaia and Rogozhskaia, were, it seemed, absolutely devastated by the fire. Vymosschennaia Street possessed the look of a great road on which there were no houses and only fences began to rise. Three-story, charred houses without roofs and windows came into sight. Only upon drawing near to the Iauzskii Bridge and the Foundling Home did I finally see residential houses which had been spared or had been restored.[5]

Statistics corroborated these eyewitness accounts. Three-quarters of Moscow lay in ruin. The fire's toll in houses was 71 percent of the 9,151 existing in the city before the disaster. Nearly 80 percent of the city's masonry dwellings were destroyed or gutted; 67 percent of the wooden buildings in the city were lost.[6]

Only a quarter of the 8,771 private buildings in the city escaped; while but 16 percent of the masonry and wooden shops survived.[7] The architectural landmarks of early classicism in central Moscow—Kazakov's Hall of Columns and his university, Bazhenov's Pashkov House—were left in ruins. Most of the mansions, great and small, along the radial thoroughfares also burned. A few of the streets were spared, and, of course, Kazakov's splendid Senate building within the Kremlin escaped. Such was the extent of the Old Capital's ruin. The architects who had aspired to build a classical Moscow would have to begin anew.

Organizing the Restoration of Moscow

Alexandrian Russia was, among other things, a vast architectural building enterprise.[8] The tsar, who had before the Moscow catastrophe committed himself to the complete renovation of central St. Petersburg, determined, nonetheless, that the work there continue. Nor was that all: Alexander decreed the refurbishing and laying out of classical cities throughout the Russian Empire. Such a broad building program offers a necessary context for assessing Moscow's restoration.

For Alexander, who had played such a dazzling role in overthrowing Napoleon, the creation of a new Moscow, the city in which the French emperor suffered his great debacle, became a compulsion. Officials in St. Petersburg conceived of this restoration in three phases: 1) creating a long-range plan for a new city; 2) providing immediately for housing and shops; and, finally, 3) embellishing the city with stately facades, monuments, and ensembles. The instrument devised to achieve these objectives was the Commission for Building, established on 5 May 1813.[9]

The Commission consisted of two departments—the survey (planning) and the archi-

---

[3] *Travels*, 246.

[4] *Journal of a tour in Germany, Sweden, Russia, Poland during the years 1813 and 1814*, 2 vols. (London, 1817):1 404.

[5] Quoted from *Istoriia Moskvy* 3, *Period razlozheniia krepostnogo stroia* (Moscow, 1954): 144–45.

[6] Budylina, "Planirovka i zastroika," 156.

[7] *Istoriia Moskvy* 3: 144. The statistics here vary only slightly from Budylina above.

[8] Cf. above, 4–7.

[9] Its dissolution in 1842 may, indeed, be taken as a symbolic end to the era of classical construction in Moscow.

tectural. The former, with a staff of two surveyors and three assistants, was responsible for the preparation of a new city plan. Its designated task brought it into conflict with the broader town planning enterprise for all Russia under William Hastie.[10] The architectural department, numbering five architects and eighteen architectural assistants, one mason and an assistant, was charged principally with alleviating the housing problem. It prescribed building standards, developed model ("*obraztsovye*") facades, conveyed designs to the builders, supervised construction, distributed building materials, and, finally, rendered financial aid to those citizens wishing to restore their homes or shops. Fortunately, this department possessed the necessary expertise to handle these various tasks, for its architects had long been associated with construction in the city.

As a first step in the formulation of an overall plan the Commission required a detailed picture of the entire city through a survey of its sections, properties, streets, squares, and lanes. This survey was a prerequisite to fixing perimetrical lines for building facades, straightening streets, eliminating crooked alleys, regulating plazas, and, finally, drawing up a comprehensive plan for Moscow.

Although the nominal head of the Commission was Moscow's controversial governor, F. A. Rostopchin, principal responsibility during the crucial years of building fell to M. D. Tsitsianov. Holding office from 1813 to 1826, the latter recruited many competent personnel, for the most part former students of Kazakov. They included surveyors like S. S. Kesarino from the then extinct Committee for Equalization of City Obligations (1802–1813), architects like the veteran Fedor Kirillovich Sokolov and Ivan Danilovich Zhukov, who had apprenticed in the old Kamennyi Prikaz of the 1770s and 1780s, and Osip Ivanovich Bove, who had worked under Kazakov in the Kremlin Department.[11] Kesarino,

as head of the planning department, and Bove appear to have played the major roles.

Restoration Plans for Moscow 1813–1817

The Great Fire offered planning opportunities unimagined by Moscow's architects during the previous half-century.[12] The Commission shifted the emphasis from estate composition, the concern of eighteenth-century planners, to perimetrical building, and in doing so made an unequivocal commitment to regular streets and plazas. Because of the varied and abundant localized planning and building, the Commission contemplated at once a grand design for the whole city and a composite of many smaller plans which focused on streets, plazas, blocks, and districts. Before the Commission's plan became a reality, however, Kesarino and Bove, the chief architects, had to contend with William Hastie, a Scotsman with long architectural experience in Russia.[13] Appointed by Tsar Alexander in 1811 to supervise town planning throughout the Empire, he, too, was charged to draft a Moscow plan, which he completed in 1813.

Because the Kremlin escaped severe fire damage Hastie concentrated on the areas outside it.[14] In the Kitai Gorod, he planned the enlargement of Red Square by annexing the first line of commercial rows opposite the Kremlin (from the Nikol'skie to the Savior Gates) and by eliminating the shops and moat along the Kremlin wall. He proposed lengthening the square by razing the buildings along its northern limits and creating a plaza around St. Basil's at the other end. For the Moskvo-

---

[10] See below, same page.
[11] Others were Domenico Giliardi, A. G. Grigor'ev, A. I. Starov, the engineer general A. de Béthencourt, and the

sculptor I. P. Vitali. Cf. Bunin, *Istoriia gradostroitel'nogo iskusstva*, 442.
[12] For the planning of Moscow the best accounts are found in Budylina, Bunin, Fedorov-Davydov, Gol'denberg, Grabar', and *Istoriia Moskvy* 3.
[13] During a half-century of Russian service Hastie had acquired particular fame for his iron bridges in St. Petersburg and his planning of Tsarskoe Selo before assuming the larger responsibilities assigned to him in 1811. See Miliza Korshunova, "William Hastie in Russia," *Architectural History* 17 (1974): 14–21, transl. L. Haskell; and Schmidt, "Hastie."
[14] See in particular Budylina, "Planirovka i zastroika," 139–44.

retskaia, from St. Basil's to the river, he advocated the open space which it possesses today. Creating this thoroughfare meant demolishing many existing shops as well as the earthen bastions enveloping both the Kremlin and Kitai Gorod, and filling the Kremlin moat. Hastie also suggested widening the Il'inka in the Kitai Gorod to reduce congestion around the Gostinyi Dvor and creating an expansive Varvarskaia Square to link with the old road to Vladimir by way of the Taganka.

Invoking the plan of 1775, the Scotsman proposed a semicircular chain of squares around both the Kremlin and Kitai Gorod. In particular, he envisioned a vast square unfolding before the Petrovskii Theater. By pulling down houses in Okhotnyi Riad Square nearby, Hastie hoped to create a new square on the Neglinnaia, one connecting the Okhotnyi Riad with Moiseevskaia Square. The latter he projected from the Great Nikitskaia to a new radial Tverskaia east of it. This Tverskaia was a startling innovation, which took little account of either the natural or man-made environment. For the same area Hastie also proposed eliminating Mokhovaia Square and widening Mokhovaia Street.

At the high end of Belyi Gorod he intended minor changes, but in the Zemlianoi Gorod they were sweeping. Arbat Square at the site of the old Belyi Gorod and the square before the governor's residence on the Tverskaia were to be left intact. Nor did he project modifications for either the old Tverskaia or the Miasnitskaia. Because of the complete devastation of the Zemlianoi Gorod, he proposed extensive alterations, e.g. the elimination of crooked alleys and the straightening of streets, but, more importantly, the location of eleven plazas at the intersection of the radial highways with the Zemlianoi Gorod rampart. Of these, seven were to have been essentially or entirely new.[15]

Hastie's completed draft differed significantly from preceding plans in that it included the area beyond the Zemlianoi Gorod. There, as elsewhere, Hastie recommended regular streets and plazas. Taganskaia Square, enlarged and straightened, was designed to filter traffic from those streets leading to the Rogozhskie, Pokrovskie, and Savior Gates along the Kamer College Rampart and to link with the projected Varvarskaia Square via the Solianka. Sennaia Square, contiguous to the newly widened plaza at the head of the Miasnitskaia at the Krasnye Gates, would be reduced in size. Hastie justified some of the new plazas beyond the Zemlianoi Gorod because they enhanced such existing architectural ensembles as Lefortov Palace and many of Moscow's monasteries. North of the Kitai Gorod beyond the Zemlianoi Gorod, Hastie planned a new square to open up a view of the Catherine Institute. In addition to these, Hastie planned fourteen squares where the main arterial highways intersected with the Kamer College Rampart.[16] This network of squares that would unite the radial streets inside the city with roads leading to provincial cities was his most original idea.

William Hastie's plan, initially approved by the emperor, was flawed for several reasons. In the first place, the architect appeared unfamiliar with Moscow, for he took little account of the historic city or even of aspects of the 1775 plan in projecting his great plazas and thoroughfare. Had he prevailed, the city center would have been wholly transformed. Secondly, his plan proved too costly for an empire which was financially strapped. Despite all these factors, Hastie's plan did constitute a link in the succession of plans before

---

[15] They were as follows: 1) a greatly expanded Novo-Serpukhovskaia Square to funnel Piatnitskaia and Ordynka traffic from the Serpukhovskie Gates to Red Square; 2) Kudrinskaia Square, origin of the new Tverskaia, at the Presnenskie Gates; 3) another square on the new Tverskaia; 4) a new plaza near the juncture of the old Tverskaia and the Boulevard Ring, by old Strastnoi Monastery and on an axis with the Miusskaia Gate at the Okhotnyi Riad; 5) a spacious square near the Krasnye Gates, where the Miasnitskaia entered the Zemlianoi Gorod; 6) a plaza by the Zachat'evskii Monastery to facilitate commerce and relieve congestion in the Zemlianoi Gorod; and 7) a square before the Military Commissariat in the Zamoskvorech'e to open a view of that building from the canal.

[16] From the south these were the Kaluzhskaia, Serpukhovskaia, Savior (*Spasskaia*), Pokrovskaia, Rogozhskaia, Prolomnaia, Semenovskaia, Preobrazhenskaia, Sokol'nicheskaia, Troitskaia, Miusskaia, Tverskaia, Presnenskaia, and Dorogomilovskaia.

1812; more importantly, it served as a foil for his opponents on the Commission.

Kesarino, the spokesman for the Commission, quite naturally led the attack. In a critique presented on 17 October 1813, he deplored the expense and the time required to realize it. Specifically, he objected to the squares and to the streets: 1) where squares were projected on privately owned land, these parcels must be purchased at additional cost. Some proposed plazas were needlessly large; others, intended for sparsely populated sections of the city, appeared to serve no useful purpose; 2) regulated streets, designed to replace old and crooked ones, would both have infringed on private property and violated the topography. And many of the existing houses, instead of facing on the new streets, would present their rear and lateral facades to them. Laying out these streets, moreover, would take much-needed labor from housing construction, while landowners whose properties were either partitioned or deprived of access to the new streets would draw on the meager housing funds.

Although other aspects of Hastie's plan raised no objections, the Commission determined to revise the entire design and seek an architect whose work would "agree with the present disposition of streets, squares and buildings."[17] Judging from his subsequent role in Moscow's restoration, Osip Bove came nearest to filling that description. The Commission, meanwhile, set to work preparing an extensive critique of Hastie's proposal. It rejected his transportation network, especially questioning his squares at the Zemlianoi Gorod and Kamer College Walls. In fact, all fourteen squares along the latter were regarded as superfluous and excessively costly; their remoteness suggested that Hastie had intended them to be more decorative than utilitarian.[18]

The Commission subjected Hastie's squares nearer the center to a similar scrutiny. While accepting those encircling the Kremlin and Kitai Gorod, it offered an important modification, i.e. a larger square before the Nobles' Meeting House and Petrovskii Theater, where an enlarged square was contingent upon covering the Neglinnyi Canal and its basins, the elimination of which would make possible a circular boulevard at the Kitai Gorod Wall. The Commission further proposed the enlargement of Nikol'skaia and the reduction of Hastie's Varvarskaia Squares. From the latter a road to the Moscow River was suggested. These recommendations did not include any alteration of the thoroughfare along the Moscow River Embankment, but for the west side of the Kremlin the Commission urged an enlargement of Mokhovaia Square, again by covering the Neglinnyi Canal. This plaza was perceived as a vital link in the chain of squares encircling the Kremlin and Kitai Gorod.

The Commission modified Hastie's Belyi and Zemlianoi Gorod plans, usually by deleting his projects. Its most notable exclusion was the new Tverskaia, which would have been both costly and destructive to the environment. The Commission also strongly reacted to Hastie's squares in the Zemlianoi Gorod and beyond.[19] In all, it recommended discarding twenty-six of his forty-seven plazas; conversely, it proposed twenty-eight, most of which already existed and required only altering. These changes, the Commission expected, would save almost 15,000,000 of the 19,500,000 rubles which Hastie had planned to spend.

Turning to the Kitai and Belyi Gorod, the Commission was in general agreement with Hastie. It proposed razing the shops and

---

[17] Budylina, "Planirovka i zastroika," 145.

[18] Kesarino estimated that realization of Hastie's plan would cost the treasury nearly 19½ million rubles; these fourteen plazas alone were estimated at 4,021,772 rubles. (Ibid., 146). Besides the cost, the hilly and marshy terrain promised structural problems.

[19] It proposed altering the Taganskaia, the Ugol'naia near the Carriage Makers' Riad, and the plazas before Lefortov Palace and the Krasnye Gates in either form or size. Designated for enlargement only were the commercial Polianskaia, Smolenskaia, Kudrinskaia, and Nemetskaia Squares. For some squares, the Commission prescribed regulation, nothing more. These were the Il'inskaia, Okhotnyi Riad, and Moiseevskaia in the center of the city, the square before the governor's palace on the Tverskaia, the Bolotnaia, Serpukhovskaia, Kaluzhskaia, Konnaia, and those squares by the Donskoi and Novospasskii Monasteries.

filling the moat along the Kremlin Wall but recommended retaining in the north end of the square those wooden buildings which were to have defined the limits of the square at the Resurrection Gates. The architects also differed on the location of buildings around St. Basil's. Whereas Hastie had intended opening the cathedral on all sides and clearing the area down to the river, the Commission advised eliminating only those buildings which obstructed the view and access and demolishing only those shops which pressed toward the Execution Place from the commercial rows opposite the cathedral. Along the Moskvoretskaia, only buildings extending beyond the facade lines were recommended for removal.

In those open spaces where the Belyi Gorod Wall had once stood and where the Zemlianoi Gorod still remained, the Commission voted to retain the existing hotels and convert other masonry buildings to new hotels. While recommending the incorporation of these hotels into a new plan, it rejected taverns and inns as a detriment to well-ordered facades. For boulevards in the Belyi Gorod, open space had to measure one hundred and forty feet; the walking area in the middle, forty-two. The same principles applied to the Zemlianoi Gorod thoroughfare, although no dimensions were specified.

This Commission paper was conveyed to Governor Rostopchin on 16 February 1814, whereupon the governor dispatched the architect Osip Bove to Petersburg to state the case. Matters did not proceed rapidly because Alexander I was with his troops driving toward Paris. Not until the end of the next year was a decision forthcoming. In November, 1815, the new Moscow governor, Tormasov, requested from the Commission an account of private lands to be procured and their probable cost. The Commission responded on 14 January 1816, with a general plan, probably completed by the surveying department during the emperor's absence from Russia. Alexander subsequently insisted upon a plan which "left out nothing"—one with complete information on buildings, blocks, and the streets to be improved. The Commission

thereupon modified its plan of 14 January, completing on 26 January 1816, a more detailed draft which differed only slightly from the Commission's 1814 critique of the Hastie plan.[20]

On 22 May 1816, the Council of Ministers, having examined this work of the Commission, responded favorably but with a few suggestions. The Council would alter the open space at the outer limits of both the Belyi Gorod and Zemlianoi Gorod. It agreed with the Commission's proposal to convert some spacious mansions on streets leading from the gates into hotels but recommended that gardens also be planted there and enclosed by grillework according to a design determined by the Commission.

Taking into account these suggestions, the Commission completed still another draft. For unexplained reasons, it was not submitted to the Council for over a year. Not until 19 December 1817, did Kesarino's successor, Cheliev, report the completion of the "Draft Plan of the Capital City of Moscow of 1817," which served as the basis for restoring and renovating the city. This general plan had virtually nothing to say about Moscow's most urgent need, housing, to which the Commission next turned its attention.

Housing: Utilitarian and Aesthetic Questions

In order to hasten restoration, the Commission divided Moscow into four regions each

---

[20] New shops facing Red Square from the Kitai Gorod were deleted, and extant ones were retained for remodeling by the architect Bove. The space unfolding before the Petrovskii Theater was again enlarged, as was Arbatskaia Square. The Nikol'skaia was changed from an oval to a rectangle, as Hastie had originally intended it to be. The size of Polianskaia Square was reduced, that of the Tverskaia increased.

For the area beyond the Zemlianoi Gorod, the corrected plan similarly altered the size and shape of plazas, as evidenced by the plans for the Taganskaia and Sennaia. It contained two additional squares, the Miusskaia-Lesnaia and the Iamskaia, by the Triumphal Gates. The building of the embankment on the Kremlin side of the Moscow River from the Moskvoretskii Bridge to the Novospasskii Monastery, as proposed by the Commission, was recorded with its varying widths. The design of the Kamer College Rampart area remained unchanged. Upon completion, the draft incorporating these changes was conveyed to St. Petersburg once again. (Budylina, "Planirovka i zastroika," 151–52).

of which had a supervising architect with assistants.[21] The first, which included the Zamoskvorech'e (in particular, the Piatnitskaia and Great Iakimanka), the Serpukhovskaia further south, and the Prechistenka and Khamovnicheskaia areas to the west, was headed by Sokolov. His task also included restoring important architectural monuments in the center of the city. A second region, assigned to Zhukov, encompassed the Sretenka, Meshchanskaia, Basmannaia, Pokrovskaia, and Sushchevskaia districts. The third—the Miasnitskaia, Iauzskaia, Taganskaia, Rogozhskaia, and Lefortovskaia—was directed by the architect V. Balashov. A fourth region consisting of the Gorodskaia, Tverskaia, Arbatskaia, Novinskaia, and Presnenskaia districts passed under the supervision of Bove and the architect Matveev.[22]

Contemporary accounts vary as to the pace of rebuilding. Some witnesses emphasized the delays and remarked upon the extensive portions of the city unreconstructed for many years after the fire. Others, however, were impressed by the vast quantities of building materials brought into the city. In late 1813, a writer marveled that "even in the most devastated streets of Zamoskvorech'e, Arbat, and Prechistenka . . . there are already quite a number of large as well as small houses, here repaired, and here completely rebuilt."[23] Robert Lyall, an English authority on Moscow of these years, observed that in the summer of 1815, in every suburb, street, and lane, workmen accomplished a great deal in cleaning and rebuilding. In the spring of the following year, "thousands of artisans and laborers were occupied in all quarters of the city" in anticipation of an imperial visit during the following summer of 1816: "Nobles and merchants vied with each other in building and

repairing with the greatest speed." During the fall of 1816 and before the snows disappeared the following spring, Lyall concluded, the citizens continued their task of repairing and rebuilding.[24]

The scope of the housing problem and the accomplishments in restoration are evident in the following statistics: for the year 1813, 1,743 houses were made habitable, having been either built anew or repaired. Of these, 1,067 were new masonry, stucco, and frame; the remaining 676 were rebuilt. Rising material and labor costs reduced by approximately one-half the number built and rebuilt during the next year; noneless, the number of out-buildings increased. Although information for 1815 is incomplete, total building—dwellings and out-buildings constructed and repaired—reached a record high of 2,957, of which 1,387 were dwellings and 1,570 auxiliary structures. The next year appeared to record a sharp decline: only 341 new houses are listed, although figures are again lacking in part.

During these three years, wooden and stucco construction, cheaper and faster, greatly outstripped masonry. Only 328 of the last were built anew (110 houses and 218 out-buildings), while 4,486 houses and out-buildings of wood were constructed. Even after adding to this figure, the 1,472 masonry houses and 715 out-buildings that were gutted but refurbished, the overall picture for masonry building remains unimpressive—especially in light of repeated official prophecies of a new Moscow in stone and brick.

Although emphasis on building in Moscow appears to have shifted by 1817, from private dwellings to important public and state buildings, the evidence still points to extensive rebuilding of dwellings and shops. The figures for that year, regrettably uncertain, indicate that 3,137 masonry houses were restored and 5,551 frame ones built.

The shops destroyed in the fire also created

---

[21] Ibid., 159.

[22] In the largely industrial and commercial sections assigned to him, Balashov became the most successful builder of housing between 1813–1816; Sokolov and Zhukov followed; few opportunities for housing construction existed for Bove in the fourth, or central, region where the accent fell on public buildings.

[23] Quote from a letter by M. Makarov (27 November 1813) in Budylina, "Planirovka i zastroika," 157.

[24] *The Character of the Russians and a detailed history of Moscow* (London, 1823), 524–25.

a crisis for Moscow. A merchant arriving in Moscow at the end of 1812 observed that "shops for trade are . . . non-extant; all are burned; and along squares temporary wooden ones were constructed; tables and mats have replaced the Gostinyi Dvor." However, within a year, the picture had changed; temporary accommodations had given way to permanent rows of shops. By 1815, with the construction of riady in the Kitai Gorod, the total number of shops made available for use approached 4,000. Between the years 1813 and 1815, 3,835 shops of masonry construction, either new or restored, opened in the Kitai Gorod alone. That number represented 75 percent of the pre-fire total there. In the Tverskaia sector, 328 shops were built or rebuilt. For the Sretenskaia District, the tally was 164, the Iakimanskaia, 177, and the Arbatskaia, 108.[25]

Impressive as the speed of restoration appeared, it was something less than the "miracle" so often proclaimed. Almost twenty years after the fire, unrepaired houses could still be seen; moreover, Moscow's population had increased by perhaps 50,000 during these two decades, and the total wooden and masonry houses did not greatly exceed the figure for 1812—from 9,151 to 9,842. That 30 percent of these were of brick or stone meant only a 2 percent increase in houses of that type over the number in 1812.[26] Official and ecclesiastical buildings and luxury town houses were typically the masonry structures. Building which did proceed with dispatch was usually of wood, a fact discouraging to those who were planning a fire-proof classical city. Since the center of the city was largely masonry, thus conforming to their program, they used that section as a criterion in judging success.

The financial operation of the Commission for Building also fell short of what had been envisioned. As a lending agency, this body received from the government 5,000,000 rubles—or 1,000,000 for each of the first five years after the fire—to be used for loans to the owners of burned houses. The five million ruble allocation in 1813 was specifically earmarked for the following: 1) restoration of those prominently located and gutted masonry houses which affected the appearance of the city; 2) restoration of the Petrovskii Theatre; 3) restoration of all barracks and construction of police buildings; 4) leveling plazas and streets throughout the city; 5) a stone or iron Moskvoretskii Bridge (replacing the wooden bridge) over both the Moscow River and Vodootvodnyi Canal; 6) lining with stone the embankment of the Moscow and Iauza Rivers and the Vodootvodnyi Canal (though in the case of the last two this was not done); 7) encasing in brick the Neglinnyi Canal and basins; 8) completion of concentric boulevards around the Kremlin, Kitai Gorod, and possibly elsewhere.[27] Subsequently, a new allocation of 3,765,832 rubles was provided for remuneration to those whose properties lay across lands projected for plazas and for the expenses of grading and paving incurred in this great rebuilding effort. The first 5,000,000 rubles hardly began to cover property losses, sometimes estimated as high as 270,000,000 rubles.[28] The Commission's charge to alleviate the city's housing problem notwithstanding, most of the poor were doubtless left to their own resources—to rebuild in wood on the outskirts of Moscow—while the wealthy secured Commission funds for townhouses in the city proper.[29] The restorers of Moscow for the most part stressed beautification over adequate housing for the city's populace.

Model Facades

The Commission, in prescribing building design in Moscow after 1812, permitted three

[25] See Budylina, "Planirovka i zastroika," 156–59.
[26] *Istoriia Moskvy* 3: 152.

[27] *Istoriia Moskvy* 3: 146–47.
[28] Ibid., 145.
[29] Government buildings naturally monopolized the center. That security was also a motive is evident by the construction of barracks and police facilities there.

years for construction on vacant plots and for the repair of burned houses. When the law was evaded or disobeyed, especially as pertaining to facades, plots of land containing the ruins of destroyed buildings were sold at public auction. For those who conformed and wished to build, money, materials, and labor were theoretically available through the Commission.

In fulfilling this aesthetic requirement, the Commission gave highest priority to both facade design and the integration of this new housing into the total urban composition. Prominent in the designs for these new houses were model ("obraztsovye") facades, which had their antecedents in Kazakov's Moscow (figs. 45a,b,46).[30] Although used sparingly in early eighteenth-century Russia, model facades became by the second half of that century an integral part of a classical program for Russian cities.

In the following century the model design proved a particularly useful device in the regulation of Moscow's alleys and secondary streets. In effect, the architects organized a street with houses of uniform facade design and fixed size. The width of the street corresponded to the height of its houses. Facades of these small though costly houses either possessed such vertical articulation as porticoes, vestibules, and loges or were notably flat, accented with horizontal lines, and severe in decor. Pastels, rather than garish colors, were prescribed in either case. Such model facades placed along carefully laid-out streets interrupted at even intervals by similar plazas assured a classical regularity for a town. The Arbat and many other sectors of Moscow were so developed after 1812.

Russian facade design in 1812 had most recently been defined in three albums, entitled

Collection of Facades Appropriate for Private Dwellings in Towns of the Russian Empire. The first two, published in 1809, were the work of William Hastie and Luigi Rusca; the third, released in 1812, was prepared by the Russian architect, Vasilii Petrovich Stasov. These designs, particularly those of Hastie and Rusca, showed a concern for strict proportion between various features of the facade. For example, the number of windows was determined by the height of the building. A single story would have no more than seven windows; a two-story no more than eleven.

The 1809 albums depicted houses of varying heights—one, two, and three stories with or without mezzanines—in masonry and wood. Some facades contained porticoes; others had rusticated and/or smooth stucco surfaces without porticoes. The architects' concern for proportional relationships was evident in their manipulation of facade decorations—columns, pilasters, archivaults, keystones, and cornices.

Stasov's designs responded to such building needs as utility buildings, greenhouses, craft shops, factories, commercial buildings, fences, and single-story dwellings for the less affluent. As noted above, standardization extended beyond dwelling facades. "Obraztsovye" albums appeared for public buildings (1803), fences, gates and city blocks (1811), inns (1819), churches (1824), jails, judicial offices, and houses for vice-governors (1828), for "the arrangement of villages" (1830), and, finally, for post offices (1831). These models were intended primarily to assist builders in the provinces where trained architects were few, if at all, but they were used to a limited extent in Petersburg and Moscow, too.

Hastie intended that model city blocks and plazas would both reduce the hazards of fire and improve urban appearances. In 1811, he produced twenty-six prototypes, nineteen of blocks and seven of squares. These plans, engraved in 1812 and published in four hundred and fifty sets, were entitled *Divisions of City Blocks into Narrow Lots.* Hastie's model block consisted of twelve plots of land with

---

[30] For model or "*obraztsovye*" projects see Beletskaia, "*Obraztsovye*" *proekty*; V. I. Piliavskii, "Gradostroitel'nye meropriiatiia i obraztsovye proekty v Rossii v nachale XIX v.," *Arkhitekturnaia praktika i istoriia arkhitektury* (Leningrad and Moscow, 1958), 21: 75–108, hereafter cited as "Gradostroitel'nye meropriiatiia"); and L. E. Chernozubova, "Iz istorii zastroiki," 15–26.

Figure 45a. Model facades for large houses of two and three stories, early nineteenth century (E. A. Beletskaia, et al. *"Obraztsovye" proekty v zhiloi zastroike russkikh gorodov XVIII–XIX vv.* Moscow, 1961); hereafter cited Beletskaia, *"Obraztsovye" proekty.*

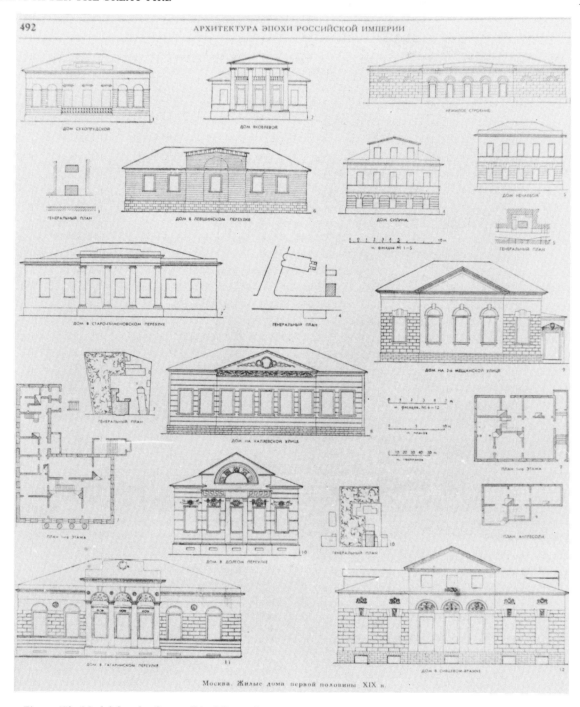

Figure 45b. Model facades for small buildings after 1812 (Brunov, *Istoriia*).

uniform construction along each of the four streets. Each contained only three variations in facades—a corner house, one with a protruding center section, and a simple rectangular dwelling. A block, conforming to con- temporary taste, encompassed a central square and, moreover, possessed a garden, an orchard, and a yard with auxiliary buildings.[31]

---

[31] See Schmidt, "Hastie," 239–43.

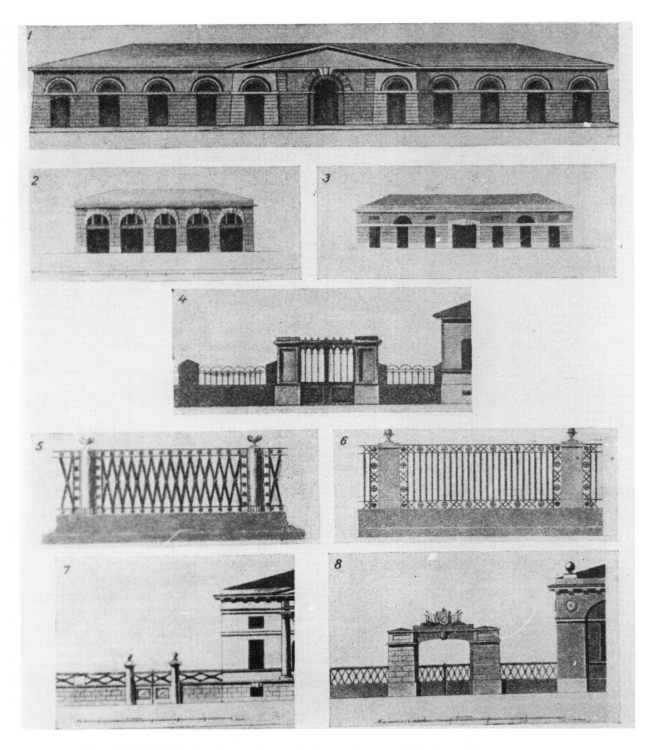

Figure 46. Model facades, fences, gates, early nineteenth century (Beletskaia, *"Obraztsovye" proekty*).

The model plazas, variously designated administrative or commercial, assumed shapes similar to those the architect had given his blocks. These block and plaza designs, backed by the law of 8 February 1812, were dispatched to provincial governors in order that "from this time on in determining city blocks and dividing these into plots of land, you are to be ruled by these designs using those patterns which appear most suitable for the comfort of the homeowners and the adaptability to the situation." Such model block plans were utilized throughout the Empire.[32]

What then was the consequence of these model facades in the reconstruction of Moscow? Unquestionably, those by Hastie, Rusca, and Stasov did guide rebuilding, a fact substantiated by the large number of new and reconstructed houses which conformed to their album designs. These facades embodied both national and classical features, differing only in detail.[33] Mezzanine and vestibule entrances added to these new houses suggested their descent from the traditional peasant cottage (*izba*). A uniformity in their decorative elements also struck a familiar cord. Some, those with porticoes, protruded; others did not. While the number of windows, stories with or without mezzanines, length of the main facade, kinds of decorative ornament,

and silhouette all varied from one facade to another, they did possess certain common features. These included a strict symmetry of composition, an uneven number of windows equally spaced, the use of columns or pilasters, consistent use of masonry, stucco, or wooden siding, and a limited use of decorative motifs. Above all, Moscow's new facades gave an element of monumentality to even small houses in the restored city.[34]

Since standardization applied only to the facades, the interiors of these dwellings could vary. However, in reality, they usually did follow a common scheme. The rooms for entertaining were situated on the street side of the house, while private or miscellaneous rooms occupied the garden side. A corridor running parallel to reception rooms separated them from private rooms. Private quarters were often located on half floors and mezzanine, accessible by stairs from the main corridor. Ornament and color also embellished these interiors. While the private rooms were sometimes adorned with bas-reliefs and ceiling murals, the larger rooms were even more resplendent with their decorative arches, cupolas, columns and pilasters. Simulated marble and/or brown, yellow, blue, and pink pastels on reception room walls contrasted with the dark and rich hues of the ceilings. The latter, moreover, were often garnished by wreaths of flowers, fruit baskets, palms, and other classical motifs.

Many model houses built after 1812 surpassed in variety the Hastie and Rusca prototypes. One group of houses had clearly articulated facades. The frame house of A. V.

---

[32] The quote is from Piliavskii, "Gradostroitel'nye meropriiatiia," 83. Cf. Schmidt, "Hastie," 226–43.

[33] A description of various types of housing of the period after the fire may be found in Chernozubova, "Iz istorii zastroiki." For wooden classicism, see A. V. Okh and M. V. Fekhner, "Novye issledovaniia po dereviannym zhilym domam nachala XIX veka v Moskve," *Arkhitekturnoe nasledstvo* 5 (1955): 115–40, hereafter cited as "Novye issledovaniia."

An interesting commentary on the importance attached to "model" projects may be seen in the efforts exerted by the architect A. A. Mikhailov in the establishment of the Society for Encouragement of Artists in Petersburg. This group was organized in 1821 in order to foster the growth of Russian art both by improving public taste and encouraging young artists and architects with talent to draw pictures of buildings. One set which received wide distribution was "Collection of Plans, Facades, and Profiles of the outstanding Buildings of St. Petersburg" (1826). The architectural editions of the Society also included "Collection of Plans, Facades, and Profiles for the Building of Masonry Churches and Model Projects of Hospitals." (See L. A. Mederskii, "Uchastie A. A. Mikhailova 2-go izdaniiakh obshchestva pooshchreniia khudozhnikov," *Arkhitekturnoe nasledstvo* 9: 139–44).

[34] Seven types of clay or carved bas-relief decoration existed for a main facade: a medallion, two torches, and a garland; three medallions on a spear twined with leaves or ribbons; a medallion and two wreaths; a medallion and two palms; a medallion and two horns of plenty; three wreaths, twined with ribbons; and a wreath and ribbons. See Chernozubova, "Iz istorii zastroiki," 24.

These dwellings contained no street entrance; access was by the rear. Carriages passed through a side gate into the yard. Invariably, auxiliary buildings were situated in this yard and opposite the house; a vegetable garden probably occupied the other side, farther back. After 1812, lots were smaller than they had been in Catherine's day; therefore, the main entrance was used for service and the size of garden plots diminished.

Iakovlev in the Piatnitskaia sector, a single story with a mezzanine and four-columned Ionic entrance, was one of these. The Gorchakov House in the Arbat, also in this architectural group, contained a huge attic with five windows across its facade and six Doric pilasters and nine windows across its main facade. M. S. Savost'ianov's Tverskaia house of masonry construction received its vertical accent from a projected and partially rusticated central section of the facade. An attic with three windows was simply an extension of it. A. I. Sukhoprudskii's frame house in the Arbat was a simpler single-story dwelling with seven windows across the facade. A pair of windows on each side of the articulated central portion were capped with semicircular niches and flanked by rusticated walls. The three middle windows, cut into a smooth wall, rose above a balustrade. The Ivanov House on the Prechistenka varied this central emphasis with a four-column portico and pediment, and a rusticated ground floor. I. I. Bekker's Tverskaia house had a six-column portico extending from the rest of the house. In the Ivan Petrov House at the Prechistenskie Gates Bove utilized two facades joined by a decorative gate. Both buildings contained similarly articulated central facade sections in front. On the larger two-story structure, there were five windows across each side section and a single on each side of a triple window in the center. A semicircular window in the parapet, supported by Corinthian pilasters, corresponded to the central section of the smaller single story. Rustication divided both buildings horizontally and vertically.

The chief characteristic of a second category of buildings was a generally flat facade. A. S. Nechaev's two-story masonry house in the Miasnitskaia area had five windows across its facade. This lack of articulation in the facade was offset by rustication, which distinguished the ground from the upper floor. The A. P. Tatarinov House in the Tverskaia—masonry, two stories, and also five windows across— received horizontal articulation from a band between the ground and first floors, a smooth foundation beneath rustication, and a plain cornice at the top.[35]

Dwellings of minor officials, tradesmen, merchants, artisans, priests, and lesser nobles—almost always more modest than those described above—conformed to the established facade designs and were constructed variously of wood, stucco, stone, or brick. Small, with either a stone or cast-iron fence around the gardens, these dwellings displayed charm, proportion, simplicity, and modest sculptural decor. Their motifs of wreaths, torches, rosettes, circles, lions, and masks were the same motifs that decorated Moscow's great houses. Like the larger houses, too, they faced longitudinally on the street, with the entrance in the rear, a carriage way on the side, and gardens within the lot. Their interior decor was also imitative of elegant Moscow homes.

Although not emphasized in the album design, soft colors no less than proportion and symmetry characterized the Moscow Empire style as it had that of Catherine earlier. Emperor Alexander himself prescribed appropriate hues for these masonry, stucco, and frame dwellings, both large and small. Observing in 1816 that many were painted in "crude colors," he decreed that "houses and fences be painted with more delicate and better colors." Specifically, he preferred gray, flesh-color, and light green. Stone houses and decorative details were to have been whitened. There followed a prohibition on dark green, red, cherry, and dark gray for houses, fences, and shops. Two years later the Commission prohibited black roofs but did permit selection by the owners of green, red, and gray. These restraints on color applied to all Russian cities, not just Moscow.

Despite all the talk about the elimination of wooden structures, many—even expensive ones—were built after the Great Fire.[36] The most attractive displayed columned porticoes or mezzanines, clay bas-reliefs, plastered

---

[35] Cf. Budylina, "Planirovka i zastroika," 161–68.
[36] See especially Okh and Fekhner, "Novye issledovaniia," 115–40.

Figure 47. The frame Polivanov House (1822) in Denezhzyi Lane near the Arbat (Schmidt).

stucco veneer, residential wings for servants' quarters, auxiliary buildings, yards, gardens, entrance gates, and, of course, fences (fig. 47). The less pretentious were shingled but generally mounted on a brick or stone foundation. Wooden construction cost less than masonry, and was quicker. Many Russians, fond of their tradition in wood and believing that masonry houses were unhealthy, frequently constructed their dwellings of wood and auxiliary buildings of brick.

Frame houses were, of course, often given the appearance of masonry by finishing the exterior in stucco or tight-fitting plank siding. Rustication, a masonry-like surface, not only provided a stone effect, but also sealed the joints of the planks at the corners of the house. Mass-produced wooden bas-relief ornament and wooden columns, dressed with fine linen and stuccoed or painted, also achieved a masonry effect. Whatever the method, the houses were required to have a classic look. The Commission regularly refused permits for the construction of cottages and is said to have denied permission to erect two-story frame dwellings; therefore, those of wood presumably conformed to the specifications and dimensions for single or single and a half stories and extended to the "red line" of the street. In such cases, entrances were placed both in front and in back.

Moscow's numerous houses in the classical mode exemplified her architects' success in achieving diversity within a uniform scheme. The disposition of portico, divisions achieved by rustication, juxtaposition of rectangular or semicircular windows, use of bas-reliefs or semi-circular arches over windows—all of these became devices by which distinction was attained. These smaller dwellings, indeed, stand among the most important accomplishments of Moscow's restorers.

While model projects facilitated the rebuilding of Moscow as well as embellishment of Russia's provincial cities, the emphasis given to them brought problems as well. Hastie seems to have been excessively committed to his models, showing little regard for history and topography. This disregard, as we have seen, was a principal reason for the Commission's rejection of his overall plan for Moscow. The model projects could seldom be implemented with ease. Straightening alleys and streets meant, for example, the subordination of property rights to a comprehensive design. Property owners, therefore, often opposed successfully or delayed interminably such alley and street regulation. The prospects for straightening residential streets and alleys improved when valuable real estate was not involved. Above all, the governor sought to effect such changes without great, if any, expenditure.

What came from all this planning? Its fruits were suggested by contemporaries. The Englishman, William Rae Wilson, in discussing "great exertions in rebuilding houses and widening streets," concluded that "the new town is on a plan quite modern and some of the streets are so completely metamorphosed that a person who had been absent a few years would hardly recognize the place."[37] On the

other hand, Robert Lyall could only observe that many winding streets and lanes still existed. Among those ordered, the Nikol'skaia, Il'inka, Tverskaia, Pokrovka, Novaia Basmannaia, and Meshchanskaia were the straightest and longest. Lyall praised the "few fine squares in Moscow," but observed that "a great number were irregular and in general not very elegant squares and public places and markets." He did admit that "if Moscow has no good squares, it still has one of the grandest in Europe—Red Square."[38]

These remarks suggest that the emergence of a new city, planned and rebuilt along classical lines, albeit diluted with the appearance of traditional wooden cottages, had softened the shock of the destruction. Indeed, a Moscow, as classical as it ever was to be, did rise from the ashes. This regeneration will be discussed in the next chapters.

---

[37] *Travels*, 116.

[38] Lyall, *Moscow*, 50.

CHAPTER IX

A New Moscow Emerges After 1812: The Central Plazas and Radial Thoroughfares

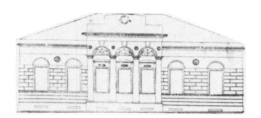 

Some old monuments remained; some that had been gutted reappeared; but most of old Moscow was gone forever.[1] Removal of both the Neglinnaia and Peter's bastions made possible an enlarged Red Square, the Aleksandrovskii Garden, and vast Theater Square.[2] Besides this reorganization of space west and north of the Kremlin, Cathedral Square within the walls and Resurrection Square, which joined Red and Theater Squares, were also rearranged. With the demolition of the bastions, Cannon Court, and the eventual disposal of the Neglinnaia, it became possible to link the space of the future Theater and Lubianskaia Squares, blocked for a century by the bastions. From the Lubianskaia, the Kitaiskii Passage facilitated traffic flow past the Varvarskie Gates alongside the Kitai Gorod Walls to the Moscow River Embankment.

The plaza chain, proposed in 1775, was virtually completed, although not as originally conceived. Spacious squares appeared at intersections of the boulevards and the radial streets when both the Boulevard and Garden Rings were finished during the 1820s and 1830s. Masonry and wooden houses, all classical, and splendid private and public ensembles multiplied, far beyond the number standing before 1812. William Rae Wilson discerned these changes when he observed that Moscow was not so bizarre as formerly, but rather more uniform. "There is something captivating," he wrote, "in this display of Grecian and Palladian architecture intermingled among the old National structures." He praised the "simplicity and grandeur" of public buildings and noted that "private individuals appear anxious to emulate the example set them by the government, each striving, as far as lies in his power, to contribute to the embellishment of the city." He concluded in a manner of flattery uncommon from visitors to Russia of that day:

And it would not perhaps be amiss if a few of our architects were to pay a visit to the two capitals of Russia which certainly contain many structures that deserve to be more generally known than at present.[3]

---

[1] Cf. A. A. Fedorov-Davydov, *Arkhitektura Moskvy posle otechestvennoi voiny*; *Istoriia Moskvy* 3; Budylina, "Planirovka i zastroika," 135–74. Principal survivors were masonry mansions and churches. Many of these, especially Moscow's seventeenth-century churches, have been demolished in recent years.

[2] The land from the Kitai Gorod Wall to Kuznetskii Bridge was leveled, divided into city blocks, and distributed to favorites, thus opening this area even more.

[3] *Travels in Russia*. 2 vols. (London, 1828) 1: 52–53. Cf. also Grabar', *Iskusstva* 8, i: 23.

The rebuilding of Moscow beckoned both an old and new generation of architects. Fedor Kirillovich Sokolov, long familiar with the Moscow building scene, supervised reconstruction of the Kremlin after the fire. Some of the new faces were Osip Ivanovich Bove (Beauvais), Dementii (Domenico) Ivanovich Giliardi, and Afanasii Grigor'evich Grigor'ev, each of whom made significant contributions to the restored city. Bove, who had studied in the Kremlin Architectural School and assisted both Kazakov and Rossi, became the chief architect of the facade department of the Moscow Committee for Construction. Giliardi, who studied both with his father and at the Milan Academy of Arts, worked extensively on restoration projects and remained in Russia until 1832. Grigor'ev, a serf until he was twenty-two, studied with the elder Giliardi and at the Kremlin School. Often working with Domenico Giliardi in the years after the fire, he turned to eclectic architectural styles toward the end of his long life.

Lesser known but active in restoration efforts were Fedor Mikhailovich Shestakov, Evgraf Dmitrievich Tiurin, A. I. Mironovskii, A. S. Kutepov, and Aleksei Nikitich Bakarev. Mironovskii had studied under Kazakov, Shestakov under Bove, and Tiurin and Kutepov under D. Giliardi. Such accomplished Petersburg architects as Andrei Alekseevich Mikhailov and Vasilii Petrovich Stasov (fig. 45) also participated in rebuilding the Old Capital.

Ensembles of Central Moscow: Kremlin and Kitai Gorod

Extensive restoration of the Kremlin proved unnecessary, for it largely escaped the fire. Upon withdrawing from Moscow, Napoleon had indeed ordered destruction of the Kremlin, but his command was only partially carried out. The French did destroy the Water (*Vodovzvodnaia*), Petrovskaia, and First (*Pervaia*) Towers and portions of the walls in five separate places. The Arsenal suffered damage on its north side along with the Kremlin Wall,

and the marquee over the Borovitskie Gates fell, apparently from the shock of the blast at the Water Tower. Within the Kremlin, fire damaged the Granovitaia Chamber, or Hall of Facets, and the Kremlin Palace. The Bell Tower of Ivan the Great escaped with a vertical crack, but the Petrovskaia and Filapetrovskaia Bell Towers nearby were shattered.[4]

Repairs to the Kremlin did not commence until 1815, and then they took twenty years to complete.[5] Significantly, no new classical ornament adorned the rebuilt fortress. Its most striking addition was the Gothic tower of light metal over the Nikol'skie Gates in 1817–1818 to replace the heavy stone one. After this, the workers whitewashed the walls as well as the Savior, Nikol'skaia, and Trinity Gate Towers; they painted the other tower spires green. Visitors to Moscow remarked, too, about the new paving within the Kremlin walls.

Even visions of a classical Kremlin Palace, which had loomed as a prospect for nearly half a century, reappeared after 1812. Rastrelli's edifice, duly redecorated and regenerated in each successive reign, had never won wide acclaim; moreover it had suffered damage in the fire. Even so, the initial decision was to refurbish it once again. Aleksei Nikitich Bakarev, A. I. Mironovskii, and Ivan T. Tamanskii began repairing it, but it was of no use. The royal entourage had simply outgrown it.

In 1816 a plan submitted by Vasilii Petrovich Stasov (fig. 48) won approval for a new second floor, which projected additions over both the central and side facades and drew attention to the Moscow River approach. Sta-

---

[4] Tikhomirov and V. N. Ivanov, *Moskovskii kreml'*, 206–08.

[5] Osip Bove presented his plans for the reconstruction in January, 1817; this work on the walls and towers was completed in 1835. Thirty years later they again showed signs of wear. The renovation which began in 1866 was under the supervision of the architects N. Shokhin, F. Rikhter, and P. Gerasimov. By the beginning of the present century the walls and towers again required attention. In 1903 a special commission for the Kremlin recommended renovating on an annual basis a tower and that part of the wall which most needed repair. By the outbreak of World War I only the Savior (*Spasskaia*) Tower had been mended. (Ibid., 208–10).

Figure 48. Portrait of the architect Vasilii Petrovich Stasov, 1769–1848 (V. I. Piliavskii, *Stasov: Architektor*. Leningrad, 1963).

Figure 49. Drawing of Stasov's Kremlin Palace (Piliavskii, *Stasov*).

sov's project, when realized, gave new expression to the entire Kremlin ensemble by accenting the hilly area up from the river, as well as the facade itself. Collaborating with L'vov, he exuberantly decorated that side, especially the two stories above the arcaded ground floor (fig. 49). The newly embellished portico, masterfully unorthodox, consisted of four pairs of Ionic columns and an entablature supporting a wide and decorated archivolt. It was pierced in the middle by a large semicircular window. Above all this rested a pediment of the plainest sort. The remainder of the facade contained the usual sculptural ornament—this time four twin columns surmounted by statues symbolizing victory. Stasov specified that these elements, perhaps in a more restrained manner, be used also for the facade in Ivanovskaia Plaza. Although the architect projected the superstructure in brick, he had to settle for wooden facing. Inside, Stasov retained the first-floor rooms which extended the length of the two facades, and in the new second story, projected a similar suite. Although he intended plastered rooms, they were lined with logs in his absence. All this notwithstanding, the interior decorations by Bakarev, Mironovskii, and Tamanskii received high praise. Sergei Glinkov in his *Guide to Moscow* asserted that the palace was decorated in "elegant beauty: the rooms are large and spacious and are marked by very symmetrical measurements."[6]

The task of enlarging the palace continued into the early 1820s; deterioration of this essentially wooden structure from dampness and general disuse increased the need to do something. Plans with several variants were prepared both by Mironovskii and Tiurin (fig. 50).[7] All proposals except one of those from Mironovskii urged the retention of Stasov's redesigned palace and construction of annexes. Some drafts kept the palace within the ensemble as a separate structure or as the symmetrical wing with a new center. Mironovskii's exception called for enlargement. Stasov, urging preservation, suggested a small addition to complete the palace square ensemble. Alexander I's death delayed a decision, for Nicholas I approved none of these plans. Stasov apparently had second thoughts about preserving the palace, for in 1828 he recommended building another. Still, he received no positive response.

The failure of either Stasov or Tiurin to achieve a completely new classical palace effectively ended the project that had begun with Bazhenov, Kazakov, and L'vov in the previous century. When, at the end of the 1830s, the palace of Rastrelli as modified by Stasov was demolished to make room for a new one, its architect, Konstantin Andreevich Ton, employed a quite unclassical Russo-Byzantine style.

Osip Ivanovich Bove, perhaps the least recognized of the important architects of classical Moscow, inspired many important changes in central Moscow after 1812 (figs. 51–52a,b).[8] His work on the Red and Theater Squares, on the Bol'shoi Theater, and in the Manezh area, determined the character of central Moscow from that day until our own. In Red Square he continued work on the commercial rows which had been initiated in the 1780s. The earlier construction had not particularly enhanced the square's appearance: the three separate rows of shops—along the Kremlin Wall, on the opposite side of the square, and, finally, those obscuring St. Basil's—had effectively transformed the square into an oblong and closed yard. Because he discerned little artistic value in these buildings and because

---

[6] See V. I. Piliavskii, "K istorii kremlevskogo dvortsa v Moskve," *Izvestiia Vysshikh Uchebnykh Zavedenii Ministerstva Vysshego i Srednego Spetsial'nogo Obrazovaniia SSSR. Stroitel'stvo i Arkhitektura* (Novosibirsk, 1962), No. 5, 145–154. A briefer account of Stasov's plan for a Kremlin palace is to be found in Piliavskii, *Stasov, Arkhitektor* (Leningrad, 1963), 76–79.

[7] Some of these variants appear in both Tikhomirov, *Kreml'* and Piliavskii, "K istorii kremlevskogo dvortsa."

[8] Osip Ivanovich Bove, or Beauvais (1784–1834), was born in Petersburg, but his family moved to Moscow before the end of the century. After initially studying under Camporesi, he worked with M. F. Kazakov in the Kremlin Department and in Petersburg under the architect Karl Ivanovich Rossi. (Cf. S. N. Sil'versvan, *Arkhitektor O. I. Bove* [Moscow, 1964], Grabar', *Iskusstva* 8, i, 191–92 and Z. V. Zolotnitskaia, *Arkhitektor Osip Bove* [Moscow, 1986]).

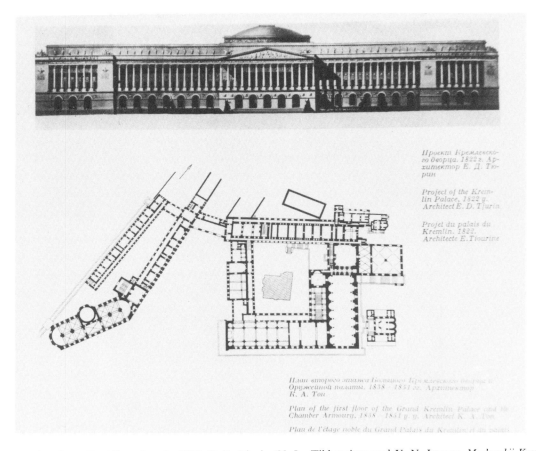

Figure 50. Project for a Kremlin palace in 1822, E. D. Tiurin (N. Ia. Tikhomirov and V. N. Ivanov, *Moskovskii Kreml'*. Moscow, 1967).

Figure 51. Red Square after the Great Fire showing ruins and the facade of the Commercial Rows (Donskoi, V-22002).

Figure 52a. Commercial Rows in Red Square as restored in 1815, architect Osip Ivanovich Bove (1784–1834). (Donskoi, V-22003).

Figure 52b. Portrait of Osip Bove (1784–1834) (Z. V. Zolotnitskaia, *Arkhitektor Osip Ivanovich Bove.* Moscow, 1986).

the fire damage had been extensive, Bove persuaded the Commission in January, 1814, to authorize razing those shops along the wall and around the cathedral and altering those on the east side, where GUM presently stands.

Bove embellished the facade of this building, the Upper Retail Row block, with twin columns, which appeared to support the arcade's archivolt and elevate the building's center. Both portico and cupola, which served no functional purpose, formed a diametrical axis with the dome of the Senate Building visible across Red Square. In emphasizing building length by introducing an architrave across the arcade and dividing the structure into three harmonious sections, Bove remained faithful to the then current architectural principle that elegant commercial buildings should be prominently displayed in the main square of the city.[9] To give it even greater dignity, the sculptor Ivan Petrovich Martos unveiled before the main portico his classical monument to the peasant heroes of the Time of Troubles, Minin and Pozharskii.

Enlarged and paved, moat and bridges gone, Red Square benefited from the changes after 1812. On the site of the moat (filled in 1817–1819), Vasil'evskaia Square appeared south of the Savior Gates, between the Kremlin Wall and St. Basil's Cathedral. From this square, an easy descent to the Moscow River was achieved by severing the crest of the hill and leveling this plaza to the point that the obstructed Konstantino-Eleninskaia Tower Gate had to be sealed. St. Basil's thus crowned the summit of a decapitated hillock. With the shops and other surrounding buildings removed, Red Square was, in part, opened to the river.[10]

Moscow's second great plaza, Petrovskaia (eventually Theater) Square, finally became a reality after 1812. Although long envisioned, the actual molding of the expanse had always been prevented by the "contemptible" Neglinnaia. After the fire, the Commission decided that insufficient water flow and pollution warranted enclosing the stream in an underground pipe. During the years 1817 through 1819, the river was replaced completely by the radial Neglinnaia Street, which had been constructed parallel to the river-canal just a short time before.

With the Neglinnaia encased, work on Theater Square began soon after the renewal of Red Square. Designing it required the efforts

of the best architects in the empire. Andrei Alekseevich Mikhailov came from Petersburg to join Bove, and the two worked on both design and construction from 1816 to 1824. Bove conceived the plaza as a true rectangle, perpendicular to the road with the longest side skirting the Kremlin-Kitai Gorod assemblage. Because the axis of the site pointed toward the center, the square even accentuated converging radial streets.

In size Theater Square surpassed even St. Peter's in Rome and the Place de la Concorde in Paris (fig. 53).[11] Okhotnyi Riad on the west side and the Theater Passage on the east formed a diametrical axis for the square, just as the Bol'shoi Theater constituted the longitudinal one. On its two long sides, the square was enveloped by four low buildings, which, except for the Little (*Malyi*) Theater on the northeast side, have been demolished.[12] Their corners, where the streets pierced the square, were cubed; the middle floors had shallow loggias with half-columns; and the lower stories, small arcades. If Theater Square had been permitted to extend longitudinally to the Kitai Gorod, it would not have been a precise rectangle. For that reason, a triangular piece of land near the wall was converted into a square facing the Bol'shoi. Resurrection Square, linked with Theater Square to the entrance to Red Square, opened a perspective to both the Aleksandrovskii Garden and Pashkov House.

In designing Theater Square, Moscow architects had an unusual building opportunity; they worked with open and hitherto unused space, thereby avoiding the need to reconcile their new creations with existing ones. A monumental structure, which would dominate both this square and adjacent buildings, was

---

[9] Bove's project was the first Upper Retail Row block and was later replaced by Pomerantsev's building in the National Style, GUM. Muscovites enjoyed perching on top Bove's structure to observe military parades in Red Square. Its splendid facade did but mask the chaotic housing that lay behind it. The Minin and Pozharskii statue now stands before St. Basil's.

[10] See sytin, *Ulits*, 85.

[11] The Plaza spanned an area of 11.6 acres.

[12] A number of other architects were involved in these. The Senate Printing (1818–1821) House (on the site of the present Stereokino) was the work of the architect I. Matveev. A. Elkinskii was responsible (1820–1824) for the merchant V. V. Vargin's home, which eventually became the Malyi Theater. The other two belonged to the Poltoratskii and Chelyshev families. The fountain in the square was I. P. Vitali's. (See *Monuments* 2:248 for a recent photograph of the fountain).

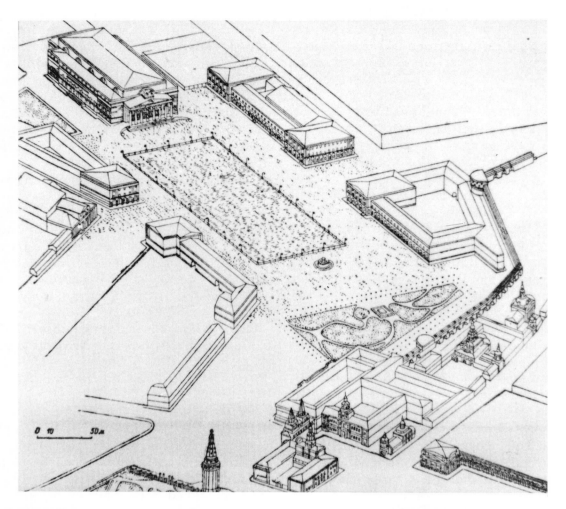

Figure 53. Theater Square (planned 1821) after building of the Bol'shoi Theater 1821–1825 (Donskoi, V-32721).

exactly what Mikhailov and Bove had in mind for the site of the burned-out Petrovskii, or Maddox, Theater. Built to a height of ninety-eight feet between 1821–1825 their Bol'shoi Theater corresponded to a one to six ratio with the length of the plaza (fig. 54a,b). By lowering all lateral wings and buildings to uniform height, they balanced the horizontal plaza against the vertical theater. Similarly, Bove and Mikhailov invited a study in contrast between the arcades at the corners of the side buildings and the theater's great portico and colonnade.[13]

The Bol'shoi Theater was originally rectangular in plan and embellished in front with an eight-column, fifty-foot Ionic portico (fig. 55). Its low lateral parts were divided into three stories with plain facades except for horizontal rustication. The middle of the building was heightened and overlapped by a hip roof, beneath which a straight cornice traversed the entire building. On the main facade this elevated portion of the building possessed a blank wall with a deep semicircular niche, in the manner of Ledoux. In it sat Apollo in his chariot, crowning the portico. A grand staircase, main foyer, five-tier audience hall, and stage, completed the interior, while a fountain on the axis with the Kremlin was placed in front.

---

[13] The theater, conceived by Mikhailov, was built by Bove. For more on the Bol'shoi Theater building, see Iu. D. Khripunov, *Arkhitektura Bol'shogo teatra* (Moscow, 1955).

Figure 54a. Theater Square after 1856 (Donskoi, VIII).

Figure 54b. View of Theater Square from the Bol'shoi Theater. Lithograph, middle of the nineteenth century (Donskoi, V-26144).

Figure 55. The Bol'shoi Theater (1821–1825), architects A. A. Mikhailov and O. I. Bove (Donskoi, VIII).

When the theater burned in the 1850s, the architect, Al'bert Katarinovich Kavos made some basic changes (fig. 56). He transformed the simple Ionic portico into a larger, deeper one and altered the facade by adding windows and pilasters to the lateral parts, rusticating the entire lower section of the building, and substituting a gable with a pediment for the hip roof. In eliminating the Apollo niche, he substituted arched windows and pilasters and brought the Apollo group to the pinnacle of the portico. Although Kavos significantly altered one of the masterworks of Russian Classicism—for much the worse—the building did retain its monumental image in the vast plaza. Osip Bove thus left his mark on Moscow: his commercial rows in Red Square pointed toward the ancient Kitai Gorod buildings and silhouetted Kremlin towers; his Bol'shoi Theater and Square, framed by elongated buildings on both sides, approached the spectacular when viewed from the walls of the Kitai Gorod.

This same architect also contributed to the Kremlin's west wall after 1812. There, on what once had been the banks of the old Neglinnaia, he set out the Aleksandrovskii Garden, called by Lyall "a magnificent ornament and an elegant promenade" (fig. 57).[14] These grounds, nearly twenty-two acres in all, took their name from the tsar, who, after visiting Moscow in 1820, determined that a garden be laid out. Previous efforts to improve the appearance of this area had met with failure; the old river bed lay filled with refuse, while the new Neglinnaia and its basins produced only a pittance of water. The protruding bastions, buttressed by rows of logs at their base and separated near the wall of the Kremlin by great earthen curtains, had inhibited all efforts to order this region. Only when the Neglinnaia was diverted into a pipe and the bastions demolished did the planting of the Aleksandrovskii Garden become feasible.[15]

Three separate gardens were artistically laid out beneath the walls and towers of the Kremlin. The Upper Garden, which opened in 1821, was approximately 383 yards in length and extended from Resurrection Square to the Trinity Gates of the Kremlin. A Middle Garden, reaching from the Trinity to the Borovitskie Gates, was 428 yards long and opened the next year. Finally, a Lower Garden, stretching 144 yards from the Borovitskie Gates to the Kremlin Embankment, opened in 1823.

An iron gate and fence, by the architect E. Paskal', bordered the Aleksandrovskii Garden in Resurrection Square. Decorative paving of the walks and cobblestone streets outside the fence and gate also enhanced the gardens' entrance. In that same location, beneath the Arsenal Tower, Bove constructed a grotto, and opposite it, an arch on an axis with the radial Great Nikitskaia (fig. 58). In such a way, the grotto, its polished Doric colonnade sharply contrasting with the rough stone around it, became an integral part of Moscow's classical center. The side gates and the fence of the gardens, conceived by architect Fedor Mikhailovich Shestakov in 1822, were lighter and not so high as those at the main entrance in the Resurrection Plaza. Shestakov therefore harmonized this gate (opposite the Manezh) with Paskal's grille in Resurrection Plaza by employing the latter's leaf motif. He also repeated this leaf design between two posts, decorated on top with iron bas-reliefs and crowned with copper balls. For a time, even the iron curbstone edging of the limestone block sidewalk contained a flower motif, associating it with the fence pattern.

Piping the Neglinnaia permitted not only creation of Aleksandrovskii Garden but also a new street skirting the gardens and Kremlin on the west side. Appropriately called Neglin-

---

[14] Lyall, *Moscow*, 525. This was also called the Kremlin Gardens.

[15] Besides the old and new Neglinnaia Rivers and the basin between Resurrection Square and the Trinity Gate, a dam by

Trinity Bridge had also to be eliminated. By the dam stood a state-owned mill used for private manufacture of brick and cement; its occupant had a vegetable garden between the Trinity and Borovitskie (formerly Predtechenskie) Gates. Other mills were located below the Borovitskii Bridge, near the Vodozvodnaia Tower late in the eighteenth century. (See *Monuments* 2: 260–62, for recent photographs of the gardens).

Figure 56. The remodeled Bol'shoi Theater (1856), architect A. K. Kavos (Donskoi, VIII-19962).

Figure 57. Aleksandrovskie Gardens and the iron gates (early 1820s) surrounding them with the Manezh in the right background, architects O. I. Bove, F. M. Shestakov, and E. Paskal' (Donskoi, OC-1978).

Figure 58. Grotto in Aleksandrovskii Garden (early 1820s), architect O. I. Bove (Schmidt).

naia (at least until the 1930s), it extended from Resurrection Square to the Borovitskie Gates and measured 998 yards in length and nearly 20 yards in width. Paved in 1820, when work on the gardens had begun in earnest, it was further enhanced by the massive classical Manezh which lined its other side.

The Manezh (*manège*, now the Central Exposition Hall), or Exercise House, was conceived by the Emperor Alexander I as a complex large enough to house and drill an infantry regiment and allow the cavalry to exercise their mounts (figs. 59a,b). It was viewed by the rest of Europe as a kind of secret Russian weapon to gain hegemony. Whatever its military merit, the Manezh as a building was massive in size though quite simple in design. One of Napoleon's generals, Auguste de Béthencourt, who headed the Authority of Roads and Public Buildings in Russia—designed the Manezh; actual construction was left to another French general,

P. L. Carbonier. Béthencourt's plan, approved by the emperor on 10 June 1817, was for a building measuring 545 × 147 feet; it was completed before the end of the year.

Thick-walled, especially at its foundation, where the columns rested, this building was distinguished by 1) a rhythmic Doric colonnade which enveloped the entire building (the walls being between the columns) and 2) an expansive ceiling, which from within had no columnar support. Powerful and arched apertures, either windows or doors, pierced the thick walls between the columns. For the ceiling, Béthencourt required wooden supports, which extended across the width of the building. These, as it happened, had to be repaired within the year and were completely replaced in 1824 when Osip Bove, by that time architect for the city of Moscow, entered the Manezh enterprise. In 1824–1825, Bove added sculpture and stucco ornament to both the inside and outside of the Manezh. He also deter-

Figure 59a. The Manezh built by P. L. Carbonier according to a plan by A. A. Béthencourt, 1817; architectural finish by O. I. Bove, 1824–1825 (Schmidt).

Figure 59b. View of the Manezh and Kutaf'ia Tower; watercolor by M. Vorob'ev, 1810s (Donskoi).

mined that no decoration should be placed in the huge pediments at either the building's east or west ends. The martial theme in these decorations typified the then current heroic and romantic sentiment.

The Manezh fascinated European visitors, curious about Russian architecture and suspicious of Russian military aspirations. Edward P. Thompson noted in the 1840s that

> The arm of power is not allowed to rest or become inactive from want of practice or from discipline which might arise from the length and severity of the winter by preventing drill and other military exercises, and therefore immense riding schools are constructed capable of permitting manoeuvres of very considerable bodies of troops. The principal one of these is really as regards its roof, an astonishing piece of architecture. . . . The Russians are undoubtedly masters in the art of of roof-building.[16]

Opposite the Manezh and facing the Kremlin from the Mokhovaia stood monumental Moscow University, dating from the 1780s. Seriously racked by the fire, it received a remarkable restoration in 1817–1819 by Domenico Giliardi (fig. 60).[17] The restored edifice brought Giliardi nearly as much fame as it had Kazakov a generation earlier (figs. 61a,b). Giliardi strengthened and raised by some twenty-one feet the central portico and topped it with a flat cupola. More notably, he substituted a Doric octastyle for its Ionic original with a raised parapet; by removing the

ters, he left the expansive facade smooth except for columns, cubicles, and bas-relief sculptures. Separate windows, framed by two-columned porticoes with parapets instead of pediments, pierced the rear and side facades, thereby breaking the monotony of the smooth walls on those sections of the building. To brighten this facade Giliardi whitewashed the columns and sculptures and washed the walls in yellow, the color most often applied then as now to these buildings in Moscow's center. Behind the columns of the main portico he placed a bas-relief representation of the triumph of science and art. The second-story windows he closed and replaced. Familiar motifs of lions' masks, shields with Medusa heads, torches, and palmettos embellished the keystones between the columns, along the axis of windows.

Giliardi's masterful restoration of the main university building has overshadowed other elements of this classical assemblage. A. G. Grigor'ev contributed the University Pharmacy in 1821. Even more significantly, Giliardi's student Evgraf Dmitrievich Tiurin transformed in 1833–1836 some of Kazakov's old buildings on the Pashkov grounds into new university structures. His most important creation was the University Church at the corner of Mokhovaia and Nikitskaia. Its "crown of columns," a colonnaded Doric half rotunda, compositionally linked the semicircular wing of Giliardi's main building to the Manezh across the plaza. In the estimation of one critic, Tiurin's building consummated this entire ensemble.

Like the university, Bazhenov's old Pashkov House also required restoration; however, in the end it changed little from its original appearance. These restorations and the completion of Theater Square, the Manezh, and Aleksandrovskii Garden imposed on the area the stamp of Empire classicism, which has endured to our time. These central squares were essentially non-residential. The Empire residences, like those of Catherine's day, occupied the radial thoroughfares leading into them.

---

[16] *Life in Russia: or The Discipline of Despotism* (London, 1848), 282. (See *Monuments* 2: 256–58, for recent photographs of the Manezh).

[17] Dementii (Domenico) Ivanovich Giliardi (1788–1845), Bove, and Grigor'ev were the outstanding architects in Moscow during the years after the Great Fire. Called Domenico, he received his first architectural instruction from his father Ivan (Giovanni) under whom he worked at the Foundling Home. After study in Italy young Giliardi returned to Russia where in 1810 he was named architect of the Foundling Home. During the course of the next twenty years he acquired fame building for the nobility and merchants of Moscow. His first important work was that of rebuilding the university, severely damaged by the fire. (Cf. Grabar', *Iskusstva* 8, i: 207–08 and E. Beletskaia, "Vosstanovlenie zdanii Moskovskogo universiteta posle pozhara 1812 goda," *Arkhitekturnoe nasledstvo* 1 [1951]: 175–90). No satisfactory biography of either Giliardi exists. (See *Monuments* 2: 249–53, for recent photographs of the university).

Figure 60. Portrait of Domenico Giliardi, 1788–1845. (Donskoi, V-6540).

The Radial Thoroughfares

The arterial highways of the Belyi Gorod and Zemlianoi Gorod contained a more diverse population after 1812. Grandees and gentry were joined by wealthy merchants, a combination that changed both the tone and appearance of the thoroughfares. Then, too, many great houses had burned, leaving only charred shells. When rebuilt, they usually emerged in a much altered form.

On the Volkhonka and Prechistenka, where such old families as the Lopukhins, Vsevolzhskies, and Khrushchevs returned after 1812, the homes once again became among the most elegant in Moscow. One such house was that of the Seleznevs, (or Khrushchevs, 1814 or 1820), said to have been the work of Grigor'ev (fig. 62a,b).[18]

_____

[18] Afanasii Grigor'evich Grigor'ev's (1782–1868) background is obscure, but it is certain that he was born a serf and

Figure 61a. Restored Moscow University (1817–1819) on the Okhotnyi Riad, architect D. Giliardi (Schmidt).

Figure 61b. Moscow University facade detail (Schmidt).

Figure 62a. Seleznev House (1814 or 1820) on the Prechistenka, architect A. G. Grigor'ev (Schmidt).

Figure 62b. Facade and columns Seleznev House (Schmidt).

Situated on the Prechistenka and flanked by Khrushchevskii Alley in front and Chertolskii in the rear, this building was judged to be among the best produced by Russia's Empire architects. Its asymmetric composition—main section, wings, and auxiliary buildings—has especially caught the fancy of admirers of the Empire mode. Because the house rested on an earlier foundation, it did not correspond to the line of Khrushchevskii Alley. To overcome this problem, the architect built a ground floor along this line and created a terrace or verandah on the first-floor level, matched by one in the rear facing the garden.

The main corpus of Seleznev House, on the corner, had two street facades. The one on the Prechistenka carried a six-column Ionic portico, resting on a lower half-story. The facade itself struck a monumental note, protruding as it did from smooth walls and delicate rustication around the windows. Conversely, the alley facade was one of greater intimacy, enhanced by a decorative portico of eight columns arranged in pairs and a metal grille which followed the line of the verandah. A pediment, level with the roof of the first story, crowned the alley portico. In contrast, the street portico substituted an open balcony with a receding mezzanine for a pediment; the balcony was covered with a two-slope roof.

The Seleznev garden facade was warm and simple like those on the Khrushchevskii and Chertolskii Alleys. Grigor'ev reiterated these qualities by placing a small pavilion on the Chertolskii along which he built a stone wall for privacy. Both the street and alley facades received bas-relief sculptures from Ivan Petrovich Vitali. The reception rooms inside lay

in a straight line, an *enfilade*, while family rooms occupied a corner in the rear of the house and the mezzanine. The interior throughout was radiant with wall and ceiling paintings.

On the opposite side of the street from Seleznev House stood the Lopukhin (Stanitskaia) House (figs. 62c and 63), a creation of Grigor'ev between1817 and 1822.[19] Somewhat less elegant than the Seleznev, the Lopukhin House with its one-story mezzanine and six columned Ionic portico reached forward to the street. Its facade was articulated by rustication around the three lateral windows, great (a story high) bas-reliefs over the windows beneath the portico, and a decorative frieze. While the proportions of this small house were excellent, the axis did not correspond to the placement of the rooms along the main facade. The enfilade of reception rooms along the street and side drive commenced from the side entrance. The mezzanine and rear ground floor accommodated the family. The interior decor of Lopukhin House, while inferior to that of Seleznev, nonetheless, possessed a very special charm.

Another Empire mansion of note in the Prechistenka was that belonging to the Samsonovs. Its first story was surmounted by a four-windowed gable and a facade dominated by a six-column, nearly full-length, portico. That of Okhotnikovs, also in the Prechistenka, was of greater dimension and more expertly designed than the Samsonov House. Distinctive features were its street facade with an octastyle Doric portico and a balustrade between columns. Platband and bas-reliefs accentuated the horizontal; voluted columns and pilasters the vertical.[20] In addition to these new houses, many antedating 1812 were restored in the Empire style.

On the Ostozhenka which forked toward the river from the Prechistenka, the aristocracy resided as before 1812. Grigor'ev built a

given his freedom in August, 1804. Having received some architectural instruction in the Giliardi home in 1802–1803, he entered the architectural school of the Kremlin Department subsequent to his manumission. (See Elena A. Beletskaia, *Arkhitektor Afanasii Grigor'evich Grigor'ev, 1782–1868* (Moscow, 1976) and V. I. Baldin, *Arkhitektor A. G. Grigor'ev* (Moscow, 1976). Among the earliest examples of his artistry were his drafts for the wings of the Indigents Hospital in 1804. (See A. G. Vvedenskaia, "Arkhitektor A. G. Grigor'ev i ego graficheskoe nasledie," *Arkhitekturnoe nasledstvo* 9 [1957]: 106–16. For recent photographs of the Seleznev House, see *Monuments* 2: 308–11).

[19] See *Monuments* 2: 315, for a recent photograph.
[20] For recent photographs of the Samsonovs and Okhotnikov mansions, see *Monuments* 2: 290, 292–93.

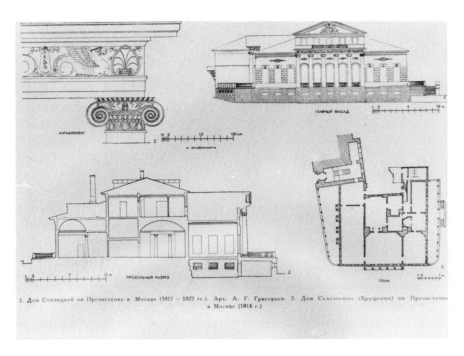

Figure 62c. Drawing of Seleznev House (Brunov, *Istoriia*).

Figure 63. Lopukhinor Stanitskaia House, architect A. G. Grigor'ev (Schmidt).

163

palatial estate house for the Grand Duke Mikhail Pavlovich. While only one wing presently remains, architectural plans and representations reveal that the original was a corpus with a great portico of six Ionic columns. A variant of this plan depicted the central section of the Grand Duke's mansion as two stories and crowned with a cupola. It contained, moreover, a ten-columned loggia resting on a rusticated ground floor. Smooth upper walls balanced the lower. Both in this variant and in the design ultimately used, the cupola served as a canopy for the round hall in the center of the building.[21]

The elegance of the Prechistenka-Ostozhenka did not apply to all Moscow's radials. Changing social configuration altered the arterial Znamenka and Vozdvizhenka almost as much as the conflagration. Merchants and minor officials occupied the smaller masonry houses built on both these streets. The same was true of the Arbat area, where smaller homes like Shchepochkina House in Spasopeskovskii Lane, gave it a pervasive classical image (fig. 64).[22] Built about 1820, it was distinguished by its non-freestanding portico of four Ionic columns linked by three arches beneath a small pediment. This exquisite house with its mid-eighteenth-century side gate represented the best of the building in the Arbat construction after 1812.

The most important Empire mansion in the nearby Povarskaia was one designed by Domenico Giliardi and built for Prince S. S. Gagarin in 1820.[23] Giliardi began this construction soon after he finished restoring the University. Like Bove's Gagarin House on Novinskii Boulevard, it differed fundamentally from the great houses. Both were smaller and simpler; neither reposed behind a grand entrance court nor extended to the street. Instead, access to each came by way of a small

garden. Giliardi's Gagarin facade, one of the loveliest in new Moscow, won distinction by the decor of its center section, an effective counterpoise to the smooth walls on each side. It was principally articulated by three large semicircular windows, divided by pedimented columns. Rustication across the entire lower floor unified the front facade. Standing as it did perpendicular to the street, the rear facade consequently became the main one. The interior of Gagarin House revealed no evident axis, although taken as a whole the building was quite symmetrical to a line. The cross-line was emphasized more than the longitudinal, especially in the central portion. Wall and ceiling paintings and drawings of garlands and wreaths enriched the interior.

Because the radial streets in the western Belyi and Zemlianoi Gorod remained predominantly residential and aristocratic, exemplars of Empire Classicism—the Seleznev, Lopukhin and Gagarin houses—were found there. Farther east the radials changed in their social configuration. The Great Nikitskaia and its adjacent alleys, having escaped heavy damage from the fire, retained their classical look even as properties there passed to minor gentry and merchants. In nearby Starogazetnyi (formerly Stroganovskii) Alley, between the Great Nikitskaia and the Tverskaia, the long-resident and princely Trubetskoi, Menshikov, Novosil'tsov, Stroganov, Naumov, Panin, and Golitsyn families gradually gave way to merchant occupants.

Mercantile people similarly invaded the Tverskaia, the appearance of which was altered somewhat after 1812 by the construction of shoe, dress, and jewelry establishments and pharmacies in masonry buildings; moreover, six of Moscow's seven hotels were also located in this street. The fire inflicted little damage on Kazakov's Tverskaia Square, yet many houses around it were subsequently taken over by merchants who used their lower floors for shops. Despite this turn to commerce, the square continued to be identified most of all with the residence of the military governor. On the Tverskaia, between the Boulevard and

---

[21] Grabar', *Iskusstva* 8, i:233–34.

[22] See *Monuments* 2: 174–75, for recent photographs.

[23] For a discussion of the Gagarin House see Grabar', *Iskusstva* 8, i: 212–13. For recent photographs, see *Monuments* 2: 312–14.

Figure 64. Shchepochkina House in Spasopeskovskii Lane (1820) (Schmidt).

Garden Rings, the most visible classical assemblages were the Razumovskii Palace and the civilian governor's house opposite it. Pushkin briefly referred to this marvelous thoroughfare in *Eugene Onegin*. Describing Tatiana's entrance into the city, he sped her carriage along the Tverskaia, past pharmacies, fashion shops, lions on a gate, and blackbirds on the crosses.[24] The lions belonged to the Razu-

movskii Palace, which after 1812 was rebuilt by Menelas as the English Club. It was prominent for not only its Doric Gates surmounted by lions, but its great eight-column Doric portico facing the Tverskaia. By 1820 stagecoaches, having replaced the "troika," raced along this street carrying passengers to and from Petersburg. All this elegance notwithstanding, the Tverskaia was not the Nevskii Prospekt, at least for visitors from the capital. The critic Belinskii wrote that

> Upon entering Moscow for the first time, our Petersburgian enters into a new world. He

[24] From 7: 38. The complete canto imparts an enchanting description of the Tverskaia, beginning at Kazakov's Petrovskii Palace on the city's outskirts.

> Farewell now, scene of grandeur humbled,
> Petrovsky Palace; onward fast!
> And presently the carriage rumbled
> Toward the shining tollgate; past
> The barrier, and on it hobbles
> Across Tverskaya's holes and cobbles,
> Past shops and lanterns, crones and youths,
> By convents, gardens, mansions, booths,
> Bokharans, sleighs, muzhiks in blouses,

> By cossacks, merchants, kitchen yards,
> Past battlements and boulevards,
> Parks, pharmacies, and fashion houses,
> Past gates where guardian lions rear,
> While daws about the crosses veer.

(This translation is by Walter Arndt, New York, 1963).

will look for the main or best Moscow street in order to compare it with the Nevskii Prospekt. He will be shown the Tverskaia and with amazement he will find himself in the middle of a crooked, narrow, upward stretching street with a square on one side. . . . One house juts out a few steps onto the street, another a few steps back, seemingly because of haughtiness or modesty depending upon its exterior. . . . An old, wooden house fits cozily and modestly between two rather large stone buildings.[25]

The arterial streets immediately east of the Tverskaia, the Dmitrovka and the Petrovka, while retaining affluence, also lost many of their aristocratic residents. This was more true of the Great Dmitrovka, where houses in the classical idiom reached two stories on the street and three toward the yard side, than of the Little Dmitrovka, which continued as a noble habitat until the second half of the nineteenth century. The Petrovka—where the Princess Lobanov-Rostovskii, the Sibirskies, and the Shcherbatovs had lived at the end of the previous century, and where, too, Bazhenov had built the Annenkova house and Bove a splendid one for Prince Shcherbatov in 1800—increasingly attracted *nouveaux riches*.

Neglinnaia Street, which had initially paralleled the canal a short distance below Trubnaia Square, assumed a new significance in the radial network of restored Moscow. By 1822 the street had merely replaced the river. As the street converged on the western fringe of Theater Square, it measured 87.25 feet in width; lots along it varied from 56 to 69 feet in width and were sold with the stipulation that masonry houses, not exceeding 30.2 feet in height, be built upon them. For this reason, Neglinnaia Street, during the 1820s, acquired many two-story houses. On the corner of Neglinnaia and Pushechnaia Streets a Military School for Orphans was built in 1822.

Although Kuznetskii Bridge developed into

a crowded commercial quarter during the nineteenth century, the thoroughfares north of it—the Rozhdestvenskaia, Lubianka, and Miasnitskaia—retained their rural look. Zagoskin described these contrasting images:

> Walk along the wide street which is called the Truba (Pipe) and you will immediately be sent to another world! Behind you, within five or ten steps, boils the city of the capital in its full debauchery. One carriage thunders after another; mobs of pedestrians crowd on the paved sidewalks; all the houses bear magnificent French advertisements; noise, tumult, crowds. . . . And in front and at your sides everything is quiet and restful. From time to time a cab will go by, a peasant with a cart, two neighbors in prehistoric coats will stop to chat. . . . Maids in simple peasant dress are going to get water with their pails. On the street there are chickens wandering around, sometimes geese, and from time to time you will have the luck to see a fat sow walking with her piglets. I, at least, have met these interesting animals not only on the Truba, but also on the Rozhdestvenskii Boulevard.[26]

After the demolition of the walls of the Rozhdestvenskii Monastery in 1782, the Rozhdestvenka had been widened from 27.9 to 62.3 feet. After the fire, the square above Theater Passage was divided into city blocks with housing heights set at the usual 29.8 feet limit. Some lots on the Rozhdestvenka lay empty until 1818, when a new plan was drawn up for the area.

East of the Rozhdestvenka, new construction changed the appearance of the Great Lubianka and Miasnitskaia after 1812. In the former, merchants in their diverse shops and dwellings continued to live in the midst of nobles' estates; in the Miasnitskaia, which continued as a haven for gentry after 1812, masonry residences were most characteristic of the reconstruction. In the Zemlianoi Gorod, where the Miasnitskaia widened to 82 feet, old stone structures which survived the fire

---

[25] Quoted in G. S. Dukel'skii et al., *Moskva: arkhitekturnyi putevoditel'* (Moscow, 1960) 205; see Belinskii, *Peterburg i Moskva*. 3 vols. (Moscow, 1949) 2: 768. See *Monuments* 2: 273–76, for recent photographs of Menelas's English Club.

[26] Quoted in Sytin, *Ulits*, 245.

Figure 65. The Adoption Council (*Opekunskii sovet*, 1823–26), architects D. I. Giliardi and A. G. Grigor'ev (Schmidt).

often obstructed attempts to regulate the street. In all, the Miasnitskaia had a pleasing appearance. Pushkin, bored with traveling, remembered it fondly:

> Can it compare with being there,
> With riding down the Miasnitskaia
> With dreaming leisurely
> Of the country, of my betrothed![27]

The Solianka, the final Belyi Gorod radial after the Miasnitskaia, terminated with an array of classical edifices at the Iauzskie Gates, where a bridge spanned the Iauza. Eventually the gates were demolished, and the Solianka continued as another street. Until 1805, the Iauzskii Bridge was wooden. Even the stone bridge which replaced it lay undistinguished among wooden houses, over which Tutolmin House towered from the hill beyond. Generally the most important houses in the Solianka dated from the eighteenth century—the

Foundling Home, the estates of the Volkonskies, Naryshkins, and General Buturlin.

The outstanding architectural creation in the Solianka after 1812 was a structure which housed the Adoption Council (*Opekunskii sovet*), a loan bank that financed the Foundling Center (fig. 65).[28] Built between 1823 and 1826 by Domenico Giliardi with the probable assistance of Grigor'ev, this ensemble facing the Solianka consisted of three two-story buildings, a main section and two wings. These wings were linked to the central corpus by a stone wall and smaller square buildings in back.[29] The main building boasted a massive eight-column portico stretching across a bare wall, capped by a low dome. Possessed of simplicity and clarity, this building rested on a rectangular base and lay latitudinally on the regulated line of the street. Steps led to the

---

[27] Quoted ibid., 256–57.

[28] See *Monuments* 2: 266–69, for recent photographs.
[29] In the 1840s the stone wall was reconstructed as a gallery and the buildings linked as one.

portals at the base of its massive portico, while the cupola extended over the vestibule, rather than the main hall. The back of the building, like the front, had smooth walls which served as a backdrop for Vitali sculptures on each side of the stairway. Bas-reliefs behind the columns, in the frieze, on the pediment, above the window in the dome drum, and over the windows of the main building's lateral facade as well as a decorative fence reduced the severity of the assemblage. Giliardi fashioned the main hall, extending along the building's longitudinal axis and divided by two rows of columns, into one of Moscow's most radiant Empire period rooms.

The post-1812 Solianka almost acquired another important edifice, a new pharmacy.[30] A pharmacy and laboratory had stood by the Foundling Home, near the Varvarskie Gates and the Solianka, since 1768. After their destruction in 1812, the task of building a new one fell to Ivan Giliardi, who opted for a location nearby, at the driveway to the Found-

ling Home. The pharmacy's design suggests that both Ivan and Domenico Giliardi engaged in the project, for it bore the mark of the younger's later work. They proposed a two-story structure with a central portico rising from the ground floor. Its facade texture and structure were diverse—smooth top story, a protruding central section, and a rusticated lower facade. The Giliardis also designed a similarly imposing portico—two columns beneath an arched entrance—for the smaller laboratory side. This effort notwithstanding the pharmacy and laboratory failed to materialize, both abandoned because of excessive costs.

The restoration of the radial thoroughfares in the Belyi Gorod revealed a changing pattern of building after the fire. While Moscow's aristocracy resided there as they had in Catherine's reign, they allowed commerce and such public buildings as the Adoption Council in their midst. This new configuration of construction did not mean a lessening of the quality of the architecture, for the thoroughfares, as before, exhibited the best of Moscow classicism.

---

[30] See N. Krasheninnikova, "Proekt apteki pri Vospitatel'-nom dome," *Arkhitekturnoe nasledstvo* 1 (1951): 197–99.

CHAPTER X

The Outer Reaches of the New Classical Moscow: The Boulevard and Garden Rings and Beyond

The concentric boulevards of central Moscow changed more dramatically after 1812 than did the radial thoroughfares. The disappearance of the Belyi Gorod Walls, gates, and towers after 1750, it must be remembered, did not result in an instant emergence of a Boulevard Ring. The Great Fire, however, swept away miscellaneous construction which had mushroomed on the site of the old rampart. Within two decades both the completed Ring and its plazas did become a reality. New and rebuilt masonry houses lined the Ring to help make it an ever-popular and "enchanting" place for strolling, as the English lady, Mrs. Wilmot, observed.[1]

The Prechistenskii Embankment and Boulevard at the Moscow River were shorn of wooden structures and completed soon after 1812. In Arbat Square, log and frame dwellings had vanished even before the fire. East of it, at the Nikitskie Gates, rose the Church of the Great Ascension.[2] Built during the 1820s by Grigor'ev, it was a pleasant, though not exceptional, edifice. Lacking the striking bell tower which its author gave to his Church

of the Trinity "in Vishniaki," it followed the plan of a Greek cross, had an Ionic portico with a grille balustrade rather than a pediment, and possessed a notable frieze on a smooth facade. Its rotunda and cupola were matched by a half cupola over the apse.

On the Nikitskii Boulevard Domenico Giliardi built between 1818 and 1823 one of Moscow's most important urban estates, Lunin House (fig. 66).[3] Three buildings formed this asymmetrical assemblage which extended to the street. Its three-story main block, visible from the Arbat, comprised a smaller two-story wing on one side and a single-floor auxiliary structure on the other. Giliardi departed from the eighteenth-century practice of placing the central block in the middle of the estate; the parts in this whole varied in form and size despite a continuous facade along the Boulevard. Most satisfying in this long frontage was the portico of the smaller wing. Because its evenly spaced columns extended farther apart at the center, the Ionic portico protruded and rested on a ground-floor podium. The windows, surmounted with wreaths but without jambs, bestowed warmth and informality on this small wing.

[1] Martha and Catherine Wilmot, *The Russian Journals*. Marchioness of Londonderry and H. M. Hyde, eds. (London, 1934), 226.
[2] See *Monuments* 2: 280, for a recent photograph.

[3] The monumental aspects of the central block and wing permitted its subsequent use as the Assignatsionnyi Bank. (See *Monuments* 2: 295–98, for recent photographs).

Figure 66. Lunin House (1818–1823) near Nikitskie Gates on the Boulevard Ring, architect D. I. Giliardi (Schmidt).

The main Lunin House block, in contrast, possessed that massiveness characteristic of Empire architecture. Here Giliardi moved the central colonnade of eight pillars into a niche, seemingly sculpted from a monolith. This effect was accentuated by the number and dimensions of the divisions and openings. A heavy cornice with sculptured horns of plenty and musical instruments, the parapet, and the smooth entablature with the grille of the loge balcony—all of these gave to the facade the stamp of Empire classicism. Since Giliardi's main concern had been the relationship of facade to street, the asymmetric front permitted Lunin House to blend with other houses on the Boulevard.

Beyond Lunin House the Tverskoi remained the showcase of the Boulevard Ring. Although suffering greatly during the period of the French occupation, it again became a fashionable promenade. A contemporary described this "wonderful Tverskoi Boulevard" after 1812. "Fragrant with mignonette and refreshed with fountains," it attracted those

who enjoyed a summer walk and entertainment with music.

> The large gallery (the "Arabian" coffee house in the middle of the Boulevard) was filled with ladies, who came there with their knitting. Men entertained them with lively jocose dialogue; laughter almost never died down; and the Boulevard was the place of most pleasant association all evening![4]

As the years went by, this traffic diminished. Pushkin noted in 1833 that "on the Tverskoi Boulevard one finds two or threefold women, a university student with eyeglasses, and Prince Shalikov, publisher of the *Ladies' Magazine*."[5] Of the stylish houses that still distinguished the Tverskoi, one was that of the Rimskii-Korsakovs, which dated from Catherine's day, and the three-story Kolgriviv House, which, after 1830, became the residence of the head of police in the city. Literary

[4] Quoted from the *Ladies' Magazine* (1826) in Sytin, *Ulits*, 302.
[5] Ibid.

giants like Gogol, S. T. Aksakov, and P. I. Chaadaev, visited D. N. Sverbeev's home there in the early 1840s. However pleasant, the Tverskoi did have its detractors: William Rae Wilson, for one, found it "crooked and steeper in some parts than Ludgate Hill."[6]

This enchantment ceased at the Tverskie Gates. Beyond that point, the future Strastnoi Boulevard remained incomplete until 1830. At the Petrovskie Gates Kazakov's mansion for Prince V. N. Gagarin, which had been gutted by fire in 1812, was rebuilt by Bove as the Catherine Hospital. The Petrovskii Boulevard Ring opened before 1812 but was swept by the fire; nevertheless, within half a dozen years both new birches and new houses appeared there. Trubnaia Square, completed in 1795 when the Neglinnaia was converted to an open canal,[7] became in the 1840s an emporium for song birds, pigeons, and small animals. In the following decade the market in flowers, seeds, and saplings was transferred to it from Theater Square. Work on the Rozhdestvenskii Boulevard, although begun before the fire, was not finished until after the conflagration. Masonry houses, more or less identical on their ground and first floors with modest Ionic porticoes and side entrances, replaced some of those of wood.

The remainder of the Ring—the Sretenskii, Chistoprudnyi, and Pokrovskii Boulevards—was completed after 1812. Vested interests delayed construction of the Pokrovskii even though its square had opened about 1800. The Pokrovskie Barracks, still standing, date from the 1830s. After 1812, brick and stone houses and shops superseded wooden ones in that square.

The Moscow River area had, during the course of the eighteenth century, changed for the better. Its earlier untidy and bucolic character faded before a regulated one of stone embankments, straight roads, and carefully-constructed canals, all of which appeared by the century's end (fig. 67). Although a classical Kremlin did not materialize, Rastrelli's old palace facade was moderately refurbished after 1812; it, along with the new bridges and masonry dwellings, also helped to impose a degree of order on this generally chaotic sector of the city.

Navigable below the Kremlin in warm weather, the river at the turn of the century invited both maritime traffic and pleasure boating. Long flat-bottomed boats, pulled upstream by eight to fifteen horses overseen by a man and a boy, inched by barks laden with firewood, floating down river from the Great Stone Bridge.[8] In the spring, boats came from the Oka and Volga to "Moscow harbor," a point of land between the Moskvoretskii and Krasnokholmskii Bridges. Even goods from such distant points as Astrakhan and Kazan were unloaded there.

The Moscow River bridges were of varying kinds. The Nikol'skii at the Krymskii Rampart and the Krasnokholmskii were "living bridges," that is, great trees simply afloat in the water. They yielded under the weight of wagons, and rose and fell with the water level. Such bridges were often removed during spring flooding, to be set out later with little difficulty.[9] In the years 1829 to 1833, stone piles replaced wooden trestles on the Moskvoretskii, and a cast-iron High (*Vysoko*) Piatnitskii Bridge with an iron trestle at the top replaced the wooden span which had been built in the Balchug sector of Zamoskvorech'e in 1786.

On that patch of land between the river and the Vodootvodnyi Canal, the fire had taken a heavy toll. Between 1813 and 1817 a number of brick and stone houses were built there, east of Moskvoretskii Bridge, to replace those which had burned. However, burned-

---

[6] *Travels in Russia*, 51–52.

[7] The aqueduct entered the square in an enclosed canal and terminated in a stone pavilion. Cf. above, 80–83.

[8] Gilbert, *Russia Illustrated*, 200–201.

[9] Ibid., 196–97. There were both "living and stone bridges" over the Iauza. The stone Iauzskii Bridge by the Foundling Home Gilbert described as "having iron balustrades with handsome stone pyramids devoted to serve as lamp posts." The other was the Dvortsovoi leading to the summer gardens at Lefortov.

Figure 67. View of the Kremlin and Great Stone Bridge, late nineteenth century (Donskoi, VIII-30456).

172

out shells lay untouched near the bridge as late as 1818. West of Moskvoretskii Bridge, fire had destroyed or gutted many houses on the Sofiiskaia and Bersenevskaia Embankments. Restoration here produced some exceptional examples of Empire domestic architecture, one of which was the Lobkov House with its four-column Doric portico on the Sofiiskaia Embankment.[10] Reconstruction of the Bersenevka occurred principally in 1817–1820; during the 1820s merchants and others of middle-class origin moved into part of the city. Bolotnaia Square was generally adapted to the design of M. D. Bykovskii's Meal Stores, construction of which began in 1842. Although this ensemble had broad planning implications for the area, it possessed an eclectic rather than classical look.[11]

In the mid-1830s, Moscow builders turned to the river front where they replaced the wooden support walls of both the Raushskaia and Sofiiskaia Embankments with stone. The Sofiiskaia Quay was built between 1836 and 1840. Although frequent flooding of the Balchug ceased, the moat near it remained until well into the century. In 1835, when the Krasnokholmskaia Dam and Locks were built at the estuary of the canal, the canal became navigable, and engineers covered the moat. The elimination of an earlier canal, called the Roushskii, permitted widening the Balchug.

The Prechistenskii Embankment opposite the Bersenevka lost its eighteenth-century edifices in 1812. Their charred remains were eventually altered or replaced by buildings in the Empire mode. Like the Tverskoi, this quay became a place for Moscow's idle rich society to walk, gossip with one another, and drink the artificial mineral waters available there. Vigel vowed that "the movement, the excellent morning air, the thundering music, and the

happy crowd of ill strollers cured me no less than the Marienbad waters I drank."[12] Construction on this embankment began in the mid-1830s, as in the Balchug, to improve navigation on the river and for the Vodootvodnyi Canal. A new wooden dam, the Babiegorodskaia, replaced the old one but had to be dismantled in times of flooding.

Zemlianoi Gorod: Zamoskvorech'e

In Zamoskvorech'e, south of the river, the fire brought new changes to this ancient district. The many frame houses in the Great Iakimanka, a habitat of merchants and minor officials, escaped the conflagration. This dusty street was not entirely ignored in the great events of 1812, for Napoleon and his distraught troops had moved along it, across its wooden plank sidewalks, and out from Moscow forever. The old rather than the new look prevailed there for years after the restoration. On the Great Polianka that influx of merchants, small landowners, officials, and clergy, which began after the liquidation of the streltsy, did not abate with the fire. The street continued as the "kingdom of merchants," although some hitherto small holdings were consolidated and subsequent building assumed a certain elegance.

Nobles and merchants, who had moved into Great Ordynka in the eighteenth century, returned after 1812 to reestablish themselves. In Great Tolmachevskii Alley, between the Ordynka and Polianka, Demidov House was restored with an Empire look.[13] Built originally during the 1780s, it was given a Corinthian portico, facade bas-reliefs, and an iron fence and gates. In 1817 Bove altered Bazhenov's nearby Dolgov House, affixing to it a new Ionic portico with a massive pediment. These additions gave it a grand entrance and effectively transformed it into an Empire edifice. Despite some remodeling at the end of

---

[10] This severity was further accentuated in the windows without jambs, but bas-relief ornament did restore a balance. Lion's head medallions topped the windows and rosettes and wreaths were added to the columns' base and frieze respectively. (See *Monuments* 2: 303, for a recent photograph).

[11] E. I. Kirichenko, "Arkhitekturnye ansambli Moskvy 1830–1860-x godov," *Arkhitekturnoe nasledstvo* 24 (1976): 18–19.

[12] Quoted from Sytin, *Ulits*, 375.

[13] See *Monuments* 2: 179–81, for recent photographs.

Figure 68. The Church of All Sorrows (*Vsekh Skorbiashchikh*) in Zamoskvorech'e, architects Bazhenov (late 1780s–early 1790s) and Bove (1828–1833) (Schmidt).

the century, it presently retains the Bove stamp.

This same architect undertook a similar remodeling of Bazhenov's Church of All Sorrows, which became an important monument of both the early classic and Empire (fig. 68). Simplicity had prevailed in Bazhenov's portion of the church, completed in the late 1780s or early 1790s. Its portico was of two paired Ionic columns supporting a modest pediment; beyond it rose a spire. The church's refurbishment between 1828–1833, not surprisingly, fell to Bove.[14] His rotunda, in particular, gave this edifice its strongest architectural accent. The cupola drum repeated the effect created by the cylindrical first floor; the frieze and cornice at both the top of the first floor and at the base of the cupola accentuated this curvature. Elongated windows, flanked by pilasters, stretched nearly to the street level.

These pilasters braced a small entablature wedged between the windows and a semicircular niche. Bas-reliefs enriched both this niche and the entablature. Bove effected in these windows the illusion of an arcade, a favorite motif with him. The entrance to the rotunda, two Ionic columns supporting a pediment, contained a richly carved frieze and cornice. This single structure embodied the evolution of Moscow classicism for a half century, from the 1780s to the 1830s.

Church architecture in the Piatnitskaia also expressed eloquently Moscow's building tradition. Grigor'ev's classical Church of the Trinity "in Vishniaki,"[15] erected about 1825, joined Evlashev's rococo St. Clement's at Klimentevskii Alley and several seventeenth-century churches in giving this street its particular character. The Trinity rotunda, capped with a lantern, was standard classical, but the splendid bell tower was among the handsomest

[14] For an earlier reference to this Bazhenov work, see above, 111–12; *Monuments* 2: 285–88, for recent photographs.

[15] Ibid., 2: 281, for a recent photograph.

built after the fire. Its monumental Corinthian entrance was surmounted by two tiers, first Ionic and then Corinthian, and finally capped with a small cupola and spire. In addition to Grigor'ev's Trinity Church, new dwellings with the usual classical ornament reached to the streets. Nobles, officials, and merchants alike took up residence in these.

In summary, the Moscow River area, which had received so much attention from late eighteenth-century planners, emerged after the fire with a classical look. New embankments, canals, roads, bridges, and restored dwellings between the river and the Vodootvodnyi Canal imposed order on the river and linked it with the restored streets and alleys of Zamoskvorech'e. Today this old suburb still retains the character given to it after the Great Fire.

Zemlianoi Gorod: The Garden Ring

One of urban Moscow's most important projects after 1812 was construction of its second concentric boulevard. It was set out on the line of fortifications of the old Zemlianoi Gorod, which had long since outlived its purpose. In some places, the walls and towers had been dismantled and the moat filled; elsewhere remnants of the rampart remained but were in an exceedingly decayed state. Because buildings of one sort or another rapidly accumulated in the open space by the walls and moat, planners in 1775 had urged that this conglomeration be swept away and the fortifications restored. In some places, this rebuilding was actually accomplished, but before long new construction spread into the cleared areas. After 1812, no serious thought was ever given to repairing the ramparts; rather, the intent was to replace them with a regulated boulevard and plazas.

Transforming ramparts and moats into boulevards and gates into plazas proved a long, arduous, and expensive task. Such a spectacular enterprise involved a major financial commitment, and this even before the Boulevard Ring was completed! Projected for

197 feet in width in order to cover the area cleared of ramparts, the boulevard required paving, lighting, cleaning, and maintenance. The economic question was finally resolved by laying streets and sidewalks that were only 69 to 85 feet wide. The remaining space was left to residents for use as flower gardens before their homes. Thus, the name, Garden Ring (*Sadovoe Kol'tso*).

The Garden Ring, which evolved between 1816 and 1830, had a circumference of 8.3 miles and bore diverse names as it passed from one police precinct to another.[16] Inevitably, property owners abused the garden space by enclosing it with high walls or cluttering it with shops, hotels, and what not. These encroachments most often occurred on the valuable properties near large plazas. Under such circumstances, land privately claimed by length of occupancy had to be repurchased by the state in order to enlarge a plaza.

In Zamoskvorech'e plazas were projected at the Serpukhovskie and Kaluzhskie Gates, which had been demolished at the end of the eighteenth century, but one thing or other delayed their completion. In the case of the Serpukhovskaia the question was the form it should assume, that of a rectangle or semicircle. As early as 1786, Governor Brius had approved establishing the Serpukhovskaia as a rectangle; a dozen years later the new governor, I. P. Saltykov, confirmed a semicircle. Yet it was a full circle which finally funneled traffic toward the center by way of the Ordynka and Piatnitskaia. In 1799 Saltykov approved a circular Kaluzhskaia Plaza, but its completion was delayed. Remnants of the old ramparts reputedly inhibited laying it out; moreover, illegal wooden and masonry construction along the walls, mushrooming whenever the planners hesitated, posed new obsta-

---

[16] The reconstruction plan of 1935 replaced these gardens by wider boulevards and the smaller houses by huge buildings; consequently, this transformation of the Sadovoe has been regarded by many as one of the most destructive acts of Soviet urban planning.

cles. A completed Garden Ring eventually brought greater clarity to both the plazas.

The clutter remained at the Krymskii Rampart until after 1812.[17] A log-paved street, which carried traffic from Nikol'skii Bridge to Kaluzhskaia Square, vaguely foreshadowed the circular boulevard at least a quarter century in the future. Flooding in the river section of the Krymskii Rampart had generally discouraged building there before the fire. Farther north along the western rampart, a sameness characterized appearances for several decades before 1812. Where decaying walls persevered, new dwellings, shops, taverns, and baths usurped the open space in the direction of the Prechistenka and Smolenskaia Square. The latter, like Kaluzhskaia, continued to be one of Moscow's important market centers during the nineteenth century. Outside Smolenskaia Square, nobility more than merchants encroached upon land formerly used for the old fortifications. In the 1790s shops burgeoned in what became Kudrinskaia Square, along both sides of the earthen wall; similar congestion engulfed the Old Triumphal Gates before 1812.[18]

Along much of the northern tier of the Zemlianoi Gorod, at the end of the eighteenth century, buildings had literally clung to the ramparts. Between 1782 and 1784 a damaged section of the old wall near the Sukharev Tower was ordered repaired by Governor Z. G. Chernyshev, but before long houses again affixed themselves to it. A contemporary's description of this location was generally applicable to much of the area along the wall:

> Here to the west of the Sukharev Tower are two movable shops for the sale of foodstuffs, stoves for travelers and nightwatchmen, the masonry two-story house of a merchant's wife, a barn of the Admiralty College, a state-

owned tavern with an icehouse, pipes of the Moscow Aqueduct, a lot with the wooden and masonry buildings belonging to a merchant, another lot with a blacksmith and house belonging to the Moscow water department, a machine of the same department, and the barn of a merchant.[19]

Shops, taverns, and the like lined the earthen wall between the Sretenka and the Miasnitskaia. Because the area east of the Miasnitskaia had for years been used for grain storage, buildings on the wall primarily served that purpose.

Beyond the Miasnitskaia in the southeastern Zemlianoi Gorod, essentially an extension of the Foreign Suburb, gentry and merchants predominated. The highly destructive 1773 fire in the Taganka necessitated replanning the blocks there. A plaza was given the shape of a triangle, which planners in 1775 scarcely altered. Early in the 1790s flour, meat, fish and grocery shops, of brick and wood alike, lined the west side of this Taganskaia Square along the old moat. In their midst was the chapel of the Pokrovskii Monastery, and on the present Little Taganskaia Square stood a tavern. In 1798, the governor, Saltykov, approved the regulation of Taganskaia Square to conform to the general plan of 1775. The street lines, however, were not so straight as intended because of the haphazard arrangement of masonry shops, which were too valuable to raze. After 1812 the burned wooden shops on the square were replaced by masonry, Bove having built on the Taganskaia's western side a columned gallery of shops.

Demolition of the Zemlianoi Gorod Ramparts in the 1820s invited construction of architectural ensembles in the freed space. Such building occurred in 1832–1835 within Krymskaia Square, at the Ostozhenka and the Boulevard, in the form of provision warehouses designed by Vasilii P. Stasov and erected by Fedor Mikhailovich Shestakov (fig. 69a,b). These warehouses, probably the best

---

[17] Krymskii Rampart (*Val*) was the setting of the Krymskii Court (*Dvor*) where Crimean Tatar diplomats resided. Specifically, this was located opposite the present-day Gorkii Central Park of Culture and Leisure.

[18] The area between the Tverskaia and Dmitrovka about 1790 was a mass of state taverns, an ice house, flour and meat shops, and gentry, merchant, and officials' homes. The deteriorating fortifications were still there as well.

[19] From the *Vedomost'* of the Surveying Office as quoted in Sytin, *Ulits*, 502.

Figure 69a. Provision warehouses (1832–1835), architect V. P. Stasov (1821); built by F. M. Shestakov, 1832–35 (Schmidt).

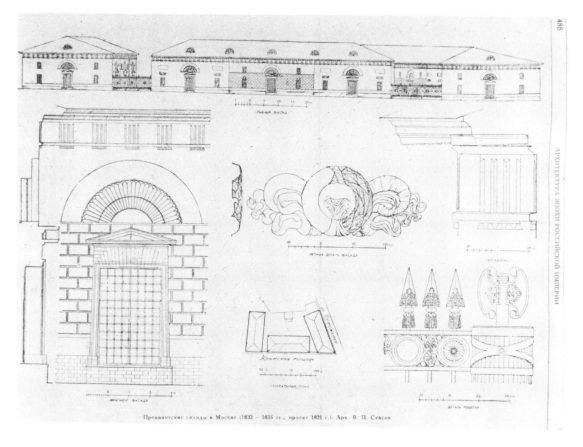

Figure 69b. Drawings of Stasov's provision warehouses (Brunov, *Istoriia*).

examples of the late classic in Moscow, consisted of three virtually identical buildings. The central one faced the street (today's Krymskaia Square) with its longitudinal side; the other two with their latitudinal facades. Large doors with pedimented classical frames surmounted by Ledoux-like semicircular windows, and rustication—all brought relief from the building's stark walls. These same walls, the doors, and a precisely-etched frieze and cornice accented the building's mass. The Stasov warehouses in both simplicity and power exemplified the utilitarian application of the classic in the new Moscow.

Beyond the warehouses, on the west Garden Ring, the Zubovskii and Smolenskii Boulevards and Smolenskaia Square were completed in the 1820s. Not far from this plaza, in Gagarinskii Alley, rose an impressive Empire house, that of Lopatin. Built in 1813–1817, it was distinguished by a four-columned portico with three small arches, instead of the usual entablature. Two windows flanked these pillars, each of which was capped with a semicircular bas-relief. The building was three-quarters rusticated, but the reliefs were backed by a smooth surface. A sharply recessed cornice and parapet articulated the facade.

North of Smolenskaia Square, once the site of the Tsar's Settlement lands and Novinskii Monastery, the Novinskii Garden Ring was set out. In the aftermath of the fire, which destroyed all the houses there, several particularly important ones were built. The house most embodying Empire elegance was that of Prince N. S. Gagarin (fig. 70). Completed in 1817 by Bove, it was situated some distance from the street and separated from it by a small garden. This Gagarin House possessed two wings attached to the main corpus by a semicircular gallery. The right wing was purely decorative, fulfilling a symmetrical purpose only. An iron grille fence accentuated the house's street orientation. Its expressive central facade featured a portico of six paired columns and a pediment with a semicircular window niche in its center. Intricate bas-reliefs, both in this niche and over the five

windows behind the columns, set the tone for the entire mansion. Bove graced each side of the semicircular pediment window with bas-reliefs of flying glory. A parapet above the pediment constituted still another unusual feature of this facade. Gagarin's interior equaled its lavish exterior: a luxurious peristyle and decorative friezes complemented the ceiling paintings.[20]

On the corner of the Sadovoe-Kudrinskii, a late eighteenth-century structure underwent a succession of remodelings before being put to new use after the fire. Once a mansion belonging to a General Glebov, it became state property in 1795 and served for a time as the Main Pharmacy. Then in 1812 the building was designated for the Widows' Home,[21] an almshouse for widows and orphans of the military and civil servants. After its main corpus was virtually destroyed in 1812, the task of reconstruction fell to Ivan Giliardi; but his son, Domenico, eventually (1818) substituted for the ailing father. Domenico Giliardi's Widows' Home, completely restored between 1820 and 1823, represented a structure totally different from that which had existed before the fire.[22] While the garden side retained the configuration of the old structure, the street facade was new. The younger Giliardi added another story, changed the right wing, and gave the facade symmetry and a monumentality in the form of an eight-columned Doric portico three stories in height. That the building receded from the street produced the effect of a rural estate house.

William Hastie had suggested razing houses

---

[20] This enchanting house, destroyed by bombing in World War II, survives only as a model in the architectural museum in Donskoi Monastery.

[21] See Sytin, *Ulits*, 482–83, and N. Krasheninnikova, "Iz neopublikovannykh rabot I. I D. Zhiliardi: Byvshii vdovii dom," *Arkhitekturnoe nasledstvo* 1 (1951): 191–96. The original Widows' Home, associated with the Foundling Home, was located in Lefortov.

[22] The facade remains virtually unaltered to this day. Giliardi's first variant provided entrances with small porches on both sides of the powerful central porch, but when implemented they were indistinct in the overall mass. At present the entrances and wings have been redone, and there is an entrance in the portico. (See *Monuments* 2: 272, for a recent photograph).

Figure 70. Architect's model of the N. S. Gagarin House (1817) in the Architectural Museum in Donskoi Monastery, architect O. I. Bove (Schmidt).

between the Great and Little Nikitskaia and laying down a thoroughfare along the courtyard facade of the Widows' Home, but this scheme necessitated dismantling the residential housing by the Zemlianoi Gorod Rampart and removing a portion of the garden in front on the Kudrinskaia. This Hastie proposal, like so many others, failed to win approval.[23]

After the demolition of the earthen wall beyond Kudrinskaia marketplace, the future Garden Ring toward the Tverskaia widened to more than 197 feet. In the 1820s its houses, belonging mainly to minor officials and the military, were small, generally no higher than two stories and obscured by the trees and gardens in front. An exception to these modest homes was the charming mansion of the Volkonskies, sometimes called Protkov House, designed by Bove and built in 1809[24] (fig. 71). Exquisite in the Empire style, it belonged to Princess Volkonskaia as late as 1826. A four-column Doric portico and bas-relief sculptures adorned its main facade; single windows flanked the front door beneath the portico

and six additional the portico itself. This variation in window design, rustication, and bas-reliefs brightened its Garden Ring facade. Volkonskii House eventually passed to Count A. F. Rostopchin, son of Moscow's wartime governor. During the era of the Rostopchins the first floor of the house became the ladies' salon and the second, a gallery for paintings. In the 1840s, the house and its large park were sold to the governor of the city, Prince A. G. Shcherbatov.

East of the Hostel for Indigents, the Garden Ring's most important eighteenth-century ensemble, stood Usachev House, another exquisite Empire mansion (fig. 72a,b,c).[25] Commissioned by Prince N. S. Gagarin, owner of the great house on the Novinskii, this residence with a park had been designed and built by Domenico Giliardi and Grigor'ev in 1829–1831. Combining features of town and estate house, it backed on the Iauza but lay situated at the Garden Ring rather than in the park. From the Ring it appeared as a severe and elongated block, two stories in height, rusticated on its lower story and plain on the upper, where the windows were without jambs. An imposing eight-column portico invited a study in contrast with the stuccoed walls behind it. Both the frieze and bas-reliefs beneath the

[23] The renovation of the square was finally achieved in 1938 with the tearing down of the residences and completion of the Novinskii Boulevard. This alteration of Insurrection (*Vosstaniia*, formerly Kudrinskaia) Square eliminated the garden in front of the Widows' Home in order to continue Herzen (formerly the Great Nikitskaia) beyond the square. The Widows' Home today is the Central Institute of Improved Medical Treatment.
[24] See *Monuments* 2: 184, for a recent photograph.

[25] Ibid., 2: 318–21, for recent photographs.

Figure 71. Protkov or Volkonskii House (1809), architect Bove (Schmidt).

Figure 72a. Usachev House (1829–1831), front view, architect D. I. Giliardi (Schmidt).

Figure 72b. Usachev House, rear view (Schmidt).

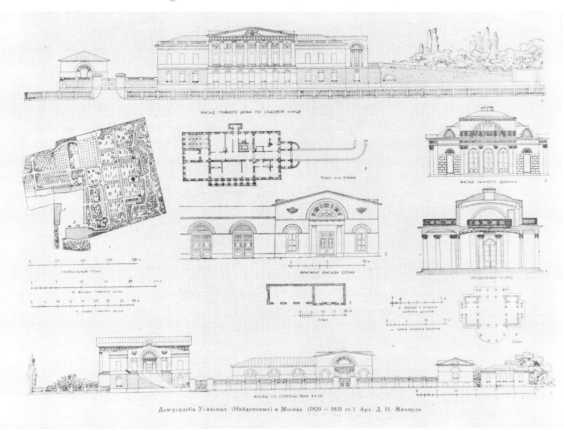

Figure 72c. Drawings of Usachev House (Brunov, *Istoriia*).

portico gave luster to, but did not diminish the severity of, the facade.

The yard facade in the rear, though without an imposing columnar portico, did possess two striking entrances. The most interesting element was a high sloping parapet into which Giliardi inserted a semicircular doorway flanked by two Doric columns and capped by an ornate architrave and tympanum. From the verandah outside this door, a walkway lined with vases led down to the garden. On the far side of the garden facade from the sweeping stairway, an entrance protected by a metal canopy and guarded by poised lions much enlivened this garden perspective of the house. As in front, this lower rear facade was rusticated, the upper smooth-textured. A similarly smooth parapet formed a background for sculpture and other decorations. The interior had an enfilade of reception rooms along the front facade separated by a corridor from the family area. The latter, facing the garden and yard, formed an essential part of the main building. An entrance led from the yard, via a vestibule and sweeping stairway.

Among the most pleasing aspects of Usachev House was its setting on the high bank of the Iauza. Giliardi planted a magnificent park, which descended toward the river in terraces and by stone staircases. Along the axis of the main lines of trees he placed pavilions richly adorned with sculpture. A charming teahouse, resembling a toy, had gleaming sculptures and finely drawn columns that formed colonnaded (four- and six-columned) porticoes, or really a semirotunda.

The Garden Ring was perhaps the most extensive and visionary undertaking by Moscow's planners and architects after 1812. While it had been, like the Boulevard Ring, an idea long discussed, no actual work on it had commenced before 1812. When completed, it proved to be much more than a boulevard encircling central Moscow. It became, as its name implies, a pleasant garden setting with both modest houses and some very fashionable mansions. The most impressive, those of the Volkonskies, the Gagarins,

and the Ushchevs, compared favorably with those of the Seleznevs and Lopukhins on the Prechistenka as the best that Empire Moscow produced. Stasov's warehouses represented superb utilitarian classic; Giliardi's remodeled Widows' Home improved upon an otherwise undistinguished and earlier edifice, which in 1812 had been but a burned shell. Otherwise, this boulevard, although more grandiose than the Boulevard Ring, was neither so inviting to the aristocrats for strolling nor identifiable with a peculiarly classical motif. Instead its breadth looked to the future, to its traffic-bearing potential, and, like the boulevards of Paris, it imposed a measure of political control on the populace.

Classical Moscow Beyond the Zemlianoi Gorod

Beyond the Zemlianoi Gorod, the fire of 1812 destroyed perhaps 70 percent of the buildings, most of which were wooden. Within five years, many of these had reappeared, again wooden. Since 1742 the Kamer College Wall had been the official boundary of the city, but growth of trade, industry, and population led to the unofficial inclusion of other districts within the administrative jurisdiction of Moscow. After 1812 many factories like the Tsindel'evskaia plant on Derbenevskaia, Titov's textile plant on the Great Kaluzhskaia, the state-owned surgical instruments plant on the Pokrovskaia, three bell factories in the Meshchanskaia District, and eleven breweries in the Novinskaia District sprang up between the projected Garden Ring and the turnpikes. These factories naturally attracted streams of workers, many of whom lived in barracks built by the owners of the factories, or in hovels which collected in the vicinity of the factories. Even though classical Moscow was not in evidence in this industrial environment, there were distinctive neighborhoods where both relatively modest dwellings and estates in classical proportions had risen, some late in the eighteenth century and some after 1812. Usually these streets—such as the Old and New

Basmannaia, the Meshchanskaia, and the Ni-kolo-Iamskaia—were not far removed from the Ring.

A notable addition to the Moscow architectural scene beyond the Zemlianoi Gorod was a triumphal arch commemorating Russia's victory over Napoleon and the French (fig. 73).[26] Not unexpectedly, it was placed in the Tverskaia, but, surprisingly, at neither the old Tverskie nor Triumphal Gates. Instead a new plaza was laid out in 1829 about a kilometer from the latter, before what is now the Belorusskii Station. The arch, designed by Bove and built in 1827–1834, gave Moscow a monumental entrance from Petersburg. Constructed of brick and faced with white stone, it was embellished with pairs of Corinthian columns on all four sides. Their capitals and bases, the carved friezes and cornices, architraves, and the sculptured figures were all of cast iron. Ivan Petrovich Vitali and Ivan Timofeevich Timofeev produced this sculpture—warriors between the columns, flying glories on the sides of the arch, female figures in the background of the high parapet, and a group representing Victory on a six-horse chariot, crowning the entire structure. Small guardhouses on each side of the arch faced the Tverskaia. Distinguished by Doric porticoes and flat cupolas, they were attached to the larger structure by semicircular-grille fencing. This complex stood in the middle of a small oval plaza and closed the perspective of the Tverskaia from Red Square.

At the opposite end of the city from this monument but at approximately the same time as his involvement with it, Osip Bove designed and built the City (*Gradskaia*) Hospital (fig. 74).[27] Erected between 1828 and 1833, it became an integral part of Kazakov's Golitsyn Hospital ensemble on the Kaluga

Road. The idea of building a city hospital in this location was first broached to Alexander I by the governor-general, Golitsyn, in 1823. A committee, formed to work on the project, recommended the site on the Great Kaluzhskaia; and although both the committee and Nicholas I subsequently approved the plan submitted by Bove in 1827, Maria Fedorovna, the emperor's mother, demanded some significant modifications.

Bove's original design for the City Hospital consisted of a central block with two wings linked to it by low fencing, embracing a central court. Both the wings and the facade of the main structure faced the street. In severity, the wings were matched by the central building, save for a massive eight-column Ionic portico and a broad staircase. Diverse sculptures adorned the front facade. Bove intended a low dome for the hospital chapel at the main entrance and designed its interior as a round hall, ringed with an Ionic colonnade and a windowed cupola above. A sculptured frieze elegantly adorned the upper vestibule leading to the church. In this, Bove repeated motifs used by Kazakov in his Golitsyn Hospital church, although Bove's generally were more decorative.

Maria Fedorovna's dissatisfaction with the church choir finally caused Bove to alter the entire plan. He redesigned both the back facade and the main stairway and subsequently changed the length and height of the building itself. To complicate matters, the frames and doors did not fit the new measurements. Bove did not present his revised plan until early 1829, and even then, it was returned to him for reconsideration because of costs. For this reason, Bove deleted interior decoration, most notably, the church colonnade. Although this hospital ensemble was completed in the summer of 1833, it fell far short of the splendid complex he had envisioned in his original plan.

In the Khamovnicheskaia Loop of the Moscow River, across from the backs and terraced gardens of Bove's and Kazakov's hospitals, lay still another early nineteenth-century assem-

---

[26] This gate was dismantled in the 1930s, carefully preserved, and reassembled on the Kutuzovskii Prospekt at the entrance to Moscow in 1968. (Cf. S. T. Palmer, "The Restoration of Ancient Monuments in the USSR," *Survey*: 174). For a recent photograph see *Monuments* 2: 259.

[27] See A. Kiparisova, "Neopublikovannye proekty: proekt Gradskaia bol'nitsa," *Arkhitekturnoe nasledstvo* 1 (1951): 127–34. See *Monuments* 2: 270–72, for recent photographs.

Figure 73. Triumphal Gates (1827–1834) on the Tverskaia, architect O. I. Bove (I. E. Grabar', *Istoriia russkogo iskusstva*. Moscow, 1963, 8:1).

blage. Its single most important element was a massive army barracks, built between 1807 and 1809. Designed by Matvei M. Kazakov, the great Kazakov's son, this extended three-story structure with Doric portico impressively dominated the Khamovnicheskaia Embankment. The ensemble also included an eighteenth-century watch house and chief's house in Khamovnicheskaia Plaza.

The palatial Iauza appropriated the Empire motif in the edifices built or rebuilt there after 1812. One of the elder Kazakov's most admired creations, the Suburban Palace, survived the fire as a shell. Domenico Giliardi, charged with its restoration, chose to retain its main walls. The most striking of the new elements which he added between 1827–1830 was a series of two-columned loges, each

Figure 74. Gradskaia or City Hospital (1828–1833), architect O. I. Bove (Schmidt).

topped by a cornice and semicircular arch, edged in white stone. Ensconced on a parapet over the central loge was a group sculpture by Vitali. With these additions the Suburban Palace received from Giliardi an Empire look while retaining its eighteenth-century hallmark, the fascinating half rotunda. Following its restoration in 1826, it served as the Remeslennyi School, one of the first technical schools in Moscow.

In this northeastern sector of Moscow, between the Red (Krasnye) Gates and the Iauza Palace complex, Evgraf Tiurin built one of the last classical churches in Moscow. This was the very substantial Church of the Epiphany "in Elokhovo" in 1837–1845.[28] Replete with bell tower, this church had a central ribbed dome on a drum, articulated with twin columns, arched windows, and bas-reliefs. Matching smaller cupolas and a uniform facade decor gave this church an impressive classic demeanor even during the twilight of the style.

On that avenue of affluence, the New Basmannaia, near the Red Gates, stood stately Perovskii House.[29] Illustrative of the Empire style in wood, it was built in 1812. Its pleasing facade had a vertical articulation from a five-window gable with a pediment and six pilasters without capitals, but substantial bas-relief ornament and horizontal divisions helped restore the balance. Perovskii House, no less than Kazakov's Demidov and Menelas's Razumovskii mansions made this section of Moscow of crucial importance for the classical aesthetic.

In summary, although facade design beyond the Zemlianoi Gorod was not so regulated as within the Garden Ring, certain neighborhoods resembled the models in the albums of Rusca, Hastie, and Stasov. Moreover, since hospitals were removed from the city's center, they continued as the suburban exemplars of classicism. After 1812, as before, Lefortov remained a retreat for the very rich. In a

[28] Ibid., 2: 289, for a recent photograph.

[29] Ibid., 302, for a recent photograph.

diverse environment of brick, stone, stucco, and traditionally wooden dwellings, some regulation of the streets occurred beyond the Garden Ring after 1812. Besides the straightening and elimination of numerous alleys, streets that had once existed independently were linked to those from the city center. Although a rural character persisted in this outer limit of Moscow, it had, even without Hastie's great squares, become a part of the classical city. The completion of the two Rings and most of the restoration by the 1830s, in a sense, marked the apogee of classicism in the architecture of Moscow. As the "golden age of the nobility" passed into history, the classicism which it fostered waned as well.

Chapter XI

Epilogue: The Classic After 1830

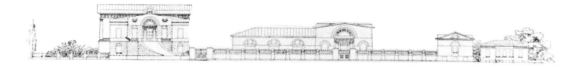

The architectural view of Moscow after 1812 was one created by its streets, plazas, and gardens as well as by its buildings. During the several decades after the Great Fire, the city showed a steady increase in principal streets and squares and a slight reduction in its concentric alleys. Streets numbered 165 in 1820, 188 in 1830, and 258 in 1840; whereas alleys, listed at 635 in 1820 and 1830, diminished to 582 by 1840. Plazas increased from 25 in 1820 to 54 ten years later, and to 79 in 1840. In addition to the 79 squares, 4 large public ones were listed for 1840. New streets and squares were naturally more prevalent in the newer sections of the city.[1]

Around the year 1830, perhaps one-sixth of Moscow was occupied by kitchen and other types of gardens. The former were plentiful between the Boulevard and Garden Rings, especially in Koz'e Marsh between the Little Nikitskaia and the Tverskaia; many also were located beyond the Garden Ring and even the Kamer College city limits. In the Khamovnicheskaia District they belonged to clerks, in the Sushchevskaia to merchants, and in the Taganskaia to monasteries. All this notwithstanding, a contemporary in 1830 could rightly observe that kitchen gardens had diminished since 1824, having been replaced by new streets. Although agrarian Moscow

doubtless waned, aspects of country life were still evident even near the center of the city. Meadowlands for grazing belonging variously to the state, monasteries, coachmen, peasants, and merchants, remained plentiful in the Khamovnicheskaia, Novinskaia, Pokrovskaia, and Taganskaia Districts.

More akin to classicism than kitchen gardens were Moscow's carefully arranged flower gardens. Splendid new public gardens became very much a part of the environment created after 1812 by the city's architects. Private gardens belonging to the rich and very rich also increased in number. In becoming an integral part of the architectural setting, they provided the aristocracy a place for walking, riding, and gossiping. Lyall remarked on the beauty of Moscow's ponds and lakes and the joys of walking along their banks. He was especially impressed by the manner in which the banks of some were laid out in lovely gardens and with them "broad gravel walks and adorned by parterres, summer houses, grottos, statues, and bridges." This entire complex was enclosed "by a fine balustrade, entered by handsome gates." Such gardens as these invited promenades when the weather permitted, and they were maintained at the crown's expense.[2] The Wilmots, commenting on the spaciousness of estate gardens, perceived that Chancellor Count Ostrowman's

---

[1] Cf. *Istoriia Moskvy* 3: 138–40 for the accounting of streets, squares, and gardens (below).

[2] *Moscow*, 49.

garden was "in the very center of Town" with "no less than fourteen English acres laid out in the Vaux Hall style."[3]

Many gardens occupied the northeastern and eastern parts of the city, especially in the Sushchevskaia, Rogozhskaia, Lefortovskaia, and Pokrovskaia Districts, where they occupied as much as a third of the available space. Around the Kremlin and Kitai Gorod, diverse gardens absorbed perhaps one-twelfth of the entire Gorodskaia District. They also prevailed in the Zamoskvorech'e, where every merchant of prominence proudly displayed his garden. The largest were those in the Lefortovskaia and Presnenskaia sectors of the city. According to a Moscow police account, the city possessed, in 1831, 12 boulevard gardens, 8 public, 1 botanical, and 1,763 private gardens. Or, in another context, of 10,000 buildings in Moscow, 17 percent contained gardens of little or no economic significance. In the 1830s Moscow also registered 141 greenhouses, located principally on estate properties, for cultivation of grapes, peaches, and apricots.

Moscow in the 1830s and 1840s

Construction in Moscow in the 1830s and 1840s gave no indication of regenerating a classicism which was losing its ascendancy elsewhere in Europe.[4] Alexander's brother and successor Nicholas I (1825–1855), had no particular taste for it. What building he encouraged was as likely to have been in another mode, perhaps Gothic, old Russian, or Byzantine. Moreover, two decades of creativity by Bove, Giliardi, and Grigor'ev did not spawn an outstanding third generation of classicists. Among the classicists who worked in Moscow during the 1830s and 1840s were Fedor Mikhailov Shestakov, one of Bove's students, and Evgraf Tiurin and A. S. Kutepov, students of

Giliardi. A. I. Mironovskii and Aleksei Nikitich Bakarev traced their tutelage to the elder Kazakov.

Shestakov, who began his career in the Commission for Building, most notably directed the building of Stasov's Provision Warehouses at Krymskii Rampart and designed the side gates and fences of the Aleksandrovskii Garden by the Manezh. Besides his exquisite University Church, Tiurin rebuilt in the 1830s the eighteenth-century Aleksandrinskii Palace. Renamed "Neskuchnoe," this Corinthian mansion was located only a short distance below Bove's and Kazakov's hospitals on the Kaluga Road (fig. 75).[5]

From Tiurin "Neskuchnoe," now the Academy of Sciences, received various alterations: a Doric guardhouse with a parapet, the main gate before the garden, a very substantial park pavilion with a Corinthian portico derived from an earlier one, and semicircular balconies on the ground floor of the palatial structure itself. These balconies, buttressed by four Ionic columns and surmounted by a small balustrade, imposed symmetry on the front facade. They also balanced the powerful central portico of four twin Corinthian columns, which supported a parapet from atop its ground floor base. Only this ground level of the facade was rusticated, but occasional bas-reliefs, semicircular windows on each side of the portico, and three arches above the four sets of columns articulated an otherwise smooth facade. Its interior, carefully preserved to this day, was one of the most elegant of the Empire era in Moscow. The excellent pilons at the entrance contained sculptures by Vitali.

The splendor of both this remodeled palace and the University Church confirmed Tiurin as an important, if not prolific, practitioner of classicism in Moscow during its twilight period. Bakarev began his career in the 1780s with the Kremlin Department. Besides assist-

[3] *Russian Journals*, 226.
[4] For a detailed examination of changes in Moscow architecture during the second third of the nineteenth century, see E. I. Kirichenko, "Arkhitekturnye ansambli Moskvy 1830–1860-x godov," *Arkhitekturnoe nasledstvo* 24 (1976): 3–19, hereafter cited as "Ansambli."

[5] See *Monuments* 2: 231–40, for superb exterior and interior photographs. Tiurin also designed a classical bell tower for the entrance to Simonov Monastery, but his plan was rejected for one in the National Style by K. A. Ton. (Cf. Kirichenko, *Ansambli*, 12–15).

Figure 75. "Neskuchnoe" Estate (Aleksandrinskii Palace, 1756). Wings by the architect E. Tiurin in the 1830s (Schmidt).

ing Kazakov, he succeeded Egotov in 1813 as director of the drafting and architectural school of the Kremlin Department. He developed a fascination for both the Gothic and the classic and brought the former to Mozhaisk and Moscow. Bakarev's propensity for eclecticism was evident in his plan for the Kremlin church of St. Catherine in Ascension Monastery near the Savior Gates. In that edifice he employed basically a seventeenth-century mode, adding a rococo cupola and a classical pediment. In his plans to redecorate the Il'inskie, Resurrection, and Nikol'skie Gates of the Kitai Gorod, Bakarev used both romantic and classical motifs, a treatment also evident in his picture gallery for the home of N. B. Iusupov, completed in 1816.

Perhaps the last important classicist in Moscow was Aleksandr Lavrent'evich Vitberg, who, according to his biographer, Alexander Herzen, was "an artist suppressed by the government with cold and unfeeling cruelty."[6]

Trained as a painter at the Academy of Arts in Petersburg, Vitberg was drawn through self-instruction to both engineering and architecture. For a time he concentrated on bridges but his crowning architectural achievement was a temple commemorating the fallen in the war with Napoleonic France. He intended this enormous three-sectional, five-dome church for the Kremlin but subsequently assented to the Sparrow Hills, which opened a view to Moscow from the south (fig. 76). Vitberg's plan greatly impressed Alexander I, who gave it almost immediate approval; construction was to have begun in 1817.

Vitberg proposed his temple-monument as a pantheon housing the bodies of all the heroes of the recent war. The three sections represented body, mind, and spirit. In its totality, the monument was to have been a memorial to Russian victory, inscribed with the names of all who had fallen. The first temple in this complex was to have been the crypt, inserted in the hill. Its outstanding feature was a monumental Doric colonnade.

---

[6] Quoted from Herzen in Grabar', *Iskusstva* 8, pt. i: 239.

Figure 76. Design of temple-monument (1817), architect A. Vitberg (Grabar', *Iskusstva*, 8, 1).

The middle temple, in the form of a Greek cross with great twelve-column porticoes on each side, constituted the base for the third temple, from which rose a vast colonnaded rotunda, capped with a great cupola (instead of the five originally proposed). This colossus, despite the initial acclaim, never became a reality. If one may believe Herzen, the young artist incurred the jealousy of the architectural establishment for the favor shown his project by the emperor. In 1826, the year after Alexander's death, a charge of embezzlement was brought against Vitberg. Relieved of the directorship of the Commission for the Construction of the Temple, he was tried, and eventually banished to Viatka in 1835. The work suspended in 1826 never resumed. Substituted for Vitberg's temple was the Temple of Christ the Savior, the work of the architect Konstantin Andreevich Ton.[7]

What caused the decline of classicism in Russia, and specifically in Moscow? There is a natural tendency for architectural styles to dissipate themselves, but several other reasons can be cited. An obvious one was the diminishing vitality of the aristocracy, a force in classicism's rise in the first place. Second, the industrial and commercial elements which came to dominate the city, were both uncaring about an ordered urban environment and philistine in taste. Third, the tsar, Nicholas I, and his successors were at best eclectic in their tastes and not at all inclined to take on grandiose building schemes as had Catherine II and Alexander I. Fourth, Russia's architects were, as noted above, of lesser ability and vision than their predecessors and more given to experimentation with revival styles. And, last, the political climate was one which encouraged a national style rather than the cosmopolitan classic.

By the 1830s, Moscow's future seemed inseparably coupled to industry and commerce,

---

[7] The late D. E. Arkin, eminent historian of Russian classicism, reflected on the symbolism of this event: Ton, employing the Russo-Byzantine, or Suzdalian style, eclipsed not only Vitberg and his temple but perhaps Russian Classicism as well. (Cf. Grabar', *Iskusstva* 8, i: 239–42, and Kirichenko, *Ansambli*, 7–11). To elaborate further on Ton's role, it was he who finally built a Kremlin palace after the many futile efforts of the classical architects to do so. Ton's was not classical but rather an eclectic mix of Gothic and Slavic Revival. (Cf. Kirichenko, *Ansambli*, 8–13).

rather than to the nobility whom it had harbored so long. Although central Moscow retained its aristocratic and official and, therefore, classical character, the city's accelerated economic growth brought both demographic and social change. Between 1846 and 1897, Moscow tripled its population to approximately 1,000,000, most of whom had migrated from the countryside. While large-scale industry, intrenched from early in the century, expanded impressively (employment increased from 46,000 in 1853 to 77,000 in 1890), so did small manufacturers and crafts. The city, having reached beyond its former boundaries, assumed a different character from the new building, paving, lighted streets, and diverse modes of local transportation. By the midnineteenth century, large factories appeared beyond the gates of the old city and in such old villages as Preobrazhensk, Semenovsk, Lefortov, Pokrovsk, and Rogozhsk.[8] Industrialists and merchants did not, like the nobility, endow the classic.

This rejection was evident especially in the Belyi and Kitai Gorod where shifting trade patterns, barely discernible during the heyday of classical Moscow, had altered the historical and architectural character of both. By the 1840s they were Moscow's two centers of commerce. The oldest and best known was the Kitai Gorod, the commercial stalls of which had originated as an open-air market within the Kremlin. Since the sixteenth century it was located in Red Square and eventually consisted of covered shops (*lavki*) housed in a primitive arcade.

In contrast to these open and covered stalls were the smart shops that appeared in the Belyi Gorod on the Kuznetskii Bridge in the mideighteenth century. French in origin, these *magaziny* were spacious and heated as opposed to the cramped, damp, and cold lavki. While the Kitai Gorod commercial rows and lavki retained dominance as late as the 1840s, commerce in the Belyi Gorod clearly was on the upswing. In such circumstances, the resi-

dential Belyi Gorod, so crucial in the evolution of classical Moscow, became the city's principal commercial district but without any definite architectural orientation. The Kitai Gorod, meanwhile, became Moscow's burgeoning financial center. The founding of the Moscow bourse in 1839 in the ancient Il'inka foreshadowed the rise of big banking and finance there during the second half of the century. Today the Kitai Gorod retains few classical reminders of its commercial past except an old and new Gostinyi Dvor.

The new mercantile role of the Belyi Gorod implied a changing social configuration in Moscow.[9] We have said earlier that gentry and grandees alike had found Catherine's Moscow a congenial environment in which to live and build. Except for such very wealthy families as the Demidovs, Sheremetevs, Shuvalovs, and Gagarins, the nobility were not really patrons of the arts; classicism for them became merely the vehicle for comfortable living, away from the court in St. Petersburg.[10] The fire which swept away much of old Moscow also disrupted their good life in the home, Nobles' Meeting House, and on the boulevards. While rebuilding was, in a sense, the triumph of the classical style in Moscow, many of the gentry had been ruined and left the city for good. Some found living cheaper in the provinces; others obtained preferment in St. Petersburg.[11] In any case, the reduced role of the aristocracy in Moscow and the corresponding rise of business and industry made classicism an anachronism. Pushkin expressed typical regret and nostalgia for the passing of the old Moscow when he observed in 1834 that

> now in a quieter Moscow the huge House of the Nobles stands sorrowfully in the middle of the vast courtyard, overgrown with weeds, and the garden, neglected and wild. . . . But

---

[8] William L. Blackwell, *Industrialization*, 111–12.

[9] Robert Gohstand, "The Shaping of Moscow by Nineteenth-Century Trade," in Michael F. Hamm, ed., *The City in Russian History*, 160–81. See also Blackwell, *Industrialization*, 427–30 for statistics on population and social structure in early nineteenth-century Russia and Moscow.

[10] Starr, "Russian Art," emphasizes that Russia's nobility seldom patronized the arts (pp. 91–92).

[11] Ibid., 97.

Moscow, which has lost its aristocratic glitter, flourishes in other respects: industry, carefully protected, has been invigorated and has developed with uncommon force. The merchants grow richer, and begin to settle in the mansions abandoned by the nobles.[12]

Since the merchant class began having an impact on Moscow life, might they not have perpetuated the style and character of a classical city? The era of the great merchant patrons, the Mamontovs and Morozovs, was still a generation away; this new class of merchants and industrialists, up from the peasantry, were, in many instances, Old Believers. Classicism with its implications of rank, leisure, and sophistication was alien and unacceptable.

A third factor in the rise and decline of classicism in Moscow was the sovereign's personal role. It had been, after all, a concern for the appearance of Russian cities that had motivated both Catherine and Alexander, and even Nicholas I, to an extent. Whatever Nicholas's politics and taste, he did have an interest in architecture, as evidenced by his encouragement of Rossi and Montferrand in St. Petersburg. Yet, his preferences were really eclectic rather than classical.[13] If he found

satisfaction in Rossi's classical ensembles, he also encouraged Ton with his Temple of the Savior. Benois's Peterhof stable was in the English Norman style, and Stackenschneider's Petersburg palaces were Renaissance. Presumably, he approved all these. In other words, he did not discourage departure from the classical mode, and for reasons stated elsewhere these various revival styles were finding an audience.[14] So at most Nicholas I was a lukewarm supporter of classicism, and after Nicholas classicism found no royal champion at all.

That classicism had no outstanding practitioner in the 1830s and 1840s was a further factor in its decline. Clearly, a "third generation" of classicists comparable to Kazakov and Bove failed to appear. Many classical architects experimented with other revival styles. Even architectural schools and the Academy, which had for years fostered classical design in the various state building projects, became arenas for competing revival styles.

Finally, classicism had in an ideological sense run its course. What had been a satisfying idiom for national glory in 1812 appeared by the 1840s excessively cosmopolitan for increasingly nationalistic tastes. As Frederick Starr has observed:

> When Briullov criticized the historian Karamzin for presenting "all tsars and no people" he was voicing a critique that had long since been advanced both by democratic opponents of autocracy and by those wishing to ground autocracy on a more ethnic ideal.[15]

A reinstituted National Style from the seventeenth century, a pre-Petrine style, seemed to fulfill this nostalgia for recapturing the pure Slav culture that had existed prior to the brutal and disorienting Peter.

---

[12] Quoted in *Istoriia Moskvy* 3: 160. This passage, from "Puteshestvie iz Moskvy v Peterburg" (1834), *Polnoe sobranie sochinenii* (Academy of Sciences, USSR, 1949) 2: 246, is quoted at greater length by Blackwell, *Industrialization*, 112–13 and Robt. Whittaker, "'My Literary and Moral Wanderings': Apollon Grigor'ev and the Changing Cultural Topography of Moscow," *Slavic Review* 42(1983): 393. Haxthausen observed that many nobles could not afford restoration of their homes after 1812: "The palaces of the nobility, with their innumerable and lazy domestics are now occupied by the manufacturers with their equally numerous workmen . . . If you ask, 'To whom does this palace belong?' The answer is 'to the manufacturer M___, the merchant C___, etc., formerly to Prince A___ or G___'" (Baron Franz August Maria von Haxthausen-Abbenburg, *The Russian Empire. Its People, Institutions, and Resources.* 2 vols. Translated from the German by Robert Farie [London, 1856] 1: 48–49). See also A. I. Kopanev, *Naselenie Peterburga v pervoi polovine XIX veka* (Moscow-Leningrad, 1957) p. 21 for similar changes in St. Petersburg.

[13] Starr "Russian Art," argues for a better image of Nicholas I than is usually accorded him. His quotation of the Russian scholar M. Polievktov, who wrote a half century ago, merits repetition: "The personal tastes of the Emperor Nicholas in the sphere of literature are of little interest . . . But things stood differently in the visual arts. Nicholas unquestionably understood art and in one field, namely architecture, he was himself a competent specialist. His love for art was crowned with a

series of positive governmental measures and undertakings directed towards the support of artistic and architectural activity. Nicholas was the last autocrat in the full sense of the word, and his reign was the last epoch in which there existed an official art" (99–100).

[14] Starr, Ibid., 100–101.

[15] Ibid., 108.

Classicism as a Constant in Russian Planning and Architecture

There remains an important postscript for classicism in Russia. Two generations after its waning in the 1830s, it emerged again as a fixture in both planning and architecture. This reappearance early in the twentieth century, then its eclipse during the Constructivist 1920s, its resurrection in the panoply of Stalinist building schemes in the 1930s and 1940s, and, finally, its most recent demise since Stalin, testify to both its durability and the numerous challenges which it has faced.

Classical planning really reemerged at the end of the last century to combat uncharted industrialism, especially in St. Petersburg, where the classical center appeared in jeopardy. In the city in which Peter the Great had banned wooden building, 65 percent of the new construction in 1890 was of wood! The artists Alexander and Leontii Benois and the young architect Ivan Fomin were among the first to propose a classical plan both as a safeguard against disordered building and for extolling the Russian Empire's greatness. Monumental cities, large in size and geometric in form, were apt symbols of martial prowess. When Alexander Benois and others in 1910 drafted plans for Petersburg, they did as their counterparts in Berlin, Vienna, and Chicago were doing, for such planning was an international phenomenon. The proposal which Benois took before the Duma in 1916 was entitled "On the Question of Planned Development of the Construction of Petrograd and Its Surroundings." What he had initially conceived as an attempt to save the city's center concluded as a plan for the entire metropolitan region. His timing was good, for the Duma approved it.[16] Alas, that sweet moment of expectation—a reckoning for the kind of state support which had produced Petersburg's great ensembles a century earlier—faded all too quickly. War and revolution saw to that,

although the center has during the Soviet period sustained its early nineteenth-century character.

This determination to preserve Petersburg-Petrograd-Leningrad by invoking the tenets of classicism had, on the other hand, a reverse effect for Moscow. Soon after the establishment of the Bolshevik capital there in 1918, planners envisioned dramatic alterations of the city. By the 1930s they exclaimed in terms of widened and straightened arterial thoroughfares and plazas, slicing through old neighborhoods, and accommodating such overpowering structures as the projected Palaces of Labor, of Industry, and, above all, of Soviets. Stalin's planners, in effect, sought to dwarf the Kremlin in the midst of these gigantic edifices, plazas, and thoroughfares. A plan for Moscow center announced in 1935 led also to the widening of the Garden Ring and ruthless straightening of the old Tverskaia, which in the process was deprived of numerous classical monuments. Bove's Triumphal Arch opposite Belorusskii Station was among these. Kazakov's governor's palace, the new Mossoviet, became unrecognizable as an eighteenth-century structure. Shorn of its wings, front altered, and two stories added, it easily melded into the new nondescript building blocks erected along this once elegant thoroughfare. Only through the arches of these massive edifices could one glimpse the charm of Moscow's classical part, lost forever in this epitome of the stolid, new classic, Gorkii Street.

*   *   *

The architecture of classicism, welcomed back to Moscow at the turn of the twentieth century, was virtually indistinguishable from that of the 1820s and 1830s. An example of such exacting reproduction was Vtorov House on Spasopeskovskaia Square, the work of the architects V. Mart and V. Adamovich in 1900 and presently the residence of the United States ambassador in the Soviet Union. Other Moscow works in the revived style of romantic

---

[16] This topic is treated in greater detail in S. Frederick Starr, "The Revival and Schism of Urban Planning in Twentieth-Century Russia," in Hamm, *The City in Russian History*, 222–42.

classicism were R. I. Klein's Pushkin Museum (1912), the "Coliseum" Cinema (1914), and Shaniavskii People's University (1913) by Illarion Ivanov-Schitz. Classicism, furthermore, became the mode for various monuments and bridges erected in 1913 to commemorate three hundred years of Romanov rule.

This classical resurgence, if so it may be called, was suppressed in the 1920s. The era of the New Economic Policy belonged essentially to the modernists, the Constructivist School of the Vesnin and Golosov brothers, of Konstantin Melnikov, of Le Corbusier and others who conceived of a truly revolutionary architecture.[17] They were joined in this enterprise by the Garden City people, who rejected the metropolis for the village. Under these circumstances the classicists either joined the modernists or bided their time. A. V. Shchusev, creator of Kazan Station before the Revolution, quickly produced an essentially classical and wooden mausoleum for Lenin in 1924 as well as a constructivist-inspired edifice for the Ministry of Agriculture before returning to the classical fold in the 1930s. I. V. Zholtovskii, less adaptable than Shchusev, fashioned next to the National Hotel on the Mokhovaia, a Renaissance-style building which for a time served as the United States Embassy and now is the Central Intourist Office.

Stalin's triumph spelled the doom for both the followers of Le Corbusier and the practitioners of "Kulak democracy." Whatever latent classicism existed in the 1920s, it came fully to life in the next decade under the architects Fomin, Shchusev, Zholtovskii, V. Shchuko, Gelfreikh, and Iofan, whose works were intended to extol the virtues of the Party and a Communist society.[18] Their opportunity came in some of the grandiose building projects approved but, fortunately, never completed. The walls of the Kitai Gorod were even partially dismantled to allow for a huge Palace of Industry which would have encroached on Red Square and reached down to the river. Even more ambitious among these classical projects was the Palace of Soviets, intended as a monument to the first Five Year Plan. Although no winner emerged in the architectural competition to build it, work went ahead under Iofan, Shchuko, and Gelfreikh. This gigantic structure, which would have resembled a multi-layered cake, was to have served as an immense pedestal for a seventy-five meter statue of Lenin rising from its top tier. The plan, moreover, called for a vast semicircular colonnade to embrace the plaza before it. Although the building was begun in the early 1940s, its appetite for steel, so necessary for the war effort, led to its abandonment. Eventually, in 1960, a vast swimming pool was constructed where its foundation had been excavated. The Palace of Soviets, curiously, was located on the site of Konstantin Ton's Temple of Christ the Savior, symbolic of classicism's earlier demise. Because the broad avenue that was to have been cut from Sverdlov (Theater) Square to the Palace of Soviets also failed to materialize, Moscow's center miraculously remained intact.

It is difficult to generate praise for the classical architecture which did rise in Moscow in the 1930s and 1940s. The chief feature of Shchusev's Moskva Hotel was its overwhelming portico and dissimilar wings. Alabyan's multi-columned Theater for the Red Army awkwardly substituted the column for any semblance of functionality. Fomin's and Arkin's Kaluga Gate, below Kazakov's Golitsynskaia Hospital appeared little more than an

---

[17] See also S. Frederick Starr, "Writings from the 1960s on the Modern Movement in Russia," *Journal of the Society of Architectural Historians* 30 (1971): no. 2, 170–78 and *Melnikov: Solo Architect in a Mass Society* (Princeton, 1978); Anatole Kopp, *Town and Revolution: Soviet Architecture and City Planning 1917–1935* (London, 1970). Transl. from the Fr. by Thomas E. Burton and first published in France in 1967; El Lissitzky, *Russia: An Architecture for World Revolution* (Cambridge, Mass., 1970, orig. published in 1930); and Berton, *Moscow*, 204–25.

[18] For more, see N. P. Bylinkin, P. A. Voldin, Ia. A. Kornfel'd, A. K. Mikhailov, and Iu. Savitskii, *Istoriia sovetskoi arkhitektury* (Moscow, 1962); Berton, *Moscow*, 226–36; Kopp, *Town and Revolution*, 222–30.

attempt to duplicate traditional triumphal arches along the arterial roads entering Moscow. In all, it was a tired and tasteless classicism that the midtwentieth century revived.

After the war this same motif appeared in the buildings and formal plazas of many devastated Soviet cities as exemplified by Ivan Fialko's axial walks and Roman temples in Volgograd (Stalingrad). In the meantime, eclectic Moscow University, replete with classical portico, soared from its surrounding geometric streets and gardens, to dominate the lovely Sparrow Hills. Only in the last two decades has there been a return to the Constructivist and Garden City formula, notwithstanding the continuing tension between those advocating urban monumentality and those promoting some aspect of the idealized village. Even as it admits such new architecture into its confines, Soviet Moscow with its wide thoroughfares, parks, plazas, and columned edifices amply reflects the durability of classicism.

Classicism and Ideology

The suggestion that classicism became for the Russian gentry an expression of incipient national consciousness appears substantiated by the heroic dimensions of classical art during and after the Napoleonic Wars. Martial glory was a prevailing theme in Imperial Russia, and classicism reflected it in its great squares, edifices, triumphal arches, columns, and statuary. Nevertheless, Great Russian nationalism, or Slavophilism, contributed significantly to classicism's demise. Despite its ideal and noble qualities, classicism in Russia was essentially neutral and really could epitomize neither the national sentiment of a people nor the policy of the state. Those who determined the doctrine of Official Nationality eventually found a better vehicle in the imagery of imperial Byzantium and old Muscovy. This was especially true of the latter, the Muscovite National Style, which had evolved from wooden architectural motifs.

By the beginning of the twentieth century this pseudo-National style had spent itself; at the same time a rational corrective to the unplanned industrial city, as noted above, lent additional impetus to the search for a new orientation in Russian architecture.[19] An important commentary in this quest for a Russian style was a work written in 1905, a year of revolution. An engineer named Apyshkov, writing on *Rationality in the New Architecture*, concluded that the time had come for a new world architecture, probably one derived from Western models and experience. Indeed, Russia's exposure at this time to Beaux-Arts, Art Nouveau, Italian Futurism, the Viennese Secession, and to such individuals as Peter Behrens, young Mies van der Rohe, and Frank Lloyd Wright suggests the scope of possibilities. In the end, however, it was classicism that once again prevailed. It did so not only because it offered a solution to the problem of a disordered urban scene, but because it was also an architectural style with which the Russians were familiar and comfortable. There was even nostalgia for it from Petersburgers and Muscovites, who, surrounded by the architecture of Catherine II and Alexander I, were reminded of these heroic reigns.

In Moscow, where the school of architecture had been fully committed to the National Style, the new classicism, as noted above, caught on rather easily. Its cause was taken up with particular enthusiasm by the architect Illarion Ivanov-Schitz and his students Konstantin Melnikov, Nikolai Ladovskii, and I. and P. Golosov—all of the Moscow School. This classical revival received impetus, too, from Ivan Fomin's article on "Moskovskii klassitsizm" in the journal *Mir iskusstvo* (1904) and his founding of the new journal, *Starye gody*, for the explicit purpose of promoting classicism.[20]

[19] Starr, *Melnikov*, 22–24.
[20] Cf. ibid., 24; E. A. Borisova, "Neoklassitsizm," in E. A. Borisova and T. P. Kazhdan, *Russkaia arkhitektura kontsa XIX nachala XX veka* (Moscow, 1970), 167–219; and I. A. Kazakova, et al., *Fomin* (Moscow, n.d.).

With classicism's revival in this century, discussion immediately ensued as to its derivation, the debt which Russia owed Europe, and the extent to which classicism was uniquely Russian. The famed Russian art historian and theoretician Igor E. Grabar' wrote early in this century of Russia's European debt, painstakingly differentiating between the French and Italian traditions in Alexandrian classicism.[21] Thomon and Rossi were the key figures, respectively, in the French and Italian phases (fig. 77). The Alexandrian period Grabar' described as one when Russia "by a strange whim of fortune . . . becomes the second motherland of the new style, for in St. Petersburg the development interrupted in France is continued."[22] Discovering antecedents of Russian Classicism in the Italian Renaissance, Grabar' gave appropriate credit to Serlio, Palladio, Vitruvius, Alberti, Vignola and many others. He perceived the influence of Piranesi and the archeological discoveries in Magna Graecia on eighteenth-century style and noted the subsequent waning of Latinism and rise of Hellenism.

Grabar' credited French Classicism with having a decisive influence on the Russian:

> In its pure form, untouched by the influences of transfer, French Classicism of the 1780s came to St. Petersburg, where it received not only its further development but also its final perfection. Ledoux's ideas lost here their baselessness . . . . the blatancy and dashing unruliness of the *grand prix* was lost but not the attractive freedom of this young and daring architecture. A new trait also appeared which was never there before—a serious, well-considered understanding, perhaps less dexterity but more depth.[23]

Grabar' regarded the French émigré, Thomas de Thomon, despite his lacking originality and his possibly plagiarizing some prize-win-

Figure 77. Architect Thomas de Thomon (G. D. Oschepkov, *Arkhitektor Tomon.* Moscow, 1950).

ning projects of the 1780s, as the principal source of French Classicism in Russia. In fact, Grabar' suggested, rather than his being only a skillful compiler who shamelessly stole from his schoolfellows, Thomon took the projects of youthful dreamers and gave them a reality in St. Petersburg.

> This alone is sufficient to grant him immense importance in the history of European and particularly Russian and French art. He was not a colossus as some represent him now; he was not a Palladio and not even a Rastrelli. And Russia has seen greater architects both before and after him. But Thomon . . . was a Prometheus, who having stolen the flame of new beauty from the gods of France, brought it to Russia where it burned for so long and so brightly as nowhere else in Europe and for this we, the Russians must be grateful to him forever.[24]

This French influence Grabar' discerned in

[21] "Rannii aleksandrovskii klassitsizm' i ego frantsuzskie istochniki," *Starye gody* (July-September, 1912): 68–96. Cf. also Leonide Ignatieff, "French Emigrés in Russia 1789–1825," unpublished Ph.D. thesis, Univ. of Michigan, 1963.
    [22] Grabar', "Rannii aleksandrovskii klassitsizm," 68–69.
    [23] Ibid., 82.

[24] Ibid., 91.

the art of Voronikhin and Zakharov, who with Thomon "gave Ledoux's ideas an entirely new direction." Even Russian classicists like Starov and Rossi of the Italian school did not divorce themselves entirely from the French.[25]

Remarks by Grabar' in his *Istoriia russkogo iskusstva* followed in the same vein. He reiterated archeology's role in effecting the shift in Europe from baroque and rococo to the new classicism and Russian Classicism's debt to this revived interest in antiquity.[26] He recognized the influence exercised on Russia by the architects of Louis XVI's France, although it had arrived circuitously, via Rome.[27] In all, Grabar' avoided chauvinism as he placed Russian Classicism clearly in the European tradition; consequently, his work on Russian art contained much more information about European antecedents than it did on the substance of Russian Classicism itself.

Grabar' believed that the imperial notion to make St. Petersburg unsurpassed in beauty among Europe's capitals began to wane by the end of the reign of Nicholas I. As building diminished, an increasingly ostentatious classicism succumbed to the revived National Style. Having abandoned Greece, Russian architects in the 1830s returned to Pompeii and the early Italian Renaissance for guidance. Grabar' perceived Nicholean Classicism to be of three types: 1) that which retained elements of Alexandrian Hellenism, as exemplified by the later Stasov; 2) that which, like the work of the artist Bruillov, looked toward Pompeii and even early Renaissance Italy for inspiration while retaining some Greek elements; 3) and that which, represented by Montferrand, looked almost exclusively to the Renaissance,

not to antiquity. Grabar' observed that this last type really paved the way for a Renaissance revival. In his summary of late classicism, Grabar' remained entirely consistent with his approach to earlier Russian Classicism; namely, that it was a European phenomenon in which Russia was but a participant.

V. Kurbatov, having traced classicism from early times to the eighteenth century, concurred with Grabar' that Russian Classicism, indeed, had many Western antecedents.[28] It served little purpose, he argued, to differentiate foreign architects like Rinaldi, Vallin de la Mothe, Cameron, and Quarenghi from the Russians Bazhenov, Kazakov, Voronikhin, and Zakharov. What mattered was that Russia, late in the eighteenth century, provided a favorable climate for the creative and productive genius of both. Foreigners were "needed not because there were not enough native builders, but because a new artistic culture and new architectural ideas were necessary." On the other hand, baroque ideas that found their greatest expression in the works of Rastrelli did not respond to the demands for "quieter and more rational architecture." In dismissing both Renaissance and baroque forms as inappropriate for Russia, Kurbatov maintained that classicism "possessed the greatest rationality and had to triumph."

Kurbatov had his preferences among the foreign influences in the development of Russian Classicism. Instead of French Classicism he hailed the Scotsman Cameron and the Italian Quarenghi as precursors of Voronikhin, Zakharov, and Rossi.[29] He noted, in particular, that "Cameron's high favor with Catherine, not achieved by her own subject Bazhenov, gave him wide influence in Russia."[30] Stressing eighteenth-century antecedents, Kurbatov played down the year 1812 as a regenerative force in Russian architecture. "It is hardly correct," he observed

to connect the flourishing of Russian archi-

---

[25] Soviet sources ignore this article by Grabar', probably because it is ideologically at variance with official views. The only reference that I have found is A. I. Nekrasov, *Russkii ampir* (Moscow, 1935) who remarked on his explanation of French and Italian antecedents and criticized an analysis based only on facades: "The author [Grabar'] denies the presence of any system in the plans of classical buildings pointing only to the tendency to avoid curves. In his work there is mention neither of volume nor space" (10).

[26] (Moscow, 1910–1915) 3: 255–62.

[27] Ibid., 468; cf. also 449–68; cf. also Grabar', "Rannii aleksandrovskii klassitsizm."

[28] "Podgotovka i razvitie neoklassicheskogo stilia," *Starye gody* (Sept. 1911): 151–73.

[29] Ibid., 172–73.

[30] "Klassitsizm' i ampir'," *Starye gody* (July, 1912): 105–19.

tecture in the 1810s and 1820s with the epoch of 1812 and the wars of Liberation. The disappointment with the Congress of Vienna was too great.

For him the human factor—Peter, Catherine, and Alexander—was paramount in the rise of Russian Classicism.[31]

In his analysis of the Empire style Kurbatov focused principally on Petersburg. What of Moscow? Moscow lived otherwise. It did not have

> to worry about the magnificence of St. Petersburg. The beautiful buildings of Kazakov are overly cozy in comparison with those of St. Petersburg and are full of the gracefulness of the dying baroque. Their facades are meant to be attractive rather than grand. Despite the architectural and decorative perfection, one feels still that the architects are inspired only by a reflected feeling. . . . Only after the Napoleonic invasion did the sentiment in Moscow rise to the same pitch as in St. Petersburg.[32]

Soviet scholars over the past several decades have perceived Russian Classicism quite differently from Grabar' and Kurbatov. They have discounted foreign influences while emphasizing indigenous Russian and "progressive" themes, citing the superior aesthetic of Russian classical architecture compared to that of Europe and the rest of the world.

The uniquely Russian character of classicism pervaded the works of D. E. Arkin and N. N. Kovalenskaia.[33] Observing that classical forms cloaked everything from modest village dwellings, servants' quarters on rural estates, and wooden churches to the splendid mansions of the aristocracy, they recalled the crucial role of the serf-architects who sometimes linked classicism to the National, or traditional, style. Instead of acknowledging West-

ern influences in Russian art, Arkin and Kovalenskaia credited the Academy of Arts in Petersburg both for its unique contributions to Russian art and for bringing Russian culture into contact with that of the West. Foreign masters who journeyed to Russia, they held, were sensitized to the high quality of Russian culture and therefore adapted their talents to it. It was this fusion of Russian and foreign genius which begat Russian Classicism. Kovalenskaia, writing independently, reiterated opinions held by other Soviet writers.[34] She believed that classicism heralded the era of great Russian architects—Bazhenov, Kazakov, Starov, Voronikhin, Zakharov, and others—who brought world renown to Russia in the field of architecture. In this respect the most important and clearly Russian contribution was the city ensemble.

Arkin, for his part, emphatically distinguished Russian from European classicism.[35] Russia produced her own masters, the students of Ukhtomskii. Their work and ideas were an "independent channel in the great international movement of classicism." Arkin disagreed that Russian Classicism was a "variant of the French classical school, an offshoot of English Palladianism, or a variety of Italian pseudoclassic." Like Kovalenskaia, he concluded that classicism constituted a great epoch in the history of Russian art and was therefore quite separate from the Western classical tradition. Almost jingoistically he proclaimed that in "European classicism we observe few national aspects; Russian Classicism grew into the national architectural style."

M. I. Rzianin, writing during the Stalin era, also dwelt on the uniquely Russian qualities

---

[31] Ibid., 117.

[32] Ibid., 118–19. Kurbatov, differentiating between revived Greek and Roman (Empire) styles, concluded that classicism in Italy, Russia, and England during the eighteenth century was Palladian; Cameron and Zakharov, Greek; and Quarenghi, Roman.

[33] See "Vvedenie," in Grabar', *Iskusstva* 6: 10–15.

[34] *Istoriia russkogo iskusstva XVIII veka*, 110–11 and 125 ff. and Kovalenskaia, *Istoriia russkogo iskusstva pervoi poloviny XIX veka* (Moscow, 1951), 17 ff.

[35] Cf. "Russkaia Klassika" in *Obrazy arkhitektury* (Moscow, 1941), 147–92. For quotes in this paragraph, see 158–60. Arkin wrote extensively on Russian classicism. Cf. his "Klassitsizm i ampir v Moskve," *Arkhitektura SSSR* (1935), no. 10–11: 82–89; "K kharakteristike russkogo klassitsizm" in *Arkhitektura: Sbornik po tvorcheskim voprosam* (Moscow, 1945), 60–80; and *Istoriia arkhitektury XVIII–XIX vv* (Moscow, 1938), in which he discusses extensively Western, especially French, classicism and its relationship to the Russian.

of both early and later Russian Classicism.[36] Dividing Russian Classicism of the second half of the eighteenth century into "early" and "mature" and then that of the late third or half of the nineteenth century into pre-1812 and post-1812 "Russian Empire" style, he insisted that such divisions did not alter Russian classicism's essential unity. He applauded the monumental architectural ensembles of Moscow and Petersburg, the more intimate gentry (*dvorianskaia*) domestic architecture of Moscow, and the scope of classical building in the provinces. Russian Classicism in architecture symbolized Russian patriotism, "the pathos of the heroic struggle of Russia with foreign enemies" (Napoleonic France). Like Arkin and Kovalenskaia, Rzianin stressed that classicism joined the mainstream of the Russian architectural tradition, "born of the social conditions of Russia of that epoch." It became, moreover, "the foremost and leading branch of the architecture of world classicism."

Like other Soviet scholars Rzianin demeaned the French classic, using such pejoratives as "formalistic dryness," "abstractness of forms," "deliberate grandeur and pomposity of forms," "severe symmetry and geometric schematism of composition," and "isolation from nature." Russian Classicism, conversely, helped solve complicated building problems of city and ensemble, which "reflected the majesty of patriotic ideas and experiences of the Russian people, in particular, of the Patriotic War of 1812."

T. V. Alekseeva also insisted that early nineteenth-century Russia's adoption of classical forms was no blind act of copying the West; rather it evidenced striking originality and genius in St. Petersburg's ensembles, the restoration of Moscow, and city-building throughout the empire.[37] Russian Classicism, exhibiting monumentality, clarity, and simplicity, repudiated the insipid rococo medium which had preceded it, although its evolution

from Ukhtomskii through his students was a unique Muscovite accomplishment.

Alekseeva believed that Russian Classicism avoided both a slavish adherence to antiquity and an inferior imitation of its revivals elsewhere. She, like other Soviet scholars, did compare it with the French "Empire style," for city-building in Paris approximated in time and daring the grandiose undertakings by Alexander I. But Bonaparte was the enemy, and she construed his architectural endeavors as retrogressive, the antithesis of those by Alexander. The French classic was the product of a reactionary despot who had compromised aesthetic as well as political principles. His monuments in Paris, eclectic and superficial imitations of ancient Rome, fell far short of the free and natural conversion of ancient forms by the Russians. French Classicism, nurtured by the Enlightenment and initially possessed with revolutionary potential, had withered on the vine. Russian, on the other hand, fulfilled these revolutionary assumptions. While the artistic level of French style suffered from its association with military dictatorship and capitalism, Russia's classicism inspired the most progressive artistic creation of its day, the architectural ensemble.

Beyond its superior aesthetic Russian Classicism, according to Arkin and Kovalenskaia, possessed ethical-moral and socio-economic qualities not evident in its rococo predecessor: they identified the rococo with an idle aristocracy and characterized it as a style unresponsive to societal needs. Its "brilliance and decorative richness . . . made this style distant from the rest of real life." In contrast, the architecture of Catherine's reign had a broader socioeconomic basis and responded through "widespread building of towns and country estates" to the needs, not only of the aristocracy, but also of governmental administration and merchants.[38]

Rzianin gave earlier Russian Classicism a firm ideological base when he distinguished between the baroque-rococo style of the

---

[36] *Pamiatniki russkogo zodchestva* (Moscow, 1950), 102–106, contains the substance of his ideas noted in text.

[37] "Vvedenie," in Grabar', *Iskusstva* 8, i (Moscow, 1963): 7–42.

[38] See ibid., 6: 10–15.

"closed dvoriane world" and the later classicism of dvoriane culture and art with its "new, progressive, revolutionary . . . and critical world outlook." Classicism, which became for him the embodiment of "enlightenment and humanism," succored dvoriane revolutionaries who achieved fulfillment, despite their failure, in the Decembrist Revolt of 1825.

For Alekseeva, the socio-economic context for Russian Classicism assumed fundamental importance. Like the rococo, classicism was the product of dvoriane culture, representing, however, not a closed system, but a liberal and revolutionary one derived from humanism and the Enlightenment. Not only was early classicism "progressive" because of this association with "dvoriane revolutionaries," it was also truly "Russian," because it synthesized traditional and classical elements. Its genius stemmed from its "rational," not blind, acceptance of antiquity. The "Empire style," as noted above, proved even easier for Alekseeva to explain. The final stage of classicism mirrored the patriotism of the Russian people and the "pathos of their heroic struggle against Napoleon." Significantly, this classicism, which initially had been inspired by an enlightened dvoriane and nurtured by aristocratic Decembrists, was also fostered by class conflict—Pugachev's peasants and the urban bourgeoisie. Russian Classicism for Alekseeva symbolized triumph over the old feudal order and embodied enlightened virtues of "self-respect, honor, and freedom and reason which generated patriotic solidarity in all strata of the Russian population in the Great Patriotic War of 1812." The style represented both a striving for a higher social good, so often negated in the course of history by a privileged few, and a protest against entrenched bureaucracy. In all, it was a firm pronouncement that class solidarity had supplanted the concept of aristocratic service. The Alexandrian appropriation of the Doric order buttressed the Soviet proposition that Hellenic democracy and progressivism were part of the same whole.

G. I. Sternin, observing that classicism in the 1830s began losing vitality and its archi-

tects, their creativity, gave the following explanation:

> In the historical evolution of the country and as progressive social opinion became more and more imbued with the ideas of ceaseless struggle with the autocratic-feudal structure, the socially solidifying feeling of the architecture of classicism lost its aesthetic support, and, in an objective sense, lost its social usefulness.[39]

Classicism, deprived of its "progressive" content, became a prop for the autocracy of Nicholas I. Ensemble building, the greatest architectural achievement of the first third of the century, was sharply curtailed. Russian Classicism "became in the eyes of architects just another variation among artistic styles." Even those architects supposedly committed to classicism used other styles. For Sternin this eclecticism and stylization in the 1830s resulted from a sinking nobility and a tasteless bourgeoisie. Only a renewal of the National (Muscovite) Style, which had flourished before Peter, saved Russian architecture after classicism's decline. This revival, Sternin stated, was not to be confused with the resurrected "Russian-Byzantine" style, a revival of pre-Muscovite forms and called by Sternin "the most reactionary movement in Russian architecture in the 1830s–1850s." This mode, associated with the work of K. A. Ton, was "forced down from the top with the direct blessing of Nicholas I."

Even when discoursing on the aesthetic and utilitarian merits of Russian Classicism, Soviet authors indulge in ideological rhetoric. For Brunov the "highest blossoming of the classical school of Russian architecture," which came during the first third of the nineteenth century, was exemplified by "new and progressive modes and methods of ensemble [building] in the development of city-building composition."[40] He perceived differences between the Russian Empire style and that of Western Europe, particularly the French. The latter,

---

[39] Ibid., 8, ii (Moscow, 1964): 28–31.
[40] N. I. Brunov, *Istoriia russkoi arkhitektury*, 516.

identified with Napoleon and the "penetration of the capitalistic interests of the bourgeoisie into architecture," led to a "lowering of the ideological and artistic level of architecture"— especially in the progressive development of ensembles. France during the seventeenth and eighteenth centuries had, he noted, pioneered city-building through ensemble architecture, but Napoleon squandered its good reputation by trying to immortalize his military successes in tasteless reproductions of ancient Rome. The Russians, on the other hand, resolved problems of city-building by utilizing methods and modes derived from their own tradition, thereby inserting Russian Classicism in the vanguard of world classicism. Outstanding among Russian accomplishments were those of planning and building the central districts of Petersburg, restoration and reconstruction of Moscow after 1812, and designing provincial cities throughout Russia.

Rzianin linked Russian Classicism to the heightened tensions caused by Pugachev's rebellion. Unlike the ostentatious baroque, classicism

> responded to the ideo-artistic form of its epoch—that of growing class tensions and revolutionary moods in dvoriane-peasant Russia. The classical epoch was one of developing critical social thought, ideas of humanism, enlightenment, and struggle of the social character of culture and art, all of which culminated finally in the Great Patriotic (*Otechestvennaia*) War of 1812.[41]

Classicism thus joined the mainstream of the Russian architectural tradition, "born of the social conditions of Russia of that epoch"; it appeared, moreover, as "the foremost and leading branch of the architecture of world classicism."

City planning and building schemes, beginning in the 1760s, were, according to Arkin and Kovalenskaia derived from "deeper artistic ideas" than early St. Petersburg baroque or Rastrelli's and Ukhtomskii's rococo. Peter's style was excessively utilitarian, too ornamen-

tal and remote from antiquity; Catherine's classicism, however, represented a compromise between the genuine antique and indigenous Russian. Its clarity and the balance of compositional and plastic elements "allowed its utilization for the most varied themes, objectives, materials and methods." Arkin and Kovalenskaia especially emphasized classicism's diverse functionality: hospitals, warehouses, blacksmith shops—nearly every conceivable edifice—could and did employ the classical motif. Russian Classicism's accent on ensemble planning admirably served the needs of town planning and lent itself to estate design and landscaping.[42]

These comments by Soviet art historians indicate the generally high regard which classicism has enjoyed among them. Having stressed the importance of classicism in Russian architectural history, the Soviets have not always cared about its preservation. Central Leningrad has been scrupulously protected, but classical edifices in provincial cities have in many cases fallen into disrepair or simply disappeared. In central Moscow, where the vogue of city planning has been most pronounced, much of the old classical city has been its victim. This was true of many individual buildings, especially churches, and of streets like the Tverskaia, (Gorkii), during the great urban remodeling in the late 1930s. In the 1960s the Kalinin Prospekt knifed through the old Arbat, thereby destroying the heart of classical Moscow.[43]

Despite its losses, Moscow of the 1812 generation remains in various individual landmarks behind the grim Stalinist facades on Gorkii Street and the slick Khrushchevian ones on the Kalinin Prospekt.[44] Classical Moscow demands of the visitor only a bit of enterprise to glimpse its remnants and comprehend its meaning.

---

[41] *Piamiatniki russkogo zodchestva*, 103.

[42] "Vvedenie," *Iskusstva* 6: 12.

[43] See Berton, *Moscow*, passim and A. J. Schmidt, "Soviet Legislation for Protection of Architectural Monuments: Background" to be published in *Law and Perestroika*, a volume in the *Law in Eastern Europe* Series, U. of Leiden, The Netherlands.

[44] See A. J. Schmidt, "Architecture in Nineteenth-Century Russia: the Enduring Classic," *Art and Culture in Nineteenth-Century Russia*, ed. Stavrou., 172–93.

Select Bibliography

The journals *Arkhitekturnoe nasledstvo* (1950–) and *Arkhitektura SSSR* have been especially useful.

Abramov, L. "Novye materialy o rabotakh V. I. Bazhenova v Gatchine." *Arkhitekturnoe nasledstvo* 1(1951): 78–85.

Alekseev, B. I. "Planirovka teatral'noi ploshchadi v Moskve v pervoi polovine XIX veka." *Ezhegodnik museia arkhitektury* 1(1937): 80–88.

Alekseev, T. V. *Russkoe iskusstvo XVIII veka.* Moscow, 1968.

Alexander, John T. *Bubonic Plague in Early Modern Russia: Public Health and Urban Disaster.* Baltimore and London, 1980.

———. "Catherine II, Bubonic Plague, and the Problem of Industry in Moscow." *American Historical Review* 79(1974): 637–70.

Alexander, Sir James Edward. *Travels to the seat of war in the East, through Russia and the Crimea, in 1829.* London, 1830.

Al'tshuller, B. L., et al. *Pamiatniki arkhitektury moskovskoi oblasti.* 2 vols. Moscow, 1975.

Anderson, M. S. "Some British Influences on Russian Intellectual Life and Society in the 18th Century." *The Slavonic and East European Review* 39(1960): 148–63.

Andreev, A. "Arkhitektura v dome Razumovskogo v Moskve." *Arkhitektura SSSR* 1955, no. 6: 32–34.

Arkin, D. E. *Istoriia arkhitektury XVIII–XIX vv.* Moscow, 1938.

———. "K kharakteristike russkogo klassitsizma." *Arkhitektura. Sbornik po tvorcheskim voprosam.* Moscow, 1945, 60–80.

———. "Klassitsizm i ampir v Moskve." *Arkhitektura SSSR,* 1935, nos. 10–11: 82–89.

———. "Perspektivnyi plan Peterburga 1764–1773." *Arkhitekturnoe nasledstvo* 7(1955): 13–38.

———. "Russkaia klassika, Bazhenov and Kazakov." *Obrazy arkhitektury.* Moscow, 1941, 146–216.

———. "Zamechatel'nyi dokument russkogo gradostroitel'stva XVII veka." *Sovetskaia arkhitektura* 6(1955): 101–10.

Auty, Robt. and D. Obolensky, eds. *An Introduction to Russian Art and Architecture. Companion to Russian Studies,* vol. 3. Cambridge, Engl., 1980.

Baedeker's Russia 1914. London, 1971.

Baldin, V. I. *Arkhitektor A. G. Grigor'ev.* Moscow, 1976.

———. ed. *Arkhitektor D. V. Ukhtomskii.* Moscow, 1973.

Balitskii, G., ed. *Pozhar Moskvy.* Moscow, 1911.

Baron, Samuel H. "The Origins of Seventeenth Century Moscow's Nemeckaja-Sloboda." *California Slavic Studies* 5(1970): 1–17.

———. "The Town in 'Feudal' Russia." *Slavic Review* 28(1969): 116–22.

———. *The Travels of Olearius in Seventeenth Century Russia.* Stanford, California, 1967.

Bartenev, I. "Stroitel'naia nauka v Rossii" (XVII v.-pervaia XIX v.). *Trudy vserossiiskoi Akademii khudozhestv.* Leningrad and Moscow, 1947, 144–60.

Batiushkov, K. N. *Sochinenie.* Moscow, 1955.

Baumgart, Fritz. *A History of Architectural Styles.* New York, 1970.

Belekhov, N. N. and Petrov, A. N. *Ivan Starov: Materialy k izucheniiu tvorchestva.* Moscow, 1950.

Beletskaia, Elena A. *Arkhitektor Afanasii Grigor'evich Grigor'ev, 1782–1868.* Moscow, 1976.

———. *Arkhitekturnye al'bomy M. F. Kazakova.* Moscow, 1950.

———. "Iz istorii stroitel'stva doma Razumovskogo." *Arkhitekturnoe nasledstvo* 9 (1959): 189–196.

———. "Neopublikovannyi proekt V. I. Bazhenova." *Soobshcheniia Instituta istorii iskusstv arkhitektury SSSR* 1(1951): 112–17.

———. *Postroiki arkhitektury V. I. Bazhenova.* Moscow, 1950.

———. "Vosstanovlenie zdanii Moskovskogo universiteta posle pozhara 1812 goda." *Arkhitekturnoe nasledstvo* 1(1951): 175–90.

———. "'Vysokie gory.' K kharakteristike tvorchestva Zhiliardi." *Arkhitektura SSSR.* 1939, no. 4: 65–68.

———, Krasheninnikova, N., Chernozubova, and Ern, I. "'Obraztsovye' proekty v zhiloi zastroike russkikh gorodov XVIII–XIX vv.* Moscow, 1961.

Beliavskaia, V. *Rospisi russogo klassitsizma.* Leningrad, Moscow, 1940.

Benesch, W. "The Use of Wood as a Building Material in Pre-Modern Russia: Its Extent and Potential Cultural Implications." *Journal of World History* 8(1964): 160–67.

Berton, Kathleen. *Moscow: An Architectural History.* New York, 1977.

Bezsonov, S. V. "M. F. Kazakov na Ukraini." *Arkhitektura radian'skoi Ukraini.* 1939, no. 5: 33.

Billington, James H. *The Icon and the Axe.* New York, 1966.

Blackwell, William. *The Beginnings of Russian Industrialization 1800–1860.* Princeton, 1968.

Blumenfeld, Hans. "Russian City Planning of the Eighteenth and Early Nineteenth Centuries." *Journal of the Society of Architectural Historians* 4(1944): 22–33.

————. "Theory of City Form Past and Present." *Journal of the Society of Architectural Historians* 8(1949).

Bogoslovskii, V. A. *Kvarengi: master arkhitektury russkogo klassitsizma.* Leningrad/Moscow, 1955.

————. "Obshchestvennaia priroda i ideinaia sushchnost' arkhitektury russkogo klassitisizma poslednei treti XVIII veka." *Uchenye zapiski Leningradskogo gos. universiteta A. A. Zhdanova. Seriia istoricheskikh nauk* 12(1955): 191–247.

————. "Obshchestvennye prichiny rastsveta russkoi arkhitektury v pervoi chetverti XIX v." *Vestnik Leningradskogo universiteta.* Leningrad, 1958, no. 2, seriia istorii, iazyka i literatury 1: 44–57.

Bol'shaia sovetskaia entsiklopediia. Moscow, 1950.

Bondarenko, I. E. "Arkhitektor Iosif Ivanovich Bove." *Ezhegodnik moskovskogo arkhitekturnogo obshchestva* 4(1914–16): 11–18.

————. *Arkhitector Matvei Fedorovich Kazakov 1738–1813.* Moscow, 1938.

————. "Arkhitektor V. I. Bazhenov i ego proekt Kremlevskogo dvortsa." *Akademiia arkhitektury.* 1935, no. 1–2: 107–12.

————. "Arkhitektura Moskvy XVIII i nachala XIX vekov." *Moskva v ee proshlom i nastoiashchem* 8(1911): 65–88.

————. *Arkhitekturnye pamiatniki Moskvy: Epokha Aleksandra.* Moscow, 1904.

————. "Uchebnik po arkhitekture vremen Kazakova." *Arkhitektura SSSR.* 1938, no. 10: 46.

————. "Zodchestvo Moskvy vosemnadtsatogo i nachala deviatnadtsatogo veka." *Putevoditel' po Moskve.* Moscow, 1913, 1–41.

Borisova, E. A. "Arkhitekturnoe obrazovanie v Kantseliarii o stroenii vo vtoroi chetverti XVIII veka." *Ezhegodnik Instituta istorii iskusstv 1960.* Moscow, 1961, 97–131.

————. "Arkhitektura serediny i vtoroi poloviny XIX v." Lectures in series *Istorii russkoi arkhitektury XVIII–XX vv.* April 9 and 16, 1986. Shchusev Museum of Architecture, Kalinin Prospect 5, Moscow.

————. "Neoklassitisizm." E. A. Borisova and T. P. Kazhdan, *Russkaia arkhitektura kontsa XIX-nachala XX veka.* Moscow, 1971, 167–219.

Borisovskii, G. "Klassicheskii order i sovremennost." *Arkhitektura SSSR.* 1958, no. 3: 45–48.

Bradley, Joseph. "Moscow: from Big Village to Metropolis" in *The City in Late Imperial Russia,* ed. Michael Hamm. Bloomington, Indiana, 1986.

————. *Muzhik and Muscovite: Urbanization in Late Imperial Russia.* Berkeley, 1985.

Braitseva, O. I. "Novoe i traditsionnoe v khramovom zodchestve Moskvy kontsa XVII v." *Arkhitekturnoe nasledstvo* 26(1978): 31–40.

————. "Ob ansamble ul. Pokrovki kontsa XVII v. v Belom Gorode Moskvy." *Arkhitekturnoe nasledstvo* 28(1980): 47–51.

————. "Ulitsy Maroseika i Pokrovka v Moskve nachala XIX v." *Arkhitekturnoe nasledstvo* 29(1981): 63–69.

Brumfield, William C. *Gold in Azure: One Thousand Years of Russian Architecture.* Boston, 1983.

Budylina, M. V., Brautseva, O. I., and Kharlamova, A. M. *Arkhitektor N. A. L'vov.* Moscow, 1961.

Budylina, M. V. "Arkhitekturno-gradostroitel'naia deiatel'nost v Moskve v poslednei chertverti XVIII-nachala XIX v." Chast' 1. Moscow, 1951.

————. "Arkhitekturnoe obrazovanie v Kamennom prikaze (1775–1782)." *Arkhitekturnoe nasledstvo* 15(1963): 111–20.

————. "Istoriia postroiki Manezha v Moskve." *Arkhitekturnoe nasledstvo* 2 (1952).

————. "Nikolai Aleksandrovich L'vov." *Sovetskaia arkhitektura* 5(1954): 75–87.

————. "Planirovka i zastroika Moskvy posle pozhara 1812 g." *Arkhitekturnoe nasledstvo* 1(1951): 135–74.

Bunin, A. V. *Istoriia gradostroitel'nogo iskusstva.* Moscow, 1953.

Catherine II. *Correspondance avec Falconet.* Ed. Louis Reau. Paris, 1921.

Catherine II. *Correspondance avec Grimm (Sbornik russkogo istoricheskogo obshchetva)* 23(1878), 33(1881), 44(1885).

Chaianova, O. *Teatr maddoksa v Moskve (1776–1805).* Moscow, 1927.

Chernov, E. G. and Shishko, A. V. *Bazhenov.* Moscow, 1949.

————. *Nekotorye osobennosti tvorchestva Bazhenova i Kazakova.* Moscow, 1946.

Chernozubova, L. E. "Iz istorii zastroiki Moskvy v pervoi polovine XIX veka." *Arkhitekturnoe nasledstvo* 9(1959): 15–27.

————. "Obraztsovye proekty planirovki zhilykh kvartalov i ploshchadei nachala XIX v." *Arkhitekturnoe nasledstvo* 15(1963): 188–92.

Clarke, Edward D. *Travels in Russia, Tartary, and Turkey.* Edinburgh, (1839) 1852.

Coxe, William. *Travels in Poland, Russia, Sweden, and Denmark.* 5 vols. London, 1802.

Custine, Marquis de. *The Empire of the Czar: or Observations of the Social, Political, and Religious State and Prospects of Russia.* 3 vols. London, 1843.

D'iakonov, M. V. "K biograficheskomu slovariu moskovskikh zodchikh XVIII–XIX vv" v kn.: *Russkii gorod,* vyp. 1, Moscow, 1976; vyp. 2, Moscow, 1979; vyp. 3, Moscow, 1980; vyp. 4, Moscow, 1981; and vyp. 5 (concluding), Moscow, 1982.

Dolgova, S. R. "Notes of an Eyewitness of the Plague Riot in Moscow in 1771." *Soviet Studies in History* 25 (1987), no. 4: 79–90.

Domshlak, M. I. *Nazarov.* Moscow, 1956.

Donnert, Erich. *Russia in the Age of Enlightenment.* Leipzig, 1986.

Dukes, Paul. *Catherine The Great and The Russian Nobility.* Cambridge, 1967.

————. *Russia under Catherine the Great. 1: Select Documents on Government and Society.* Newtonville, Mass. 1978.

Dutton, Ralph. *The English Garden.* London, 1937, 2nd ed. 1950.

Egorov, Iu. A. *Ansambl' v gradostroitel'stve SSSR: Ocherki.* Moscow, 1961.

————. *The Architectural Planning of St. Petersburg.* Athens, Ohio, 1969.

Ehret, Joseph. "Domenico Gilardi von Montagnola; ein Wiedererbauer Moskaus nach dem Brande von 1812." *Zeitschrift für schweizerische Archäologie und Kunstgeschichte.* Basel Bd. 15, Heft 1(1954): 33–54.

Evangulova, O. S. *Dvortsovo-parkovye ansambli Moskvy pervoi poloviny XVIII-go veka.* Moscow, 1969.

————. "Kazakov i Kvarengi." *Pamiatniki kul'tury: issledovanie i restavratsiia.* 2 vols. Moscow, 1959.

Evsina, N. A. "Arkhitektura pervoi treti XVIII v." Lecture in series *Istoriia russkoi arkhitektury XVIII-nach. XX v.* February 5, 1986 at Shchusev Museum of Architecture, Kalinin Prospect 5, Moscow.

————. "Arkhitektura serediny XVIII v." Ibid., February 12 and 19, 1986.

Fedorov-Davydov, A. A. *Arkhitektura Moskvy posle Otechestvennoi voiny 1812 goda.* Moscow, 1953.

————. *Fedor Alekseev.* Moscow, 1956.

Fekhner, M. "Dom A. S. Griboedova v Moskve." *Pamiatniki kul'tury* 1(1959): 123–42.

————. "K istorii stroitel'stva Mariinskoi bol'nitsy dlia bednykh v Moskve," *Arkhitekturnoe nasledstvo* 31(1983): 12–16.

Fomin, I. "Moskovskii klassitsizm." *Mir iskusstva.* 1904, no. 7: 149–98.

————. "Moskovskii klassitsizm." *Starye gody* 12(1904): 187–98.

Gaisinskii, Abram Iakovlevich. *Arkhitektura inter'era paradnykh pomeshchenii epokhi russkogo klassitisizma.* Moscow, 1946.

Gerasimov, Iu. N. "Arkhitektura epokhi stanovleniia klassitsizma." Lecture in series *Istoriia russkoi arkhitektury XVIII-nach.*

XX v. February 26, 1986 at Shchusev Museum of Architecture, Kalinin Prospect 5, Moscow.

Giedion, Sigfried. *Spätbarocker und romantischer Klassizismus.* Munich, 1922.

Gilbert, Linnie. *Russia Illustrated.* London, 1844.

Gladkova, E. "Roboty russkikh rezchikov XVIII veka v prigorodnykh dvortsakh." *Arkhitekturnoe nasledstvo* 4(1953): 166–76.

———. *Naberezhnaia Moskvy.* Moscow, 1940.

Gohstand, Robert. "The Shaping of Moscow by Nineteenth Century Trade." *The City in Russian History,* ed. M. Hamm. Lexington, Ky., 1976.

Gol'denberg, P. *Staraia Moskva.* Moscow, 1947.

Gol'denberg, P. and B. *Planirovka zhilogo kvartala Moskvy XVII, XVIII, XIX vv.* Moscow and Leningrad, 1935.

Gorbachev, V. *Arkhitekturnyi analiz inter'era grazhdanskikh sooruzhenii kontsa XVIII veka v Moskve.* Moscow, 1958.

Grabar', Igor Emmanuilovich. "Les débuts du classicisme sous Alexandre et ses sources françaises." *Starye gody* (July–Sept., 1912): 68–96.

———. "Fedor Alekseev." *Starye gody.* 1907, no. 7–12: 357.

———. "Gagarinskii osobniak v Moskve." *Pamiatniki iskusstva, razrushennye nemetskimi zakhvatchikami v SSSR.* Moscow, 1948, 433–48.

———. *Istoriia russkogo iskusstva.* 3 vols. Moscow, 1910–15.

———, et al. *Istoriia russkogo iskusstva.* 13 vols. Moscow, 1953–68. See 6 (Moscow, 1961); 8, i (Moscow, 1963); 8, ii (Moscow, 1964) for excellent bibliographies.

———, et al. *Neizvestnye i predpolagaemye postroiki V. I. Bazhenova.* Moscow, 1951.

———. "Rannii aleksandrovskii klassitsizm." *Starye gody* (1912), no. 7–9.

———. *Russkaia arkhitektura pervoi poloviny XVIII veka.* Moscow, 1954.

———. "U istokov klassitsizma." *Ezhegodnik instituta istorii iskusstv* (1956).

Gransberg, Alina Khristoforovna. *Arkhitekturnoe tvorchestvo N. A. L'vova.* Moscow, 1952. Dissertation.

Grech, A. *Dereviannyi klassitsizm v Moskve.* Sbornik obshchestva izucheniia russkoi usad'by, Moscow, 1928.

Grimm, G. *Arkhitektura perekrytii russkogo klassitsizma.* Moscow, 1939.

———. "Issledovanie nekotorikh ordernykh kompozitsii V. I. Bazhenova i M. F. Kazakova." *Voprosy teorii arkhitekturnoi kompozitsii* 1(1955): 77–129.

Grintsevich, O. S. "Proekty planirovki Peterburga vtoroi poloviny XIX-nachala XX vekov." *Arkhitekturnoe nasledstvo* 9(1959): 51–58.

Guliantskii, N. F. "Cherty preemstvennosti v kompozitsii tsentrov russkikh gorodov, pereplanirovannykh v XVIII v." *Arkhitekturnoe nasledstvo* 29(1981): 3–17.

———. "Gradostroitel'naia osnova tvorcheskogo metoda V. P. Stasova." *Arkhitekturnoe nasledstvo* 25(1976): 116–30.

———. "Gradostroitel'nye osobenosti Peterburga i cherty russkoi arkhitektury serediny XVIII v." *Arkhitekturnoe nasledstvo* 27 (1979): 12–21.

———. "O kompozitsii zdanii v ansamblevoi zastroike Moskvy perioda klassitsizma." *Arkhitekturnoe nasledstvo* 24(1976): 20–40.

———. "Moskva Iauzskaia." *Arkhitekturnoe nasledstvo* 34(1986): 34–43.

———. "Russkii reguliarnyi gorod na traditsonnoi osnove." *Arkhitekturnoe nasledstvo* 33(1985): 3–13.

———. "Sintez professii i metod zodchero v russkoi arkhitekture kontsa XVIII v." *Arkhitekturnoe nasledstvo* 30(1982): 24–31.

———. "Traditsii klassiki i cherty renessansa v arkhitekture Moskvy XV-XVII vv." *Arkhitekturnoe nasledstvo* 26(1978): 13–30.

———. "Tvorcheskie metody arkhitektorov russkogo klassitsizma pri razrabotke ordernykh kompozitsii." *Arkhitekturnoe nasledstvo* 22(1974): 30–52.

Hamilton, George H. *The Art and Architecture of Russia.* (1954, 1975) Baltimore, 1983.

Hamm, Michael, ed. *The City in Russian History.* Lexington, Ky., 1976.

Haxthausen, Baron von. *The Russian Empire and Its People, Institutions and Resources.* 2 vols. London, 1856.

Hiorns, Frederick. *Town-Building in History.* London, 1956.

Hitchcock, Henry-Russell. *Architecture: Nineteenth and Twentieth Centuries.* Baltimore, 1967.

Hittle, J. Michael. *The Service City: State and Townspeople in Russia 1600–1800.* Cambridge, Mass., 1979.

Honour, Hugh, *Neo-Classicism.* Baltimore, 1968.

Ialova, N. T. *Raboty russkikh arkhitektorov kontsa XVIII v. i nachala XIX v.* Leningrad, 1949. Dissertation.

Ignatieff, Leonide. "French Emigrés in Russia, 1789–1825: the Interaction of Cultures in Time of Stress." Univ. of Mich. Ph.D. dissertation. 1963.

Ikonnikov, A. V. "Planirovochnye pradtsii v narodnom zodchestve." *Arkhitekturnoe nasledstvo* 14(1962): 159–184.

———. *Kamennaia letopis Moskvy: Putevoditel'.* Moscow, 1978.

Il'in, M. A. *Arkhitektura Moskvy v XVIII veke.* Moscow, 1953.

———. *Bazhenov.* Moscow, 1954.

———. "Eskizy V. I. Bazhenova dlia Tsaritsyna." *Arkhitekturnyi Arkhiv* 1(1946): 109–17.

———. "'Facadicheskii' plan Moskvy M. F. Kazakova." *Arkhitekturnoe nasledstvo* 9(1959): 5–14.

———. *Kazakov.* Moscow, 1955.

———. *Matvei Fedorovich Kazakov.* Moscow, 1944.

———. *Moskva.* Moscow, 1963.

———. *Moskva: Pamiatniki arkhitektury XVIII-pervoi treti XIX veka/ Moscow: Monuments of Architecture 18th and First Third of 19th Century.* 2 vols. Moscow, 1975. Cited as *Monuments.*

———. "Nasledie Palladio i russkaia arkhitektura kontsa XVIII veka." *Arkhitektura SSSR* 10(1938): 35–40.

———. *O russkoi arkhitekture.* Moscow, 1963.

———. "Osip Ivanovich Bove." *Liudi russkoi nauki* 2 (Moscow and Leningrad, 1948): 1185–92.

———. *Podmoskovie.* Moscow, 1966.

———. "Russian Parks of the Eighteenth Century." *The Architectural Review* 135(1964): 100–11.

———. "Usad'ba O. I. Bove." *Sbornik obshchestva izucheniia russkoi usad'by* 3(1927): 17–19.

——— and Moiseeva, T. V. *Moskva i Podmoskov'e.* Moscow, 1979.

Istoriia Moskvy. Ed. S. V. Bakhrushin, et al. 6 vols. Moscow, 1952–57.

Johnston, Robert. *Travels Through Part of the Russian Empire and the Country of Poland.* New York, 1816.

Robert E. Jones. *The Emancipation of the Russian Nobility.* Princeton, 1973.

———. "Urban Planning and the Development of Provincial Towns in Russia, 1762–1796." *The Eighteenth Century,* ed. J. G. Garrard. Oxford, 1973: 321–344.

Kabuzan, V. M. *Narodonaselenie Rossii v XVIII-pervoi polovine XIX v.* Moscow, 1963.

Kaplun, A. "K istorii postroiki proviantskikh skladov v Moskve." *Soobshcheniia Instituta teorii i istorii arkhitektury Akademii arkhitektury SSSR.* 1947, no. 6.

———. "Moskovskie proviantskie sklady." *Arkhitektor V. P. Stasov.* Moscow, 1950, 55–70.

Kaufmann, E. *Architecture in the Age of Reason.* Cambridge, Mass. 1955.

———. "Three Revolutionary Architects: Boullée, Ledoux and Lequeu." *Transactions of the American Philosophical Society,* n. s., pt. 3, vol. 42 (1952).

Kazhdan, T. *Tvorchestvo V. I. Bazhenova v 70-x gg. XVIII v.* Moscow, 1952. Dissertation.

Kelly, Laurence, ed. *Moscow: A Travellers' Companion*. New York, 1984.

Kharlamova, A. M. *Kolonnyi zal Doma soiuzov*. Moscow, 1954.

———. *Zolotye komnaty doma Demidovykh v Moskve*. Moscow, 1955.

Kholmianskii, L. *Plastika inter'erov moskovskogo klassitsizma kontsa XVIII i nachala XIX vv.* Moscow, 1954. Dissertation.

Khozerov, I. "Novye dokumenty o tvorchestve D. Zhiliardi." *Arkhitektura SSSR*. 1941, no. 2: 63.

Khripunov, Iu. D. *Arkhitektura Bol'shogo teatra*. Moscow, 1955.

Kimball, Fiske. "Romantic Classicism in Architecture." *Gazette des Beaux-Arts* 25(1944): 95–112.

Kiparisova, A. A. "Akvarel' M. F. Kazakova. Prospekt stroiushchegosia goroda Tveri." *Arkhitekturnyi arkhiv* 1(1946): 122–24.

———. "Barochnye otrazheniia v planirovkakh Kazakova." *Ezhegodnik Muzeia arkhitektury* 1(1937): 69–79.

———. "Chertezhi i proekty M. F. Kazakova v Tsentral'nom voennoistoricheskom arkhive." *Arkhitekturnoe nasledstvo* 1(1951): 119–34.

———. "Gradskaia bol'nitsa." *Arkhitekturnoe nasledstvo* 1(1951): 127–34.

———. "Neopublikovannye proekty moskovskikh zodchikh kontsa XVIII i nachala XIX vekov." *Arkhitekturnoe nasledstvo* 1(1951): 108–19.

———. "Novye materialy o tvorchestve russkikh zodchikh." *Arkhitektura SSSR* 12(1946).

———. "Stat'i ob arkhitekture v russkikh zhurnalakh vtoroi poloviny XVIII v." *Arkhitekturnoe nasledstvo* 22(1974): 19–26.

———. "Stanovlenie nekotorykh tipov sooruzhenii moskovskogo klassitsizma v tvorchestve D. V. Ukhtomskogo." *Arkhitekturnoe nasledstvo* 29(1981): 33–40.

Kirichenko, E. I. "Arkhitekturnye ansambli Moskvy 1830–1860-x godov." *Arkhitekturnoe nasledstvo* 24(1976): 3–19.

———. "Dokhodnye zhilye doma Moskvy i Peterburga (1770-1830-e gg)." *Arkhitekturnoe nasledstvo* 14 (1962): 135–158.

———. *Moskva: Pamiatniki arkhitektury 1830–1910-kh godov*. Moscow, 1977. (Russian and English)

———. *Moskva: na rubezhe stoletii*. Moscow, 1977.

———. "Ob osobennostiakh zhiloi zastroiki poslepozharnoi Moskvy." *Arkhitekturnoe nasledstvo* 32(1984): 54–62.

———. "Zhilaia zastroika Peterburga epokhi klassitsizma i ee vliianie na razvitie arkhitektury." *Arkhitekturnoe nasledstvo* 16 (1967): 81–95.

Kohl, J. G. *Russia and the Russians in 1842*. 2 vols. London, 1842.

Kopp, Anatole. *Town and Revolution: Soviet Architecture and City Planning, 1917–1935*. London, 1970.

Korb, Johan-Georg. *Diary of an Austrian Secretary of Legation*. 2 vols. in one. Transl. Count MacKonnell (Latin, 1700; English, London, 1863; reissued New York, 1968).

Korshunova, Miliza. "William Hastie in Russia." *Architectural History* 17(1974): 14–21.

Kovalenskaia, N. "Arkhitektura russkogo klassitsizma." *Arkhitektura SSSR*. 1938, no. 9: 74–81.

———. *Istoriia russkogo iskusstva XVIII v.* Moscow and Leningrad, 1940.

———. *Istoriia russkogo iskusstva pervoi poloviny XIX v.* Moscow, 1951.

———. *Martos*. Moscow and Leningrad, 1939.

———. "Proekt Ekateringofskogo dvortsa V. I. Bazhenova." *Arkhitektura SSSR*. 1937, no. 3: 59.

Kozhin, N. "Novye materialy ob arkhitektore M. F. Kazakove i ego uchenike arkhitektore A. N. Bakareve." *Akademiia arkhitektury*. 1935, nos. 1–2: 112–17.

Krasheninnikov, A. F. "Redkii dokument arkhitekturnoi kritiki v Rossii XVIII v." *Arkhitekturnoe nasledstvo* 22(1974): 27–29.

Krasheninnikova, N. L. *Ansambl' Golitsynskoi bol'nitsy*. Moscow, 1955.

———. "Iz neopublikovannykh rabot I. i D. Zhiliardi." *Arkhitekturnoe nasledstvo* 1(1951): 191–201.

———. "K voprosu ob atributsii byvshego doma Dolgova na 1-oi Meshchanskoi ulitse." *Arkhitekturnoe nasledstvo* 1(1951): 86–93.

———. "Proekt apteki pri Vospitatel'nom dome." *Arkhitekturnoe nasledstvo* 1(1950): 197–99.

———. "Sobstvennye doma V. I. Bazhenova v Moskve." ibid.: 105–107.

———. (N. Krasceninnicowa and Maria Gibellino). *L'Architettura Russa nel passato e nel presente*. Roma, 1963.

Krivoruchko, M., Kurlat, F., Mikhailov, M., and Sokolovskii, Iu. *Po ulitsam Moskvy. Putevoditel'*. Moscow, 1962.

Kruglyi, A. "Reka Neglinnaia v kontse XVIII i nachale XIX stoletii." *Kommunal'noe Khoziaistvo*. 1927, nos. 9–10: 40–44.

Kudriavtsev, M. P. "Nekotorye printsipy i kompozitsonnye priemy gradostroitel'stva Moskvy XVII v." *Arkhitekturnoe nasledstvo* 33(1985): 23–30.

———. "Opyt privedeniia kompozitsii Moskvy kontsa XVII v. k idealizirovannoi skheme." *Arkhitekturnoe nasledstvo* 30(1982): 13–23.

———. "Prostranstvennaia kompozitsiia tsentra." *Arkhitekturnoe nasledstvo* 25(1976): 19–24.

———. "Sistemy prirechnykh ansamblei Moskvy XVII v." *Arkhitekturnoe nasledstvo* 34(1986): 17–25.

Kudriavtseva, T. N. "Kadashevskaia sloboda v Moskve i ee razvitie v kontse XVII–XVIII vv." *Arkhitekturnoe nasledstvo* 27(1979): 38–48.

———. "Kompozitsiia ulits drevnerusskikh gorodov." *Arkhitekturnoe nasledstvo* 33(1985): 14–22.

———. "Struktura i kompozitsionnye osobennosti slobody v russkom gorode XVI–XVII vv." *Arkhitekturnoe nasledstvo* 32(1984): 13–25.

Kunitskaia, E. R. "Men'shikova bashnia." *Arkhitekturnoe nasledstvo* 9 (1959): 157–168.

Kurbatov, V. Ia. "Klassitsizm i ampir." *Starye gody*, July–Sept., 1912, 105–19.

———. "K voprosu o Brenne." *Starye gody*, May, 1912.

———. "Podgotovka i razvitie neoklassicheskogo stilia." *Starye gody*. July–Sept., 1911, 151–73.

———. *Sady i parki. Istoriia i teoriia sadovogo iskusstva*. Petrograd, 1916.

Lavedan, Pierre. *French Architecture*. Middlesex, 1944, 1956.

Lavrov, V. A. *Razvitie planirovochnoi struktury istoricheski slozhivshikhsia gorodov*. Moscow, 1977.

Lees, Andrew. *Cities Perceived: Urban Society in European and American Thought, 1820–1940*. New York, 1985.

Leiboshits, N. Ia. "Materialy k tvorcheskoi biografii A. I. Mel'nikova." *Arkhitekturnoe nasledstvo* 9(1959): 117–38.

Libson, Vladimir, Ia. *Arkhitektura inter'era teatra epokhi russkogo klassitsizma*. Moscow, 1947.

———. "Triumfal'naia arka." *Vozrozhdennye sokrovishcha Moskvy*. Moscow, 1983.

———, Kuznetsova, A. I. *Bol'shoi teatr SSSR*. Moscow, 1982.

Lincoln, W. Bruce. "The Russian State and Its Cities: The Search for Effective Municipal Government, 1786–1842." *Jahrbücher für Geschichte Osteuropas* 17, no. 4 (1969): 531–54.

Liubavskii, M. K. "Moskovskii universitet v 1812 gody." *Obshchestvo istorii i drevnostei rossiiskikh*. Moscow, 1912, 57–118.

Lopez, Robert. "The Crossroads Within The Wall." *The Historian and The City*, ed. Oscar Handlin and John Burchard, Cambridge, Mass. 1966: 27–43.

Lukomskii, G. K. *Arkhitektura russkoi provintsii*. Moscow, 1916.

Lundberg, E. "A. I. Gertsen i A. L. Vitberg." *Akademiia arkhitektury*. 1934, nos. 1–2: 122–25.

Lyall, Robert. *The Character of the Russians and a Detailed History of Moscow*. London, 1823.

———. *Travels in Russia, the Krim, and the Caucasus*. London, 1825.

MacMichael, William. *Journey from Moscow to Constantinople in the Year 1817, 1818*. London, 1819.

Madariaga, Isabel de. *Russia in the Age of Catherine The Great.* New Haven, 1981.

Marker, Gary J. *Publishing, Printing and the Origins of the Intellectual Life in Russia, 1700–1800.* Princeton, N.J., 1985.

Matveev, A. "V. P. Stasov." *Arkhitektura SSSR.* 1939, no. 10: 62–67.

Mederskii, L. A. "Pervaia postroika Andreia Mikhailova." *Arkhitekturnoe nasledstvo* 7(1955): 177–78.

———. "Uchastie A. A. Mikhailova 2-go v izdaniiakh obshchestva pooshchreniia khudozhnikov." *Arkhitekturnoe nasledstvo* 9(1959): 139–42.

Mikhailov, A. I. *Arkhitektor D. V. Uktomskii i ego shkola.* Moscow, 1954.

———. *Bazhenov.* Moscow, 1951.

———. "Natsional'nyi kharakter russkoi arkhatektury XVIII i nachala XIX vv." *Russkaia arkhitektura.* Moscow, 1940, 70–92.

———. "Zapiska V. I. Bazhenova o Kremlevskoi perestroike." *Arkhitekturnyi arkhiv* 1(1946): 118–21.

Mikhailova, M. B. "Printsip zavisimosti ot obraztsa pri vozvedenii monumental'nykh zdanii klassitsizma." *Arkhitekturnoe nasledstvo* 31(1983): 3–11.

———. "Tipy sooruzhenii antichnosti v arkhitekture russkogo klassitsizma." *Arkhitekturnoe nasledstvo* 26(1978): 3–12.

Monas, Sidney. "St. Petersburg and Moscow as Cultural Symbols." *Art and Culture in Nineteenth-Century Russia,* ed. Theofanis G. Stavrou. Bloomington, Ind., 1983: 26–39.

Morenets, N. "Novye materialy o V. I. Bazhenove." *Arkhitekturnoe nasledstvo* 1(1951): 94–104.

Moskalets, E. "Chertezhi A. L. Vitberga." *Arkhitektura SSSR.* 1957, no. 12: 41.

Moskva: entsiklopediia, "Gradostroitel'stvo i arkhitektura." Moscow, 1980.

Nekrasov, A. *Russkii ampir.* Moscow, 1935.

———. "Russkoe zodchestvo epokhi klassitsizma i ampira." *Akademiia arkhitektury.* 1936, no. 1: 28–39.

Nikolaev, Evgenii V. *Klassicheskaia Moskva.* Moscow, 1975.

Okh, A. V. and Fekhner, M. V. "Novye issledovaniia po dereviannym zhilym domam nachala XIX veka v Moskve." *Arkhitekturnoe nasledstvo* 5(1955): 115–40.

Ol', G. A. *Arkhitektor Briullov.* Leningrad, 1955.

Ol'khova, A. "Reshetka i vorota Aleksandrovskogo sada v Moskve." *Arkhitekturnoe nasledstvo* 9(1959): 197–200.

Oshchepkov, G. D. *Arkhitektor Tomon.* Moscow, 1950.

Ozhegov, S. S. *Tipovoe i povtornoe stroitel'stvo v Rossii v XVIII—pervoi polovine XIX v.* Moscow, 1957.

Pallas, Peter Simon. *Travels through the Southern Provinces of the Russian Empire in the Years 1793 and 1794.* 2 vols. London, 1812.

Pamiatniki arkhitektury Moskvy. Moscow, 1982.

Paul, Robert B. *Journal of a Tour to Moscow in the Summer of 1836.* London, 1836.

Pegov, A. M., ed. *Imena moskovskikh ulits,* rev. ed. Moscow, 1975.

Perry, John. *The State of Russia Under the Present Czar.* London, 1716 (DeCapo reprint, New York, 1968).

Petrov, A. N. *Arkhitektor V. P. Stasov.* Leningrad, 1950.

———. "Iz materialov o V. I. Bazhenove." *Ezhegodnik Instituta istorii iskusstv.* Moscow, 1958. 57–82.

Pevsner, Nikolaus. *Academies of Art, Past and Present.* Cambridge, 1940.

———. "The Egyptian Revival." *Architectural Review* 119(1956): 242–54.

——— and Lang, S. "Apollo or Baboon." *Architectural Review* 104(1948): 271–79.

Piliavskii, Vladimir Ivanovich. "Gradostroitel'nye meropriiatiia i obraztsovye proekty v Rossii v nachale XIX veka." *Nauchnye trudy Leningradskogo inzhenerno-stroitel'nogo instituta.* vyp. 21. Leningrad and Moscow, 1958. 75–112.

———. "Ivan Kuz'mich Korobov." *Arkhitekturnoe nasledstvo* 4(1953): 41–62.

———. "Iz istorii obshchestvennoi stroitel'noi tekhniki." *Izvestiia vysshikh uchebnykh zavedenii.* MVO, SSR 1958, no. 6.

———. "K istorii kremlevskogo dvortsa v Moskve." *Izvestiia vysshikh uchebnykh zavedenii,* no. 5. Novosibirsk, 1962.

———. "Odna iz pozdnikh rabot K. I. Rossi." *Arkhitekturnoe nasledstvo* 4(1953): 119–22.

———. "Postroiki V. P. Stasova v usad'bakh pod Riazan'iu, Kalugoi, i Torshkom." *Arkhitekturnoe nasledstvo* 9(1959): 79–103.

———. "Proekty triumfal'nykh sooruzhenii D. Kvarengi v Rossii." *Arkhitekturnoe nasledstvo* 28(1980): 71–79.

———. *Russkie triumfal'nye pamiatniki.* Leningrad, 1960.

———. *Stasov: Arkhitektor.* Leningrad, 1963.

———. *Vydaiushchiisia russkii zodchii Vasilii Petrovich Stasov.* Leningrad, 1951.

———. *Zodchii Rossi.* Moscow, Leningrad, 1951.

Podol'skii, R. "Dom i shkola arkhitektora M. F. Kazakova." *Arkhitektura SSSR.* 1953, no. 5: 20–22.

———. "Neizvestnyi pamiatnik arkhitektury moskovskogo klassitsizma (dom Tolstogo na Zemlianom valu)." *Arkhitekturnoe nasledstvo* 20 (1972): 70–74.

———. "Petrovskii dvorets na Iauze." *Arkhitekturnoe nasledstvo* 1(1951): 14–55.

Posokhin, M. V. *Perspektivy razvitiia Moskvy.* Moscow, 1973.

Poulsen, Thomas M. *The Provinces of Russia: Changing Patterns in The Regional Allocation of Authority 1708–1962.* Univ. of Wisconsin, Ph.D. dissertation. 1962.

Praz, M. "Herculaneum and European Taste." *Magazine of Art* 32(1939): 684–93.

———. Pribul'skaia, G. "Proekt zhilogo doma v Peterburge V. P. Stasova." *Arkhitekturnoe nasledstvo* 9(1959): 104–105.

Prizemlin, V. *Moskovskii stil' ampir.* Moscow, 1911.

Prokhorov, M. F. "The Moscow Uprising of September 1771." *Soviet Studies in History* 25 (1987), no. 4: 44–78.

Proskuriakova, T. S. "O reguliarnosti v russkom gradostroitel'stve XVII–XVIII vv." *Arkhitekturnoe nasledstvo* 28(1980): 37–46.

Raeff, Marc. *Imperial Russia 1682–1825: The Coming of Age of Modern Russia.* New York, 1971.

———. *Origins of the Russian Intelligentsia: The Eighteenth-Century Nobility.* New York, 1966.

———. "The Enlightenment in Russia and Russian Thought in the Enlightenment." *The Eighteenth Century in Russia.,* ed. J. G. Garrard, Oxford, 1973.

———. *The Well-Ordered Police State.* New Haven, 1983.

Razrushennye i oskvernennye khramy: Moskva i sredniaia Rossiia s poslesloviem "predely vandalizma." Frankfurt/Main, 1980.

Ransel, David L. *Mothers of Misery: Child Abandonment in Russia.* Princeton, 1988.

Reau, Louis. "Un grand architecte français en Russie: Vallin de la Mothe." *L'Architecture.* 1923.

Reinbeck, Georg. *Travels from St. Petersburg through Moscow, Grodno, Warsaw, Breslau, etc. to Germany in the Year 1805.* London, 1807.

Repnikov, A. N. "Novoe o V. I. Bazhenove." *Arkhitekturnoe nasledstvo* 9(1959): 65–68.

Ritchie, Leitch. *A Journey to St. Petersburg and Moscow.* London, 1836.

Rogger, Hans. *National Consciousness in Eighteenth Century Russia.* Cambridge, Mass., 1969.

Rowland, Benjamin, Jr. *The Classical Tradition in Western Art.* Cambridge, Mass., 1963.

Rusakov, Iu. "Predvaritel'nyi variant proekta Proviantskikh skladov." *Arkhitekturnoe nasledstvo* 4(1953): 108–10.

Russkii Biograficheskii Slovar'. (New York, 1962, reprint.)

Rzianin, M. I. *Arkhitekturnye ansambli Moskvy i podmoskov'ia XIV–XIX veka.* Moscow, 1950.

———. *Pamiatniki russkogo zodchestva.* Moscow, 1950.

———. *Russkaia arkhitektura.* Moscow, 1947.

Samoshlova, N. A. *Arkhitekturnaia kompozitsiia i order v moskovskom ampire*. Moscow, 1947.

Savitskii, Iu. *Moskva: istoriko-arkhitekturnyi ocherk*. Moscow, 1947.

———. *Russkoe klassicheskoe nasledie i sovetskaia arkhitektura*. Moscow, 1953.

Schmidt, Albert J. "Architecture in Nineteenth-Century Russia: The Enduring Classic." *Art and Culture in Nineteenth-Century Russia*, ed. Theofanis G. Stavrou. Bloomington, Ind., 1983: 172–193.

———. "Soviet Legislation for Protection of Architectural Monuments: Background." Paper presented at Univ. of Bridgeport Soviet Law Symposium, 15 Nov. 1987 and to be published in *Law and Perestroika*, ed. A. J. Schmidt, in Univ. of Leiden's *Law in Eastern Europe* series.

———. "The Restoration of Moscow after 1812." *Slavic Review* 40(1981): 37–48.

———. "William Hastie, Scottish Planner of Russian Cities." *Proceedings of the American Philosophical Society* 114, no. 3 (1970): 226–43.

Sedov, A. P. *Egotov*. Moscow, 1956.

Shamurin, Iu. A. *Ocherki klassicheskoi Moskvy*. Moscow, 1912.

———. "Ocherki klassicheskoi Moskvy." *Baian*, 1914, no. 4: 5–72.

Shaw, J. Thomas, ed. *The Letters of Alexander Pushkin*. 3 vols. Bloomington, Ind. and Philadelphia, 1963.

Shchenkov, A. S. "Struktura russkikh gorodov XVI–XVII vv. i ikh esteticheskoe vospriatie." *Arkhitekturnoe nasledstvo* 32(1984): 3–12.

Shchenkova, O. P. "Kitai-gorod-torgovyi tsentr Moskvy v kontse XVIII-pervoi polovine XIX v." *Arkhitekturnoe nasledstvo* 33(1985): 31–39.

———. "Kitai-gorod v strukture tsentra Moskvy XVII v." *Arkhitekturnoe nasledstvo* 29(1981): 56–62.

Shchusev, A. V. *Arkhitektor V. P. Stasov*. Moscow, 1950.

Shilkov, V. F. "Proekty planirovki Peterburga 1737–1740 godov." *Arkhitekturnoe nasledstvo* 4(1953): 7–13.

———. "Raboty A. V. Kvasova i I. E. Starova po planirovke russkikh gorodov." *Arkhitekturnoe nasledstvo* 4(1953): 30–34.

———. "Russkii perevod Vitruviia nachala XVIII veka." *Arkhitekturnoe nasledstvo* 7 (1955): 89–92.

———. "Zodchii Timofei Usov." *Arkhitekturnoe nasledstvo* 4(1953): 63–65.

Shkvarikov, V. *Planirovka gorodov Rossii XVIII i nachala XIX veka*. Moscow, 1939.

———. "Planirovka i stroitel'stvo russkikhh gorodov." *Russkaia arkhitektura*, ed. V. A. Shkarikov. Moscow, 1940, 7–26.

———. "Stroitel'stvo russkikh gorodov v XVIII i nachale XIX vv." *Arkhitektura SSSR* 8(1939): 49–59.

Shkvarikov, V., Baranov, N., et al. *Moskva: Planirovka i zastroika goroda, 1945–1957*. Moscow, 1958.

———, et al. *Ocherk istorii planirovki i zastroiki gorodov*. Moscow, 1954.

Shvidkovskii, D. O. "Arkhitektura poslednei chetverti XVIII v." Lecture in series *Istoriia russkoi arkhitektury XVIII-nach. XX v.* March 5, 1986 at Shchusev Museum of Architecture, Kalinin Prospect 5, Moscow.

———. "Russkoe gradostroitel'stvo XVIII-nach. XIX vv." Ibid. March 12, 1986.

Silverstein, S. N. *Arkhitektor O. I. Bove*. Moscow, 1964.

Smirnov, V. *Arkhitektura krupneishikh teatrov Rossii vtoroi poloviny XVIII i nachala XIX vv.* Moscow, 1950. Dissertation.

Snegirev, V. "A. L. Vitberg i ego arkhitekturnye roboty." *Arkhitektura SSSR* 7(1939), no. 7: 79–82.

———. *Arkhitektor A. L. Vitberg*. Moscow, 1939.

———. *Arkhitektor V. I. Bazhenov*. Moscow, 1937.

———. *Moskovskie slobody*. Moscow, 1956.

———. *Moskovskoe zodchestvo XIV–XIX vekov*. Moscow, 1948.

———. *Znamenityi zodchii Vasilii Ivanovich Bazhenov*. Moscow, 1950.

———. *Zodchii Bazhenov*. Moscow, 1962.

Sobolev, N. N. *Chugunnoe lut'e v russkoi arkhitekture*. Moscow, 1951.

Sokovnin, Andrei N. *Moskovskii ampirnyi zhiloi dom*. Moscow, 1947.

Solov'ev, K. A. *Russkii khudozhestvennyi parket*. Moscow, 1953.

Sorokin, V. Z. "Obezglavlennaia Moskva." *Russkoe vozrozhdenie* 14, ii (1981): 155–76.

Starr, S. Frederick. *Melnikov: Solo Architect in a Mass Society*. Princeton, 1978.

———. "The Revival and Schism of Urban Planning in Twentieth Century Russia." *The City in Russian History*, ed. M. Hamm. Lexington, Ky., 1976.

———. "Russian Art and Society 1800–1850." *Art and Culture in Nineteenth-Century Russia*, ed. T. G. Stavrou. Bloomington, Ind., 1983.

———. "Visionary Town Planning during the Cultural Revolution." in *Cultural Revolution in Russia 1928–31*, ed. Sheila Fitzpatrick. Bloomington, Indiana, 1978.

———. "Writings from the 1960's On the Modern Movement in Russia." *Journal of The Society of Architectural Historians* 30(1971): 170–78.

Stemparzhetskii, A. *Risunok i tsvet dekorativnykh tkanei v inter'ere arkhitektury russkogo klassitsizma, vtoraia polovina XVIII-nachalo XIX vv.* Leningrad, 1956. Dissertation.

Summerson, John. *The Classical Language of Architecture*. London, 1963.

Suslova, E. N. "Uchenicheskie gody Iu. M. Fel'tena." *Arkhitekturnoe nasledstvo* 9(1959): 69–72.

Svin'in, Pavel Petrovich. *Sketches of Moscow and St. Petersburg*. Philadelphia, 1813; London, 1814; 2nd ed., 1843.

Sytin, P. V. *Iz istorii moskovskikh ulits*. Moscow, 1959.

———. *Istoriia planirovki i zastroiki Moskvy*. 2 vols. 1: 1147–1762. Moscow, 1950. 2: 1762–1812. Moscow, 1954.

———. *Po staroi i novoi Moskve*. Moscow-Leningrad, 1957.

Sytina, T. M. "Russkoe arkhitekturnoe zakonodatel'stvo pervoi chetverti XVIII v." *Arkhitekturnoe nasledstvo* 18 (1969): 67–73.

Taleporovskii, V. N. *Kvarengi*. Leningrad and Moscow, 1954.

———. *Russkie arkhitektory*. Moscow, 1953.

Taylor, Bayard. *Travels in Greece and Russia*. New York, 1859.

Thompson, Edward P. *Life in Russia*. London, 1848.

Tikhomirov, N. Ia. *Arkhitektura podmoskovnykh usadeb*. Moscow, 1955.

———, and Ivanov, V. N. *Moskovskii kreml'*. Moscow, 1967.

Tverskoi, L. M. *Russkoe gradostroitel'stvo do kontsa XVII veka*. Leningrad and Moscow, 1953.

Vagner, G. "Ischeznuvshii pamiatnik shkoly M. F. Kazakova." *Arkhitekturnoe nasledstvo* 16 (1967): 96–98.

———. "K biografii M. F. Kazakova." *Arkhitektura SSSR*. 1957, no. 3: 62.

Vasil'ev, B. "K istorii planirovki Peterburga vo vtoroi polovine XVIII veka." *Arkhitekturnoe nasledstvo* 4(1953): 14–29.

Vernadsky, George et al., ed. *A Source Book for Russian History from Early Times to 1917*. 3 vols. New Haven, 1972.

Vigel', F. F. *Zapiski*. 2 vols. Leningrad, 1928.

Vinograd, V. *Moskva: Arkhitekturnyi putevoditel'*. Moscow, 1960.

———. "Pis'ma i drugie dokumenty V. I. Bazhenova o stroitel'stve v Tsaritsyne." *Arkhitekturnyi arkhiv* 1(1946): 103–108.

Vlasiuk, A. I., Kaplun, A. I., Kiparisova, A. A. *Kazakov*. Moscow, 1957.

Vol'tsenburg, O. "Novye materialy k biografii V. I. Bazhenova." *Soobshcheniia gos. Ermitazha* 15(1959): 17–20.

Voyce, Arthur. *Moscow and The Roots of Modern Culture*. Norman, Okla., 1964.

———. *The Moscow Kremlin: Its History, Architecture, and Art Treasures*. Berkeley, 1954.

Vvedenskaia, A. G. "Arkhitektor A. G. Grigor'ev i ego graficheskoe nasledie." *Arkhitekturnoe nasledstvo* 9(1959): 106–16.

———. "Iz istorii planirovki russkoi derevni XVIII i pervoi

poloviny XIX vv." *Trudy gos. Istoricheskogo muzeia* 15(1941): 77–120.

Weber, Friedrich Christian. *The Present State of Russia*. 2 vols. London, 1722–23; reissued New York, 1968.

Whittaker, Robert. "'My Literary and Moral Wanderings': Apollon Grigor'ev and the Changing Cultural Topography of Moscow." *Slavic Review* 42(1983): 390–407.

Wilmot, Martha and Catherine. *The Russian Journals*. London, 1934.

Wilson, William Rae. *Travels in Russia*. 2 vols. London, 1828.

Zabelin, I. E. *Istoriia goroda Moskvy*. Moscow, 1905.

Zel'ten, L. *Promyshlennaia arkhitektura Rossii XVIII-nachala XIX vekov*. Leningrad, 1952.

Zemtsov, S. M. *L'vov*. Moskva, 1956.

Zolotnitskaia, Z. V. *Arkhitektor Osip Ivanovich Bove k 200-letiiu so dnia rozhdeniia (1784–1834)*. Katalog vystavki, Moscow, 1986.

———. "Arkhitektura Moskvy pervoi treti XIX v." Lecture in series *Istoriia russkoi arkhitektury XVIII-nach. XX vv.* March 26, 1986 at Shchusev Museum of Architecture, Kalinin Prospect 5, Moscow.

———. "Arkhitektura podmoskovnykh usadeb XVIII-pervoi treti XIX v." Ibid. April 12, 1986.

Zombe, S. "Neopublikovannye i maloizvestnye portrety arkhitektorov." *Arkhitektura SSSR*. 1939, no. 7: 83.

———. "Proekt plana Moskvy 1775 goda i ego gradostroitel'noe znachenie." *Ezhegodnik instituta istorii iskusstv 1960*. Moscow, 1961: 53–96.

———, and Beletskaia, E. "Arkhitektor Grigor'ev." *Arkhitektura SSSR*. 1939, no. 5: 66–71.

Zucker, Paul. *Town and Square*. New York, 1959.

Zviagintsev, E. A. "Rost naseleniia v moskovskikh slobodakh XVIII veka." *Moskovskii krai v ego proshlom*, pt. ii. Moscow, 1930.

———. "Slobody inostrantsev v Moskve XVIII veka." *Istoricheskii zhurnal* (1944): nos. 2–3: 81–86.

Index